GLOBAL VIGILANTES

DAVID PRATTEN • ATREYEE SEN

editors

Global Vigilantes

HURST & COMPANY, LONDON

First published in the United Kingdom by
HURST Publishers Ltd,
41 Great Russell Street, London, WC1B 3PL
© David Pratten, Atreyee Sen
and the Contributors, 2007
All rights reserved.
Printed in India

A catalogue data record for this volume is available
from the British Library.

ISBNs
978-1-85065-837-5 *casebound*
978-1-85065-838-2 *paperback*

www.hurstpub.co.uk

CONTENTS

CONTENTS

THE CONTRIBUTORS

Ray Abrahams is a retired member of staff of the Department of Social Anthropology and a Fellow of Churchill College Cambridge. He is author of *Vigilant citizens: vigilantism and the state, Cambridge* (1998).

Jennifer Burrell is Assistant Professor in the Anthropology Department at the University at Albany, State University of New York. Her research examines local politics, power and state formation in Todos Santos Cuchumatán, a Mam-speaking community in north-western Guatemala.

Lars Buur is Senior Researcher at the Danish Institute for International Studies where he works on democratic decentralisation, state and citizenship, and security, law and order in Southern Africa. He is co-editor of *The Security-Development Nexus: Expressions of Sovereignty and Securitization in Southern Africa* (2007).

Conerly Casey is Assistant Professor of History, Sociology and Anthropology at The American University of Kuwait. She is co-editor of *A companion to psychological anthropology: modernity and psychocultural change* (2005).

Leo Chavez is Professor of Anthropology and Director, Chicano Latino Studies Program at the University of California, Irvine. He is author of *Covering immigration: popular images and the politics of the nation* (2001), and *Shadowed lives: undocumented immigrants in American society* (1992).

Mark Galeotti is Senior Lecturer in International History at Keele University, and Director of the Organised Russian and Eurasian Crime Research Unit. He is managing editor of the journal *Global Crime*, and editor of *Global crime today: the changing face of organised crime* (2005).

Daniel M. Goldstein is Assistant Professor in the Department of Anthropology at Rutgers University. He is author of *The spectacular city: violence and performance in urban Bolivia* (2004).

Neil Jarman is Director of the Institute for Conflict Research, an independent research organisation which specialises in working on issues related to conflict, social transformation and social justice. He is author of *Material Conflicts: Parades and Visual Displays in Northern Ireland* (1997).

Steffen Jensen is Assistant Professor in the Department of Geography and International Development Studies at the University of Roskilde, Denmark. He is co-editor of *The Security-Development Nexus: Expressions of Sovereignty and Securitization in Southern Africa* (2007).

Tobias Kelly is Lecturer in Social Anthropology at the University of Edinburgh. He is author of *Law, Violence and Sovereignty among West Bank Palestinians* (2006).

Helene Maria Kyed is a doctoral student in the Department of Geography and International Development Studies at the University of Roskilde, Denmark. Her thesis examines decentralisation, state formation and changing forms of authority in Mozambique.

David Pratten is Lecturer in the Social Anthropology of Africa at the University of Oxford, and Fellow of St Antony's College. He is author of *The Man-Leopard Murders: History and Society in Colonial Nigeria* (2007).

Rosellen Roche is a post-doctoral research fellow at the School of Anthropological Studies, Queens' University Belfast. Her research focuses on the impact and role of sectarianism in everyday life in Northern Ireland.

Dennis Rodgers is Senior Research Fellow in the Brooks World Poverty Institute, University of Manchester. His research focuses on violence, crime, youth, local responses to political and economic crisis and urban poverty.

Alpa Shah is Lecturer in Social Anthropology at Goldsmiths College, University of London. Her research interests include the state and politics, indigenous movements and development, the environment and migration. She is currently writing a monograph *In the Shadows of the State: Indigenous Politics in Jharkhand, India*.

Atreyee Sen is Research Council United Kingdom (RCUK) Fellow in Conflict, Cohesion and Change, CIDRA, University of Manchester. She is author of *Shiv Sena Women: Violence and Communalism in a Bombay Slum* (2007).

Jonathan Spencer is Professor of the Social Anthropology of South Asia at the University of Edinburgh. He is author of *Anthropology, Politics, and the State: Democracy and Violence in South Asia* (2007).

Gavin Weston is a doctoral candidate in the Department of Anthropology at the University of Sussex. His thesis explores the causes and effects of lynchings in Todos Santos Cuchumatán in the north-west highlands of rural Guatemala.

FOREWORD

When Ray Abrahams published his monograph *Vigilant Citizens* in 1998, he had to draw heavily on material from social history in order to contextualize the relatively small anthropological literature on contemporary vigilantism. Things have changed considerably since then, especially because of the strong literature that has emerged on different manifestations of popular justice in parts of Africa. This collection adds some tremendously vivid material, almost all of it based on very recent fieldwork. As a social phenomenon, vigilantism raises questions for scholars working in a number of fields: socio-legal studies, development studies and comparative politics, as well as socio-cultural anthropology and social history. The spectacle of groups of people (usually men, often young men) 'taking the law into their own hands' obviously begs questions about the perceived failings of formal institutions of justice, in rapidly changing political regimes. The popular use of violence in pursuit of justice challenges and disturbs the feel-good political assumptions which lie unexamined at the heart of much recent academic writing on power and resistance. Deep moral anxiety about the threat of others links Guatemalan lynch-mobs, gangs of West African youths - and the denizens of gated communities in some of the most affluent parts of the world. This capacity to raise deeply troubling questions about justice and morality in a globalizing world is one of this volume's greatest strengths. Another is the broad geographical and social canvas it employs, which forces the authors of individual chapters to speak to much wider audiences than the regional specialists most work on this theme is addressed to. The editors are to be congratulated on the appearance of this brilliantly provocative collection.

In the spring of 2007 a movie opened in the US called 'Shooter'. Starring Mark Wahlberg, it told the story of a US combat veteran

called Bob Lee Swagger who suffers repeated betrayal by the powers-
that-be, first as a Marine sniper in a turbulent African state, then in a
set-up to assassinate the President of the USA. As the assassination
plot fails, Swagger and his gun are cut loose against the dark forces at
the heart of American power. The movie itself is, I gather, unremark-
able except for one thing—it takes the familiar pop culture motif of
the lone hero pursuing a violent quest for justice in an amoral world,
but fuses it with a vaguely left-wing critique of the bad guys responsible for the unsavoury adventures of recent US foreign policy.

There are three reasons to draw attention to this otherwise for-
gettable moment in movie history. First of all it reminds us of the
continuing cultural spell cast by fantasies of popular justice, while
raising the possibility that the allure of the lone avenger may yet
appeal to progressive as well as reactionary audiences. Secondly, like
its predecessors in the Rambo series, it reminds us again how potent
the idea of taking the law into one's own hands is in the *American*
political imaginary, occupying that space where the central principle
of the sovereignty of the people finds its expression in the Second
Amendment to the Constitution. (Tocquevillian readers will note
that many of these recent explorations of issues of popular justice in
the USA concentrate on the *individual* qualities of the avenger, in
contrast to the collective action analysed in most of the cases in this
volume.) Thirdly, all this together raises questions about what we
mean by globalization and where we expect to track its effects, questions which are explored in the excellent collection which follows.

For many of its political critics, globalization is little more than
a euphemism for the global spread of American popular culture. So
when, for example, the anthropologist Paul Richards found young
fighters in the Sierra Leone civil war drawing inspiration from repeated viewings of Rambo videos, we might simply assume this to be
an unexpected but relatively trivial accident of mass cultural dissemi-
nation.[†] But if there is a deep political structure in these fantasies of

---

† Richards, P. 1996. *Fighting for the Rainforest: War, Youth and Resources in Sierra
Leone.* Oxford: James Currey.

popular justice and popular violence—a structure of feeling which combines issues of justice, violence, democracy, sovereignty, and possibly masculinity too—then the global manifestations of vigilante violence so brilliantly charted in this volume may draw on equally widely distributed anxieties and suspicions about law, violence and the state. The fantasies themselves may often take place on the margins of the state, but their appeal is by no means combined to the populations of frontier zones or so-called 'failing states': these are also, I suggest, central motifs in the political imaginary of the world's most powerful state. As with the best kind of political anthropology, this volume promises to unsettle and destabilize our view of our own political and legal arrangements. Whoever 'we' may be.

Jonathan Spencer, University of Edinburgh
April 2007

I

GLOBAL VIGILANTES: PERSPECTIVES ON JUSTICE AND VIOLENCE[1]

Atreyee Sen and David Pratten

Vigilantism is global: 'South African vigilantes fill police gap', 'N. Ireland's 'alternative police forces', 'Nepal's rising vigilante violence', 'Nigerians turn to vigilantes', 'Australian 'vigilantes' plan coastal patrols', 'Mob justice in rural Guatemala', 'Vigilantes set for Mexico border patrol'. Contemporary news headlines are replete with accounts of global vigilantism. The stories these headlines report capture a broad range of incidents and processes in which ordinary folk have taken the law into their own hands to prevent theft and crime, insurgency and immigration. These stories speak to some of the key themes of this volume. Whether as localized self-policing of crime and culture, or as trans-local surveillance of trafficking and terrorism, vigilante movements and ideologies have widespread appeal in many parts of the world. But can a link be drawn between the apparent proliferation of vigilantism and the dynamics of globalization with its associated forces of political and economic liberalization?

Vigilantism has yet to be framed within understandings of the dynamics and meanings of globalization, or the localized discourses on global terrorism. The aim of this book is to draw into focus a range of judicial and violent social practices that are linked to concepts of

---

1 This volume arises from the proceedings of a workshop, 'Global Vigilantes' held at the University of Sussex on 8-9 July 2005. We would like to thank all of the participants for their contributions and the Wenner Gren Foundation and The British Academy for their generous support.

vigilantism and which operate within, and are articulated to, a shifting global political economy. Rather than presenting a set of papers recounting instances of the same narrowly defined form of vigilantism in different parts of the world, the emphasis here is on the forms that vigilante-style justice and violence take in a contemporary global context. The aim then is to reach an understanding of the complexity of vigilante dynamics in a context of increasingly polarized global rhetorics of security and insecurity, order and disorder.

From a global perspective the relationship between vigilantism and globalization would appear almost self-evident. Seen on a macro scale the global political order wrought by neoliberalism has created unparalleled opportunities and motives for citizens to take the law into their own hands. If the politics of deregulation, the franchising of sovereignty, and the 'privatization of indirect government' are the signature features of the current international economic regime, then vigilantism is both a logical response and an integral aspect. The appropriation of sovereignty from the state, through privatization on the one hand and seizure on the other, may therefore be seen as a reflex of globalization and neoliberalism.

Globally policing has 'entered a new era, an era characterized by a transformation in the governance of security.'[2] This new paradigm of privatized and decentralized policing contradicts our common understanding of the state's provision of security, its monopoly of force, as the essential function of government. As policing is restructured even distinctions of private and public, centralized and decentralized become problematic, since contemporary trends separate the authorization of security and the activity of policing.[3] Is it 'private' or 'public' policing when a government legislates to authorize village defence forces or to sponsor vigilante groups; is it 'private policing' or 'local government' when communities grasp opportunities within the law to organize their own protection even though they are not explicitly authorized to do so? These dichotomies are collapsing in part

---

2 Bayley and Shearing, 2001 p.1.

3 Ibid. p.5.

because governments in recent years have facilitated, encouraged and required non-state groups to assume policing activity through the creation of legal opportunity, by outsourcing, and by supporting the community policing movement of the 1980s and 1990s.

'Rather than being passive consumers of police services,' Johnston suggests that citizens 'engage in a variety of productive security activities'.[4] Analysts of policing and security around the world now speak of complex patterns of 'overlapping agencies',[5] of 'plural networked policing',[6] and no longer accept the conceptual priority of the state in these new security networks. Increasingly questions of accountability and legitimacy in policing are less important than 'what is available', 'what works best', and 'what can I afford'.[7] Vigilantism is a cheap form of law enforcement.

Neoliberalism's effects on criminal justice are felt on a global scale. The free-market doctrine precludes the need for programmes of social justice and welfare. The resulting social fragmentation creates uncertainty and rootlessness and alienates categories of the vulnerable—the deskilled, the part-time, immigrants and unemployed—who occupy a 'carcereal social zone'. While governments are less able to effect social and economic outcomes within their own jurisdictions, privatization is rapidly becoming part of state repressive arsenals. Accounts of the privatization of national police forces abound. In China commentators write of the 'commodification of policing' as police have become private security companies wholly owned as subsidiaries of local ministries; in Poland police officers are ironically heralded as leaders in labour 'flexibility' since their services are open to the highest bidder; and in Brazil the continual circulation of personnel between private security, vigilante organizations and government agencies serves to disguise the perpetrators and victims of urban violence.

---

4 Johnston, 2001 p.965.

5 Baker, 2004.

6 Loader, 2000.

7 Baker, 2004

Commentators on globalization, indeed, argue that the negative side of the inexorable resource-hungry demands of neoliberalism is violence and conflict. There are those who link violence to globalization on other levels too. Appadurai, for instance, links violence to local logics of identity formation that have been distorted by the flows of images, capital and people circulating within the new global political geography.[8] Precisely how the distortions introduced by diasporas into the large-scale identities produced by modern nation-states take place has occupied other scholars in their endeavour to determine a 'phenomenology of affect' in the analysis of collective violence.[9]

The consequence of globalization is not the disappearance of sovereign states, but their loss of leverage over economic life and a fragmentation of their control of organized violence. Deregulation and the privatization of violence are integral aspects of this process in which the line between licit and illicit business, law and lawlessness is increasingly finely drawn. Where regimes have conceded their monopoly on violence new cartographies of disorder have emerged. Bayley and Shearing argue that governments are not just devolving power in this manner, but 'accepting new bases of legitimate government.'[10] Emerging forms of privatization of lawful violence are not automatically indicators of chaos either, as Mbembe reminds us. Rather, it is important to see them as struggles aimed at 'establishing new forms of legitimate domination and gradually restructuring formulas of authority built on other foundations.'[11] But what are these evolving formulas of authority, and can a direct link be drawn between the primacy of the market and the rise of private military, paramilitary and jurisdictional organizations?'[12]

---

8 Appadurai, 1996 p.154.

9 Das and Kleinman, 2000.

10 Bayley and Shearing, 2001 p.8.

11 Mbembe, 2001 p.76.

12 Ibid. pp.78-9.

Contemporary states across the globe confront a paradox. On the one hand states are saturated in self-imaginings grounded in the law. New geographies of production have generated new heterodoxies for which legislation, constitutions and new cultures of legality are seen as the universalizing levelling counterpoints. On the other hand, we witness the deregulation and decentralization of the law predicated on the ideology and practice of 'outsourcing' life services to the market and to volunteers. The interstices of these parallel movements—legal fetishization and formal outsourcing—are pregnant with creative possibilities. This twilight space accommodates a 'culture of productive deception' and an elision of the law and lawlessness. Betwixt and between an alternative citizenry 'stands in' for the state, conversant in 'languages of stateness', and able to represent the state precisely because it moves with impunity between appeals to the form of law and forms of extra-judicial practice that are clearly construed as lying outside or prior to the state.[13]

The link between vigilantism and globalization is a powerful argument then, but only a partial one. From above, on a macro scale, private security and vigilantism can look like a reflex of wider, global discourses and dynamics. From below, however, the reflex link is much harder and more complex to delineate since vigilantism obeys not only the logics of neoliberalism but its own historical and cultural logics. The chapters of this volume do not contest the salience and insight of the macro perspective in examining the faultlines and features of globalized inequalities. Political and economic shifts in the light of the new mobilities of capital and population have produced resonances within vigilante activity. In post-Soviet Russia, or Bolivia after the neoliberal reform package, opportunities are derived from state deregulation and states of mind of volunteer activism. Yet even in these situations it is clear that long historical trajectories, and particular cultural repertoires, are the proximate and pressing imperatives behind vigilante violence. Indeed, what the papers collected here contest is the explanatory potential of

---

13 Das and Poole, 2004.

a perspective that emphasizes the link between globalization and vigilantism in illuminating vigilantism's modes and meanings, or its imperatives and legitimacy.

This collection brings together scholars who share a concern with investigating the localized meanings and imperatives of vigilantism and a methodology which focuses on an examination of the 'theoretical nature, everyday popular uses, public discourses and empirical reality of vigilantism.'[14] Hence, it is necessary to explore vigilantism as practice rather than as an object of analysis with clear-cut conceptual and empirical boundaries. In this sense these papers move beyond an argument that vigilantism is straightforwardly a popular response to the vacuum left by state collapse, failure or instrumentalized disorder. Here, as elsewhere, vigilantism 'cannot be reduced to either expressions of the mob or to mere antidotes to formal law'.[15] Elements of this thesis appear in each paper, of course, and each contributor is emphatic in claiming that police resourcing and corruption contribute materially to the emergence and continuing legitimacy of vigilantes.

Nevertheless, the papers collected here present an alternative perspective, one that sees vigilantism from within localized cultural and historical frameworks, and in which vigilantes are seen within a range of 'longstanding ethics and practices concerned with the protection of their communities'.[16] Each of the chapters examines the ways in which historical registers of justice and violence are inflected in contemporary practice. As Whitehead insists, 'Why we should choose to be violent, or how we can be induced to act violently will obviously differ culturally and historically.'[17] Non-state or self policing has a very long historical trajectory to which the history of state policing, not just state failures, has contributed in large measure. As Baker argues with regard to Africa, decades of 'autocratic predation

---

14 Buur and Jensen, 2004 p.140.

15 Ibid.

16 Leach, 2004 p.ix.

17 Whitehead, 2005 pp.55-56.

with little concern for legality or Socialist leadership in which law served the interests of the state provoked alienation from the official law and the development of informal legal orders...'[18]

Diffused in crowds and mobs and concentrated in groups and gangs, 'popular' violence tends to obey moral imperatives and is often structured in terms of 'legitimate' targets and appropriate punishments. It is important to account for the different moral and aesthetic evaluations people in different contexts make of their actions on the bodies of others.[19] These various moral communities produce notions of justice and law with different kinds of imaginaries from those available in the official sites and representations of justice and law.[20] In her comparative evaluation, Martha Huggins notes that vigilantism in Latin America is 'essentially conservative or reactionary: It represents demands for return to a real or idealized social past, whether or not that vision of the past actually serves wider social good, or even the interests of the vigilantes themselves.'[21] Indeed, views of justice captured by vigilantes are often 'retrospective vision[s] of a world restored to its proper order',[22] but this is not to say that they are based on unchanging notions of cultural norms and practice. Rather, the complexity of lived experience inflects both past and imagined futures into an ambiguous, dynamic and very powerful notion of the moral order and of the routines by which it should be upheld.

The definitional issues surrounding vigilantism are many and varied. These persistent questions concern matters of scale, of ethics, and of state complicity among others. These issues raise significant problems in the study of vigilantism. How significant is the organization of violence? Are there analytical distinctions to be drawn between the violence of vigilante organizations and lynch mobs, for instance?

---

18 Baker, 2004 p.166.
19 Spencer, 2003 p.1568.
20 Das and Poole, 2004 p.22.
21 Huggins, 1991 p.5.
22 Spencer, 2003 p.1570.

Does paying for protection voluntarily or under duress undermine a vigilante ethic? And what does it mean when the state authorizes the use of non-state violence? Many of the chapters deal with organisations whose members call themselves vigilantes. Others, however, refer to militia, military, paramilitary, lynch mobs, street gangs and private security firms. In retaining flexibility in our own definitions it is equally necessary to account for the ways in which the labelling of vigilantism itself contains a politics of language, and how language is employed to legitimate or oppose vigilante activity.

The chapters are organized around four inter-related themes: 'boundaries and belonging', which focus on the ideologies associated with vigilante practice; 'personhood and punishment', which highlights the significance of conceptions of deviance and inscriptions of embodied violence; 'protection and politics', which reassesses the relationship between vigilantes and state institutions; and 'transitions and trajectories', which explores the historical inflections and institutional pathways of vigilante groups and practices.

Ideologies of vigilantism

As Mary Douglas emphasized, '… all margins are dangerous. If they are pulled this way or that the shape of fundamental experience is altered. Any structure of ideas is vulnerable at its margins.'[23] The volume examines the ways in which vigilante groups and ideologies produce and reproduce themselves within shifting climates of hate and fear to patrol and police borders of belonging, of citizenship, and of constituency. These papers ask to what extent the content of an ideology is important to vigilante practice, and whether the boundary-making function of community inclusion and exclusion is the determining factor. The language of justice and morality by which community boundaries are constructed, and in which vigilantism is cloaked and legitimated, is often presented as an unproblematic

---

23 Douglas, 2002 p.145.

given. The ethnographic insights from these papers, however, illustrate that this is a complex and contested terrain.

Boundaries are of central importance to the Minuteman Project on the US-Mexico border in Tombstone, Arizona. Leo Chavez links this initiative to a sense of frustration with new global realities that have reduced the power of national borders to delimit the nation state as an autonomous territory. Chavez locates the Minutemen within the history of media discourse on the US-Mexico border. History is key to this spectacle of borderland 'theatre' since the Minuteman label recalls vigilantes of an earlier era and draws to itself the legitimacy of those who would build and shape the nation. Here vigilantes attempted to signal the ways in which a border zone was historically configured as a place of danger, how illegal Mexican immigration was represented within a symbolic opposition of citizen versus enemy, and how citizenship and sovereignty might be re-enacted in a rite of policing non-citizens.

In contrast to this definition of a hierarchy of citizenship defined through vigilantism, Steffen Jensen shows how in South Africa intra-community boundaries configured along the lines of emergent inter-generational tensions are shaped by vigilantism. Everyday policing in Nkomazi sees elders distinguish their authority on the basis of property and tradition, while young men draw on the historical legitimacy of the 1980s anti-apartheid movement. Here elders police sexuality, drunkenness and theft in their confrontations with young men, while they confront their elders through accusations of witchcraft and mob violence. The definition of crime in the context of Nkomazi has therefore become a shifting signifier that defines boundaries of a moral community. Moral transgressions, Jensen argues, are not just infractions of legal codes, which are themselves unstable, but we are urged rather to identify who defines these codes and on what basis of authority.

In her chapter on the Hindu nationalist strategies of the Shiv Sena women's wing in India, Atreyee Sen pursues Kathleen Blee's pioneering work on the role of women, not as a passive legitimating force, but as active agents and 'sentinels' of vigilante movements.[24] Sen's study shows that Hindu nationalism in its violent opposition to Muslim communities can only be seen as a partial explanation for the popularity and legitimacy of the Aghadi women's movement. As important is the protection and retribution, the material and economic security these groups provide for women negotiating a new flexibility and autonomy within the home, in the workplace and in public spaces. Vigilantism in this context is directed against both Muslims and men, and like Blee, Sen argues that while the Shiv Sena movement as a whole is conservative and reactionary it nevertheless offers women a space to articulate progressive views and practices on gender roles.

While Sen's case study illustrates how a Muslim 'other' serves to delineate the struggles of an imagined Hindu nation, so Conerly Casey's chapter shows how vigilantism has been a central aspect of the renewal and reform of 'affective citizenship' for Muslim communities in northern Nigeria. Within a historical framing of emergent cultures of surveillance in the city of Kano, which inflect a global Muslim protest against recent Israeli and US policies, Casey discusses how reformist projects by the Hausa Ulama promoted an autochthonous, ethnic and religious exclusion backed by the often violent 'policing' of street gangs (*'yan daba*) and *sharia* implementation brigades (*'yan hisba*). As part of a process in which Nigerian vigilante movements have refracted geographical affiliation, language, ethnicity and religion into 'fetishized cultural codes of belonging', Casey argues that in stratifying citizenship between Muslims, non-reformist Muslims and non-Muslims, vigilantes pursued an imperative to clarify and purify the blurred boundaries of the contemporary Nigerian state.

Each of these examples therefore provides a localized and historicized reflection on Appadurai's observation that where the lived experience of 'large labels' becomes unstable, indeterminate and socially volatile, violent action can become one means of satisfying

---

24 Blee, 1991; Blee, 2002.

one's sense of one's categorical self.[25] It is to definitions of self and other, configured through ontologies and practices of personhood that subsequent chapters turn.

Deviant categories and registers of justice

Vigilantes perform exemplary acts of violence in order to make and mark community boundaries. The semiotic potential of violence makes it a powerful signifier in this situation. It is imperative therefore to understand the cultural construction of violence given the violent construction of community that appears in so many of the settings described in the following chapters. To what extent does violence, day-to-day violence, become central to the moral order? Does violence orient norms and normality? To what extent are identities recovered through violence? Violence is generative of worlds and structures of meanings. Daniel, for instance, has encouraged us to perceive violence not as an end point to be explained but as a productive starting point.[26]

In this light it is important to examine the persistence of ontological frameworks, or what Sen, after de Certeau, refers to as the 'tenacity of ethics' in explaining the repertoires of violence, the improvised procedures of justice, and the oppositional categories that are embedded in vigilante practice. Here categorical distinctions are inscribed in punishment on the body as a primary site representing parameters of otherness and violent closure.[27] These chapters each point to the various registers of personhood upon which identities of vigilante and perpetrator are configured.

In his analysis of the Amadlozi vigilante group in Port Elizabeth, South Africa, Lars Buur argues that citizenship should be seen not as a status but as a process in which vigilante justice performs a powerful defining role. In holding informal tribunals Amadlozi 'take re-

---

25 Appadurai, 1998.
26 Daniel, 1996.
27 Appadurai, 1998 p.193.

sponsibility', as they put it, for domestic abuse and a range of crimes and misdemeanours. Their findings are based on seeking consensus from the community at large and their verdicts and punishments are delivered as the accused stands in what Buur refers to as the 'space for transformation'. It is in this context that personhood is not conceived *a priori* but is fluctuating and contingent, and Amadlozi punishment can radically reorder the status of persons by 'transforming' them as moral beings to rejoin their family and normal reproductive relations or strip them of their relational identities and expel them as outlaws. Buur's argument then shows that by abjecting and de-humanizing criminals the Amadlozi operate within alternative ontologies of personhood that undermine South Africa's constitutional conception of universal citizenship and autonomous individuals.

This theme of the seizure of 'popular sovereignty', based on the social and symbolic construction of insiders and outsiders, is pursued in Tobias Kelly's chapter which emphasizes the significance of oppositions between 'martyr' and 'collaborator' in the context of the Palestinian *intifadas*. Here claims to rule in the name of 'the people' are made tangible through the taking of life. Palestinian collaborators with the Israeli security forces are configured within a concept of *jawasis* connoting the corruption and moral weakness of a distorted self, which contrasts with the nation-building concept of *shahid*, martyrdom. In tracing the shifting trajectory of these concepts in the highly contested sphere of the West Bank, Kelly, informed by Benjamin's theoretical insights on law-making and law-preserving violence, shows that the execution of collaborators serves to conserve popular claims to authority at the same time as producing a new moral and political order.

This conception of the imperatives of vigilante violence does not concern state failure so much as the construction of abject bodies beyond reform. David Pratten similarly argues for the historically contingent and culturally specific logics of being a vigilante, and how they are contrasted with conceptions of thieves in Annang villages in Nigeria. In this context vigilante practices are shaped by the representation of deviant types in terms of a moral evaluation of character often seen as a set of dispositional attributes that are 'inherent, unalterable and irremediable'.[28] Inflections of the aesthetics and politics of former traditions not only shape the mode of contemporary Annang vigilantism but also provide its imperative for violence, since the thief is conceived in embodied and discursive practices analogous to familiar representations of malevolent, non-human ancestral spirits.

The importance of tacit cultural codes to define and punish deviants is stressed in Rosellen Roche's analysis of punishment beatings in Northern Ireland. Set against new demographic and cultural shifts in the post-ceasefire era, Roche provides a visceral account of the experience of beatings and community policing among young people from both Republican and Loyalist communities who find themselves identified as joy-riders and drug-takers by former paramilitaries. Mediated by the proximity and density of social relations, codes of warnings, weapons and restraints on violence are shared across the religious and political divides. Hence, as distinct from hired, privatized security, objections to excess violence are tempered by a network of familiarity and tacit support.

States and sovereignty

It seems clear that contemporary vigilantism relates both to the fragmentation of the sovereignty of nation-states and to the dependence that states have on the vigilance of their citizens. Recent ethnographic evidence decentres our understanding of the state and the relationship between vigilantes and state institutions. As Das and Kleinman have argued, 'Although many have theorized that this is the era of declining states... there are ... contradictory aspects in which the state is encountered in the context of violence.'[29] One of these key contexts has been vigilantism. In contemporary Iranian politics, for example, vigilantes are known as pressure groups (*guruh-i fishar*) and

---

28 Heald, 1986 p.76.
29 Das and Kleinman, 2000 p.6.

act on behalf of hard-line factions using violence, intimidation and assassination to affect government policy.[30] Since the 1997 election of President Khatami's government, therefore, conservative sponsors of these groups have been able to forestall any internal reform or external rapprochement.

In this light, the papers here point emphatically to the enmeshing, complicity and mutual encompassment that vigilantism generates. Edmund Leach, of course, pointed us to consider the continuities between the state and criminal enterprise, showing that history provides many examples of how 'legitimate' actions of the state become the 'criminal' actions of the enemy, and as Taussig suggests, 'There is something insufferably attractive about the margin of law where the state re-creates the very terror it is meant to combat.'[31] These transitions and transgressions are examined throughout these chapters.

Lynchings, Daniel Goldstein argues, represent a 'privatization' of justice that incorporates the organizational and cultural logics of neoliberal, transnational capitalism which has saturated the Bolivian political economy and public culture. A continuum of violence emerges, he argues, which links the deficiencies of the neoliberal state to the cultural logics of privatization, flexibility and self-help in which citizen groups are urged to shoulder responsibility for the administration of justice. It is no accident, Goldstein observes, that the upsurge in the number of lynchings in Bolivia in 2000 coincided with a wave of popular discontent with the introduction of neoliberal structural reforms which included drastic cuts in police budgets.

Parallel dynamics in post-Soviet Russia have witnessed a long-standing tradition of *samosud* vigilantism sublimated into what Mark Galleoti describes as a 'more pernicious compound' linked to the market economy. With the rapid growth of the Russian private security industry (currently 40 per cent annually) both the police and the private sector provide protection, *krysha* (a roof), at a price. In this context private hiring of serving law enforcement officers, and the formation of

---

30 Rubin, 2001.
31 Taussig, 2003.

sections of the police precisely to service private leasing arrangements, take police away from their duties at a time when they are most sorely needed. New forms of 'outsourced vigilantism' are no longer personal, redemptive or reintegrating. Rather, citizens are faced with making a cost-benefit analysis of security provision in which the state's legitimacy depends on it competing effectively with the private sector.

Alpa Shah's chapter also illustrates the importance of retaining flexibility in our definitions of vigilantism. Her account of the Maoist Communist Centre, a modern incarnation of the Naxalite peasant and worker uprising of the late 1960s which has been labelled as a terrorist group by the Indian state since 2001, demonstrates how a militia movement incorporates both informal policing of public morality and protection rackets for local elites. The Marxist-Leninist pro-poor ideological trajectory of the movement is subsumed, Shah suggests, in favour of the policing of middle-class sensibilities (with regard to alcohol and adultery) and for gaining access to state resources. By seeking to control a 'market of protection' the MCC contributes to a climate of fear that is productive of new relationships and obligations that require us to recognize the mutually beneficial co-existence and dependence of protector and protected.

In a review of vigilantism in South Africa, Burr and Jensen conclude that 'The first thing that becomes evident … is that vigilantes do more than simply substitute for the functions of the state.' [32] These chapters illustrate, nevertheless, that justice at the margins of the state is not simply a matter of 'folk' notions of law and justice versus state sanctioned ideas of justice. Though they are locked in unequal relations, they are enmeshed in one another.[33] What these cases illustrate, then, is that vigilantism does not solely involve the desperate falling back on their own physical resources in the face of state failure, but a more complicated process in which the state becomes one of a range of options which citizens can purchase.

---

32 Buur and Jensen, 2004.
33 Das and Poole, 2004 p.21.

Vigilantes in transition

It is often asserted that crime and disorder are related to transitions within political systems—from authoritarianism to democracy, from military to civilian rule, from communist regime to market economy, or from civil war to peace.[34] This assertion applies equally to the role of vigilantism. With the constraints on post-transition states in delivering justice, communities will seek alternative forms of protection. The relationship between crime, vigilantism and political transition, however, is a complex one and one that is difficult to prove. Comparative evidence is therefore limited, but nevertheless points to the importance of ruptures and disruptions in social organization and crime control as the most pressing causes of crime and vigilantism in transitional states.

Vigilante groups, as institutions, have their own historical trajectories too, and are likely, over time and as they develop control in a particular locale, to become involved in a diverse range of activities including forms of illegal accumulation. What distinguishes long-running vigilante groups and practices from those that slip over into extortion and criminality themselves? Can the autonomy of vigilante groups be maintained over the long term or are scenarios of cooption or criminality inevitable? In the *rondas campesinas* ('peasants who make rounds') of Starn's eloquent ethnography, for example, nightwatches established by small numbers in 1983 to combat cattle rustling boasted universal able-bodied male membership within a year.[35] Emboldened by their success, the *rondas* soon established informal tribunals, *arreglos*, to settle disputes over land, water, debt, and wife beatings. By 1986 they had expanded into public works and mobilized in protests over interests rates. By the early 1990s Starn was moved to observe that with thousands of *rondas campesinas* operating in Peru's northern Andes they had become 'one of the largest and most sustained rural movements in

---

34 Shaw, 2000.
35 Starn, 1999.

late twentieth century Latin America.'[36] As vanguards of alternative modes of political vision and identity, the trajectory of these groups encapsulated a new spirit of local cooperation and autonomy.

The vigilante trajectories related in this volume do not capture them as progressive reformists, however, but within more complex narratives. In the context of post-1994 Northern Ireland, for instance, Neil Jarman traces paramilitary trajectories from vigilantism to community policing, and from punitive to restorative justice. Restorative justice projects and community policing initiatives set up to monitor sectarian rioting and anti-social behaviour shed considerable light, he shows, on the contested fault-line between vigilantes' autonomy from the state and their accommodation within it. A British government report which suggested that these initiatives should engage formally with state probation and youth justice bodies in 2005, for instance, was met with political and media criticism for attempting to legitimize vigilante activity and modes of justice based on the threat of the use of paramilitary force.

These ambiguities of vigilante practices are also highlighted in Dennis Rodgers' study of *pandillerismo* (youth gangsterism) in a poor neighbourhood of Nicaragua's capital, Managua. In contrast to Jarman's account of the socially positive trajectories of paramilitarism, Rodgers identifies a dramatic shift in the role of gangs that were formed out of the demobilization of Contras and Sandinistas. During the 1990s gang membership became an index of community, and established localized but variable regimes of order within the wider conditions of insecurity in post-revolutionary Nicaragua. By 2002, however, with what Rodgers describes as the 'contingent compatibility' of gangs and drugs, and with an upsurge in cocaine trafficking and dealing, a gang which had protected and 'loved' its neighbourhood turned rapidly to prey upon it.

The effects of long-term militarization are a common theme in these contributions and inflections of violence associated with the civil war loom large in Guatemala. Jennifer Burrell and Gavin

---

36 Starn, 1992 p.90.

Weston, in their chapter on post-1996 lynching cases, contest an emerging consensus that these acts can be explained as a continuation of violence from the civil war or as failings of a transitional judicial system. They argue for an ethnographic and micro-political perspective and for the need to examine more proximate factors in order to set lynchings against the specific local details of political contests and rumours. In this way, therefore, we see that there is no direct link to be made with the past; rather, there are ways in which vigilantism operates to discredit rival candidates in forthcoming elections, and articulate localized anxieties about wider forces of social change (*los cambios*).

These discourses on the continuities of violence in transition states are contrasted in Helen Maria Kyed's chapter with the role of vigilantes in securing a post-war settlement. Kyed argues that the state-franchising of vigilante patrols in Mozambique, along with the engagement of chiefs in new roles and responsibilities, represents not only a policy of decentralized self-policing at work, but also modes by which the Frelimo-led government is able to involve vigilantes and chiefs as 'collaborators' within new networks of surveillance over former opposition regions. International discourses of community policing are therefore articulated to the state-sponsorship of vigilante movements in former Renamo opposition strongholds, to define a conflation of criminals and Renamo supporters who are represented in opposition to new categories of affiliates to the Frelimo state. Hence, while it is commonly assumed that outsourcing weakens the state, Kyed examines ways in which vigilantism and popular justice are both implicated in the state's project and manufactures new modes of state allegiance.

Overall, as Ray Abrahams points out in his afterword, vigilantism connotes an unstable, labile and awkward borderland concept that is veiled in secrecy and serves as a cloak of deception. Rather than anticipate greater precision in our definition of vigilantism through comparative analysis, we argue that the comparative study of justice and violence illustrates the need to confront precisely these ambiguities with all their conflations and elisions. We share Abrahams' resistance to refocusing any definition onto those frequently recurring features of vigilante activity, since the chapters that follow illustrate that vigilantism is a shifting concept that articulates to ever-changing social realities.

While globalization shapes these new realities in significant ways, its logics do not provide a complete or satisfactory explanation for the questions raised by the contributors to this volume. The perspective on justice and violence that stresses a reflex link between globalization and vigilantism is critically over-determined. The effects of community policing reforms, of privatized security industries, and of state-sponsorship of vigilante groups are each mediated by localized cultural and historical repertoires. From these perspectives global vigilantes are shaped by the imperatives to define boundaries of belonging, by cultural templates of popular justice, by political and economic opportunity, and by institutional trajectories.

Appadurai, A. *Modernity at Large: Cultural Dimensions of Globalization*, Minneapolis, Minn., 1996.

—— 'Dead Certainty: Ethnic Violence in the Era of Globalization', *Public Culture* 10(2), 1998, pp. 225-47.

Baker, B. 'Protection from Crime: What is on offer for Africans?', *Journal of Contemporary African Studies* 22(2), 2004, pp. 165-88.

Bayley, D. and C. Shearing. 'The New Structure of Policing: Description, Conceptualization and Research Agenda', National Institute for Justice, 2001.

Blee, K.M. *Women of the Klan: Racism and Gender in the 1920s*, Berkeley, 1991.

—— *Inside Organized Racism: Women and Men in the Hate Movement*, Berkeley, 2002.

Buur, L. and S. Jensen. 'Introduction: Vigilantism and the Policing of Everyday Life in South Africa', *African Studies* 63(2), 2004, pp. 139-52.

Daniel, E.V. *Charred Lullabies: Chapters in an Anthropography of Violence*, Princeton, NJ, 1996.

Das, V. and A. Kleinman. 'Introduction', in *Violence and Subjectivity*, V. Das, A. Kleinman, M. Ramphele and P. Reynolds (eds), Berkeley, 2000, pp. 1-18.

Das, V. and D. Poole. 'Introduction', in *Anthropology in the Margins of the State*, V. Das and D. Poole (eds), Oxford, 2004, pp. 2-32.

Douglas, M. *Purity and Danger: an Analysis of Concepts of Pollution and Taboo*, New York, 2002.

Heald, S. 'Witches and Thieves: Deviant Motivations in Gisu Society', *Man* 21(1), 1986, pp. 65-78.

Huggins, M.K. (ed.). *Vigilantism and the State in Modern Latin America: Essays on Extralegal Violence*, New York, 1991.

Johnston, L. 'Crime, Fear and Civil Policing', *Urban Studies* 38(5-6), 2001, pp. 959-76.

Leach, M. 'Introduction to Special Issue: Security, Socioecology, Polity: Mande Hunters, Civil Society, and Nation-States in Contemporary West Africa.' *Africa Today* 50(4), 2004, pp. vii-xvi.

Loader, I. 'Plural Policing and Democratic Governance', *Social and Legal Studies* 9(3), 2000, pp. 323-45.

Mbembe, A. *On the Postcolony*, Berkeley, 2001.

Rubin, M. *Into the Shadows: Radical Vigilantes in Khatami's Iran*, Washington, DC, 2001.

Shaw, M. 'Crime and Policing in Transitional Societies—Conference Summary and Overview' Paper presented at the Crime and Policing in Transitional Societies, University of Witwatersrand, 2000.

Spencer, J. 'Collective Violence', in *Oxford India Companion to Sociology and Social Anthropology*, V. Das (ed.), Delhi, 2003, pp. 1564-80.

Starn, O. 'I Dreamed of Foxes and Hawks: Reflections on Peasant Protest, New Social Movements, and the Rondas Campesinas of Northern Peru', in *The Making of Social Movements in Latin*

America: Identity, Strategy, and Democracy, A. Escobar and S.E. Alvarez (eds), Boulder, Colo., 1992, pp. 89-115.

—— *Nightwatch: the making of a movement in the Peruvian Andes*, Durham, NC, 1999.

Taussig, M.T. *Law in a Lawless Land: Diary of a "Limpieza" in Colombia*, New York, 2003.

Whitehead, N.L. 'Cultures, Conflicts and the Poetics of Violent Practice', in *Violence*, N.L. Whitehead (ed.), Sante Fe, NM, 2005, pp. 2-23.

BOUNDARIES AND BELONGING

2

SPECTACLE IN THE DESERT: THE MINUTEMAN PROJECT ON THE US-MEXICO BORDER[1]

Leo R. Chavez

On 1 April 2005, volunteers began arriving along the Arizona-Mexico border, converging on Tombstone, the site of the historical Wild West shootout at the OK Corral between Wyatt Earp's men and a gang of roughneck cowboys.[2] These modern-day vigilantes came in search of another confrontation, another example of cowboy justice, only this time the scofflaws were 'illegal' immigrants. These men came to be part of the Minuteman Project, a name with immediate appeal because it called forth the patriotic volunteers who fought against British rule of the American colonies. The Minuteman Project's ostensible goal was to monitor the Arizona-Mexico border in the hopes of locating clandestine border crossers. However, this surveillance operation also had a larger objective, which was to produce a spectacle that would garner public media attention and influence federal immigration policies.

The Minuteman Project's start date of 1 April is known as April Fool's Day in the United States and is a time to play a joke on someone else. In a sense that is what their spectacle in the desert did. It

---

1 This paper has benefited by the generous comments of Lisa Garcia Bedolla, Jesse Cheng, Louis DeSipio, Susan Bibler Coutin, and Juliet McMullin. Any errors or errors in judgement rest with the author alone.

2 Claudine LoMonaco, 'Minutemen gather in Tombstone for border watch', *Tucson Citizen*, 1 April 2005, p. A-7.

made the press into the unwitting co-conspirators of the Minuteman Project's attempt to shape public policy. As they were given something—a spectacle—to cover, the media broadcast the Minuteman Project's message about a need for greater border surveillance.

Like many spectacles, this one had costumes. The Minutemen volunteers came equipped with military fatigues, binoculars, bulletproof vests, aircraft, walkie-talkies, even guns, since it is legal to carry firearms in Arizona.[3] The Minuteman Project had all the trappings of a military campaign, which is not surprising given that many of the volunteers had served in the military, serving in places such as Vietnam and Iraq.[4] Jim Gilchrist, the founder of the Minuteman Project, was himself wounded in Vietnam.[5]

This chapter attempts to contextualize the pseudo-military operation at the Arizona-Mexico border. The Minuteman Project's April 2005 offensive to monitor the Arizona-Mexico border is examined in relation to Michel Foucault's contrasting concepts of 'spectacle' and 'surveillance'.[6] The Minuteman Project engaged in practices of both spectacle and surveillance to achieve its goals, especially the larger objective of targeting public opinion and the federal government's immigration policies. The Minuteman Project's border surveillance is viewed here as a practice of power that defines the juridical border between 'citizens' and 'Others', that is, 'illegal aliens'.[7]

Michel Foucault's concepts of 'spectacle' and 'surveillance' provide a useful theoretical and analytical framework for assessing the

---

3 Michael Riley, '1,000 activists to patrol Arizona border for migrants', *The Denver Post*, 31 March 2005, pp. A-06. Arthur H. Rotstein, 'Volunteer border watchers cause concern', *Ventura County Star*, 27 March 2005, p. 1.

4 Ioan Grillo, 'Minute patrol off to a slow start', *Houston Chronicle*, 2 April 2005, p. A8. Michael Coronado, 'Volunteers arrive to monitor border', *The Orange County Register*, 2 April 2005, p. News 1.

5 Jennifer Delson, 'Profile of James Gilchrist', *Los Angeles Times*, 11 April 2005, p. B2.

6 Foucault, 1977.

7 See Coutin, 2005 for a discussion of surveillance and power in relation to the sanctuary movement, which also occurred in Arizona.

Minuteman Project and its goals. In *Discipline and Punish*, the spectacle is isomorphic with the scaffold, the public execution of prisoners in 18th century France. The spectacle was a public performance that enacted upon the body of the prisoner the power of the sovereign, and thus clarified the distinction between the sovereign and those he governed. 'Its [the spectacle's] aim is not so much to re-establish a balance as to bring into play, as its extreme point, the dissymmetry between the subject who has dared to violate the law and the all-powerful sovereign who displays his strength.'[8] A key to the spectacle of public torture was 'above all, the importance of a ritual that was to deploy its pomp in public.'[9] These two aspects of the spectacle, that it demarcates power positions and does so in a public way, are central to the activities of the Minuteman Project on the US Arizona border. In this case, the public performance is one that emphasizes the power and privileges of citizenship, which is controlled by the democratic state now standing in place of the sovereign. The subjects in this spectacle are the 'illegal aliens' who dared to violate the law and in doing so put the privileges of citizenship into question, at least for the Minuteman organizers and participants.

For Foucault, the move toward less public executions is coterminous with the emphasis on surveillance as a means of discipline. Surveillance, especially the totalizing practices represented by Foucault's use of the Panopticon, was a practice of power that instilled discipline in subjects, producing docile bodies. Rather than opposing these two practices, this paper views the Minuteman Project's border monitoring as a practice that combines both spectacle and surveillance. In short, the Minuteman Project used surveillance to produce a spectacle on the Arizona-Mexico border. Finding clandestine border crossers became part of the 'show', and what one might describe as a 'media circus'. In the final analysis, the success of Minuteman Project was not in numbers of border crossers found and detained, but in the

8 Foucault, 1977 pp. 48-9.
9 Ibid. p.49.

attention the project received and the disciplining it achieved, that is, the ability to force governmental reaction aligned with its cause.

Before turning to the events in Arizona, the Minuteman Project must also be contextualised historically. The following section examines the representation the Mexican immigration and the US-Mexico border in public discourse as threats to the nation.

The US-Mexico border as a place of danger

The Minuteman Project must be viewed in relation to decades of public discourse in the United States that has constructed and represented the US-Mexican border as a place of danger and threat to US society and culture. Research on national US magazine covers and their accompanying articles found that alarm is conveyed through images and text that directly or metaphorically invoke crisis, time bombs, invasion, reconquest, floods, war, and border breakdown.[10] A few of examples will have to suffice.

In December 1974, the cover of the *American Legion Magazine* depicted the United States being overrun by 'illegal aliens'. Most of the cartoon people in the image are Mexicans storming, en masse, across the US-Mexico border, breaking down a sign that states 'USA BORDER' and another one that states 'KEEP OUT'. Other immigrants are landing by boats along the east coast, flying in and swimming from the Caribbean, parachuting across the Canadian border, and all of them are converging upon, and inundating, the nation's institutions, most notably

---

10 Chavez, 2001.

welfare, education, housing, jobs, and medical aid. Such images would become more frequent on the nation's magazines over the next three decades and they contributed to an increasingly alarmist discourse on Mexican immigration.

It should also be noted that the *American Legion Magazine* serves the US armed services, which underscores the salience of the threat to US society posed by Mexican immigration and the possible need for the military to be ready for action. As noted, the Minuteman Project was a quasi-military action in which ex-military people played an important role, as did the ideology of protecting the nation.

On 4 July 1977, *U.S. News & World Report*'s cover again focused attention on Mexican immigration. The cover's text reads: 'TIME BOMB IN MEXICO: Why There'll be No End To the Invasion of 'Illegals'.' The use of 'invasion' on the cover of a mainstream national magazine is a noteworthy escalation in the alarmist discourse on Mexican immigration.[11] Invasion is a word that carries with it many connotations, none of them friendly or indicating mutual benefit. Friends do not invade; enemies invade.

The invasion metaphor evokes a sense of crisis related to an attack

on the sovereign territory of the nation. Invasion is an act of war, and puts the nation and its people at great risk. Exactly what the nation risks by this invasion is not articulated in the image's message.

The war metaphor is enhanced by the prominence of the words 'Time Bomb'. The text conjures up an image of Mexico as a bomb which, when it explodes, will damage the United States. The dam-

---

11 Ibid.

age, the message makes clear, will be the unstoppable flow of illegal immigrants to the United States.

The 'Mexican invasion' theme was the focus of both *U.S. News & World Report* (7 March 1983) and *Newsweek* (25 June 1984). *U.S. News & World Report*'s cover announced: 'Invasion From Mexico: It Just Keeps Growing.' The image on the cover is a photograph of a line of men and women being carried by men across a canal of water. At the head of the line was a woman being carried to the US on the shoulders of a man. *Newsweek* had a similar cover, a photographic image of a man carrying a woman across a shallow body of water. The woman is wearing a headscarf and a long shawl. The man carries the woman's handbag, which suggests she is travelling somewhere, moving with a purpose and for an extended amount of time. She holds a walking stick. The text states: 'Closing the Door? The Angry Debate Over Illegal Immigration. Crossing the Rio Grande.'

Featuring women so prominently on the covers of these two national magazines while warning of an 'invasion' sends a clear message about fertility and reproduction. Rather than an invading army, or even the stereotypical male migrant worker, the images suggest a more insidious invasion, one that includes the capacity of the invaders to reproduce themselves. The women being carried into US territory carry with them the seeds of future generations. The images signal not simply a concern over undocumented workers, but a concern with immigrants who stay and reproduce families and, by extension, communities in the United States. These images, and their accompanying articles, allude to issues of population growth and use of prenatal care, children's health services, education, and other social services related to reproduction.

Newsweek's 25 June 1984 feature story characterized the public as deeply concerned with undocumented immigration and yet conflicted in their attitudes and views about what to do about it. *Newsweek* alerts us to the 'fact' that 'America has 'lost control' of its borders' (p. 18). The report cites President Ronald Reagan, who envisioned the nation in grave peril because of this loss of control: 'The simple truth is that we've lost control of our own borders, and no nation can do that and survive' (p. 18).

Immigration and 'reconquest' came together in *U.S. News & World Report*'s 19 August 1985 cover. Its headline announces: 'The Disappearing Border: Will the Mexican Migration Create a New Nation?' The accompanying article, entitled 'The Disappearing Border', provides fully embellished rendition of the 'reconquest' theme:

Now sounds the march of new conquistadors in the American Southwest.... By might of numbers and strength of culture, Hispanics are changing the politics, economy and language in the U.S. states that border Mexico. Their movement is, despite its quiet and largely peaceful nature, both an invasion and a revolt. At the vanguard are those born here, whose roots are generations deep, who long endured Anglo dominance and rule and who are ascending within the U.S. system to take power they consider their birthright. Behind them comes an unstoppable mass—their kin from below the border who also claim ancestral homelands in the Southwest, which was the northern half of Mexico until the U.S. took it away in the mid-1800s (p. 30).

In the mid-1980s, the framing of the US-Mexico border as something that is 'lost' and across which 'invaders' come coincided with calls from prominent political leaders to further militarise the border. In 1986, San Diego's sheriff publicly called for Marines to be stationed every 15 or 20 feet, day and night, along the border.[12] Then-Senator Pete Wilson also publicly supported this idea, should immigration reform not work to reduce the flow of undocumented immigrants across the border.[13] Duncan Hunter, a member of the House of Representatives from San Diego, suggested that rather than the Marines, the National Guard should be stationed on the border.[14] Not surprisingly, the military's involvement has steadily

---

12 J. Stryker Meyer, 'Sheriff urges posting Marines along border', in *San Diego Union*, 6 April 1986, p. A3.

13 Joe Gandelman, 'Wilson would back Marines on border if reform move fails', *San Diego Union*, 6 April 1986, p. A3.

14 Patrick J. McDonnell, 'Hunter asks for National Guardsmen along border', *Los Angeles Times*, 24 June 1986, p. B3.

increased since this initial controversy, with National Guard and US Marines regularly deployed along the border. [15]

The invasion metaphor was subtly referenced in *The Atlantic Monthly*'s May 1992 feature article by William Langewiesche, which is a first-hand account of Langewiesche's travels on the American side of the border. In addition to characterising the border as an unpleasant and dangerous place, the author includes images of a militarized border and metaphors of war throughout the article. For example, a Border Patrol officer is quoted as he compares his nightly vigilance against illegal border crossers to Vietnam, a war in which 'we didn't win there either' (p. 74). The author describes the high level of technology used along the border to 'fight' smuggling, and the various contributions of US military personnel to the anti-drug smuggling effort. In remote deserts, the author finds that the Army carries out training exercises designated in part to intimidate would-be drug smugglers. In southern Arizona, the National Guard, the reserve army, searches vehicles. A frustrated Customs agent also compares his work trying to stop the entry of drugs to his Vietnam experience: 'It's a civilian version of Vietnam. That makes it the second losing war I've fought' (p. 84). The recurring Vietnam metaphor not only helps to characterize the US-Mexico border region as a war zone, but heightens the level of frustration and anxiety over problems associated with the region. It suggests a deep sense of hopelessness about the government's ability to successfully secure the borders and protect citizens from the various 'problems' (immigrants, drugs, now terrorists) that manage to cross it clandestinely. The ideology (below) of the Minuteman Project also expresses the despair inherent in the Vietnam analogy. At the very least, in relation to Mexican immigration, raising the Vietnam analogy challenges Americans not to lose another 'war'.

---

15 Peter Andreas, *Border Games: Policing the U.S.- Mexico Divide*, Ithaca, 2000; H.G. Reza, 'Patrols Border on Danger', *Los Angeles Times*, 29 June 1997, p. A1; Dunn, 1996; Dunn, 1999.

SPECTACLE IN THE DESERT

The problem of moving from the metaphor of the border as a war zone to acting as if this were actually the case became painfully obvious on 20 May 1997. On that day, a Marine corporal shot to death 18-year-old Esequiel Hernandez Jr., an American citizen, who had been herding his family's sheep on a hilltop near his family's home on the US side of the border near Redford, Texas. The corporal and three privates were stationed along the border to help the Border Patrol detect drug smugglers under an agreement with a federal agency called Joint Task Force Six, which was established in 1989. The Marines were to observe and report to the Border Patrol. However, Esequiel Hernandez Jr. carried a .22-calibre rifle and was shooting at rocks as he passed the time guarding his sheep. Feeling themselves under attack, the Marines, who were hidden from view, observed the young man for 23 minutes, determined that he was tending his flock, but then killed Hernandez when he looked as if he was going to fire his .22 again. Controversy developed over the length of time the Marines watched Hernandez, and the fact that Hernandez was shot in the side, not in the chest, indicating he was not facing the Marines as he shot his rifle. In addition, the Marines never identified themselves, nor did they render first aid to the dying Hernandez. Medical assistance was not called until the Border Patrol arrived 20 minutes later, but by then it was too late for intervention.[16]

Despite the inherent problems raised by the militarization of the US–Mexico border, pundits continued to portray the border as under assault. In 2000, Samuel P. Huntington repeated the alarm of a Mexican reconquest. 'The invasion of over 1 million Mexican civilians is a comparable threat [as 1 million Mexican soldiers] to American societal security, and Americans should react against it with comparable vigour. Mexican immigration looms as a unique and disturbing challenge to our cultural integrity, our national identity, and potentially to our future as a country.'[17]

---

16 Julia Prodis, 'Texas town outraged at Marines over shooting of goat herder', *The Orange County Register*, 29 June 1997, p. News 10.

17 Samuel P. Huntington, 'The Special Case of Mexican Immigration: Why

The harsh reality between the metaphor of a war zone and the actual practice of increased militarization of the border region raises a number of issues, including those of human rights.[18] At the very least there is the incongruence between military personnel trained for war and the job of the Border Patrol, which more often than not involves servicing unarmed civilians seeking work or to reunite with their family. The idea of untrained civilian border guards or militia, such as the Minutemen, expands these concerns exponentially.

The relationship that must be underscored between the public discourse examined here and the increased militarization of the border region is not that the anti-immigrant discourse *caused* this push for militarization to occur. However, the discourse of invasion and the loss of US sovereignty, and the representation of Mexican immigrants as the 'enemy', surely contributed to an atmosphere that helped to justify increased militarization of the border as a way of 'doing something' about these threats to the nation's security and the American way of life. The Minuteman Project's enlistment of citizens to conduct surveillance along the border in Arizona is a logical consequence of this decades-long maelstrom of rhetoric associating Mexican immigration with narratives of threat, danger, invasion, and destruction of the American way of life.

The Minuteman Project

In early 2005, Jim Gilchrist put a call out for 'citizens' to come to the Arizona-Mexico border to monitor and report 'illegal' immigrants.[19] Although he was a resident of California, Gilchrist's motivation for his call to action was the failure of the Bush administration and the US Congress to provide the funds necessary to secure the borders against the 'millions of illegal migrants' flowing into the United States from Mexico, a powerful theme in the post-9/11 political

---

Mexico is a Problem', *The American Enterprise*, December 2000, pp. 20-2.

18 Dunn, 1999.

19 Chris Strohm, 'Activists to flock to border, set up citizen patrols', National Journal Group Inc., 28 March 2005, pp. 1-5.

debate over security.[20] They chose Arizona because by 2005, this was the area where a disproportionate number of undocumented migrants crossed. Of the 1.1 million unauthorized border crossers apprehended in 2004, one-fifth were caught in one Arizona county, Cochise County, alone.[21] Such statistics are, as Jean and John Comaroff put it, part of the 'alchemy of numbers' that helps construct the rhetoric of fear discussed above.[22] For example, Mike McGarry, the Minuteman Project's media liaison, commented: 'We have something in the neighbourhood of three million people from all over the world breaking into the country. And we have an out-of-control—by any definition could be termed an invasion.'[23] Although such statistics can be used to signify 'invasion' and 'threat', they do not illuminate the political economy that creates a demand in the American labour market for immigrant labour.[24] But they are useful to motivate the enlistment of Minutemen.

Gilchrist had the following goals for the Minuteman Project: a) draw attention to 'illegal immigration' and the lack of border security; b) reduce the number of apprehensions along the border where they monitor; and c) influence the US Congress to put a 10-year moratorium on illegal immigration and cap the number of legal immigrants at 200,000 per year.[25] Although monitoring the US-Mexico border was Gilchrist's immediate objective, the larger goal was to use the 'citizen patrols' on the border to draw attention to Gilchrist's larger aim of influencing public opinion and federal immigration policy.

The government's immediate reaction to the Minuteman Project, before it actually began its operations, was not favourable. President

---

20 Ibid.

21 Amy Argetsinger, 'Immigration Opponents to Patrol U.S. Border: Rights Groups Condemn "Minuteman Project"', *The Washington Post*, 31 March 2005, p. A-3.

22 Comaroff and Comaroff, 2006.

23 democracynow.org, 'Vigilantes or Civilian Border Patrol? A Debate on the Minuteman Project', 5 April 2005.

24 Inda, 2006.

25 Strohm, 2005, ibid.

George W. Bush took a strong position: 'I'm against vigilantes in the United States of America. I'm for enforcing law in a rational way. It's why we've got the Border Patrol, and they ought to be in charge of enforcing the border.'[26] At the time Bush made this statement, he was meeting with Mexico's President, Vicente Fox, with whom Bush had discussed immigration reform early in 2001, during his first administration and before the 9/11 attacks.[27] The organizers of the Minuteman Project were outraged by Bush's use of the term 'vigilantes', which carries a negative connotation, identifying a group of individuals who operate outside the law, or 'rational' law enforcement, by taking action into their own hands. Gilchrist continually stressed that the Minuteman Project was a non-violent protest along the lines of Martin Luther King.[28] However, one of the main concerns of the Minuteman Project organizers in the days leading up to 1 April was the possibility for violence, given that many of the volunteers would carry guns. Moreover, one of the organizers, Chris Simcox, had been convicted on federal weapons charges and the white supremacist group Aryan Nation was recruiting Minuteman volunteers.[29] In addition to President Bush's condemnation of the Minuteman Project, Joe Garza, spokesman for the Border Patrol's Tucson sector, dismissed the Project's impact, stating that the agency was not planning to change any operations as a result of the Minutemen's activities.[30]

Despite such official reservations about the Minuteman Project, Jim Gilchrist was proclaiming success a few days before the Minuteman Project volunteers were even to begin arriving in Arizona: 'I

26 Strohm, 2005, ibid.

27 James F. Smith and Edwin Chen, 'Bush to Weigh Residency for Illegal Mexican Immigrants', *Los Angeles Times*, 7 September 2001, p. A-1.

28 David Kelly, 'Border Watchers Capture Their Prey—the Media', *Los Angeles Times*, 5 April 2005, p. A-1.

29 Michael Marizco, 'Abusive acts vs. entrants are ignored, activists say', *Arizona Daily Star*, 29 March 2005, pp. A-1.

30 Strohm, 2005, ibid.

struck the mother lode. It has already accomplished what we want to accomplish: nationwide awareness. And we haven't even started the project yet.'[31] Gilchrist's emphasis on nationwide awareness underscores the public spectacle nature of the Minuteman Project and its goal of disciplining the federal government.

It is easy to see why Gilchrist was claiming success before the Minuteman Project began operations. On 30 March 2005, two days before the official start date of the Minuteman Project, the Bush administration announced that more than 500 additional Border Patrol agents would be deployed along the Arizona-Mexico border, bringing the total to about 2,900, and additional aircraft. In addition, top Homeland Security officials would be arriving in Tucson, Arizona to add to the visible display of the administration's efforts to enforce the border.[32] Government officials claimed there was no connection between the minutemen and this new deployment of resources to the Arizona border.[33] However, a spokesman for the Minuteman Project, Bill Bennett, pointed to these deployments as a sign of success: 'President Bush called the Minuteman Project a bunch of vigilantes—but if it's the case that this [federal crackdown] did start because of the Minuteman Project, then the project is a success. I find it very interesting that this is all coinciding.'[34]

April 2005 on the Arizona–Mexico border

Minuteman volunteers officially began operations on 1 April 2005. Organizers expected 1,300 volunteers.[35] By 2 April, however, only about two hundred volunteers had shown up and were stationed in seven

---

31 Strohm, 2005, ibid., p.1.

32 Ricardo Alonso-Zaldivar, 'U.S. to bolster Arizona border security', *Los Angeles Times*, 30 March 2005, p. A-12.

33 Amy Argetsinger, 31 March 2005, *Los Angeles Times*.

34 Alonso-Zaldivar, 30 March 2005, *Los Angeles Times*.

35 Claudine LoMonaco, 'Minutemen gather in Tombstone for border watch', *Tucson Citizen*, 1 April 2005, p. A-7.

outposts along a 23-mile stretch of border.[36] One newspaper described the Minutemen's activities this way: 'In four member teams, they rode out caravan-style for several miles along red-dirt roads flanked by rocks and prickly brush. They fanned out hundreds of yards apart along a skimpy barbed wire fence at the Mexico border, eager to catch men and women trying to sneak into the United States.'[37]

The volunteers' motivations for coming echoed the discourse on Mexican immigration discussed above. 'We have an illegal invasion of our country going on now that is affecting our schools, our healthcare system and our society in general. No society can sustain this.'[38] Another said about immigration, 'It's destroying America.'[39] Another noted, 'I'd like to see my brother get a wheel chair lift rather than an illegal alien get a free education. I just think you've got to take care of your own.'[40] Yet another noted, 'I think all of this will put the federal government on notice as to where we stand as citizens.'[41] Such comments clearly delineate simple dichotomies, such as us/them, invaders/invaded, destroyers/victims, illegal/'our own' or legitimate members of society, and citizens/non-citizens, that define both citizens and those in a position of 'illegality'.[42]

Although the number of Minutemen was less than anticipated, the media turned up in full force. In fact, as the *Los Angeles Times* observed: 'The number of media members here Friday to cover the volunteer border patrols nearly outnumbered the Minutemen. Reporters from around the world descended on Tombstone, popu-

---

36 David Kelly, 'Citizens Border Patrols Hurry Up ... and Wait', *Los Angeles Times*, 3 April 2005, p. A-20.

37 Margaret Talev, 'Minuteman Volunteers Give Motives: Middle Aged Whites Express Frustrations with Illegal Crossings', *The Modesto Bee*, 4 April 2005, p. A-10.

38 David Kelly, 'Minutemen prepare to lay down the law', *Los Angeles Times*. 2 April 2005, p. A-15.

39 Talev, 4 April 2005, ibid.

40 Talev, April 2005, ibid.

41 Kelly, 3 April 2005, ibid.

42 Ngai, 2004.

lation 4,800. Along with journalists came some filmmakers work-ing on documentaries about the U.S.-Mexico border.'[43] Ironically, Chris Simcox, editor of the *Tombstone Tumbleweed* and one of the organizers of the Minuteman Project, seemed to blame the media for manufacturing the event: 'The media has created this frenzy and this monster. They are looking for Bigfoot, the Loch Ness monster, the vigilante.'[44] However, Jim Gilchrist was more candid: 'We have already accomplished our goal a hundredfold in getting the media out here and getting the message out.'[45] As Gilchrist's comment indicates, the Minuteman Project's goal of creating a spectacle is clearly elevated above other objectives originally elaborated for the Minuteman Project. Indeed, the other goals seemed to have been forgotten, perhaps reflecting the fewer than expected volunteers. Or perhaps this lays bare the point being made here, that media atten-tion was their only real objective in staging this spectacle.

On 3 April, the media reported on still larger increases in surveil-lance power along the Arizona-Mexico border. The Department of Homeland Security upped the ante to more than 700 additional bor-der patrol agents to the area.[46] In addition, the US Senate approved an amendment to hire 2,000 border patrol agents, a direct affront to President Bush's 2006 budget, which called for only an additional 216 new border patrol agents.[47] Both the new deployments of agents and the new hiring goals came just as Minutemen were beginning to monitor the border.

By 5 April there appeared to be fewer clandestine border crossers in the areas monitored by the Minuteman. Chris Simcox was quick to claim another success: 'We've shut down the whole sector. That's

43 Kelly, 5 April 2005, ibid.

44 Kelly, 5 April 2005, ibid.

45 Kelly, 5 April 2005, ibid.

46 Samantha Levine, 'Border guard shift questioned', *Houston Chronicle*, 3 April 2005, p. A-16.

47 Levine, 3 April 2005, ibid.

success.'[48] However, the reduction in numbers of clandestine border crossers was also influenced by other factors, not the least of which was the Mexican police force, Grupo Beta, patrolling the Mexican side of the border, warning would-be migrants of the Minutemen's presence.[49] Two weeks into the project, the Border Patrol had apprehended about the same number of clandestine border crossers as during the same period the year before.[50] However, such considerations did not deter Jim Gilchrist from bragging: 'None of this would have happened if it wasn't for the Minuteman action. This thing was a dog and pony show designed to bring in the media and get the message out and it worked.'[51]

Although the Minuteman Project was to be a month long monitoring exercise, Jim Gilchrist claimed 'victory' and formally ended the project's border monitoring on Wednesday, 20 April 2005.[52] Border monitoring was to continue, however, under the guise of Civil Homeland Defense, headed by Chris Simcox. Also, the Minuteman Project spawned related projects along the US-Mexico border in Texas, New Mexico and California, and far from that border in Idaho and Michigan.[53] The fallout from the Minuteman Project also had other ramifications. On 19 April Arnold Schwarzenegger, Governor of California, caused quite a political furor when he announced that closing the borders was a good idea. 'Close the borders in California and all across, between Mexico and the United States...be-

48 Michael Coronado, 'Wary groups in border watch', *Orange County Register*, 5 April 2005, p. News 1.

49 Coronado, 5 April 2005, ibid.

50 Chris Richard, 'The Buzz on the Border', *The Press-Enterprise* (Riverside, CA), 14 April 2005, p. A-01.

51 Kelly, 2005a, ibid.

52 Michael Coronado, 'Minutemen quit patrol early but declare victory', *The Orange County Register*, 19 April 2005, p. B-1.

53 Susan Carroll, 'Border watch to widen: Minuteman Project plans to patrol more states', *Republic Tucson Bureau*, 19 April 2005, p. 1; Jerry Seper, 'Border patrols inspire imitation—Other civilians take up cause', in *The Washington Times*, 16 April 2005, p. A-01.

cause I think it is just unfair to have all these people coming across,' adding that border enforcement was 'lax'.[54] In mid-August (12 and 15 August respectively) the governors of New Mexico and Texas went even further, declaring their respective counties along the US-Mexico border 'disaster areas', thus freeing up government funds to spend in the region.[55] Although the Minuteman Project's April offensive ended prematurely, it helped to turn the public debate on immigration reform decidedly toward increased border enforcement, eclipsing guestworker programmes, legalization programmes and other issues.

Jim Gilchrist managed to turn his 15 minutes of fame into an extended spotlight on 'illegal aliens' and the US-Mexico border by running as the American Independent Party's candidate for the US Congress in Orange County, California. The 48th Congressional District is solidly Republican, but Gilchrist managed to use his one-issue campaign to stir up politics. His campaign attracted media attention and a war chest of about $500,000, both of which helped him win third place in the 29 November 2005 primary election, with 15 per cent of the vote.[56] Gilchrist still came third in the final election on 6 December 2005, but he increased his share of the electorate to 25 per cent.[57] In the course of the campaign, the favourite candidate and eventual winner, John Campbell, had to insist that he, too, was tough on immigration. Two votes Campbell cast as a member of the California legislature became favourite Gilchrist targets. One vote was in favour of allowing undocumented students who grew up in California to pay in-state tuition rather than the more costly tuition charged students from foreign countries when attending public col-

---

54 Herbert A. Sample, 'Governor talks of closing Mexico border', *The Sacramento Bee*, 20 April 2005, p. A-3.

55 Nicole Gaguette, 'Border troubles divide US states', *Los Angeles Times*, 18 August 2005, p. A-1.

56 Jean O. Pasco and Dan Weikel, 'O.C. race a border skirmish', *Los Angeles Times*, 4 December 2005.

57 Jean O. Pasco, 'Campbell wins seat; Gilchrist takes 3rd', *Los Angeles Times*, 7 December 2005.

leges and universities. The other vote concerned Mexican consulate cards and their use as valid identification in California. By the time of the final election, Campbell had repudiated these votes and joined Gilchrist in opposing a guestworker programme and other moderate immigration reforms.[58] Immediately following his defeat at the polls, Jim Gilchrist assured his followers of his intentions to continue to seek elected office and to focus attention on 'illegal immigration'.[59] In other words, he would continue to use the spectacle of surveillance to garner media attention.

The spectacle revisited

Renato Rosaldo has observed: 'The U.S.-Mexico border has become theatre, and border theatre has become social violence. Actual violence has become inseparable from symbolic ritual on the border—crossings, invasions, lines of defence, high-tech surveillance, and more.'[60] To this list I would add the Minuteman Project. The border theatre that occurred in Arizona was, indeed, a symbolic ritual of surveillance.

However, the Minutemen's monitoring may not have provided a great deterrent to clandestine border crossers in the long run. First of all, the demand for immigrant labour continues to act as a magnet for Mexicans and others. This demand results from a complex set of interacting factors, none of which is carefully examined in the Minuteman Project's public discourse. For example, rarely if ever discussed are the effects of low fertility rates and an ageing American population, especially during periods of economic expansion; middle and upper class Americans' desire for cheap commodities, food, and services; economic pressures related to globalization and low-wage production in developing countries; or the economic benefits of immigration, not the least of which is immigrants' con-

---

58 Mark Z. Barabak and Jean O. Pasco, 'Election as immigration bellweather', *Los Angeles Times*, 8 December 2005, p. B-1.

59 Barabak and Pasco, 8 December, 2005, ibid.

60 Rosaldo, 1997.

sumption of US goods, or as *BusinessWeek* magazine put it on its 18 July 2005 cover: 'Embracing Illegals: Companies are getting hooked on the buying power of 11 million undocumented immigrants.' Simply increasing surveillance along the US-Mexico border does little to address these salient factors creating a demand for the type of labour supplied by undocumented migrants. Consequently, the Minuteman Project's monitoring of a small area along that border probably resulted in potential unauthorized border crossers moving elsewhere, seeking less guarded areas.

Without a doubt, however, the spectacle of surveillance was very effective in reaching the target audience, the public. The Minuteman Project's April 'offensive' on the Arizona-Mexico border was a media success, or as one newspaper put it: 'Sifting hoopla from hard facts can be tricky, but Minuteman Project has succeeded in key goal—shifting nation's eyes to illegal immigration.'[61] Not only did the media turn out in full force, but stories on the Minuteman Project saturated newspapers nationwide.

As the chart below indicates, newspaper stories on the Minuteman Project went from a few score a month in February to almost six hundred in April. While there was a precipitous drop in the number of citations to the Minuteman Project in the months after April, the number did not fall to pre-March levels for the rest of the year. There continued to be an interest in Minuteman activities for months after the April spectacle, rising sharply again in December with coverage of Jim Gilchrist's run for Congress.

From the perspective of critical cultural analysis, the spectacle in the desert has many connotations. The Minuteman Project grew out of a sense of frustration with new global realities that reduce the power of national borders to delimit the nation-state as an autonomous territory.

---

61 Richard, 14 April 2005, ibid.

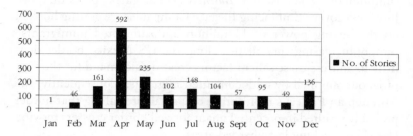

Newspaper Stories on the Minuteman Project, January to December 2005.[62]

Anthropologists have been arguing that these flows reflect the unmoored or deterritorialized nature of contemporary post-nation-state realities that make national borders permeable in many ways.[63] Indeed, the world is now on the move as capital, culture, people, and information flow across once ponderous national borders at an increasingly rapid pace.[64] The organizers and sympathizers of the Minuteman Project viewed its activities as a stand against the destruction of the nation-state symbolized by the inability of the state to control the flow of unauthorized border crosses. For the Minutemen, the 'breakdown' of border, as they perceived it, was an empirical assertion that the border was, for all practical purposes, a legal fiction.[65] Their dramatics were an attempt to reaffirm the contours of the nation-state, which from their perspective was in danger of being 'lost'. Through their actions, the Minutemen hoped to restore the nation-state's clearly defined border around its territory. The spectacle of surveillance on the Arizona-Mexico border drew the line, as it were, along the US-Mexico border.

The Minuteman Project engaged in a performance that inscribed citizenship and the nation similar to the way anthropologists have

---

62 America's Newspapers Online Database.

63 Gupta and Ferguson, 1997.

64 Appadurai, 1996; Inda and Rosaldo, 2002.

65 Coutin, 2005.

shown for gender.[66] Through the dramatics of their 'hunt' for non-citizen 'prey', the Minutemen enacted a rite of policing non-citizens, an act of symbolic power and violence that defined their own citizen-subject status. At the same time, the spectacle in the desert was a nation-defining performance. Unauthorized border crossers, those 'space invaders' as Puwar might put it, were kept in their own national territory.[67] For a couple of weeks in a small area along the 2,000-mile US-Mexico border, the danger to the nation posed by people out of place was averted.[68] The Minutemen's monitoring of the border was a corporal spectacle and for many the Minutemen came to embody the citizen exerting power to preserve the privileges, and purity, of citizenship and the integrity of the nation-state.

Appadurai, A. *Modernity at Large: Cultural Dimensions of Globalization*, Minneapolis, Minn., 1996.

Butler, J. *Bodies that Matter: on the Discursive Limits of "Sex"*, New York, 1993.

Cassell, J. 'Doing Gender, Doing Surgery: Women Surgeons in a Man's Profession', *Human Organization* 56(1), 1997, pp. 47-52.

Chavez, L.R. *Covering Immigration: Popular Images and the Politics of the Nation*, Berkeley, 2001.

Comaroff, J. and J.L. Comaroff, 'Figuring Crime: Quantifacts and the Production of the Un/Real ', *Public Culture* 18(1), 2006, pp. 209-46.

Coutin, S. 'Being en Route', *American Anthropologist* 107, 2005, pp. 195-206.

Douglas, M. *Purity and Danger: an Analysis of Concepts of Pollution and Taboo*, London, 1966.

---

66 Butler, 1993; Cassell, 1997.

67 Puwar, 2004.

68 Douglas, 1966.

Dunn, T. J. 'Military Collaboration with the Border Patrol in the US-Mexico Border Region: Inter-Organizational Relations and Human Rights Implications', *Journal of Political and Military Sociology* 27(2), 1999, pp. 257-77.

Dunn, T.J. *The Militarization of the U.S.-Mexico Border, 1978-1992: Low-Intensity Conflict Doctrine Comes Home*, Austin, 1996.

Foucault, M. *Discipline and Punish: The Birth of the Prison*, London, 1977.

Gupta, A. and J. Ferguson. 'Culture, Power, Place: Ethnography at the End of an Era', in *Culture, Power, Place: Explorations in Critical Anthropology*, A. Gupta and J. Ferguson (eds), Durham, NC, 1997, pp. 1-29.

Inda, J.X. *Targeting Immigrants: Government, Technology, and Ethics*, Malden, Mass., 2006.

Inda, J.X. and R. Rosaldo. *The Anthopology of Globalization: a Reader*, Malden, Mass.; Oxford, 2002.

Ngai, M.M. *Impossible Subjects: Illegal Aliens and the Making of Modern America*, Princeton, NJ, 2004.

Puwar, N. *Space Invaders: Race, Gender and Bodies out of Place*, Oxford, 2004.

Rosaldo, R. 'Cultural Citizenship, Inequality, and Multiculturalism', in *Latino Cultural Citizenship: Claiming Identity, Space, and Rights*, W.V. Flores and R. Benmayor (eds), Boston, 1997, pp. 27-38.

3

POLICING NKOMAZI: CRIME, MASCULINITY AND GENERATIONAL CONFLICTS

Steffen Jensen

Since 1994, South Africa has witnessed an increased interest in vigilantism. Vigilantism is commonly understood as activities performed by citizens who organize themselves into groups to take the law into their own hands in order to reprimand criminals and protect their community. According to this understanding, vigilantism is likely to occur when the state is unable or unwilling to fulfil its part of the social contract. Whether the upsurge in this interest emanates from increasing occurrences of vigilantism is debatable, as vigilantism has existed in many different forms for at least a century.[1] Nevertheless, two inter-related political issues seem to structure the current South African sense of urgency regarding vigilantism. Firstly, during the anti-apartheid struggle, the regime's counter-insurgency strategy employed vigilante groups to fight against the opposing 'comrades'; to be involved in vigilantism meant being on the wrong side of history.[2] Secondly, in recent years, organizations such as People Against Gangsterism and Drugs (Pagad)[3] in Cape Town, and Mapogo-a-Mathamaga in present-day Limpopo Province,[4] have challenged the

---

1 For an elaboration of historical forms of vigilantism, see Crais, 1998; Seekings, 2001; Burman, 1989.

2 Buur and Jensen, 2004.

3 For elaboration see Jensen, 2005; Dixon and Johns, 2001.

4 For elaboration see Oomen, 1999; Oomen, 2004.

47

legitimacy of the ANC government, as it is perceived to have failed to protect the citizens of South Africa. In the eyes of the new democratic state, these foremost representatives of vigilantism threaten the precarious South African miracle. In this way, crime fighting organizations hailed as vigilantes have faced potential delegitimization.

The political framing has been shaped by theoretical assumptions, which are largely inspired by Western literature on the subject. In this framing, vigilantism becomes the (understandable) response to the state's inability and/or unwillingness to secure the lives and property of its citizens. What is at stake, then, is the challenge posed by vigilantism to the Weberian state's monopoly over the use of legitimate violence.[5]

The specific South African political and theoretical framing of vigilantism has consequences for the study and understanding of contemporary vigilante activities. Firstly, casting it as the evil remnants of a horrible past effectively renders vigilantism as exceptional. Secondly, these understandings limit the exploration of vigilantism as anything other than as challenges to a (legitimate) state. Hence, we fail to explore vigilantism in its normality and everyday practice.[6] I have in recent writings suggested the use of the term 'everyday forms of policing'.[7] This expression focuses attention on practices identified through ethnographic study of people's daily life, their attempts to police their own communities, to secure livelihoods and property, as well as to survive an often violent and threatening everyday. This then allows for the analysis of diverse

---

5 See for instance Abrahams, 1998; Baker, 2002; Adler and Steinberg, 2000.

6 The study of vigilantism in South Africa would benefit from looking north in the African continent for inspiration. Here, a number of studies have emerged in recent years that do not take their point of departure in failures of the Weberian ideal state. While recognizing that vigilantism is indeed an important phenomenon with a wide range of repercussions for both political and social life in Africa, their departure points are anchored in the ethnographic studies of *inter alia* the marginalization of young men (Gore and Pratten, 2003), masculinity (Heald, 1986; Heald, 1999), and public authority (Lund, 2001).

7 Buur and Jensen, 2004; Jensen and Buur, 2004.

forms of policing within different communities, each understood to fit under the same conceptual umbrella and belonging to popular understandings of law enforcement.

Based on the concept of everyday policing, this paper explores three interrelated arguments. Firstly, it argues that everyday policing is not only concerned with formal and legal conceptions of criminal behaviour. Rather than crime being only transgressions of the law structures, everyday policing reacts to moral transgressions perceived to threaten the community. As community is a hotly contested entity, different forms of everyday policing target different forms of moral transgression from economic crimes to witchcraft.[8] Secondly, crime is not entirely a stable category; whether particular acts are categorized as criminal depends as much as on who has the power to define it as crime as on the act itself. In this way, crime is an effective political language that allows certain groups to act decisively to stop it to save the community. In Waever's words, it is a 'speech act' and its primary reality is the utterance.[9] Thirdly, some of the most important social conflicts in South Africa and in Africa in general, which are negotiated in everyday policing, are gender and generational conflicts inside particular areas.[10] Through the language of crime, particular younger indigent men and older, economically well-off men fight to gain or sustain authority, respect and livelihood in a time of socio-economic upheavals and change. Although accusations of criminality levelled at the opposition and practices to stop them are not the only arena in which this battle is fought, everyday policing remains an important political language and performance in settling the conflict between the young and the old.

I explore these three propositions in Nkomazi, South Africa. Nkomazi is in many ways typical of former South African homelands. It is located in the far north-eastern corner of South Africa,

---

8 Heald, 1986.

9 Waever, 1997, p. 222.

10 Oomen, 2004; Gore and Pratten, 2003; Heald, 1999.

bordering Swaziland to the south, Mozambique to the east and the Kruger National Park to the North. For years an impenetrable and dangerous wild-land, it was named the ethnic home of the Swazi people in South Africa in the 1950s. Thousands of people were forcibly removed from the Kruger National Park (a true wild land where humans had no business if they were not tourists) and from what became some of the richest agricultural land in South Africa. After the 1950s, successive waves of migrants (from later forced removals and from the war in Mozambique) washed over Nkomazi and transformed it into a highly complex and overcrowded social field. The fall of apartheid potentially heralded a new period of hope for people living in Nkomazi. However, many of these hopes have been dashed. While new opportunities have emerged for some, many residents of Nkomazi have shared in the downhill course of other poor Black South Africans facing the new processes of reconfiguration of class structure that have brought about rising inequalities. Furthermore, the AIDS pandemic causes daily ravages. Most of Nkomazi's estimated 500,000 residents live under traditional authorities that continued to be involved in intense power struggles with the democratically elected local government structures.

Nkomazi, then, is a battleground for multiple power struggles based on tensions created through differences between generations, class, gender, ethnicity, or governance. As we shall see, practices of everyday policing play a pivotal role in these power struggles. Based in ethnographic work in two villages[11] in Nkomazi, this paper begins by describing the multiplicity of different forms of everyday policing, before it examines how everyday policing works as a political language through which conflicts are fought.

---

11 Each of these villages contains around 20,000 inhabitants. In the former homelands the concept 'village' denotes first and foremost peri-urban areas that are ruled by traditional authorities. These authorities were formalized by the apartheid regime and perpetuated into the democratic dispensation (Oomen, 2000).

Multiplicity of forms

Evidently, the state and the police are the primary responsible parties in policing Nkomazi. However, there are at least three different actors involved in providing security: influential neighbours, the tribal authority and young men. Although the state and the police constitute important actors, this article focuses on the more or less formalized structures performing everyday policing. 'Influential neighbours' or 'concerned citizens', as one of them, Mr Khumalo, called himself, are important actors. As part of a larger endeavour aimed at understanding the different ways people in South Africa address concerns about security, a survey[12] was administered in two sections of Nkomazi: the rural area Flagstaff[13] and the peri-urban town KaMhluswa. This survey revealed significant differences in the ways different members of each community dealt with security issues. In response to a question regarding whom people would go to in times of trouble, approximately half of the respondents from KaMhluswa stated that they would go to the police, whereas only one quarter of the respondents in Flagstaff mentioned the police as their choice. In contrast to this, more than sixty per cent of the Flagstaff respondents said that they would consult influential neighbours. In both study areas, the local councillor rated second in the list of answers. Actual rates of reporting of incidents seem to confirm the trends emerging from this survey. In KaMhluswa fourteen out of thirty incidents had been reported to the police, whereas only one out of twenty-nine incidents in Flagstaff had led to help being sought from the police in a criminal matter. The second most common answer recorded by respondents was simply to do nothing or to go to a neighbour. Only two respondents in this section of Flagstaff went to the tribal authorities. One reason so few went to the police or to the chief was

---

12 The survey attempts to capture in more quantitative terms how people deal with security issues, crime levels, attitudes and use of police, and whom people go to in terms of trouble. Lars Buur carried out a corresponding survey in Port Elizabeth to assess difference in terms of rural and urban settings.

13 Flagstaff is an invented name.

that half of the residents come from Mozambique. Many of them are without official immigration documentation and as a group they are ostracized. In this regard, with their fears of exposure, Mozambicans will tend to go to neighbours when seeking help in a criminal matter, before going to the state or tribal structures.

The tribal authorities have traditionally played a role in policing the community, although less so in Flagstaff. However, in the adjacent village of KaMgweni which the chief considers his core constituency, the tribal authority plays a pronounced role in policing, especially after the emergence of the *Khukula*, which in SiSwati means the 'cleaning'. The *Khukula* was initiated by a group of older, socially and economically influential residents, all with close connections to the tribal authority and the chief. The *Khukula* began operating after a series of car thefts leading across the border (2 kilometres away) into Swaziland. Since then, the *Khukula* extended its mandate to include other categories of crime. After the initial spur of action the *Khukula* waned, only to resurface in 2002 after the murder of two young men. The local police endorsed the *Khukula*. As the station commander noted, 'That is also why the sub-forum works well. They are really working hard. They do case handling. They investigate cases, apprehend the suspects and then hand them over to the police. So as a result we only have had one case in the last month.'

Finally, crime is dealt with through young men acting in mobs. These young men are normally the targets of everyday policing. The occurrence of mobs remains rare. In Flagstaff, the latest reported incident involving a mob took place in 2003, a decade after the previous incident.[14] However, across Nkomazi mob activity is relatively more frequent. During one year I registered five incidents throughout Nkomazi. These incidents involving the mob are relatively short-lived explosions of fear, anger and frustration towards perceived threats—often in the form of witchcraft killings—that need to be dealt with by the community. In the case of Flagstaff, such incidents once led to the killing of an elderly man, whereas others resulted

---

14 Jensen and Buur, 2004.

in evictions. Despite their relative rarity, mob activities occupy an important position in local imaginaries because of the violence the community associates with them. Furthermore, as with the tribal authority, they draw on and are structured by local history. Whereas the local tribal authorities draw on cultural notions of respect, the young men of the mobs draw on and structure their anger and actions in line with the 'youth revolt' of the 1980s in which young men managed to supplant authority in the rural areas.[15] Today these protectors of the community are also referred to as the 'comrades' or the 'youth', and the political history of comrades continue to influence their struggles for recognition and livelihood.

Crime, criminals and the community

Across the board, municipal workers, police officers, tribal authorities and ordinary residents of Nkomazi agree that local crime is increasing. Typical remarks made today by local citizens link an ideal of a peaceful yesteryear, where authority and property were respected, with the greed, disrespectfulness and misbehaviour of today. Nonetheless, when I presented my research at the local police station in Flagstaff, the station commander said to me, 'I must tell you, Flagstaff is not a high crime area. It is very peaceful.' At first, it might seem difficult to reconcile this with the perceptions of increasing crime rates and the associated deep-seated anxieties and fears of theft, robbery and bodily harm most informants expressed in interviews. However, compelling explanations of the discrepancy exist. Firstly, the comments made by the station commander were based on the station's official statistics, which do not capture all criminal activity. Secondly, the commander's statement is based on notions of formal law where definitions of crime are formed according to penal codes. However, what constitutes a crime for people in Nkomazi is not so easily determined.

---

15 Delius, 1996; Ritchken, 1995; Niehaus, Mohlala and Shokane, 2001.

The multiple forms of everyday policing tend to target certain criminal activities in particular. Theft is considered to be the main form of criminal activity. Most thefts involve the robbery of food and bear the imprints of poverty. Other theft incidents concern the robbery of farming and household equipment such as wheelbarrows and building material. There are also other categories of crime that emerge from the narratives of informants. In one particular meeting, called by several respected individuals because 'there were some problems with criminals', the residents discussed issues of sexuality. Members of the local community were increasingly concerned about the apparent proliferation of relationships between older women and younger men. One informant remembers, 'All the young men were put in the middle, and their parents were allowed to beat them with belts. Only the boys were beaten, but that was a mistake. The women should also have been punished.' Also, the *Khukula* officially emerged as a result of a spree of car-smuggling to neighbouring Swaziland. However, according to several accounts provided by young men in the community, the *Khukula* beats them up severely for theft of sugar cane and for loitering in the streets after nightfall or drinking in one of the taverns. Neither the policing of sexuality nor that of perceived excessive drinking is limited to Nkomazi. In different settings, Buur and Bozolli illustrate the extent to which sexuality and perceived excessive alcohol consumption are and have been policed in the townships of New Brighton and Alexandria in Port Elizabeth and Johannesburg respectively.[16] They are complemented by Oomen who argues that older men beat up younger men for many different transgressions in Limpopo Province.[17]

Witchcraft, or the evil forms of the occult, is also policed.[18] There are two different forms of witchcraft accusation. Young men turn their wrath towards better-off and older men, whom they accuse of being engaged in such harmful occult activities, while other forms of

---

16 Buur, 2005 and Bozzoli, 2004.
17 Oomen, 2004.
18 Jensen and Buur, 2004.

everyday policing target the perceived detrimental jealousy of kin and neighbours.[19] In one such incident a man attacked his neighbour, a poor elderly woman who had knowledge of medicinal plants, because he believed her to have killed his bread-winning father. As a consequence of the attack, she was forced to move to another section of Flagstaff. Very few or none of these transgressions would have been recorded in the annals of the state, and in some cases the state might even have had to prosecute the protectors of the community, as they beat up night prowlers and burn the houses of alleged witches. Heald has forcefully argued that the links between crime and witchcraft are often overlooked.[20] Thieves and witches are, as she notes, bracketed together amongst her informants; their 'trials' follow the same accusational patterns, and the killing of either sort of transgressor is viewed as a service to the community.[21] The difference between each category of transgression is their being embodied in different people. Whereas witchcraft is located amongst the old and the poor, theft is seen as the domain of the young. By exorcizing those embodying danger, Gisu society has been able to preserve strict notions of manhood and morality in a time when both are under threat.[22]

The highly differentiated forms of transgressions illustrate that crime is a category that is negotiated and contested. As Durkheim once suggested, 'We must not say that an action shocks the common conscience because it is criminal but rather that it is criminal because it shocks the common conscience'.[23] Taking this quote of Durkheim as her point of departure, Carol Greenhouse suggests, '[C]ategories of crime do not derive from some universal scale of evil or public consensus as to interests, but from the way systems of authority make themselves known and maintain themselves. [...] The interests of authority and its needs for self-legitimization determine *crime*, then,

---

19 Heald, 1986.
20 Heald, 1999.
21 Ibid., p. 74.
22 Ibid., p. 89.
23 in Greenhouse, 2003, p. 269.

not the nature of the acts in question.'[24] Hence, crime as a category relates intimately to authority. In Nkomazi, crime as a discourse of accusation traverses, maintains, and challenges the structures of authority. Crime becomes a moving signifier that potentially disallows the communal recognition of those individuals it taints. In this way, crime is the constitutive outside of the moral community. It constitutes the outer boundaries of the polity in negative terms: Crime is all that the moral community is not. As crime is polyvalent, it serves different renditions of the moral community. Hence, the moral community and crime's personification, the criminal, are locked in struggles that disallow mutual recognition. Some versions of the moral community hold sway over others, especially the tribal leadership, vested with the authority of tradition, and often in a strategic alliance with the state against particularly young men.[25] As Heald points out above, these conflicts are inexorably linked to issues of generation and masculinity; at stake is how to become a man in Nkomazi.[26]

Generation and masculinity

After years of having been ignored, inter-generational conflicts assume an ever-larger place in scholarly debates regarding African politics.[27] As Jean and John Comaroff assert, 'Generation, in fact, seems to be an especially fertile site into which class anxieties are displaced'.[28] Generational conflicts in South Africa have a long history and particularly came to the fore with the youth-led struggle against the apartheid regime and its allies in the traditional structures

---

24 Ibid., p. 276

25 Oomen, 2004. One other vilified group in Flagstaff is the group of Mozambican refugees from the war, to whom South Africans attribute most of the crime. However, it falls outside the scope of this article to explore their coping strategies to survive the harsh stereotyping. For elaboration, see Jensen, forthcoming; Crush, 2002.

26 Heald, 1999

27 Durham, 2000.

28 Comaroff and Comaroff, 2000, p. 306. For a theoretical elaboration on the issues of youth in Africa, see Durham, 2000.

of authority in the 1980s.[29] In 1986, within just a few months, the 'Comrades' utterly replaced the traditional structures of authority in most rural areas.[30] Although the traditional structures were not entirely dismantled, the youth revolts of the 1980s had many lasting effects such as instituting a political language that had not existed before. Ever since, the 'youth' of Nkomazi—as polyvalent as 'community'—have been locked in conflict with representatives of the local traditional structures of authority. In ways recalling the analyses provided by Gore and Pratten, and Suzette Heald, crime, as a moral category of community destruction, constitutes an important arena for these localised struggles.[31]

In Nkomazi, crime control initiatives most often focused on young men. As one of the concerned residents who engage in everyday policing asserted, 'Those who steal are not the old people. It is the young—those in school or just after school. They are very difficult. I cannot begin to say how difficult they are.' Furthermore, the *Khukula* and the tribal authorities were deeply preoccupied by the problems associated with the behaviour of the young men in the area. The villages were continually policed to keep the youth off the streets at night and away from the taverns. As one member of the *Khukula* observed, crime most often occurred when the young men were returning from the taverns late at night. However, theft was not the only concern. Sexuality and the perceived disrespect of the young must also be policed.[32] In her analysis of Mapogo a Mathamaga, Oomen brings the point home when she asserts that Mapogo policing needs to be understood as a way of asserting generational control in a time when age hierarchies no longer—in the post-1994 moment—constitute privileged modes of authority.[33] Finally, everyday policing initiatives often emerged out of business environments.

---

29 Seekings and Everatt, 1993; Bozzoli, 2004.

30 Delius, 1996; Niehaus, Mohlala and Shokane, 2001.

31 Gore and Pratten, 2003; Heald, 1999.

32 Buur, 2003.

33 Oomen, 2004.

STEFFEN JENSEN

The *Khukula*, for example, had a history of protecting property and privileged access to resources.[34]

Most often, older men (whom I shall call the gerontocracy) succeeded in asserting authority in the community. Young men succumbed to their decisions and violence imposed both in everyday encounters and during special sessions where their behaviour became the focal point of performances to assert the community. In reference to a particular incident where young men were punished publicly, an elderly man stated: 'We did it because we got emotionally relieved. We can't just continue to talk. But it helped that the boys were beaten in front of the whole community. The parents are relieved because something is done for the victims as well.' In this regard, ritualized enactments of generational hierarchies function as a means of reaffirming a particular social order, which posits older, propertied men above young men who are weak on resources. Furthermore, everyday policing performs and confirms gendered hierarchies, as the dominant masculinity becomes that which is based on a particular social status. By submitting young men to everyday policing and the almost inevitable corporal punishment, the older men posit young men as not having achieved maleness.

Young, indigent men had few avenues through which to contest the power of the gerontocracy in everyday life. Nevertheless, they occasionally succeeded in temporarily overthrowing the local generational hierarchies of power. Most often this was achieved through the use of accusations and charges of witchcraft and sorcery.[35] In such events, the elderly and the powerful were publicly accused of

---

34 Buur, 2005 details the extent to which property is central to everyday policing. In situations where the recovery of goods takes prominence over seeing perpetrators brought to justice, structures of everyday policing can prove its importance, as a central activity (and selling point) is their ability to retrieve stolen property.

35 I use the two terms interchangeably. I take my cue from Stewart and Strathern, 2004, p. 2, who argue that instead of making strict definitions, we should note how they are used locally. In Nkomazi few people distinguished and witchcraft became the common denominator of evil through occult means.

performing acts of sorcery against the poor and disenfranchised.[36] In Nkomazi, witchcraft becomes the primary explanation for misfortune and is often associated with incidents of increased poverty or unexpected death. Most of the time, nobody acts on the suspicions. When people reacted to the suspicion there was invariably an intervention from young, indigent men. This analysis resonates with Comaroff and Comaroff who suggest: 'Many young black men, their masculinity ever more at risk, blame their incapacity to ensure a future for themselves on an all-consuming, aged elite' who turn them and other poor people into zombies, working the fields or the shops of the rich.[37] In this way, targeting the immoral gerontocracy becomes a way of dealing with the crisis of masculinity. Furthermore, through their accusations of witchcraft, the young men come to embody another moral community—a moral community representing the poor and powerless constituted in opposition to predators who literally suck their lifeblood by turning them into zombies that work the field of the rich at night; in this way, the accusations form part of a political language of gendered morality.

In November 2003, in the eastern part of Nkomazi[38], a relatively successful man had been suspected of getting rich by killing his kin and neighbours and turning them into half-living nocturnal creatures to work his fields. The man in question was involved in other

---

36 Witchcraft accusations can also be reversed and the rich (or better off) accuse the poor of witchcraft. In these events, the better off accuse the weak of jealousy of success. In one case from Nkomazi, a family almost killed an older lady whom they accused of killing the head of household who had just secured a well-paid job in the public sector. Niehaus, Mohlala and Shokane, 2001 also convincingly show that witchcraft accusations often, almost always, are levelled at the poor. However, in the case to be presented the accusations were levelled at the better-off.

37 Comaroff and Comaroff, 1999, p. 289. See also Geschiere, 1998.

38 The following narrative is partly reconstructed from interviews with the aggrieved family and other residents. It links multiple deaths to witchcraft. However, it can be argued that the deaths are HIV/AIDS related. As few people in Nkomazi accept AIDS as a cause of death, other reasons are sought. In many instances witchcraft is said to be the cause of death, but illnesses are also stated. See also Ashforth, 2001.

economic endeavours but community attention focused solely on his sugar cane farm. From the mid-1990s the new national and provincial governments expanded upon previous homeland initiatives, and invested money and political capital in the formation of a black rural elite in commercial sugar cane farming. The local chiefs were in charge of land allocation in Nkomazi and the land for these sugar cane projects was given to the oldest residents who had come to Nkomazi first, when the white government had forced them off their land. Thus the sugar cane projects continued to perpetuate traditionally established land privileges, as land was assigned to those already in possession of farmland. At the time, sugar cane promised enormous economic returns and helped reconfigure class structures in the former homeland areas. Yet from their inception, the success of these sugar cane projects has been clouded by rumours of witchcraft. A recurring rumour describes the rattle of dead children working the fields being heard as one passed the sugar fields at night. These rumours can, as Stewart and Strathern assert, lie unused for years but [...are resources] that can be pulled out in subsequent contexts of change and conflict.[39] In the case of the accused sugar cane farmer, despite recurring rumours of misdeeds, it was only as members of the family next door began to die that the rumours were persistently put to use. First the grandfather died, followed shortly afterwards by his son. Within a month of the son's death, a young sixteen-year-old girl fell seriously ill. The family then began to suspect the sugar cane farmer across the road of using witchcraft against them. They went to the local chief, asking for a letter granting them permission to consult a diviner (a *sangoma*) who could tell them if indeed their neighbour was using occult means to kill members of their family. The chief reluctantly conceded to their demand under mounting pressure from the village community to act against the sugar cane farmer.

The family and the sugar cane farmer went to the diviner together, sharing the costs amounting to more than US$1,000 for transport and the consultation. In a highly dramatic session, the diviner pointed

---

39 Stewart and Strathern, 2004, p. 39.

to the sugar cane farmer and said, 'You are a witch. You have killed before. You use a dog [as familiar].' According to the aggrieved family, the entire community felt vindicated in their suspicions. Shortly after the young girl's death and in blatant disregard for the mourning family, the sugar cane farmer allegedly slaughtered a cow to celebrate the girl's death and her ensuing contribution to his shadowy labour force. This proved to be intolerable to the village community and the next morning, approximately a thousand people, led by the youth, congregated outside his house in protest. As more and more people assembled the police were called and after hours of negotiation the police, the young men heading the crowd and the sugar cane farmer agreed that the latter should leave the village and move to the nearby town where he had family. When asked if this outcome was satisfactory, the family replied that they were no longer afraid of him. The youth and the community had assisted them, and the threat had been defeated. This event is a prime example confirming the existence of another moral community, one that has to defend itself against the greed of a predatory individual of the rural elite.

The role of the tribal authorities in this case remains ambiguous and the aggrieved family was doubtful of the depth of their support. When asked whether they had support from the chief, a member of the family replied hesitantly, 'It would seem that we did...'. They were right to be uncertain. After the sugarcane farmer moved to live with his uncle, the tribal authority had gone with great enthusiasm to apologize to the farmer and his uncle for their poor behaviour, and begged that the issue should be considered finished and that the farmer would not take any further action in this case. The uncle played a central role in the negotiations. Not only was he the head of the family, he was also considered to be a wealthy and powerful man in the community. He had strong links with the ANC (links that were said to have saved the farmer's life), he owned a hardware store and a service station, as well as farmland. Furthermore, he was among the first to be resettled in Nkomazi. In every way, he was an ideal representative of the new rural elite. The revolt against his nephew, instigated and driven by young men crowding outside his house, was arguably a protest against the gerontocracy. Other members of the gerontocracy were aware of this and did not (or dared not) intervene, knowing that the explosion of violence would be short-lived. When the crowd dissipated, the gerontocracy could leave its hideouts and resume daily business activities. This particular incident led to the eviction of one member of the community elite, but the gerontocracy in the long run maintained its position of authority and its control in the community. As the uncle asserted, 'There is no reason to dig into the past. I have given my word and it is all over now.'

The examples illustrate how the two different moral communities occupy different positions in terms of the power they can exercise upon the community. Although the gerontocracy's definitions of a moral community remain dominant, it cannot guard itself against temporary challenges to its position of authority. The two different renditions of who constitutes the moral community draw on different political registers. The gerontocracy bases its legitimacy on reified notions of tradition and culture. Civil status (including paid up *lobola* or bride wealth[40]), land ownership (or other forms of resources), control of one's underlings (children and women) and the respect of one's peers (in the tribal council or other institutionalized forms of culture) are central to the political language. These are the artefacts of a patriarchal masculinity. This form of masculinity was severely threatened during the struggle against apartheid where the institutions of traditional authority, which the regime created or empowered as a means of control, were under attack. Although initially opposed by the ANC, these institutions have regained much of their influence with and respect from the post-apartheid South African state.[41] These are also the institutions most favoured by the police, which see them as their natural allies in the rural areas.

---

40 In many cases, young black men are unable to honour the quite substantial demands of bride wealth, which might amount to sixteen cows or 16,000 rand. Hence many couples live without having paid *lobola* to the family of the wife.

41 Oomen, 2000.

In opposition to the gerontocracy, the young men draw their legitimacy from the revolutionary strain of 1980s youth politics and its promise of justice, freedom and equality. Still referred to as either 'comrades' or 'youth', they occupy a sacred position in South African non-white political imaginary. They were the ones who fought the mighty state and prevailed; they were the ones who, in the words of Adler and Steinberg talking of civics more generally, were 'the sole and legitimate representative of the people, a sacred and untouchable place of democratic sovereignty'.[42] However, the comrades movement or the youth was riddled with contradictions and fears. As Belinda Bozzoli argues, when the term 'comrades' was universally applied from around 1985, it 'became a catch-all phrase for young militants' to include every young man who professed to fight the regime, including criminals.[43] However, for those involved in formal structures the term 'comrade' only applied to those in organisations who acted in a moral and disciplined way.[44]

These same tensions existed in Nkomazi when the struggle reached its border in April 1986. Despite the organized and disciplined cadres' attempts to prevent it, the youth of Nkomazi were involved in witch hunting and burning in several villages. In these episodes, which took place over a period of several months, local concerns expressed through witchcraft merged with the revolutionary zeal of the comrades, to instil both fear and hope in the people of Nkomazi. This was a time when the social hierarchies were reversed. As Bozzoli argues in relation to the people's courts, which were run by the comrades, 'The reversal was what rendered [...them] capable of subverting the social order in ways which made them both frightening and capricious.'[45] For a few brief moments, the youth were in control and the age hierarchies subverted.

---

42 Adler and Steinberg, 2000, p. 7.

43 Bozzoli, 200,4 p. 95.

44 Ibid., pp. 97-110.

45 Ibid., p. 152.

In present day Nkomazi, the same contradictions and ambiva-
lences regarding the youth or the comrades prevail. Most people in
Nkomazi are just as unsure about the young men's promise of liberat-
ing the oppressed from the exploitation of the rich as they were about
the youth of 1986. On the one hand, they do wish for justice and the
safety against bodily exploitation promised by the young men. On
the other hand, they remain fearful of the potential chaos and the
terror these young men cause as they attempt to enforce justice in
the community. As one woman said, 'You must know that when we
hear the comrades today, we all think of 1986—and most of us are
scared'. Nonetheless, the language of comrades and youth remains
a potent political tool. The problem for the young men is that these
revolts last but briefly. As Heald notes in relation to young men in
Uganda targeting wealthier people and the chiefs (slashing fields and
beating up chiefs), such forms of revolt were often short-lived and
'constituted temporary stock markets of influence'.[46]

Despite the relative predicament young, indigent men find themselves in, recalling Gore and Pratten's analysis, these incidents of
reversing social order potentially act as a deterrent on the exercise
of power.[47] Furthermore, it can be argued that these gendered inter-
generational conflicts are embedded in irreconcilable and widening
divides in social class structures. As long as these divides exist, the
struggles between the gerontocracy and the young men will remain.
In the struggles for power links between gendered criminality, bodily
harm and moral communities will remain one of the privileged sites
in which these conflicts are played out.

Conclusion

Vigilantism has in recent years captured the imagination of South
Africa's public and political world. For many officials of the state
and leading members of the ANC, vigilantism speaks both of past

---

46 Heald, 1986, pp. 456, 64.
47 Gore and Pratten, 2003.

betrayals and of today's threats. In order not to fall prey to political and theoretical framing, this paper has proposed to explore what I termed 'everyday policing', that is, the multiple different practices of policing, rather than solely focusing on formal vigilante organizations. I explored the different ways in which people in Nkomazi deal with their security concerns, and how these resulting forms of policing traverse and undermine or perpetuate the social order. Although crime is an issue that impacts on people's everyday lives in often devastating ways, it is also an emic category that does not always correlate with formal definitions provided by state law. Accusations and policing of witchcraft in this regard provide the most radical example, but the policing of adolescent sexuality also illustrates the ways in which crime becomes the constitutive outside of a moral community. Finally, the chapter shows that there exist different versions of who belongs to the moral community, each competing with one another through different forms and practices of everyday policing. The gendered inter-generational conflicts between generic groups of young men and the gerontocracy are important in this regard. Each group draws on a different political language—one cultural and the other 'revolutionary'. Because of the recent extra-ordinary political and economic transformations on the rural frontier, the tensions seem to be permanent. In the allocation of guilt for social unease, death and poverty, everyday policing becomes one of the ways in which to create a separation between the 'good' community and the evil outsiders.

Abrahams, R. *Vigilant Citizens: Vigilantism and the State*, Cambridge, 1998.

Adler, G. and J. Steinberg. *From Comrades to Citizens: the South African Civics Movement and the Transition to Democracy*, New York, 2000.

Ashforth, A. 'AIDS, Witchcraft, and the Problem of Power in Post-Apartheid South Africa.' Paper presented at the School of

Social Science, Institute for Advanced Studies, Princeton, NJ, 2001.

Baker, B. 'Living with Non-state Policing in South Africa: the Issues and Dilemmas', *Journal of Modern African Studies* 40(1), 2002, pp. 29-53.

Bozzoli, B. *Theatres of Struggle and the End of Apartheid*, Athens, Ohio, 2004.

Burman, S. 'The Role of Street Committees: Continuing South Africa's Practice of Alternative Justice', in *Democracy and the Judiciary*, H. Corder (ed.), Cape Town, 1989.

Buur, L. 'Crime and Punishment on the Margins of the Post-Apartheid State', *Anthropology and Humanism* 28(1), 2003, pp. 23-42.

—— 'The Sovereign Outsourced: Local Justice and Violence in Port Elizabeth', in *Sovereign Bodies: Citizens, Migrants, and States in the Postcolonial World*, T.B. Hansen and F. Stepputat (eds), Princeton, NJ, 2005, pp. 192-217.

Buur, L. and S. Jensen. 'Introduction: Vigilantism and the Policing of Everyday Life in South Africa', *African Studies* 63(2), 2004, pp. 139-52.

Comaroff, J. and J.L. Comaroff. 'Occult Economies and the Violence of Abstraction: Notes from the South African Postcolony', *American Ethnologist* 26(2), 1999, pp. 279-303.

—— 'Millennial Capitalism: First Thoughts on a Second Coming', *Public Culture* 12(2), 2000, pp. 291-343.

Crais, C. 'Of Men, Magic, and the Law: Popular Justice and the Political Imagination in South Africa', *Journal of Social History* 32(1), 1998, pp. 49-72.

Crush, J.a.D.M. *Transnationalism and New African Immigration to South Africa*, Southern African Migration Project (SAMP)/ Canadian Association of African Studies, Cape Town, 2002.

Delius, P. *A Lion amongst the Cattle: Reconstruction and Resistance in the Northern Transvaal*, Oxford, 1996.

Dixon, B. and L. Johns. *Gangs, Pagad and the State: Vigilantism and Revenge Violence in the Western Cape*, Johannesburg, 2001.

Durham, D. 'Youth and the Social Imagination in Africa: Introduction to Parts 1 and 2', *Anthropological Quarterly* 73(3), 2000, pp. 113-20.

Geschiere, P. 'Globalization and the Power of Indeterminate Meaning: Witchcraft and Spirit Cults in Africa and east Asia', *Development and Change* 29(4), 1998, pp. 811-37.

Gore, C. and D. Pratten. 'The Politics of Plunder: The Rhetorics of Order and Disorder in Southern Nigeria', *African Affairs* 102(407), 2003, pp. 211-40.

Greenhouse, C.J. 'Solidarity and Objectivity', in *Crime's Power: Anthropologists and the Ethnography of Crime*, P. Parnell and S. Kane (eds), New York, 2003, pp. 269-91.

Heald, S. 'Mafias in Africa: the Rise of Drinking Companies and Vigilante Groups in Bugisu, Uganda', *Africa* 56(4), 1986, pp. 446-67.

—— *Manhood and Morality: Sex, Violence and Ritual in Gisu Society*, London and New York, 1999.

Jensen, S. 'Above the Law: Practices of Sovereignty in Surrey Estate, Cape Town', in *Sovereign Bodies*, T.B. Hansen and F. Stepputat (eds), Princeton, NJ, 2005, pp. 218-40.

—— 'Security and Violence on the Frontier of the State: Vigilant Citizens in Nkomazi, South Africa', in *Violence and Non-Violence: African Perspectives*, L. Bethlehem, R. Ginio and P. Ahluwalia (eds), London, 2007, 105-24.

Jensen, S. and L. Buur. 'Everyday Policing and the Occult: Notions of Witchcraft, Crime and "the People"', *African Studies* 63(2), 2004, pp. 153-71.

Lund, C. 'Precarious Democratization and Local Dynamics in Niger: Micro-politics in Zinder', *Development and Change* 32(5), 2001, pp. 845-69.

Niehaus, I.A., E. Mohlala and K. Shokane. *Witchcraft, Power, and Politics: Exploring the Occult in the South African Lowveld*, Cape Town, 2001.

Oomen, B. 'Vigilante Violence in Perspective: The Case of Mapogo a Mathamaga', *Acta Criminologica* 12(3), 1999, pp. 45-53.

────── *Tradition on the Move; Chiefs, Democracy and Change in Rural South Africa*, Leiden, 2000.

────── 'Vigilantism or Alternative Citizenship? The Rise and Fall of Mapogo a Mathamaga', *African Studies* 63(2), 2004, pp. 153-72.

Ritchken, E. 'Leadership and Conflict in Bushbuckridge: Struggles to define Moral Economies in the Context of Rapidly Transforming Political Economies', PhD thesis, University of the Witwatersrand, 1995.

Seekings, J. 'Social Ordering and Control in the African Townships of South Africa: An Historical Overview of Extra-state Initiatives from the 1940s to the 1990s', in *The Other Law: Non-State Ordering in South Africa*, W. Schärf and D. Nina (eds), Landsowne, Cape Town, 2001, pp. 71-97.

Seekings, J. and D. Everatt. *Heroes or Villains?: Youth Politics in the 1980s*, Johannesburg, 1993.

Stewart, P.J. and A. Strathern. *Witchcraft, Sorcery, Rumours, and Gossip*, Cambridge, New York, 2004.

Wæver, O. 'Conceptualizing Security', Doctoral Dissertation, University of Copenhagen, 1997.

4

EVERYDAY AND EXTRAORDINARY VIOLENCE: WOMEN VIGILANTES AND RAW JUSTICE IN THE BOMBAY SLUMS

Atreyee Sen

'Ordinary' women's involvement in right-wing activism has not only challenged theoretical models of women's resistance developed by feminist scholars, it has also opened up an analytical space which re-examines the gendering of violence and aggression. My research centres around the activities of women slum dwellers affiliated with the violent, Hindu nationalist Shiv Sena movement in Bombay. These low-income working class women played an instrumental role in coordinating communal riots and other public demonstrations of religious hate and hostility. This essay, however, will focus on their recent (and simultaneous) initiative to sustain a system of raw justice in the slum localities, primarily to favour poor women. My ethnography will show how marginalized right-wing women can strategically position themselves within multiple categories of social identity offered within a larger discourse of political violence, so as to confront, complicate and often change the everyday practices of patriarchy that structure social processes in urban slums.[1]

Unemployed and underemployed slum women constitute the primary membership of the Sena women's front, the Mahila Aghadi.

---

1 A part of the ethnography for this paper has been drawn from my forthcoming monograph *Shiv Sena Women: Violence and Communalism in a Bombay Slum*, London: Hurst & Co., 2007.

The front started out (in the 1980s) as a passive support group within an aggressive, ethno-nationalist movement. The combative activities of the Sena women's squads became prominent, especially their organized assaults on migrants and Muslims. The Aghadi women emerged finally as autonomous 'sentinels' of the streets of Bombay, openly patrolling their borders with Muslim slums. The front's militant actions came into the limelight during the 1992-93 Bombay riots, when the Sena women led attacks on Muslim ghettoes after Islamic organisations protested against the planned destruction of a mosque by Hindu nationalists in north India. Over a period of two decades, the Sena women gained substantial legitimacy as anti-minority religious 'warriors'. This essay explores how the cadres used their martial image and their notorious reputation within the politics of urban fear to develop an everyday mechanism that served and protected slum women.

The Sena supremo Bal Thackeray lauded the Aghadi's militancy during situations of communal violence in the slums; but he consistently glorified the more restricted roles of 'everyday Sena women' as carriers of domestic and religious culture. As a crucial wing of the party, the women had to show adherence to his preferences; yet, their daily functions incorporated activities involving structured violence, digressing considerably from Thackeray's vision of an ideal Aghadi woman. I suggest that the Aghadi's venture into vigilantism was a ploy to counter restrictive decrees on women issued by nationalist movements in particular, and society in general. Walking a tightrope between domesticity and public aggression, the Sena women used their greater nationalistic credentials to violently wrest practical social and economic benefits for poor women (ranging from material benefits, like illegal taps and electricity, to more intangible advantages like women's safety and mobility in the face of male predatory behaviour). While discussing diversionary practices within operational models of popular culture, de Certeau points out how people 'develop countless ways of refusing to accord the established order the status of law, an ultimate meaning or a fatality', suggesting instead that such popular tactics embody, in fact, 'an ethics of tenacity'.[2] This essay shows how the independent actions of a women's wing within a manifestly male political organization enabled it to operate as a new-age vigilante group, 'tenaciously' adapting to and evolving within changing climates of terror. The Sena slums, thus, exemplified a human habitation marked by conflict, poverty and questions of survival where 'routine, ordinary and normative violence of everyday life coexisted with sudden eruptions of extraordinary, pathological, excessive or gratuitous violence'.[3] The Sena women, however, concealed their gender concerns and continued to project their local militarism as 'religious valour'.[4]

Sharing loyalties, serving women: interviewing a 'notorious' Aghadi leader

From an anthropologist's diary:

Yogita gave me a call in the morning and asked me to visit her. I must have been irritatingly persistent, begging for a meeting... because she had that tone... 'OK come and see me pest'... I am getting used to it now. I put on a saffron *salwar kameez*. I hate doing this when I go to visit a new *shakha* (local party office), but it was a waste. She was not a member of the hardcore saffron brigade I had thought her to be. I walked straight into her tiny LIG (low income group) flat. The door was wide open and there were five women sitting on the floor. There were Walt Disney cartoon characters painted on the walls; a children's slide and water tub was pushed against a corner. The women smiled at me, they must have known I was planning to visit and one of them popped their head into the adjoining room and announced: 'Yogita*tai*, that girl from England (*woh Englandwali ladki*) has come.' Yogita walked into the room in a pale blue *salwar kameez*. She sat in one of the two chairs while I occupied the other. 'What is there to tell about me,' she began when I brought out my infamous notepad. 'I am *shakha pramukh* (local office chief) in Bhayander area for fifteen years now. I am bored.'

---

2 De Certeau, 1984, p. 26.

3 Scheper-Hughes and Bourgois, 2004, p. 5.

4 I have changed the names of my informants to protect their identities.

Yogita looked at the women around her and said: 'I am training these women to be my successors. Initially I used to take them along wherever I went for work. Now they go on their own.'

Radha: 'I am her neighbour. When I came into this neighbourhood, I was such a docile housewife. My husband did not let me go anywhere. Yogita*tai* convinced my family to let me join the Sena... (hesitant pause)... for a better cause of course. Now she says 'Be my successor'! I get a lot of freedom now, but even today my husband says if you go anywhere for work, make sure you take Yogita*tai*'s name. Everyone here fears her.'

A: 'What was the better cause?'

Radha (looking at Yogita): 'Uh... social work, *Hindutva* (pan-Indian Hindu nationalism)...'

In the following sections I will show how the Sena Mahila Aghadi used a range of strategies (persuasion, raw justice, threats, ostracism etc.) to gain the sympathy of poor women and partially modify their life-cycles in urban slums. Under the aegis of 'Uh... social work, *Hindutva*' the Sena women with various social and economic histories tried to develop a shared identity as a women's collective. The Aghadi members initially approached women who were partially free from male guardianship. This target group consisted of women who were heads of their households, widows, women abandoned by brothers/husbands and, often, unwed mothers. In the case of single mothers, the Sena leaders approached 'uncontroversial' women, on whom traditional sanctions had eroded over time. The leaders also pressured unmarried women and older women living among kinsmen, usually with no hope of marriage, to join the women's wing. Some women felt isolated in a life of poverty, and vulnerable because of the absence of protectors in their household. Some others were house-bound women with sick husbands, or workers who had acquired a degree of freedom after establishing their economic productivity. These women felt protected and 'empowered' to be part of a martial women's organization. After establishing a strong group of women in the *shakha* (the local Shiv Sena party office), the Aghadi

72

pursued slum women restrained at home and persuaded them to take part in the front's activities without offending their immediate families. By their own admission, mobilizing women and developing strategies for an everyday gendered vigilantism was not a unilinear process. The women did not organize popular courts. Their vigilante activities were based on women's formal and informal complaints, and on the Aghadi's nexus of accruing and circulating information within their localities.

Consolidating a system of brute justice

Yogita: 'During the rail riots, I took my women and burned a whole train. The corporation did not give us any water on Holi day (a festival of colours)… we could not bathe… everyone was so angry! I knew the local police would not dare to touch me. But unfortunately the matter came up with the Railway Police in Delhi and they arrested me. On the day of my trial, some of the Aghadi women from my area got into a jeep and whisked me away while I was entering the courthouse. I lay down on the floor of the jeep and the women sat on me. Later people told me that they thought a group of women were just picnicking around the area! The women took me to Thackeray's house where I stayed in a cellar for two months. After two months, I left the city and went to live with my uncle in the districts. The police frantically hunted for me… and finally the search orders were lifted. See these newspaper cuttings… (the headlines read: 'Yogita abducted from courtroom', 'Massive manhunt launched for Yogita', till finally 'Yogita's case dismissed by judge'). I did not see my family for months.'

The Aghadi tried to project itself as a general-law enforcing body, which did not operate exclusively for women. Yogita led all sections of affected people during the infamous Bhayander water riots (March 1998) into violence.[5] *Shakha* leader Surekha once received a complaint that a local shopkeeper dumped plastic bags into the drain, which clogged the sewerage system. Surekha and her mates marched

---

5 During the festival of Holi, when men and women were smeared in murky colours, the municipal corporation could not provide water to the local houses for the whole day in Bhayander. This angered the residents. They were led into rioting by the Sena leader Yogita Patil, and the residents burned all the trains stationed in the area.

to the man's shop, assaulted him, dragged him out, and made him climb down into an open sewer and clear the bags. On another occasion the Aghadi leader Laxmi smashed a cigarette-betel nut shop because the shopkeeper, a *chakkha* (a eunuch/gay), would lecherously say '*Aaja raja*' (come my king) to tease small boys. I also went with the Aghadi women for a sit-in demonstration against the municipal authorities trying to evict illegal tenants from government owned land. The group slogan I had to shout at regular intervals was:

'If Pakistanis and Bangladeshis can come and stay on our land, why can't we who serve the country stay on this land? (Twice) Down with the government, up with the Shiv Sena (Clap your hands).'

The women then went on to break the iron railing set up by the corporation to mark their territory. I watched while one of the cadres told me: 'Stay with us, you will learn so much'.

The Aghadi, however, gave special attention to women's grievances. Most slum women remembered with pride and relief how a man who raped his daughter received a battering from Aghadi leader Mohini and her squad. One day a Sena leader from Jogeshwari, Rita, called me and I asked whether I would go with the women to a local school, where a clerk had been consistently harassing a teacher. I arrived a little late and was directed to the school premises. When I walked into the office I saw this clerk kneeling on the floor, with Rita, perched on his desk, occasionally poking a measuring scale into his testicles. The man flinched in pain. He was made to apologize to the teacher, several times, and then had to say 'this teacher is my sister' and 'all women are my sisters'. After this entire drama was over, the Sena cadres left in a hurry. Before she sailed out of the room, Rita yelled: 'Make sure you are not a sister-fucker!' and slammed the desk into the man's chest.

This event greatly hurt my sensibilities and I stood around speechless for a while. A few days later, while travelling to Central Bombay to meet another Sena woman leader, I was 'teased' by a man on the train. He began to follow me to my destination. It was getting dark, the road was empty and the man did not leave my side. I stopped at a shop and asked for directions to this Aghadi leader's house. My 'stalker' turned pale and to my relief ran as fast as his legs could carry him. This event did not offend my sensibilities in the least and I cheerily rattled off the story to the Sena leader when I finally found her residence. There is a point in elaborating my dilemma. Sena women saw brute justice as an extension of the system of serving and protecting women's interests that they had developed over the years. The Aghadi's aggression became legitimised in a violent discourse, which perceived notoriety and rough justice as a prerequisite for the survival of poor women. And its 'benefits' were also enjoyed by the anthropologist. The demands for gender justice kept pouring in.

Poor women vigilantes were far more effective in delivering justice than men. During my stay in the Bombay slums, I saw women busying themselves assisting people in 'distress'. Men rarely addressed 'insignificant' local problems and became agile during larger political turmoil. Yet, even during Thackeray's arrest over his role in the Bombay riots, the women were more active in resisting officials sent to produce the Sena supreme leader in court. Though the Aghadi cooperated with both men and women in the slums, the women were far more passionate about their association with the front. Yogita, in her fifteen years of social service in Bhayander, had won over the loyalty of the women cadres to such an extent that the latter were willing to risk their lives to stage a dramatic getaway for their local leader. According to Rani: 'She rescued us from so many situations, how could we let her languish in jail?'

Yogita: 'We do the most for women because it is always a woman who has to deal with mundane affairs. This woman here (she points to a woman in the floor who was busy putting *vada*s on a plate which I later discovered was for me)... her husband left her with a child. She was helpless and came to me for help. I kept her as a maid in my house.'

Rani: 'After sometime Yogita*tai* told me that I was a good cook and should start my own business to support my child. She threatened some bank official and got a loan sanctioned even though I did not have any assets. I started a *vada pao* (salty doughnuts and bread) stall and now I have bought a small flat. I just have to pay Rs 20,000 to clear my loan. I am sold to her for life.'

When the Aghadi women were clearing sewage systems, controlling misdemeanours, protesting against evictions and procuring loans from banks, they used and promoted physical and destructive violence. They would not, however, blatantly contest the practice of 'customs' even though they were willing to use aggression to set limits to their practice. For example, in cases of torture over inadequate dowry, Sena women would ferociously protect young brides, and it would often lead to incidents of violent confrontations with the groom's kin. Seema, Aghadi leader, said:

'It is hard to fight age-old customs on the face. What I did was simple. My team we almost broke the backs of a few men who treated their wives badly for getting insufficient or no dowry. Now, we just visit all the weddings in my locality and make a survey of the dowry and declare that it is enough. None of men would dare to demand more after that or beat their wives.'

The Aghadi women were not battling for an abolition of the system of dowry; they claimed that exchange of gifts was auspicious during a wedding. Their inhibitions could be determined by their own desire to demand dowry while marrying off their male children. The Aghadi also remained concerned about its popularity as a social service group with limited resources, and probably tried to strike a balance between tradition and radicalism. The wing tried to relieve the bride's kin from the pressure of gift-giving. Chandrika, a cadre, said: 'We did not want the men to use the idea of inadequate dowry as an excuse to beat up their wives.' The system of raw justice aimed to redefine the concept of dowry to free it from commercialism and thereby curb cruelty to women.

Smita: 'Our girls are not always radical. Once we got news that a cadre, a young bride, was being beaten up by her husband. We went and rescued her at once and sent her back to her family. After a few days we discovered she was back with her husband. All our effort went waste and we were laughing stock for a few days. But we cannot blame the girl really. She must have been ill-treated in her family home as well. It's natural that she was not used to the idea of being a married woman staying with her parents. Since we do not run destitute homes or something like that, we cannot be judgemental about her behaviour. Over time, she will know that her situation is unbearable and then if she comes to us, we will help her again.'

The Aghadi leaders seemed aware of their limitations as temporary relief teams offering no real alternative support structures to women. Smita was affected by her loss of face, but she realized that the cadre involved was not yet prepared for any extreme action. She would wait for that moment when the young bride felt pushed to the brink. However, the comfort of belonging to a collectivity was unconditionally offered to the girl. I sensed that people were drawn to Smita because she sympathized with the aspirations of poor people, she claimed to 'understand' their circumstances. 'Oh, that must be taken into account. Only then my work can be legitimate. And the strategies can be effective,' she said. The women leaders were aware that programmes imported from alien cultural settings—from the West, from elite institutions or from male-centred Hindu nationalism—would fail when applied to the gendered, patriarchal, patrimonial systems operating in marginalised urban slums. The Aghadi tried to develop indigenous channels of social work, which took into consideration cultural factors like the role of the family, attachment to one's roots, kinship groups, emotional dimensions of poverty and community involvement, and reinforced rather than distorted them.

Yogita: 'Why did I start a creche in my own house? I used to teach in a Christian school in the area. They threw me out because I worked with the Shiv Sena. They can exert their Christian identity and I cannot exert mine? I promised myself that I would start a children's school in seven days' time. And I did. I painted the walls and invested the money for other playthings.'

The rivalry between the Aghadi women and members of other religious communities was at the very grassroots level. The women wanted to oust Muslims from the slums for more land, to eradicate competition in businesses, etc. It was clear that the larger issues of 'serving historical justice' were manipulated to resolve local level rivalries. Sometimes enmities arose over minor conflicts. After a Sena meeting, I went with some Aghadi cadres to a crowded beach to have *gola*s (crushed ice dipped in syrup). The women looked around for a spot to rest and their eyes fell on a group of Muslim women. After loudly accusing the women of reproducing rapidly and probably being married to the same man, the Aghadi cadres took off their slippers and started to throw them at the *burqa*-clad group of women. The latter, in a state of shock (as I was), gathered their belongings and ran as fast as their legs could carry them. The people on the beach looked on nonchalantly; they seemed to be used to the Aghadi's antics, or they probably endorsed anti-Muslim behaviour. The Sena women sat on the cleared spot and patted an area on the sand for me to join them. This attack on minority women was a case of pure harassment to acquire some space to sit, but the women projected it as a spontaneous display of religious nationalism. The Hindu women threw slippers, the Muslim women fled, the spectators, probably Hindu, did not intervene: this whole public performance of honour and humiliation reflects how nationalism gets refreshed and rearticulated as local vigilantism. At the end of the day it seemed to be a battle for space, be it the mosque at the national level, housing space at the slum level or just a place to sit at the insignificant level of an outing by the sea. The Sena women had a simple justification: the majority wins.

These actions, which appeared to be outbursts of irrational social behaviour, were forms of ritualized violence—a brief demonstration of the Aghadi's obedience to the Sena and to the religion. Displaying hostility towards Muslims allowed the Aghadi to gain a forceful visibility in their surroundings. Girard argues that the internal divisiveness and conflict within a group or collectivity may drive its members to seek out a scapegoat and sacrificially kill it to gain an uncertain unity within the group, making this a cleansing and a sacred act of generative unanimity.[6] The Sena women were aware that they did not experience a real threat from their impoverished Muslim neighbours; yet they needed to gain a more central role within a violent, anti-Muslim nationalist movement. So they exploited the more the general insecurities created by an understanding of the 'Islamic world' as

---

6 Girard, 1977, p. 23.

promoters of world terrorism. Since 'ideological fantasies were often forms of knowledge about the other, that appeared as a construction beyond argument or falsification',[7] the women would circulate myths about their neighbours (the Muslims had guns hidden in their tin shacks; they were eating *biriyani* to celebrate the death of local Hindus) keeping wider hostilities towards the Muslim community in perspective. In his writings on torture and the Putumayo, Taussig makes it clear that cultures of terror are largely dependent on the circulation of myth in which 'the fanatical stress on the mysterious side of the mysterious flourishes by means of rumour and fantasy woven in a dense web of magical realism. It is also clear that the victimiser needs the victim for the purpose of making truth, objectifying the victimiser's fantasies in the discourse of the other.'[8] The Aghadi *needed* to sustain a communal conflict and keep alive the threat of the Muslim other, so as to gain a more lasting status as women warriors. This strategy, when implemented successfully, allowed the women to offer better practical solutions to gender concerns within slum areas. The Aghadi's participation in a fundamentalist movement became more about claiming civil and political space for women, while couching it in chants of '*Jai Shri Ram*' (Victory to God Ram) and '*Jai Maharashtra*' (Victory to Maharashtra).

Yogita: 'Who are you?' (A man walked in with fresh bruises on his face.)

Man: 'Yogita*tai*, by accident I hit a man with my autorickshaw this morning. He and his friends turned out to be some rich man's sons and they beat me up so badly. I kept apologizing with folded hands, but they went and complained to the police against me! Please help me out.'

Yogita: 'Leave the FIR number with the *shakha*. Get your butt to a hospital first. Nothing will happen to you.'

AS: 'How do you know this man is telling the truth… he could be…'

---

7 Žižek, 1989, p. 24.
8 Taussig, 2002, p. 166.

Yogita: 'Poor people do not need to lie about such things... I have worked with these people for ages... they are all criminals in your eyes... but they are all fighting to survive.'

The primary reason for the popularity of the Aghadi was that they quickly redressed grievances, especially for the poor, in a society marked by 'untrustworthy' institutions of justice. Before my time in Bombay, news spread that local women employed in Middle Eastern countries as domestic servants were victimized by their employers. Some of these maids, who had been bundled back to Bombay, went to women's NGOs for help. With no aid from either the government or the embassies, the NGOs finally gave up on their case. A few weeks later the women informed the NGOs that their problems had been settled. The maids had decided to approach the Aghadi. The Sena women located the employers' relatives in Bombay, marched to their homes, threatened/thrashed them and recovered the sums due for the maids. Setalvad, in her comparative study of Hindu nation- alist women in northern and western India, also cites examples of the Aghadi's activities which involved '*gherao*-ing' a senior advocate in Thane, north of Bombay, and preventing him from appearing in court on behalf of a priest accused of sacrificing a child.[9] Over time, the Aghadi task squads were enormously glorified as covert and swift revenge groups.

The Aghadi's strong-arm image and philosophy of brute justice made women realize the possibility of countering exploitation and 'protecting' their jobs as a group. For example, the more aggressive Aghadi leaders could make sure that women got work round the year by threatening or, at times, thrashing building contractors, fac- tory owners or shop owners in their locality. They would also attack and abuse men accused of sexually harassing women employees. In this context, the slum women witnessed the everyday successes of collective violence. It is significant that the militant, mobile Aghadi women did not want to mass produce other women in their image. The fluidity in the organization and the flexibility in its approaches

---

9 Setalvad, 1996, p. 238.

to incorporation of women from varied backgrounds reflected the Aghadi's desire for sympathy, support and an extensive base of cadres. This phenomenon had parallels with the operations of other 'fascist' organizations, such as the KKK (Ku Klux Klan) in America, where the swearing-in oath for both men and women into the Klan stated: 'Female friends, widows and their households shall ever be the special objects of our regard and protection'.[10] In this context, Blee argues that there was a marked difference between the propagandist messages of the Klan and the real motivations for women to join the women's wing of the KKK, Kamelia. While the official line was to attack the racial others (African Americans, Jews etc.), women were drawn into the movement for 'much more mundane concerns like education, physical safety and family life'.[11] This is true of the Sena, because the women surely benefited, physically and financially, from their association with the Aghadi. Though there is little scholarship on Kamelia, a substantial difference with the Aghadi was probably that the latter women were consciously and conspiratorially protecting their own gender interests even while projecting a selfless, self-effacing image as nationalist women.

Most Sena cadres felt that the internalisation of violence was an existential reality in the lives of women. From an early age, girls would see their mothers and sisters getting thrashed by their in-laws. Many of them had faced marital violence themselves, had been raped by other men in the family, had been abandoned and also subjected to male supervision in the workplace. This kept them constantly vulnerable to sexual and emotional violence. Besides, life in illegally constructed slums required a state of preparedness for all forms of violence. There were several agencies striking them from all quarters, trying to uproot them from their life of subsistence. For the senior Sena women, migration and dislocation was also an experience of violence against women. One of the Sena cadres put it this way:

---

10 Quoted in Annan, 1967, p. 266.
11 Blee, 2002, p. 113.

'When a home burns down during riots, everyone shouts "violence, violence". When a home so carefully held together by a woman is blown away by storms, or maybe razed to the ground by bulldozers, then it is not violence?'

The popularity of some films was also an indicator of women's apathy for turning to state institutions for help. For example, the film *Zakhmee Aurat* (wounded woman) was extremely popular in the slums. It focused on a raped police officer, who organized a team of victims to castrate rapists let off by the law.[12] I took some of the Aghadi women to see *Pukar* (the call), a film about an unjustly court-martialled hero and his lover who foiled a terrorist operation by Pakistani militants. The hero delivered nationalistic dialogues as such 'A small country Pakistan, I will squelch it under my shoe... I don't need to be part of the army to do that'; the Sena women cheered and clapped. Setalvad argues that many state institutions, especially the police, the army and the bureaucracy, were perceived to be redundant, or incapable of providing prompt succour for common grievances (a case in court takes a decade to get settled), so that an organization that offered ready justice, whatever the means applied, enjoyed a special appeal.[13]

Rani (in the absence of Yogita): 'Did you know what she did once? She went to her village and was sleeping with her aunts and uncles. Some dacoits attacked the house and injured everyone. They hit her in the stomach with a rifle butt. In that state, she drove her uncle's motorcycle to the next village and came back driving a jeep. She piled all the bodies of her kin into the jeep and drove it straight to the hospital. Since it was night, the doctors refused to come, but she dragged the doctor out of his house at the point of a knife. The doctor saved all the family members and when he came out of the operating theatre and announced the good news, she collapsed from pain in her stomach.'

Yogita walks in and scolds Rani: 'How dare you talk about this event to anyone? (Rani looks at the floor.) I was supposed to be awarded for national bravery, but they did not give me the award because I was an Aghadi woman and had threatened the doctor into saving the lives of the people I love.'

---

12 Setalvad, 1996, p. 239.

13 Ibid.

From Rani's narration, it was apparent that she immensely admired Yogita's heroism. I realized the Aghadi's system of delivering justice through organized violence allowed women to be equal participants in a masculinist discourse. Not just as valued accomplices in public; the use of guns and knives or the freedom to drive vehicles also gave the women a chance to overcome pervasive feelings of envy against men. During my stay in Bombay, there was a spate of killings where Sena men were being targeted. (It was only after I left the field that Aghadi women were also killed by contract killers.) Most of the male leaders at that time had security guards carrying sophisticated arms. At a Sena meeting, I asked a guard whether I could hold his gun and shoot at a tree. He saw people swarming around the tree I wanted to kill, promptly turned down my request, but permitted me to hold his gun. When I put the strap across my chest, I found myself surrounded by Aghadi women who had been observing the exchange from a distance. They applauded loudly but quickly dispersed when I accidentally pulled the trigger. Luckily the safety lock was on. On the one hand, I could identify with the Sena women in the childlike glee at having handled a toy that usually boys played with, which was equivalent to crossing a frontier. On the other, I shied away from a collective glorification of the image of an armed woman in public. This is where one's 'status' as a woman stands out against one's 'identity' as a woman, which has been very poignantly described by Mies while discussing the methodological problems faced by female researchers studying provincial women's struggles.[14] According to Aruna, a cadre: 'We are heroines. We prove our might in the face of adversity. We *also* deserve an ovation.' The Aghadi's system of raw justice thus became an effective means of countering the efforts of men to recreate particularistic, non-competitive and unadaptive social structures in the slums of Bombay.

Yogita: 'Priya here is an interesting girl. She keeps quiet at home all the time like a good housewife. Her folks thought she was the docile, obedient sort. After joining the Sena, she was very active in all our violent operations.

---

14 Mies, 1979, pp. 13–17.

She would shout and scream during the Sena protests. Her family was quite shocked. But they could not complain because she was socially active for a good cause and she does not open her mouth in the house.'

Priya: 'At least, they should not take me for granted no? They know that I have many sides to my character now. I may be docile in the house, but I am capable of more.'

Several families in the slums saw women's raw aggression as a form of deviancy. Some women joined the Aghadi to show their families that they were *capable* of deviant behaviour, even though women were silenced at home. Priya, for example, used the vigilante politics of the Aghadi as a platform to raise consciousness in her own home about her subjugation, and show that she retained the capability to fight back. Hence complete domesticity did not come 'automatically' to most slum women, even though they had been practicing it for years. They were willing to be part of a collective strategy to wrest more public space, though this kind of endeavour without a support group appeared frightening to them. The women were also content to achieve their end in phases, without toppling their immediate family structures.

Jenkins, while studying ethnic problems in Northern Ireland, commented that the vision of a researcher studying ethnic communities could be structured to *see* an intense solidarity among the group, especially if the group is forcefully displaying it all the time.[15] I often sat among the Aghadi members and wondered whether I was missing sharp differences of opinion among them. There were arguments and clash of ideas, but there was a sincere effort to organize all kinds of slum women. There were no fixed policies. Initiation of new members seemed to add vitality to the wing. There was all-round excitement and sweets were given out to reinforce the group solidarity. There were no formal incorporation rituals and the inflow of women was an outsider-insider, a cadre-leader continuing process. Some of the women would tell me how the process would reawaken a cadre's

---

15 Jenkins, 1997.

sense of responsibility to the group and would also reassure her that she operated within a structure on which she could depend. The intensity of the reciprocal relationship apparently made the women feel 'invulnerable' to the world outside. According to Sandhya, a senior cadre,

Each new face reminds me that this girl has come because she believes in what I believe in… and makes me think afresh about what I want… and since I am already an old member of the group, I feel more responsible because there are new faces that will depend on me… and it will be my job to keep them with the wing, protect them from the world outside and also help them face it…

The estrangement that came with relocation into a peripheral urban setting slowly faded with support from a clearly defined group. Neha, a new member, said: 'I want to stay in a small, stable and less mobile community. I want to stay in the Aghadi.' The women in the Aghadi sought unity, but also did not want to be depersonalized to the extent to which they believe Muslim women in *burqas* experience uniformity. Jaba said, 'In our culture we do not make our sexuality apparent. But they (Muslim women) look like a flock of black crows! You can't tell one from the other.' The Aghadi women obviously enjoyed their visibility, and the fact that their vigilantism marked them out as women to be seen and feared.

Rewards for 'bad conduct'?: male leaders endorsing Aghadi solidarity

The Shiv Sena's upper male leadership had noticed the functionality and powerful impact of women operating in solidarity, and some of the male leaders conspired with the Aghadi to create an everyday space where women could interact freely and assert their presence without coming under suspicion.

The Aghadi had played a visibly aggressive role during the Bombay riots, which had benefited the Sena men. Madhukar Sarpotdar, a notorious Sena corporation member, was arrested for supplying arms to Hindu rioters. The Aghadi slum women in Sarpotdar's constituency demonstrated in front of the police station and shouted slogans until the police were 'forced' to release him. Some women even lay down on the ground preventing police vans from entering the station premises. The women felt that men could not have achieved this effect since they would have been dispersed easily by a police '*lathi* (stick)-charge'. Women on the other hand were imagined to be 'frailer' and traditionally safeguarded from bodily harm in public.

The local police chief had failed to retaliate against the demonstrating Sena women. He spoke to me about the soft line toed by the legal system towards women's criminality, which was a subtle form of lamenting the protectionist attitude of patriarchy towards women. A male policeman 'touching' a woman was interpreted as violation of women's physical and sexual honour in public. Ridd, while discussing the symbolic and covert powers gained by women caught in conflict, said: 'Women seen as political innocents can on occasion use their immunity to take initiatives and responsibilities of a covert political nature'.[16] It became fairly obvious through my interaction with the Aghadi members and the policemen that women's manipulation of this feminine immunity, often to shelter Sena men, was a disturbing yet palpable 'public menace'.

In the context of women in struggle, Ridd further argues that women's powers can take on various symbolic forms. A society directing all its resources towards sustaining a violent movement may exploit the power of women to represent to the outside world its determination on its struggle, in which even women and children play their part.[17] This principle has been used effectively in a few Shiite Muslim communities, where the media filmed veiled women who had their fists clenched while shouting for Ayatollah Khomeini in the streets of Tehran.[18] Some of these arguments have been taken further by Giles and Hyndman, who highlight the prevalent representations of women in conflict situations. Through the writings of

16 Ridd and Callaway, 1986, p. 12.
17 Ibid.
18 Mernissi, 1987.

a network of feminist scholars, the authors assemble various images of 'a woman with a rifle over her shoulder and a baby on her back, or in similar fashion, images of nationalist Croatian or Serbian mothers and daughters protesting on the street to prevent relief trucks from reaching zones belonging to the enemy'.[19] The authors expressly blame the state institutions, media, and military organizations for manipulating these images as iconic representations or symbols of women in violence. The activities of the Sena women also appear to comfortably juxtapose the seemingly conflicting notions of the protected female and the militant woman. Instead of being manipulated by the party or the media, the women claimed that they had knowingly demonstrated in public, often going against the party dictates. The primary aim was to establish women's indispensability in prolonging an ethno-nationalist struggle, where the presence of women in locations of violence could (a) draw attention to the movement and (b) save the Sena men from 'returning home in gunny bags' (leak-proof sacks for carrying mangled dead bodies).

Among the male leaders, Sarpotdar decided to develop physical support structures to ensure that Sena women's strength and solidarity did not get eroded within daily slum life. When Sarpotdar became MLA (Member of the Legislative Assembly), he was allotted an amount of money to extend civic facilities to the people in his assembly. He invested a part of that money in building three decorative Ganapati[20] temples with expensive bathroom tiles. This appeased the Sena women, because it gave them a fancy place to meet and sing *kirtan*s (devotional songs) in the evening. Women were not condemned for gathering in these temple areas, and hence they could freely exchange their ideas for recruitment and raw justice. I often went to these *kirtan* sessions and though I did not put my vocal skills to test, I enjoyed the energy of the place when all the women sang, laughed, cried and conspired together. Most women,

---

19 Giles and Hyndman, 2004, p. 4.
20 Ganesha, an elephant-headed Hindu God popular in western India.

who mourned the lost vitality of community life in villages, seemed to have regained their traditional group solidarities.

The Aghadi's world of protective vigilantism gave the slum women a chance to assimilate into a new social and political network, within which they could resolve their urban insecurities and experiences of alienation. And some male leaders in their limited capacity helped the Aghadi increase their scope for mobilizing these women.

Choices and sanctions

The Aghadi concentrated on earning merit within their surrounding network of Sena members. The cadres first took advantage of the built-in choices available to women (such as trips to the market) and then exploited the choices developed for them (attending the Aghadi meeting while out shopping). 'Choices usually curtail or reinforce one another.'[21] In the case of Yogita's 'loss of face', a woman did have the choice of ending an abusive marriage, but since she could not support herself or return to her natal home, her choice became devoid of meaning. The Aghadi was aware that 'disadvantaged' women could not relate to feminist stands.[22] Instead, the Aghadi turned itself into an alternative organization, informing women about the 'unconventional' choices available to them. For example, the Aghadi ran catering factories which solely employed slum women, thereby offering a 'men-free' space in which women developed emotional bonds and acquired a source of income. These factories reinforced partially the choices available to women because they realized the value of financial and emotional fallbacks when faced with personal crises. However, the Sena women's front did not rest on their laurels and remained concerned about the future of the Aghadi; women's strategies were oriented to gain long-term sustainability for the organisation.

---

21 Dube, 1997 p.9.

22 The vigilante activities of the Aghadi challenged the feminist movement in many ways, a debate which remains beyond the scope of this paper. However, it has been discussed further in my forthcoming book.

The Aghadi did not always represent an image of a patient and benevolent giver of social and economic goods. In situations of crisis, the refusal of cadres to contribute to collective action, whether actively or through support functions, was penalized by the Aghadi through systems of formal or informal sanctions like collective ostracism. In such situations, there were few choices available to women. During the Bombay riots, for example, a Sena mob attacked a bus and dragged out six passengers identified as Muslims. While five of them tried to escape, one man received a head injury and fell down and fainted. As he lay unconscious, the mob poured kerosene on him and torched him. While the man lay burning, the Sena women threw stones at the Muslim passengers fleeing from the scene. One of the women later approached a *Mashwara*, a legal aid centre, to avoid a police crackdown on her pro-Sena family. She claimed she took part in the violence to avoid being branded a deserter, which was common if cadres did not respond to the call of the Aghadi. She chose not to remain ostracized from the Aghadi's comforting and constructive social and financial network in the slums. So, while trying to instil discipline in its operations as deliverers of immediate, social or historical justice, the Aghadi functioned through a system of positive *and* negative incentives. This was in keeping with the ideals of the Aghadi to develop a reputation as a martial women's organization. The stress on intolerance of any breach of discipline during displays of group action upheld the Aghadi's faith in structured violence.

The Aghadi's ultimate goal was to create a militaristic Hindu society, where women had the freedom of mobility, assertiveness and association. This 'freedom' would remain couched in women's nationalistic credentials. When Abu Azmi, a member of the Samta Party, which was originally the Muslim League, made a comment against Hindus in India, all the Aghadi leaders marched to the town centre and burned Azmi's effigies. After a few days, when the agitation did not subside, Azmi apologized in public and withdrew his comment. There was revelry after the public apology was issued and the success of the Aghadi movement was extolled. The women's wing had displayed its anger against an imaginary alien so that the women's battle against the enemy within, their patriarchal fetters, remained submerged in the din of protests and celebrations of success.

Conclusion

In this paper, I have tried to explore the ways in which the Mahila Aghadi functioned as a vigilante group, and restructured its environment in terms of power and autonomy for women.

According to Mernissi, 'the public visibility of women terrifies and angers most men'. Though she was referring to the male-female dynamics in a Muslim fundamentalist society, this terror at seeing women in public roles seems to be partly at the base of ideological revitalization of suppressive religious movements in an urban setting, where socio-economic shifts are compelling women to enter the labour force in greater numbers. Though the thrust of a right-wing movement is to recreate a moral order where simplifying reality would dilute role conflict between the sexes, the Aghadi operated differently. Since a large proportion of the Sena women consisted of workers, it was difficult for the Aghadi to develop a gender discourse which put women squarely within the home. Even though the Sena supreme leader emphasized the role of women in upholding tradition, the Aghadi expressed support for the large numbers of Sena women who have entered the public realm to provide for their families. The popularity of the women's wing was related not just to its political standing and achievement, but also to its grass-roots activities, which made its emergence and the legitimization of its authority possible for women.

Women were mobilized into the Aghadi, and desired the stability that came with a shared identity and common interests within an organization. At the same time, they did not desire the stability which remained embedded in clearly defined sex roles, a family life and passive religious orientation. Thus women created and organized the Aghadi according to these desires. While recreating the moral universe as 'committed' members of the violent *Hindutva* brigade, women were trying to conceive a more flexible construction of womanhood. The Sena men only saw the 'culture masks of women'[23] because they uncritically assumed their claims *on* women. The Aghadi saw the real faces of women marked by multiple insecurities and made claims *for* them, which forms the basis of women's vigilantism. On the one hand, the Sena women had a pragmatic and utilitarian approach towards political participation. On the other, the Aghadi negotiated to create a transitional space between the harsh reality of the current community and the imagined Hindu nation, where women's honour was tied to women's autonomy. The ambiguous notions of nation and culture allowed the women to manipulate these two concepts and keep up the pretence of a struggle for a Utopian Hindu community; if that goal is reached, and peace reigns, then all Hindu women return to their homes. This means that the autonomous space for women lay in perpetuating a violent struggle, and not in reaching the end. So in the case of the Aghadi women, organization and mobilization entailed the creation of an 'artificial reality', i.e. women needed to struggle for the greater Hindu community to come into being. This parallel universe was created in response to what the women felt was an 'actual reality', i.e. women violently wresting social and economic benefits through their visibility within a struggle. This paper has tried to recognize the transformative potential in such mass actions by uncovering the internal dynamics of women's vigilantism.

☸

Annan, D. 'The Ku Klux Klan', in *Secret Societies*, N.I. MacKenzie (ed.), London, 1967, pp. 222-37.

Blee, K.M. 'The Gendered Organization of Hate: Women in the U.S. Ku Klux Klan', in *Right-wing Women: from Conservatives to Extremists around the World*, P. Bacchetta and M. Power (eds), New York, 2002, pp. 101-14.

---

23 Moghadam, 1994.

De Certeau, M. *The Practice of Everyday Life*, Berkeley, 1984.

Dube, L. *Women and Kinship: Comparative Perspectives on Gender in South and South-East Asia*, Tokyo and New York, 1997.

Giles, W.M. and J. Hyndman. *Sites of Violence: Gender and Conflict Zones*, Berkeley, 2004.

Girard, R. *Violence and the Sacred*, Baltimore, 1977.

Jenkins, R. *Rethinking Ethnicity: Arguments and Explorations*, London; Thousand Oaks, California, 1997.

Mernissi, F. *Beyond the Veil: Male-female Dynamics in Modern Muslim Society*, Bloomington, 1987.

Mies, M. *Towards a Methodology of Women's Studies*, The Hague, 1979.

Moghadam, V.M. *Gender and National Identity: Women and Politics in Muslim Societies*, London, 1994.

Ridd, R. and H. Callaway. *Caught up in Conflict: Women's Responses to Political Strife*, Basingstoke, 1986.

Scheper-Hughes, N. and P.I. Bourgois. 'Introduction', in *Violence in War and Peace: an Anthology*, N. Scheper-Hughes and P.I. Bourgois (eds), Malden, Mass., 2004, pp. 1-31.

Setalvad, T. 'The Woman Shiv Sainik and Her Sister Swayamsevika', in *Women and Right Wing Movements: Indian Experiences*, T. Sarkar and U. Butalia (eds), Delhi, 1996, pp. 233–44.

Taussig, M. 'Culture of Terror—Space of Death: Roger Casement's Putumayo Report and the Explanation of Torture', in *Genocide: An Anthropological Reader*, A. Hinton (ed.), Oxford, 2002, pp. 164-91.

Žižek, S. *The Sublime Object of Ideology*, London, New York, 1989.

5

'POLICING' THROUGH VIOLENCE: FEAR, VIGILANTISM, AND THE POLITICS OF ISLAM IN NORTHERN NIGERIA[1]

Conerly Casey

In the years 1999 and 2000, the implementation of Shari'a criminal law in twelve states across northern Nigeria brought violent conflicts over the legal bounds of civility and criminality, and heated public debate about the place of ethnicity, religion and region in Nigerian governance. New cultures of surveillance emerged in northern cities such as Kano, where an Independent Shari'a Implementation Committee recruited *'yan hisba*, the watching, enforcing tier of the Committee, from ward vigilantes, some of whom were also *'yan daba*

1 I am grateful for the assistance of Aminu Shariff Bappa, Usman Aliyu and Show Boy, and for the *'yan daba*, *'yan hisba* and families who allowed me into their lives. For reasons of confidentiality, they shall remain unnamed, but I greatly appreciate my experiences with them. I would like to thank Salisu Abdullahi, Abdulkarim Dan Asabe, Phillip Shea, Murray Last, Istvan Patkai, Aminu Taura Abdullahi, Aminu Inuwa, and Umar Sanda for their important contributions to my thinking about this project. I thank faculty in the Departments of Psychiatry and Sociology, Bayero University and in the Department of Anthropology, University of California, Los Angeles for research affiliations and a sense of home base. I am greatly indebted to Allen Feldman and Uli Linke for their mentoring and inspiration for this project. However, the project would have been impossible without the generous support of the Harry Frank Guggenheim Foundation, and the skilful guidance of Karen Colvard, followed by a Fulbright IIE Lecturing/Research Award.

(urban ward gang members).[2] *'Yan daba* agitated for the immediate implementation of Shari'a law, threatening and enacting violence to persuade the Governor, Rabiyu Kwankwaso, to sign it into law. *'Yan daba* violence, though necessary for the radical break with secular law, was at the moment of violence outside Shari'a law, so that *'yan daba* affectively broke with all law, and became the primary focus of *'yan hisba* intervention. Likewise, *'yan hisba* declared informal Islamic 'states of emergency' to justify their violence against non-conforming Muslims and Christians; they, too, through violence effectively placed themselves outside of Shari'a law.

The way in which Shari'a law was implemented illustrates the power of Nigerian armed youths to instigate and resolve conflict through violence—to 'police' through violence. The implementation of Shari'a constituted and reflected conflations of identity, morality, and ward and state security, which led to violence towards Muslims and Christians, along with the exclusion and arrests of Muslims whose moral aesthetic values and behaviour were not those of the reformist Muslim Hausa Ulama. Moral aesthetics, and the power of their classifications, were strengthened, in Kano, by the inseparability of what is seen from what is unseen, or the world of spirits. Reformist Muslims, while condemning aesthetics and behaviour—such as adornments used in animist-Islamic or Sufi rituals, or the playing of musical instruments—that signify or incite breaches in the demarcation between the worlds of humans and spirits, nonetheless reinforced the power of this relationship; they employed realist interpretations of Qur'anic scripture as 'truth', to project visual/spiritual profiles of

---

2 The change in 1999 and 2000 involved a re-imposition of the criminal code of Shari'a that had been in place during the colonial period (under the control of British who outlawed *hadd* punishments which they found 'repugnant'), but had been excised at independence (Kumo, 1993:7-8). Following the implementation of Shari'a criminal law in November 2000, the Kano State government formed the Kano State Shari'a Implementation Committee to address charges that *'yan hisba* of the Independent Shari'a Implementation Committee were abusing their powers. The government committee retained most of the *'yan hisba* from the Kano Independent Shari'a Implementation Committee, but provided increased supervision and a code of conduct.

the 'enemies' of Islam into popular consciousness. *Yan hisbah*, who identified themselves as 'Nigerian Orthodox Muslims', an uneasy alliance of reformist Shia and Sunni Muslims,[3] vigilantly profiled Muslims living in ethnically plural spaces, Muslim ethnic minorities, and people who, by virtue of their region of origin, religion, or ethnicity, were 'marginal Muslims' or polytheists, and thus, 'out of place'. *Yan hisbah* considered Muslim *'yan daba*, *'yan Bori* (followers of *Bori*)[4], non-reformist Sufis, and non-Hausa Muslims, particularly Muslim Yorubas, to be political, spiritual saboteurs who disallowed the re-enchantment of orthodoxy and its ability to function as an Islamic collective memory, a history of perception that would unify Nigeria's Muslims and draw them more fully into world networks of reformist Muslims. Through preaching and surveillance, *'yan hisba* inserted visual/spiritual profiles of the enemies of Islam into concepts of Muslim piety, Muslim Hausa 'indigene' versus 'settler', 'tenant' or 'alien', enforcing a Hausa ethnicization of Islam, along with ethnic

---

3 Prior to the implementation of Shari'a law, there was a concerted effort to reconcile Kano Muslim sects and factions. I use the locally employed term 'Nigerian Orthodox Muslims', rather than 'Islamist' or 'political Islam' to emphasise reconciliation and Nigerianisation..

4 'Bori' is widely regarded as animism or a spirit possession cult that predated Islam (Besmer, 1983; Bourguignon, 1968; Callaway, 1987; Greenberg, 1947; Masquelier, 1993; Onwuegeogwu, 1969; Palmer, 1914; Tremearne, 1914; Wall, 1988). Scholars describe the Bori spirit possession rituals, practiced in Kano State, as religious opposition to Islam (Besmer, 1983; Onwuegeogwu, 1969) and as alternative or oppositional gender experience and expression (Callaway, 1987; Wall, 1988). Through my work with *sarakuna Bori* (leaders, literally, kings of *Bori*) and *malamai* (Qur'anic scholar-healers), I have found a link between the beliefs and practices of *Bori* and a sect of Islam that diverged during the 1400s over the use of magic or *shirk* (polytheism: associating partners such as humans or *jinn* with the work of Allah). This sect believed that Allah gave the Prophet Sulayman the power to 'tie' or 'bind' spirits to humans, thus legitimating contemporary Bori spirit possession practices. In all writings about Bori, the *jinn*, Sulayman, is the spirit king or leader of spirits. For these reasons, I refer to *Bori* as a fusion of animism and Islam. I am not addressing the origin of *Bori*, but rather the historical power and contentiousness of contemporary narrations about *'yan Bori* and *Bori* practices. *Yan Bori* consider themselves Muslims, while Kano Sufis, Sunnis and Shias variably refer to them as 'fallen Muslims', 'marginal Muslims' or 'pagans'.

95

customary legal claims to land and resources. The reformist Hausa Ulama promoted an autochthonous, ethnic, religious exclusionism, backed by the often violent 'policing' of *'yan daba* and *'yan hisba*. Through the Shari'a Implementation Committee, the reformist Hausa Ulama presented Islamic moral and political accountability as a democratic alternative to a Nigerian nation-state, increasingly co-opted by the United States government and by non-Hausa Nigerians, particularly Yorubas, who have strong representation in the Federal Government.

This chapter builds upon studies of vigilantism in Nigeria,[5] media and the institutional channelling of emotion,[6] and theories of collective violence,[7] in particular, those of Feldman and Taussig who trace the 'prosthetic' terror of the visibility and invisibility of security forces as 'paranoiac mystique' or the 'magic of the state' which can be turned back upon the state by its opposition.[8] In the struggle for political power, *'yan daba* and *'yan hisba* conflated identity, morality and security, projecting images and acts of violation and terror, seen and unseen, as simultaneous weapons and justifications for their use. In this chapter, I draw out the relations of *'yan daba* and *'yan hisba* and the ways in which they produced and reproduced themselves, as 'legitimate' vigilantes, within Kano State's historical shift to Islamic reformism and to Shari'a criminal law. I focus on the construction, meaning and communication of identity, fear and respect, self/other differentiations, and the politics of self- and other-policing through violence, concluding with an analysis of the imperatives of vigilantism, local and global, that frame and underpin the politics of belonging, power and legitimacy in today's Kano.

---

5 Dan Asabe, 1991; Gore and Pratten, 2003; Harnischfeger, 2003; Smith, 2004; Ya'u, 2000.

6 Ado-Kurawa, 2000; Casey, 2001a; Casey, 2001b; Casey and Edgerton, 2005; Huyssen, 2001; White, 2005.

7 Bauman, 1991; Daniel, 1996; Douglas, 1966; Durkheim, 1995; Malkki, 1995.

8 Feldman, 1991; Feldman, 1997 and Taussig, 1997.

With the demilitarization of Nigeria in 1999, and a crippled police force, youth groups all over Nigeria have entered into the realm of 'policing'.[9] Nigerian journalists variably portray the militant wing of the southern and south western Yoruba O'odu'a People's Congress (OPC), the south eastern Igbo Bakassi Boys, now officially disbanded,[10] and northern Hausa *'yan daba* as either mercenaries navigating a fragmented political space or as 'vigilantes', 'ethnic militias' or 'tribal armies'. In the year 2000, the author of a lead story in the Muslim-funded *Weekly Trust* described *'yan daba* as a future Islamic Army:

The *'yan daba*, a reserve army of unemployed youths, have acted in ways that suggest that they can metamorphose into a tribal army some day. In 1999, when Hausa residents of Sagamu town in Ogun State had a clash with their Yoruba hosts, it was the *'yan daba* group that organised a reprisal attack against Yoruba residents in Kano.[11]

Residents of Kano explain their increased reliance on *'yan daba* and on newly formed ward vigilantes and *'yan hisba* as a public response to a corrupt nation-state that fails to provide security and to account for growing political, economic insecurities, inequities and injustices. In Nigeria there has been widespread regional support, and even state sanctioning, for vigilantes such as the Bakassi Boys and the OPC, who, at least initially, demanded social justice and government accountability, even when these groups employed violence as enforcement.[12] However, working with the Bakassi Boys in south-eastern Nigeria, Smith suggests that 'despite its massive popularity as an alternative to the perceived failure of the government and its policing institutions, vigilantism effectively deflected or obscured the role of politicians and the state in perpetuating the conditions that produced crime, insecurity, and inequality.'[13] Nigerian forms of vigi-

---

9 Baker, 2002; Gore and Pratten, 2003; Harnischfeger, 2003; Smith, 2004; Ya'u, 2000.

10 Smith, 2004.

11 *Weekly Trust*, 4-10 August 2000, pp. 1-2.

12 Gore and Pratten, 2003; Smith, 2004.

13 Smith, 2004, p. 431.

lantism are not simply reactions to government corruption or violent crime, but local responses to the politics of ethnicity, religion and region that characterize the postcolonial transition to 'democracy' in many parts of Africa, and decentralized struggles over the codification of rights and privileges that result in political economic power.[14] Armed youths are at the forefront of such struggles.

Perspectives on vigilantism and the increasingly violent forms of 'policing' associated with the politics of identity and power in postcolonial Africa, parallel explanations of collective violence as anxiety about failing or blurred identities and the desire to purify them,[15] or as constitutive of identities and solidarity.[16] According to Abrahams a rise in vigilantism is a common response to ambivalence about the authority of the state, a major source of anxiety for Nigerians since the implementation of Shari'a criminal law in northern Nigeria and the increased emphasis on Hausa ethnicity and the Muslim religion in determining Kano State citizenship and access to resources.[17]

On 11 May 2004, ethnic, religious exclusionism and violence in Kano reached an apex when Muslim Hausa 'yan daba, 'yan hisba and almajirai (Qur'anic students) joined together to brutally murder their neighbours and fellow residents, calling them arna (unbelievers), Kiristoci (Christians), and baki (strangers).[18] The crisis followed several

---

14 Argenti, 1998; Baker, 2002; Gore and Pratten, 2003; Mamdani, 2001; Mbembe, 2001a.

15 Douglas, 1966; Bauman, 1997; Daniel, 1996; Malkki, 1995.

16 Durkheim, 1995; Feldman, 1991.

17 Abrahams, 1996; Abrahams, 1998.

18 The majority of residents living in Kano identify themselves as Muslim Hausa or Muslim Hausa-Fulani. Current use of the term 'Hausa' extends beyond ethnicity to describe cultural and language communities on both sides of the Niger/Nigeria border. People commonly refer to the ha'be, 'Aborigines; indigenous tribes' (Bargery, 1993, p. 432), as the only 'pure Hausa'. Following the 19th century Islamic jihad in northern Nigeria, Muslim Fulanis conquered the Hausas and established themselves as a ruling class (Paden, 1986; Palmer, 1914; Robinson, 1896; Tremearne, 1914). Marriages between Hausa and Fulani became increasingly common, but people make a distinction between marriages with ancestors of the Fulani ruling class and those with 'cattle Fulani'

months of communal violence in Plateau State that Muslim residents of Kano felt had been condoned through the inaction of the Christian Governor of Plateau State, Joshua Dariye, and the Christian Head of the Nigerian State, General Olusegun Obasanjo. There were passionate and vivid international components—protests over the killing of Palestinian leaders by the Israeli Army and the brutal treatment of prisoners in Iraq by the US Army—that culminated in a public burning of the effigies of Ariel Sharon and George Bush. The language of Muslims and Christians, 'indigenes' and 'strangers', used to describe the identities of victims and killers, the spiritual and material power associated with them, and the spatial patterning of the violence led to an increased conflation of identity, morality and security, with Nigerian Christians held responsible for the actions of Plateau residents and the Nigerian, United States, and Israeli Presidents.[19]

In Nigeria, allegiances and jurisdictions correspond to the plurality of the forms of territoriality, so that an interlacing of social ties is never reducible to family relationships, ethnicity or religion. Ethnic, religious conflicts, when they do occur, rarely cross national borders, but are closely tied to reclassifications of localities within Nigeria, a process based upon colonial associations of family ties, ethnicity and religious proximity.[20] In the early 1990s, Sani Abacha, then military Head of State, exacerbated ethnic tensions by creating new states, effectively undermining certain cross-ethnic coalitions while strengthening others. Demilitarization in 1999, the lack of an effective police force, ongoing conflicts between the police and military, and a sharp increase in armed robberies worsened political conflicts, public insecurities, and ethnic, religious, and regional struggles for politi-

---

who are nomadic. People who wish to emphasize ancestral connections to the Fulani ruling class use the term 'Hausa-Fulani' more often. Though this is not meant to describe ethnic, cultural and language distinctions in their entirety, nor as representative of all Kano communities, it is a reference to majority identifications and the complexities and implications for inclusion and exclusion based upon locally defined concepts of status and power.

19 Casey, forthcoming-b.
20 Mbembe, 2001b.

cal power. The Igbo Bakassi Boys, the militant wing of the Yoruba Odua'a Peoples Congress (OPC), *'yan daba*, and *'yan hisba* began to reflect, produce and act out physical and metaphysical insecurities as identity politics, refracting geographical affiliation, language, ethnicity, and religion into fetishized cultural codes of belonging.[21] Global and national religious networks, Muslim and Christian, placed additional pressure on refractions of identity through evangelism, charity and the consequent conversions, contributing to additional insecurities at physical and metaphysical levels.

When asked what would happen if the OPC came to Kano, a *'dan tauri* (person who makes and uses ritual herbal medicine to prevent injuries from a variety of weapons) heading a group of *'yan daba* said:

They would be finished. If our leaders, or the authorities give us the go ahead, Lagos is not far. We can go in buses or trailers to meet them...They have guns, but I swear the guns will not work (because of *tauri* herbal medicines and ritual practices)...Can you recall how many hours we were in Kaduna? Didn't they have different types of guns? The infidels were going to kill people, but *Kanawa* (people of Kano) took away the guns with *tauri*.[22]

Nigerian ethnic, religious and regional divides are kept alive in traumatic memories of colonization and the colonial amalgamation of the Muslim north and Christian south, and of the Igbo Biafran succession, which resulted in the Nigerian Civil War.[23] Regional divides have been aggravated by the betrayals that emerged through what

---

21 In 2002, the Federal Government disbanded the Bakassi Boys. Smith (2004) points to both the brutal murder of Barnabas Igwe, President of the Anambra chapter of the Nigerian Bar Association and a leading critic of the Anambra state government's support of the Bakassi Boys, and public disenchantment with the Bakassi Boys' corruptibility and daily violence, as catalysts for the government's actions.

22 This is taken from an interview with a *'dan tauri* in *'Yadda 'Kwari* (5 November 2000). *Tauri* literally means 'toughness'. In this case, it is used to describe the power of *tauri* herbal medicines and ritual practices to make a *'dan tauri* invulnerable to guns.

23 Casey, forthcoming-b; Casey, forthcoming-a.

Mamdani refers to as the 'decentralised despotism'[24] of colonialism and the mosaics of ethnic, religious, and regional politics, made worse again by the 'petro-Capitalism' and 'spoils politics' that have emerged since Nigeria's independence in 1960.[25] The 1999 election and political leadership of President Olusegun Obasanjo, a Yoruba born-again Christian whom reformist Muslims refer to as 'the US's boy', further deepened antagonisms, leading to conflations of identity, morality and security with Nigerian national and world insecurities.

'Affective' rememberings and forgettings of violence, and the capacities of violence to generate and to resolve conflicts, find new means of political expression through Nigerian anti-colonial, anti-imperial, Islamic movements, from whom most of the *'yan hisba* were selected, hence reviving identification with 19th century jihadists to reform and to unify Nigeria's Muslims, to establish Nigeria as a Shari'a state, and to protest against the violence of the West. Islamic reform movements gain momentum through extensive uses of, and responses to, media and telecommunications, embedded in the profiling stratifications of state violence, violence sanctioned by the governments of the United States, the Nigerian nation-state and Kano's Shari'a State, and state, legal and media legitimizations of violence towards 'enemies of the state' under 'wars' and 'states of emergency'.

While there is growing documentation of the contributions of Islamic reform movements in Nigeria and in Niger, particularly of *'yan Izala*, to open debate over reigning political and moral orthodoxies and the legacies of colonialism,[26] such movements, as they seize on the signs, objects, and practices they seek to reform, create a 'precarious oscillation of democracy and despotism.[27] In Kano, reformist muslims advocated the 'democratic' implementation of Shari'a law, set limits on government accountability, and opened new domains for public sentiment and debate that cut across longstanding community barriers; yet they also stratified

---

24 Mamdani, 1996.

25 Watts, 2001.

26 Loimeier, 1997; Masquelier, 1999; Umar, 1993; Westerlund, 1997.

27 Comaroff and Comaroff, 2000, p. 29.

citizenship among Muslims, 'marginalizing' non-reformist Muslims and non-Muslims.[28] They offered new opportunities for Islamic identification and participation, yet, through self- and community 'policing', these reform movements increased anxiety about sustenance, salvation, and the potential for evil, political and religious, to enter oneself and one's community through a lack of commitment to Islamic reform.

Among northern Nigerians, the relations of political, ethnic, religious antagonism, forged during the 19th century Islamic *jihad*, British colonization, the Nigerian Civil War and subsequent violence, intersect with media portrayals of violence against Muslims within and outside Nigeria's national borders. Such antagonisms are rooted in, reproduce, and transform the ideologies and feelings of 'affective citizenship',[29] fusions of personal, ethnic, religious and regional citizenship, based on ethnic customary law *and* on religious law, *and* on the historical perceptions of enclosure and exclusion that underpin memories of belonging—backed by law, but a law that, historically, has been arbitrary and violent in its application. *Yan hisba* and *'yan daba*, unified as 'Nigerian Muslims' to force the implementation of Shari'a law and to protest against the violence of the US government's war on Iraq and War on Terror, nonetheless responded to different histories and configurations of identity, morality and security, and to dissimilar ideas about legitimate 'policing' and the tensions between majority rules and individual human rights.[30]

Kano: postcolonial histories and identities

In July 2000, I returned to Kano, an ancient city of northern Nigeria, with a population of several million.[31] Located in the north of Nigeria

---

28 In many parts of Africa, the violence of European 'civilizing missions' and more recently, ideologically charged 'development' industries, those that link technological 'development' to changes in peoples' cultures and psychologies have an enormous impact on the use, and deployment, of terms such as 'morality', 'civility' and 'democracy' in arousing public debate.

29 In Casey, forthcoming-b, I define 'affective citizenship' as displays of feeling about belonging to, and having agency within, the state.

30 Ibid; Casey, forthcoming-a.

31 The research for this project builds upon four years of dissertation research

towards the border with Niger, the city of Kano, as the commercial and religious centre of the north, serves a vast area stretching from Burkina Faso in the west to Chad and Cameroon in the east. Much of this region has been under cultivation for centuries, and is covered by a network of towns and villages, the latter often just a mile or two apart. On the main road heading south, the next major centre is Kaduna, and beyond that lie Abuja, the Nigerian capital, and then Lagos on the coast.

While the people of Kano have been predominately Muslim Hausa for the past six centuries, aligned with one of two *Darika* (Sufi) brotherhoods, Qadiriyya and Tijaniyya, Kano has incorporated large communities of Yorubas, about half of whom are Christian and the other half Muslim, and Igbos, who are predominately Christian. It includes well-established communities of Muslim Lebanese, and smaller communities of people from other parts of Nigeria and Africa, and from the Middle East, Europe and Asia.

Muslim Hausas have social and familial networks that extend into rural farmlands, other cities, and other countries. Many of those who live in the city have regular contact with relatives in villages, or maintain farms to assure their family's food supply. One's religion, ethnicity, language, and geographical affiliation are linked in complicated ways, with certain signifiers brought forward through day-to-day life. Kano spoken Hausa is considered 'standard', while that from other areas, by default, is non-standard, so that many ethnic minorities and Hausa living outside of the city feel 'downgraded' or excluded by language. Hausas living in the city joke about people from the 'bush', considering them uneducated or culturally unsophisticated,

---

between 1991 and 1996, and postdoctoral research, for my study *Youthful Martyrdom and Heroic Criminality: The Formation of Youth Groups in Northern Nigeria*, which took place from 2000 until 2002 and in the year 2004. During the span of this latter project, I interviewed a hundred *'yan daba, 'yan hisba, 'yan tauri*, hunters, *'yan Bori* and *mallams*, Sufi and reformist Shia and Sunni, policemen, Drug Enforcement Agency officers, and judges. The *'yan daba, 'yan hisba, 'yan tauri*, hunters and policemen were perpetrators and victims of communal violence. I also interviewed twenty Christians who were the victims of violence on 11 May 2004.

yet anyone who can afford to build a home in their family's village does so, and there is some sense that people living in villages have a greater knowledge about witchcraft, spirit possession, and *tauri*, alternative sources of power, because of their access to herbal medicines and the rituals surrounding these practices. There are strong links between rural areas and the city, these links animated by flows of people, spirits and material culture that are, themselves, associated with differently streaming levels of power.

Yan daba frequent villages to attend hunting expeditions with *mafarauta* (hunters) and *'yan tauri* ritual specialists. All of the *'yan daba* I met in Kano city described affiliations between their ward gangs and one of two small rival villages about 40 minutes south of the city: 'Yadda 'Kwari (whose name means the place where one drops arrows), and Kura (the Hausa term for a female hyena, an animal considered to have special magical powers). *Yan daba* spoke of 'Yadda 'Kwari as the 'black team', with Kura as the 'white team', simultaneously indicating a mirroring east/west division between affiliated ward gangs in Kano city.

At the heart of the old city, or Gari, is the Emir's ancient palace, and the Central Mosque attached to it. Surrounding the Gari, remnants of twenty feet high walls built during the twelfth century create weathered hills that are crossed by indented walkways. Most of the *'yan daba* hangouts and *'yan hisba* positions of surveillance are around the gates and walkways of their wards, points of visual power, security and escape.

Beyond the predominately Muslim Gari is the congested sprawl of greater Kano, more cosmopolitan by far, a maze of commercial and industrial sections interspersed between newly developed residential quarters for the rich. Two miles from the old walls is the tree-lined Government Residential Area (GRA), its colonial stone houses a contrast to newer, Arabic-style residences. Unlike the Gari, there is a level of ethnic, religious and regional diversity within this quarter, for it is mainly populated by the Kano middle and upper classes who work in the professions, small business and manufacturing, and government service. There are tensions between Muslims who live in the single family compounds of the GRA and their extended family relatives in the Gari who complain that the Westernization and elitism associated with life in the GRA result in an unruly selfishness that separates Muslim Hausa families. No *'yan daba* have historically congregated in the GRA, although in the years 1999 and 2000 the GRA became one of the main sites of political, religious protest and violence, especially violence associated with the profiling and 'states of emergency' implemented to regulate 'prostitution' and the consumption of alcohol, the other areas being wards on the outskirts of the Gari such as Doraye and Tudun Wada, whose populations are also culturally mixed but tend to be poor, and Sabon Gari (the new city), including a large market and residences of mainly southern Christians.

'States of emergency'

Before Shari'a criminal law was introduced its supporters, including *'yan hisba* and the majority of *'yan daba*, had been hopeful, even idealistic about Shari'a, suggesting that its implementation was the only way to restore public security and faith in any Nigerian system of governance. Shortly thereafter, *'yan daba* became increasingly marginalized, and a split within the Independent Shari'a Implementation Committee emerged between Muslims who insisted upon the enforcement of Shari'a law prior to the establishment of jobs, social services and provisions for people such as *'yan daba*, and those who believed that it was impossible for the poor, marginalized or otherwise disadvantaged to obey Shari'a law in its entirety without these amenities. The Kano State government, responding to charges that *'yan hisba* were 'abusing their powers', created the Kano State Shari'a Implementation Committee, yet the division between those who supported 'policing' versus those who emphasized social services continued to deepen through the politically motivated enforcement of Shari'a law; Shari'a law was applied to particular groups of people—unmarried women, *'yan daba*, *'yan Bori*, non-Hausa Muslims, and Christians—at times specially chosen for the implementation of and public support for Shari'a criminal law.[32]

While perspectives on reformist Islamic interventions in moral, social order are widely associated with conservative ideologies of gender and family, the Shari'a Implementation Committee simultaneously 'arranged' marriages for unmarried women, and developed strong educational programmes for women, persuading women to participate in politics. Muslim Hausa women, marrying and having babies, were a major front in the domestic politics of democracy as majority rules, but they also participated in protests and other public displays of reformist political affiliation. In December of 2000, the wives of the Kano Hausa Ulama and members of the Shari'a Implementation Committee led a protest of several thousand women in front of the Governor's mansion, requesting a stricter implementation of Shari'a law. These women were particularly vocal about the continued use of alcohol and the 'womanizing' of Muslim Hausa men who repudiated the responsibilities of marriage. They thought a strict implementation of Shari'a would increase their husbands' and sons' identification with reformist Muslim Hausa morality and security, providing their families and communities greater cohesion, attention and security. Evaluating the women's protest, a 'dan hisba, told me:

Women are the people to bring all moral conduct. It is for them to teach children. They are our mothers, so we like them to be in front. They are the figureheads of everything moral.[33]

Yet, referring to the women's protest, another 'dan hisba said:

Politics is there for the religion. All of the questions raised by women were supposed to be raised by men. But, when men start raising an alarm, it won't be looked on with gentle eyes. People would be dead.[34]

---

32 The Kano State government continually asserted that Shari'a criminal law was not to be applied to Christians, yet as State law, it absolutely affected the rights and privileges of Christians.

33 Interview with a 'dan hisba, Kano, Nigeria, 15 January 2001.

34 Interview with a 'dan hisba, Kano, Nigeria.

To avoid arrest by *'yan hisba*, Sufi and reformist Muslims who ventured out to consume alcohol changed from Muslim Hausa *riguna* (tunics or gowns) into Western cut shirts tucked into trousers, a style Muslim Hausas jokingly referred to as *zanzaro* (wasp), transferring their immodest 'immorality' to Muslim Yorubas and Christians. Concerned with the 'visibility of immorality', *'yan hisba* arrested their age mates and the poor more often than their elders for consumption of alcohol and for wearing clothes, such as short skirts, associated with 'prostitution', strata of society less able to hide in cars or 'guest houses'. *Yan hisba* complained about Muslim Yoruba and Christian women who, not practicing the partial seclusion (*kulle*) of Muslim Hausa women, were 'too independent', available attractions for Muslim men. Unmarried women and women who live alone are commonly referred to as 'prostitutes', bound to men only through sex and money, potential sources of communal betrayal. There is a widespread sentiment among Muslim Hausa that ethnic others, spirit and human, and members of the opposite sex, men and women, are 'uncontrollable'— that, without volition, their erotic desires and sexual activities inevitably overflow the boundaries of marriage. *Yan hisba* preached to unmarried women, arranging marriages for them, while silently encouraging *and* openly condemning *'yan daba* attacks and rapes of Muslim women, married and unmarried, who ventured out of their homes unaccompanied.

In March 2001 the Deputy Governor, Dr Abdullahi Ganduje, announced an Islamic 'state of emergency' referring to the inability of Shari'a criminal law, as it was being practiced in Kano State, to stop 'prostitution' and the sale and consumption of alcohol. He led *'yan hisba* on a series of raids on local hotels, restaurants, and 'cool spots', where the *'yan hisba* abused patrons, destroying millions of dollars' worth of alcohol. Because Christian Igbos and Muslim and Christian Yorubas owned most of these businesses, these raids bankrupted some, scaring others into a mass exodus of Christians and Muslims who feared increased violence. Establishments stayed indefinitely closed or operated odd hours or with armed guards patrolling the gates. Jokes about 'dying for a drink' became a permanent fixture as humour rose to meet increased levels of anxiety. Rumours about the arming of Muslims and Christians came more frequently. In response General Olusegun Obasanjo, the Nigerian Head of State, called Dr Ganduje to Abuja, stating in public that the Deputy Governor had endangered Nigerian state security, thus, reframing Kano's 'state of emergency' as a national 'state of emergency'. Debates about the constitutionality of Shari'a criminal law continue to be assessed by lawyers and by the National Assembly, so at the time Dr Ganduje went home with a mere warning.

The Deputy Governor's 'state of emergency' spawned other forms of Islamic state-preserving 'states of emergency'. In the summer of 2002, secondary school students, Muslim and Christian, girls and boys, were having an end of school party. They were dancing and playing music, when *'yan hisba* knocked loudly on the door and began preaching to them about the evils of 'mixing' with the opposite sex. According to *'yan hisba* who were present, the students listened respectfully to their preaching, yet refused to end their party. *'Yan hisba* left the house, gathered additional *'yan hisba* from a nearby village, and returned to the ward. A few *'yan hisba* tried once again to 'persuade' the youths to end their party, but they refused. Minutes later, one of the *'yan hisba* yelled *'Allahu Akbar'*, raising the 'passions' of other *'yan hisba* who rushed down a hill, broke the door to the house and entered to fight the students. According to the students, *'yan hisba* beat them with sticks, then stole their watches and cameras, breaking all the furniture in their house.

A member of the *'yan hisba*, involved in this raid, denied that *'yan hisba* had stolen property, but said it was necessary for *'yan hisba* to declare the party an 'emergency condition' because 'a party is something that happens only from time to time, so you have to make your move'.[35] He differentiated this from other crimes, like gambling, that are daily 'habits' that the *'yan hisba* can address on any given day.

---

35 Interview with a *'dan hisba* from the Kabuga quarters of Kano, 3 August 2001.

When asked about an incident of *'yan hisba* burning down a Christian owned hotel that had been in operation on a daily basis for several years, he said:

They (*'yan hisba*) made a mistake. Any human can make a mistake...But, this *'yan hisba* militant group is here to stay. We have to confront the evildoers. The *'yan hisba* exist and have 100% support from God. Most of the vices committed by poor people...are because of the poor leadership in America, England and Switzerland. Why did they allow our leaders to go and take our money there?[36]

There were other 'states of emergency' used during the early implementation of Shari'a criminal law as justifications for attacks on *'yan Bori* in Kumbotso, a town just outside of Kano, and in surrounding villages. A *dan hisba* said, 'I heard they clashed and the Bori people slashed some of them with knives. But, it is said that Bori has been stopped.'[37] Days later, in Tsamiya, the late Umar Sanda, a Sarkin Bori renown for his healing of *mahaukata* (mad people), held a ritual involving spiritual power called *Kashe Kabewa* (smashing the pumpkin). Several hundred people were attending the ritual, many of whom were *mafarauta*, *'yan tauri* and *'yan Bori*, so that even though *'yan hisba* arrived armed, in convoys of buses, they were put down by Umar Sanda's supporters, and driven out of the village.[38]

While *'yan daba* joined *'yan hisba* in confronting *matan zamani* (modern women), they were reluctant to 'police' Nigerians who sold or used alcohol, or engaged in the spirit possession or *tauri* rituals *'yan hisba* considered 'unIslamic'. *'Yan daba* enjoy these practices and have friendships in communities where alcohol, spirits, and *tauri* medicines are used. Yet, increasingly, *'yan daba* joined the Shari'a state in violent confrontations with non-Hausa Muslims and Christians, exacerbated by the autochthonous, ethnic, religious exclusionism promoted by the reformist Ulama.

---

36 Ibid.

37 Ibid.

38 Interview with *Sarkin Bori*, Umar Sanda, in Tsamiya, a village thirty minutes outside of Kano, 12 August 2001.

'Yan hisba, 'yan daba and their Almajirai recruits

Last identifies four periods when Muslim youths have come to power in northern Nigeria within the last two hundred years: 'with the Sokoto jihad of 1804-1808, at the time of the British colonial takeover ca. 1900-10, in the 1950s with the advent of party politics in the run-up to independence, and recently when local government councils and the enforcement of *shari'a* law started being largely run by 'the young'.'[39] In Kano State, traditional youth groups, such as *'yan farauta* (hunters) and *'yan tauri*, a warrior class during the colonial era, emphasized bravery and skill with weaponry and forms of magical protection sanctioned by most Muslims. During the colonial occupation joining these groups was banned, but they continued illicitly as forms of youth development, entertainment and economic survival. The roles of these youths changed during the 1950s with the emergence of partisan politics in northern Nigeria.[40] The leaders of an opposition party, faced with harassment and arbitrary arrests by the Native Authority policemen, recruited hunters as bodyguards (*'yan banga*). Other parties followed suit, and clashes between *'yan banga* of different parties became routine. In 1966 the army took over and banned all partisan politics, eliminating most *'yan banga* activities in the process. In 1978 the ban was lifted, the emerging parties once again recruited *'yan banga* from *'yan farauta* and from ward *'yan daba*, and conflicts resurfaced.[41]

Party politics were further complicated, in the late 1970s, when a man whom Nigerians nicknamed Maitatsine (the one who curses) came to Kano from Cameroon. Maitatsine claimed that Kano Muslims had no *kibla* (direction), and he repeatedly shouted at them, 'May Allah separate you from all of His blessings!'[42] Maitatsine considered himself a Prophet, while his followers, *'yan Maitatsine*,

---

39 Last, 2004 p.37.

40 Dan Asabe, 1991.

41 Ibid.

42 Personal communication with Professor Phillip Shea, Department of History, Bayero University, Kano, Nigeria, 19 July 2004.

were 'original' Muslims, uncorrupted by the *bidi'a* and *shirk* of Kano Muslims. *'Yan Maitatsine* refused to accept watches, bikes or other material goods emblematic of modernization and urbanization.[43] They took over the Kano goat market, lived in cave-like dwellings and trenches, kidnapped and shared young women, while killing their enemies. Maitatsine and his followers were *'yan tauri* who made and used ritual herbal medicine against piercing from weapons. Unable to stop *'yan Maitatsine* from their criminal and recruitment activities, the local police enlisted the aid of other *'yan tauri* and the Nigerian military who eventually killed Maitatsine. During this time, checkpoints around Kano, manned by armed young men, looking for the stomach tattoos of *'yan Maitatsine,* contributed to an emerging fear of Kano youths and 'strangers'.[44] People feared youths who had joined Maitatsine's movement and those who, alongside the Kano State and the Federal Government, had armed themselves to fight against *'yan Maitatsine*—analogous fear and ambivalence to those directed at the moral aesthetics and behaviour of *'yan hisba* and *'yan daba* who fight for and against the state.

In 1995, large numbers of Wahhabis from Saudi Arabia came to northern Nigeria to develop Islamic schools and social services. Well-funded at a time when the Nigerian national government was in a state of crisis and unable or unwilling to provide such services, Wahhabis became rapidly absorbed with the needs of Muslims, converting hundreds of Sufis to Wahhabi orthodoxy, fuelled by an explicit critique of colonization and neo-colonial, imperial politics. Anti-American media reports became increasingly common; the authors of these reports argued the need for Shari'a as a way for Muslims to separate—physically, psychically, and economically—from 'infidels', especially Nigerian Christians and imperialists, but also from 'marginal' Muslims who break spiritual/political unity and solidarity. Muslim journalists highlighted the arrogance and brutality

---

43 Dan Asabe, 1991, p. 99.

44 Personal communication with Professor Phillip Shea, Department of History, Bayero University, Kano, Nigeria, 19 July 2004.

111

of the United States' bombings in Iraq, holding the US government responsible for untold deaths and destruction. They recounted the plight of Palestinians, and the need for Muslims to fight against social injustice. Osama bin Laden stickers began to adorn Kano buses, while hundreds of youths joined the 'yan hisba and wider networks of separatist Muslims.

'Yan hisba, who number from about ten to forty per ward, and 'yan daba, whose ranks have swollen from between fourteen per ward in 1991 to between 50 and 200, are the main caretakers of younger male siblings and almajirai (Qur'anic students).[45] Almajirai leave their families and come into the city from across northern Nigeria to study the Qur'an at a Kano mosque. Like younger siblings, almajirai, who may be as young as five years, serve as errand boys while playing at the mosque or along the borders of 'yan daba joints. Through 'yan hisba and 'yan daba caretaking, almajirai form the main pool of youths from which 'yan hisba and 'yan daba recruit.[46] Almajirai moral aesthetics and behaviours develop through ambiguous attachments to social rituals and daily life at the mosque, and to those of 'yan daba and the daba street economy.

'Yan daba recruits speak about getting even with people who have 'downgraded' or 'underrated' them. Insults and injuries are taken as re-enactments of earlier acts, variably related to personal experience and to cultural or political abstractions, but nonetheless excusing violence. Forceful acts of domination are accompanied by outbursts of ribaldry and derision that seem to mock and mimic officialdom, while creating new forms of officialdom altogether.[47] For instance,

---

45 Watts, 1996.

46 Dan Asabe, 1991 describes the social services 'yan daba have historically provided for their neighbourhoods, including labour for community projects, protection, sporting and cultural events for community entertainment, and enforcing the community discipline of children, adolescents and women who may go out at night or leave their marital homes. 'Yan daba provide almajirai with most of their food and places to sleep, which, especially for children, signifies the care of a family.

47 Ya'u, 2000.

crowd control during festivities at the Emir's palace involves whipping youths, the guards chasing and striking youths while they run, shrieking through tears or laughter. A *'dan daba*, dressed lavishly in a Muslim-style *riga* (dress), smoking a joint reminiscent of Cheech and Chong, slaps an *almajiri* to the ground for forgetting to say his prayers. Once again, the crowd cheers and laughs. Through the systematic application of pain, *'yan daba* produce fear that 'reinforces certain moral values within society'.[48]

Yan daba speak of attractions to power, physical and metaphysical, and the fear they will generate through their associations with *daba*. Recruits say they are impressed with *'yan daba* fighting, a form that uses two sticks enabling someone to beat opponents who are larger or stronger. They say they are impressed with the money and clothes *'yan daba* flaunt, their party lifestyle, and with girls they date. One recruit said he became impressed with the collective nature of *daba* hemp smoking because 'people are afraid of *'yan daba* who are high, so they don't follow or meet them with useless talk'. *Daba* recruits fear *'yan daba* who use *tauri* medicines, and who perform the ritual acts and prohibitions that make them invulnerable to their enemies. They enjoy frightening married women into staying home. The felt and expressed qualities of fear and respect emerge as an entanglement with what Mbembe refers to as the 'banality of power', part of which is a 'distinctive style of political improvisation, by a tendency to excess and lack of proportion, as well as by distinctive ways identities are multiplied, transformed and put into circulation'.[49]

Yan daba self-identify with wards, hanging out in particular joints, but they shift among modes of violent opposition to other wards, tolerant separation and eclecticism. They identify with *'yan farauta*, particularly men from 'Yadda 'Kwari and Kura, whom they consider expert hunters, *tauri* ritualists and fighters. Nonetheless, this relationship is tenuous, and in some cases is another source of

---

48 Mbembe, 2001b, p. 102.
49 Dan Asabe, 1991, p. 99.

'yan daba marginalization. For instance, a *mafarauci* (hunter) from 'Yadda 'Kwari described *daba* as:

...an acquired habit, not a profession or tradition...stealing, drinking, smoking hemp, and general anti-social behaviour is not the culture or subculture of hunters...what is paining us is that these groups of *'yan tauri* and *'yan daba*, even in the eyes of the law and the Emir, they see them as hunters, which is not so. To us, *'yan daba* are hooligans.[50]

While predominately Muslim Hausa, *'yan daba* have incorporated youths of other ethnic and religious backgrounds. They often take non-Hausa words, like 'scorpion' or 'pusher', or words combining Hausa with references to people elsewhere, such as *kayaman* (reggae man) or *Takur Sahab* (person who has a leader in India) as street names. *'Yan daba* have adopted a style of dress they associate with 'Westside niggers', or Los Angeles-based rappers. In their sunglasses, chains and baggy jeans, *'yan daba* show a broad interest in world youth cultures, questioning me, through whirls of Indian hemp, about the impact of rappers like Tupac Shakur and the revolutionary politics of his Black Panther mother.

'Yan daba hired as *'yan banga* serve as the vanguard for local political and religious leaders, earning the major part of their incomes from politically motivated thuggery. Until the emergence of vigilantes in 1999, and the *'yan hisba* in 2000, *'yan daba* were the main protectors of their wards, safeguarding them from armed robberies, communal violence, and crimes committed by the *'yan daba* of other wards. *'Yan daba* who participate in violence are typically the leaders of a *daba* and the inner core of members who have *zuciya* (heart) for their *dabas* and for particular political leaders. This inner core of *'yan daba* differentiate themselves from the majority of *'yan daba* who restrict their *daba* involvement to business—mainly to selling petrol and Indian hemp. Business-oriented *'yan daba* support the inner core by paying them a portion of their earnings for protection. When attacked, however, business-oriented *'yan daba* join those with *zuciya* to defend their wards and businesses.

---

50 Interview with a hunter from 'Yadda 'Kwari, 26 October 2000.

With the implementation of Shari'a criminal law and the increased crackdown on prostitution, drugs and alcohol, and black market petrol sales, 'yan daba suffered increased poverty, finding it difficult to obtain money for food and clothing, dating or marriage. Petty theft was down, but the rates of rape and violent crimes against individuals increased and were more often attributed to 'yan daba 'rampages', even though there was no evidence tying 'yan daba to these increases.[51] What emerged was a competition between 'yan daba and 'yan hisba to provide 'legitimate policing' and social services for their communities.

'Yan daba and 'yan hisba quickly developed languages, sets of codes and acts that were meant to signify their participation in democracies, local, national and global, a framing necessary for their assertion that the implementation of Shari'a criminal law as State Law was constitutional. However, in the wake of Shari'a implementation, whether one belonged or was excluded was increasingly tied to the concept of blasphemy which for Bhabha is 'a moment when the subject-matter or the content of a cultural tradition is being overwhelmed, or alienated, in the act of translation.'[52] A Muslim Hausa critic of 'yan hisba said, 'They ('yan hisba) are migrants or aliens, but they were never original indigenes...some are non-Nigerians, some are unemployed and lastly some are from poor families.'[53] A teenage dan daba took me to see daba graffiti on the wall of a run-down hotel that read: "We are made to be criminals, not because of what we have done, but

---

51 Many 'yan daba participate in 'daukar amarya (literally, carrying away a bride), kidnapping and raping women whom they feel have 'slighted' or disrespected them. 'Yan daba admit kidnapping groups of 'prostitutes' from hotels, brutally raping them in uninhabited areas of Kano. However, these rapes are rarely reported. According to a Magistrate Judge in Gyadi Gyadi, cases of reported rape increased six-fold between the implementation of Shari'a criminal law in November of 2000 and January of 2001. The Judge attributed this to a decrease in the number of 'prostitutes' available for older men, who had instead begun 'turning to young girls' (personal communication, 12 January 2001).

52 Mbembe, 2001b, p. 102.

53 Interview with a Muslim Hausa critic of 'yan hisba who lives in the Kabuga quarters of Kano, 3 August 2001.

because of what we stand for.'[54] Like elsewhere in the world, these armed young men, recruited into revolution, were unspoken heroes *and* outcasts as a result of their violence.

Political Islam, democracy and vigilantism

While *'yan hisba* and *'yan daba* consider Shari'a criminal law to be a democratic form of governance, they differ in the emotional attachments they have to democratic values. *Yan hisba* tend to equate Shari'a with a democracy of majority rules, while *'yan daba*, concerned with their own marginality, advocate social justice and individual human rights. A *'dan hisba* said:

We are a democracy. We are the majority. And, the Islamic injunction is superior to any other injunction. So they say it's a government of the people, for the people, by the people—Abraham Lincoln, American President... since this is a democracy, we can use it (Shari'a) as a political weapon, to make sure that someone who is conscious of Shari'a is elected.[55]

By contrast, a response I commonly heard among *'yan daba* is reflected by the statement:

We are all Muslims. Shari'a will help us to know each other better. In this way, crimes will be reduced and the rich and poor will be the same under the law.[56]

To a great extent, these differing perspectives reflect and constitute *'yan daba* and *'yan hisba* experiences of violence, with *'yan daba* routinely the objects and perpetrators of violence.[57] It belies their varied

---

54 Interview with a teenage *'dan daba* living in a hotel near the Sabuwar Kofa gate in Kano, 3 July 2000.

55 Interview with a *'dan hisba* living in the Kabuga quarters of Kano, 3 August 2000.

56 Interview with a *'dan daba* living in the Nassarawa quarters of Kano, 13 October 2000.

57 During the summer of 2001, two *'yan daba* that I interviewed had been arrested by the police for selling black-market petrol. They were taken to the police station, hung upside down for several hours, over a period of three days, while beaten with large sticks. Their bloodied eyes and bodily bruises were testament

experiences with EuroAmerican NGOs or reformist Islamic organizations whose secular and religious social services are riddled with the moral codes and languages of democracies, secular and religious.

'Yan daba and 'yan hisba described their hopes for jobs and schooling, for health care and for personal or social reforms like changes in patterns of substance abuse or marriage, forms of idealism reflected in wider discourses of support for Shari'a law. In these official narratives, 'yan daba and 'yan hisba spoke of hope and the desire to participate in building a society of opportunity. However, alongside these official narratives 'yan daba activities revealed mistrust, feelings of betrayal and anger. 'Yan daba developed systems of 'lookouts' who monitored their wards for 'yan hisba. Some said discretion was their best protection from the 'yan hisba because 'Shari'a works with eye-witnessing a crime.'[58] Others said they would allow 'yan hisba to preach to them, but would not change. A 'dan daba smoking Indian hemp on the side of Bayero University Road, a busy two lane road connecting the city with Bayero University, joked about 'yan hisba:

These 'yan hisba are hypocrites. They do these things, but they hide in their houses. We do it in the open because we only fear God. We fear God, while they fear other people. We are the only true Muslims.[59]

'Yan daba and 'yan hisba were concerned with masculine power and the moral authority to secure an area. A dan daba who was a strong supporter of Shari'a said:

'Daba actions and mode of life do not conform with what society wants, so people like the 'yan hisba are the ones who abuse them. If they come and meet 'yan daba committing an offence, they will try to arrest them, thus

---

to this form of police brutality. Another 'dan daba was shot by a policeman after the policeman caught him with his girlfriend. While these were the most severe cases of police brutality that I witnessed, 'yan daba were routinely beaten by the police for selling black-market petrol or Indian hemp which, according to 'yan daba, the police confiscated to sell or use themselves.

58 Interview with a 'dan daba living in the Nassarawa quarters of Kano, 14 March 2000.

59 This is a statement made by a 'dan daba while hanging out with other 'yan daba in the Nassarawa quarters of Kano, 12 September 2001.

117

there is this kind of indirect abuse or small talk between them...But, *'yan daba* will not stop because they would be labelled as cowards.[60]

Another *'dan daba* said:

We can stop our activities perhaps...but you should remember that if a person is just killed without committing any offence, do you think if the Shari'a doesn't do anything about it that we will let the matter rest? To me, you cannot give advice to *'yan daba* after such a thing...The Shari'a says if you kill a man, you should be killed too. So why should you kill and not be killed?[61]

'Yan daba, who were often on intimate, joking terms with *'yan hisba* from their wards, responded to the *hali*, or personal character, of *'yan hisba* in face-to-face confrontations. They most respected *'yan hisba* whom they perceived, following the tenets and restrictions of Shari'a law, to be generous, fair and sincere about their social roles as *'yan hisba*. *'Yan hisba* witnessed *'yan daba* beating up or lashing their own members who had broken Shari'a law. Under such circumstances, *'yan daba* who had been punished for breaking Shari'a law, by a Shari'a court or within a *daba*, seemed to feel that it was justified, not as law or rational sentiment, but as personal, situational respect that was 'for real'. This was a subtle process, however, because *'yan daba* also beat *daba* members who had broken Shari'a law as a way to get *'yan hisba* 'off their backs'. By doing so, *'yan daba* were able to maintain a unified presentation to *'yan hisba*, avoiding, for instance, the wrath of particularly disliked *'yan hisba* whom they felt might be 'out to get them'.

Concluding remarks

Conflations of identity, morality, and security transform the politically unseen, the *talakawa* or peasantry, what Feldman refers to as the 'blind spot' of visual power, into the politically unseeable, a microcosm of a

---

60 Interview with a *'dan daba* living in the Nassarawa quarters of Kano, 29 January 2001.

61 Interview with a *'dan daba* living in the Nassarawa quarters of Kano, 23 February 2000.

world politics rooted in social injustice and violence. During the years 1999 and 2000, 'yan daba, 'yan Bori and non-Hausa Muslims were threatening to reformist Muslims because, as religious 'innovators' and as 'settlers', 'tenants' and 'aliens', people who incorporate, or ask to be incorporated into, the spiritual and social lives of others, they disallow the re-enchantment of Islamic 'orthodoxy' and its ability to function as collective memory and political/spiritual unity. The making of political/spiritual enemies maps onto us/them concepts of 'indigenes' versus 'migrants', 'settlers', 'tenants' and 'aliens' and the (dis)allocation of land and other resources under Hausa ethnic customary law. These local politics, framed by global 'Wars on Terror' along with a polarization of Muslim/Christian identities, fuel many forms of vigilantism, based on a conflation of identity, morality, and security, that hide the politics of the state—whether the United States, Nigeria, or Kano State—in perpetuating violence against perceived "enemies of the state", typically ethnic and religious minorities.

While the concept of Muslim unity was a common goal for 'yan daba and 'yan hisba living in northern Nigeria, it was based on the paradoxical notion of an Islamic state, founded by and through violence that effectively placed 'yan daba and 'yan hisba outside of Shari'a criminal law. Acting on behalf of the Kano Hausa Ulama, 'yan hisba violence emerged as a result of communal fear that the spiritual/political body would become contaminated by the *shirk* or *bidi'a* of non-Hausa Muslims and Christians, or destroyed through Nigerian national and international governance and 'policing'. 'Yan daba feared the reverse—that the spiritual/political body would stagnate because of rigid spiritual and human relations. 'Yan hisba sought an Islamic democracy of majority rules, while 'yan daba, ambivalent or even sceptical about Islamic state governance, considered the protection of individual human rights fundamental to democracy in pluralist societies, reserving their right to use force against the government if necessary. 'Yan hisba and 'yan daba supported a Kano State citizenship based on Hausa ethnic identity *and* the Muslim religion, marginalizing and endangering the lives of non-Hausa Muslims and

CONERLY CASEY

non-Muslims living in Kano. As outlaws with different visions of Shari'a law and of democracy, 'yan daba and 'yan hisba, along with the local and world leaders who targeted or supported them, were in constant 'states of emergency', recreating and re-enacting collective memories of unity, morality and security through violence—policing through violence.

'Dan Asabe, A. "Yan Daba: The "Terrorists" of Kano Metropolitan?' *Kano Studies, Special Issue: Youth and Health in Kano Today*, 1991, pp. 85-110.

Abrahams, R. 'Vigilantism: Order and Disorder on the Frontiers of the State', in *Inside and Outside the Law: Anthropological Studies of Authority and Ambiguity*, H. Olivia (ed.), London, 1996, pp. 41-55.

——*Vigilant Citizens: Vigilantism and the State*, Cambridge, 1998.

Ado-Kurawa, I. *Shari'ah and the Press in Nigeria: Islam versus Western Christian Civilization*, Kano, 2000.

Argenti, N. 'Air Youth: Performance, Violence and the State in Cameroon', *Journal of the Royal Anthropological Institute* 4(4), 1998, pp. 753-83.

Baker, B. 'When the Bakassi Boys Came: Eastern Nigeria Confronts Vigilantism', *Journal of Contemporary African Studies* 20(2), 2002, pp. 223-44.

Bargery, G.P. *A Hausa-English Dictionary*, Tokyo, 1993.

Bauman, Z. *Modernity and the Holocaust*, Ithaca, NY, 1991.

——*Postmodernity and its Discontents*, New York, 1997.

Besmer, F.E. *Horses, Musicians and Gods: the Hausa Cult of Possession-trance*, South Hadley, Mass., 1983.

Bourguignon, E. 'World Distribution and Patterns of Possession States', in *Trance and Possession States*, R. Prince (ed.), Montreal, 1968, pp. 3-34.

Callaway, B.J. *Muslim Hausa Women in Nigeria*, Syracuse, NY, 1987.

Casey, C. 'The Formation of Cultural Enemies: Media and Perceptions of Cultural Aggression among Nigerian Youths.' Paper presented at the Society for Psychological Anthropology, Decatur, Georgia, 2001a.

—— 'Security and Morality in Northern Nigeria: Youth Gangs as the Keepers and Breakers of Shari'a Law.' Paper presented at the American Anthropological Association, Washington, DC, 2001b.

—— 'Marginal Muslims: Politics and the Perceptual Bounds of 'Islamic Authenticity' in Northern Nigeria', *Africa Today*, forthcoming-a.

—— 'Mediated Hostility: Media, "Affective Citizenships", and Genocide in Northern Nigeria', in *Genocide, Truth and Representation: Anthropological Approaches*, A.L. Hinton and K. O'Neill (eds.), Duke University Press, forthcoming-b.

Casey, C.C. and R.B. Edgerton (eds). *A Companion to Psychological Anthropology: Modernity and Psychocultural Change*, Malden, Mass., 2005.

Comaroff, J.L. and J. Comaroff. 'Introduction', in *Civil Society and the Political Imagination in Africa: Critical Perspectives*, J.L. Comaroff and J. Comaroff (eds), Chicago, 2000, pp. 1-43.

Daniel, E.V. *Charred Lullabies: Chapters in an Anthropography of Violence*, Princeton, NJ, 1996.

Douglas, M. *Purity and Danger: an Analysis of Concepts of Pollution and Taboo*, London, 1966.

Durkheim, E. *The Elementary Forms of Religious Life*, New York, 1995.

Feldman, A. *Formations of Violence: the Narrative of the Body and Political Terror in Northern Ireland*, Chicago and London, 1991.

—— 'Violence and Vision: The Prosthetics and Aesthetics of Terror', *Public Culture* 10, 1997, pp. 24-60.

Gore, C. and D. Pratten. 'The Politics of Plunder: The Rhetorics of Order and Disorder in Southern Nigeria', *African Affairs* 102(407), 2003, pp. 211-40.

Greenberg, J.H. *The Influence of Islam on a Sudanese Religion*, New York, 1947.

Harnischfeger, J. 'The Bakassi Boys: Fighting Crime in Nigeria', *The Journal of Modern African Studies* 41(1), 2003, pp. 23-49.

Huyssen, A. 'Present Pasts: Media, Politics, Amnesia', in *Globalization*, A. Appadurai (ed.), Durham, NC, 2001, pp. 57-77.

Kumo, S. 'Shari'a under Colonialism in Northern Nigeria', in *Islam in Africa: Proceedings of the Islam in Africa Conference*, N. Al-kali, A. Adomu, A. Yadudu, R. Moten an H. Salihi, (eds), Ibadan, 1993, pp. 1-22.

Last, M. 'Towards a Political History of Youth in Muslim Northern Nigeria, 1750-2000', in *Vanguard or Vandals: Youth, Politics and Conflict in Africa*, J. Abbink and I.v. Kessel (eds), Leiden, 2004, pp. 37-54.

Loimeier, R. 'Islamic Reform and Political Change: The Examples of Abubakar Gumi and the 'Yan Izala Movement in Northern Nigeria', in *African Islam and Islam in Africa: Encounters between Sufis and Islamists*, E. Rosanders and D.Westerlund (eds), Athens, Ohio, 1997, pp. 286-307.

Malkki, L.H. *Purity and Exile: Violence, Memory, and National Cosmology among Hutu Refugees in Tanzania*, Chicago, 1995.

Mamdani, M. *Citizen and Subject: Contemporary Africa and the Legacy of Late Colonialism*, Princeton, NJ, 1996.

—— *When Victims become Killers: Colonialism, Nativism, and the Genocide in Rwanda*, Princeton, NJ, 2001.

Masquelier, A. 'Narratives of Power, Images of Wealth: The Ritual Economy of Bori in the Market', in *Modernity and its Malcontents, Ritual and Power in Postcolonial Africa*, J. Comaroff and J. Comaroff (eds), Chicago, 1993, pp. 3-33.

—— 'The Invention of Anti-tradition: Dodo Spirits in Southern Niger', in *Spirit Possession, Modernity and Power in Africa*,

H. Behrend and U. Luig (eds), Madison, WI, 1999, pp. 34-49.

Mbembe, A. 'At the Edge of the World: Boundaries, Territoriality, and Sovereignty in Africa', in *Globalization*, A. Appadurai (ed.), Durham, NC, 2001a, pp. 22-51.

—— *On the Postcolony*, Berkeley, 2001b.

Onwuegeogwu, M. 'The Cult of the Bori Spirits among the Hausa', in *Man in Africa*, M. Douglas and P.M. Kaberry (eds), New York, 1969, pp. 279-306.

Paden, J.N. *Ahmadu Bello, Sardauna of Sokoto: Values and Leadership in Nigeria*, London and Portsmouth, NH, 1986.

Palmer, H.R. 'Bori among the Hausas', *Man* 14, 1914, pp. 113-17.

Robinson, C.H. *Hausaland, or, Fifteen Hundred Miles through the Central Soudan*, London, 1896.

Smith, D.J. 'The Bakassi Boys: Vigilantism, Violence and Political Imagination in Nigeria', *Cultural Anthropology* 19(3), 2004, pp. 429-56.

Taussig, M.T. *The Magic of the State*, New York, London, 1997.

Tremearne, A.J.N. *The Ban of the Bori*, London, 1914.

Umar, M. 'Changing Islamic Identity in Nigeria from the 1960s to 1980s', in *Muslim Identity and Social Change in Sub-Saharan Africa*, L. Brenner (ed.), London, 1993, pp. 154-78.

Wall, L.L. *Hausa Medicine: Illness and Well-being in a West African Culture*, Durham, 1988.

Watts, M. "Islamic Modernities? Citizenship, Civil Society and Islamism in a Nigerian City', *Public Culture* 8, 1996, pp. 251-89.

——'Petro-Violence: Community, Extraction, and Political Ecology of a Mythic Commodity', in *Violent Environments*, N.L. Peluso and M. Watts (eds), Ithaca, NY, 2001, pp. 189-212.

Westerlund, D. 'Reaction and Action: Accounting for the Rise of Islamism', in *African Islam and Islam in Africa: Encounters between Sufis and Islamists*, E. Rosanders and D.Westerlund (eds), Athens, Ohio, 1997, pp. 308-34.

White, G. 'Emotive Institutions', in *A Companion to Psychological Anthropology: Modernity and Psychocultural Change*, C.C. Casey and R.B. Edgerton (eds), Malden, Mass., 2005, pp. 241-54.

Ya'u, Y.Z. 'The Youth, Economic Crisis and Identity Transformation: The Case of the Yandaba in Kano', in *Identity Transformation and Identity Politics under Structural Adjustment in Nigeria*, A. Jega (ed.), Uppsala, 2000, pp. 161-80.

PUNISHMENT AND PERSONHOOD

6

FLUCTUATING PERSONHOOD: VIGILANTISM AND CITIZENSHIP IN PORT ELIZABETH'S TOWNSHIPS

Lars Buur

Introduction

Modern citizenship is conventionally understood in terms of the status held under the authority of a state. This involves the production of a codified set of formal rights and duties that defines membership of a particular political community, i.e. a nation-state.[1] This formalistic understanding has been expanded progressively to include economic, socio-cultural and political struggles for recognition, entitlements and redistribution of resources.[2] Citizenship as a *process* rather than a *status* has changed 'the rules of the game', to paraphrase Bourdieu,[3] so that we are increasingly forced to consider and explore how changing power-relations are linked to context-specific processes of state and citizen-formation. One way of doing this is to focus on 'how states and citizens are represented in public ritual, and how these rituals reflect particular political projects and struggles over state-citizen relations'.[4] This article will explore how, through a set of semi-formal, codified practices and speech-acts, the ritualized quasi-court setting

---

1 See Stepputat, 2004, p. 244.
2 See Honneth, 1995; Isin and Turner, 2002.
3 Bourdieu, 1990, pp. 66-7.
4 Stepputat, 2004, p. 245.

of the vigilante group Amadlozi embodies particular understandings of how citizenship and personhood are configured in the poor black townships surrounding Port Elizabeth in the Eastern Cape.

The relationship between state and citizen-formation is no trivial matter. Citizenship is after all grounded in 'the guarantee of legal and political protection from raw coercive power, whether that power comes in the form of the sword blade or gun barrel of soldiers, the fist of abusing spouse or parent'.[5] Citizenship understood as rights is based on 'the active or passive membership of individuals in a nation-state'.[6] This implies that citizenship begins with determining who is eligible for membership of a nation-state, or, in other words, with establishing national 'personhood'. I consider how in South Africa 'personhood' adheres to both an ideology and a bill of individual rights that formally encompass everyone, irrespective of ethnicity, race or class. Can we assume that, in practice, citizens are primarily or solely conceptualized as rights-bearing individuals?

The position of the individual in South Africa is puzzling, be-cause the ideology of individual rights assumes that, in a hierarchy of legal forms, individual rights overrule other forms of law. Part of what Comaroff and Comaroff have called 'an almost fetishised faith in constitutionality and the rule of law' in South Africa has been the constant ritualization of that country's Constitution as the most elaborate, transparent, participatory and modern in the world.[7] While it is indeed a remarkable achievement, it is worth exploring what this ritualization achieves, as a process aimed at 'setting some activities off from others, for creating and privileging a qualitative distinction between the 'sacred' and the 'profane','[8] and the ways in which more quotidian activities—ways of adopting or appropriating the new credo of rights in specific contexts—are played out.

---

5 Janoski and Gran, 2002, p. 13.

6 Ibid.

7 Comaroff and Comaroff, 2004a, p. 515.

8 Bell, 1992, p. 74.

From what is citizenship, defined as rights and as the new sacred domain, distinguished or set apart? The colonial distinction between citizens with rights and membership of the political community on the one hand, and subjects governed indirectly through a range of different arrangements on the other, continues to underlie practices of citizenship in the new South Africa, as Mamdani[9] in particular has argued. As other scholars have pointed out, it may be better to conceptualize the discrepancy between *de jure* and *de facto* rights as 'conditional' citizenship.[10] The new ANC government has tried to address this discrepancy symbolically in a range of nationalized public spectacles such as the first national and local elections, South Africa's Truth and Reconciliation Commission and new public holidays celebrating human rights, gender and youth. Symbolic revocations are one thing, however; the configuration in specific contexts of the ideology of individual rights is quite another.

This paper proposes that the legal notion of a 'universal individual' is inadequate if we want to understand how personhood and citizenship as rights are configured in South Africa. Important characteristics of citizenship and personhood become clearer when we focus on the specific position of the person and the particular ideology to which such a conception of personhood belongs in different domains of the South African reality. My analysis of the Amadlozi quasi-court reveals a township understanding of 'the individual' where personhood is constructed in terms of relations rather than substance.[11]

The Amadlozi quasi-courtroom

The discussion that follows is based on the proposition that personhood and citizenship can be analyzed as the performance of status roles and spatial practices in the context of the organizations of space. This is not a privileged entry point, but one of many that are possible.

---

9 Mamdani, 1996.
10 Comaroff and Comaroff, 2004b, p. 191.
11 See Buur, 2003; Buur, 2005; Buur, 2006.

As Fiona Wilson has stated in a another context: 'People think and move within definitions of social space that are by no means natural or universal, but are underpinned and supported, structured and contained by concepts and practices of spatial politics that have their own historical trajectories.'[12] The space I am concerned with here is 'quasi-courtrooms', by which I mean rooms and venues modelled on a courtroom. They do not look exactly like a 'proper' courtroom, but they draw on many of the spatial-organizational practices characterizing court-rooms.

The space used as a court by the Amadlozi in 2003 was a classroom at Molefe Primary school.[13] Although the crime-fighting organization was not officially approved, the fact that a state school was used without charge was seen as an important marker of official acceptance and approval. It gave court sessions considerable symbolic status, *as if* they were official. Different references were made to a formal court system, to the Law, for instance, in an unspecific manner. People attending the sessions often, but not continuously, referred to the chairperson as 'the judge'. The quasi-court deals with crimes positioned somewhere between criminal cases in the legal sense and civil cases, including *petty crimes* such as family-related disputes (over gender, marriage, inheritance, pregnancy), generational conflicts (about sexuality, schooling, disrespectful language), theft (of smaller items from other youngsters' clothes to cell-phones), and failure to repay loans and return borrowed goods. A list of *serious crimes* might include murder, rape (of both women and children), burglary (mainly house break-ins), and theft (everything from stock to electronic and other kinds of households goods). On most days, petty and serious crimes are discussed interchangeably, often as disturbances preventing the community from accessing development funds.[14] Cases are handled

---

12 Wilson, 2004, p. 529.

13 During my six-month stay with the Amadlozi in New Brighton, near Port Elizabeth in the Eastern Cape, my two local research assistants and I followed roughly 40 court sessions or meetings.

14 See Buur 2003: 23-24; 2005: 200)

in a manner that resembles court-work: investigation, presentation of cases before apparently 'neutral' arbiters and so on. The venue was arranged in much the same way for each meeting, as in Figure 1. According to Amadlozi leaders, the main organizing principle was to ensure space for as many community members as possible, and to enable the orderly conduct of the session.

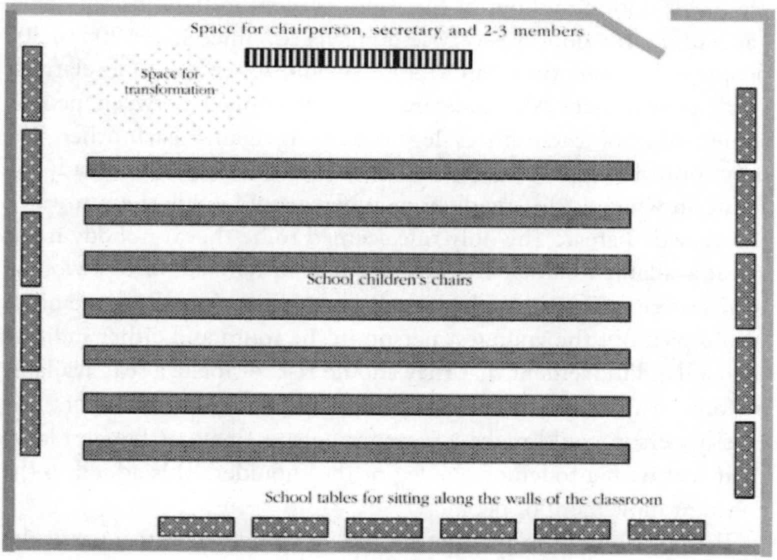

Figure 1

The only clearly demarcated area was that for the chairperson, the secretary and a few Amadlozi persons to the left as one entered the room. Amadlozi members attending the session sat on the tables along the walls or stood in front of them, or sat on classroom chairs in the middle of the room, indistinguishable by spatial pattern or movement from other community members if one did not know who they were.[15] Similarly, people attending the meetings—ordinary community members, people who had been summoned, complainants or witnesses—seemed to lack allocated spaces, although elders generally tended to occupy chairs in the middle of the room closer to the chairperson, while most youngsters sat or stood against the walls.

The role of chairperson could be played by up to four different people during a meeting, and the general flux and movement of people inside and in and out of the room gave an initial sense of disorganization. The door was very seldom closed. Since about 200 to 300 people—and sometimes up to 400—would squeeze into a relatively small room, there was constant physical contact between people, some sitting on each others' legs or leaning against each other. The only control of movement was when someone entered an already full room, in which case Amadlozi members would guide them towards less crowded areas. The only rule seemed to be that if nobody made a seat available to an elderly person (male or female), or to a woman who was pregnant or with a small child, then Amadlozi members would pick out the youngest person in the room and either indicate with a hand movement that they should rise, or make a seat available by force. This authority was not confined to Amadlozi members; any elderly person could make a younger person (male or female) leave their seat with a touch on the leg or the shoulder. This added to the constant movement of people.

The position of the chairperson did, of course, refer to a particular status-role and a more or less fixed set of conventions for how to behave and conduct the meeting. However, no rules were clearly articulated or written down; procedures depended on the initiative of the acting chairperson, whose experience of conducting meetings might come from forums such as political parties and civic organizations, and who might base participation on recollections of the

---

15 At one stage in the history of the Amadlozi, members wore a yellow T-shirt with the word 'Amadlozi' in black, along with three political groupings: the ANC, AZAPO and the Democratic Movement. As this had not been sanctioned by these political groupings, the T-shirt slowly disappeared from the sessions.

makgotla system, on which present-day township courts are partly building.[16] Despite the lack of overt rules, a session would follow more or less the same procedure. First, an undifferentiated group of community members (ordinary members, complainants, witnesses and summoned people) would gather in the room and take seats. As they arrived, people would move around and greet those they knew. Then the chairperson of the meeting (usually a man but sometimes a woman) would enter the room and take his or her place behind or in front of the tables that clearly marked his/her space at the front. When the chairperson had greeted the secretary and who ever else needed to be attended to (often quite a few people), everybody would rise and sing a Christian hymn or chorus. Still standing, all would bow their heads while the chairperson or an elder delegated by the chairperson said a prayer. The content of the prayer varied, but often hinted at particularly difficult challenges confronting the community and the meeting (we will return to this point).

Here followed 'listening to reports' from 'working groups', after which the chairperson began 'case handling' by indicating the case presenters. Summoned people or complainants raised their hands to indicate that they had a case to be addressed. People normally stood up to speak. A man would remove his hat or cap voluntarily or as prompted by the chairperson or an Amadlozi or community member. During case processing, the chairperson would normally guide the questioning and let the different parties speak in turn. The chairperson would go on to ask the audience for comments and further questions. Finally, after a session bringing new cases to public attention, the gathering would slowly disperse. At times, if the gathering retained some composure, the chairperson would close with a prayer. Occasionally, the procedure was amended to integrate new and urgent cases into the agenda described above. The demarcation of the

---

16 *Makgotla* (*lakgotla* in the singular) were originally 'elders' courts in the rural areas' (Seekings, 2001 pp.81-2) which over time became part of urban life, until people's courts emerged during the radicalization of the internal struggle against apartheid (see Buur, 2005 pp.194-5).

proper place of the chairperson by three or four tables was not strict. The chairperson's function could, as mentioned, be assumed by up to four different individuals during a session. The concrete fulfilment of the role was up to each incumbent. Some exercised firm rules for when to speak and what they wanted to listen to. For example, if a speaker dwelt on details, the chairperson might intervene and ask the person to stick to the salient features of the story, always out of concern for the many waiting community members: 'We cannot waste people's time on minor details, we are not paid for this. We are here out of concern for the well-being of the community, so please be brief.' Generally, however, chairpersons were more relaxed in their management of the flow of exchanges, allowing community members considerable control over the proceedings.[17]

One consistent element was language: the way people addressed each other would be rigidly managed, with firm conventions for respectful address by age group. An older person would address boys or younger men by the term '*bhuti*' (brother)[18] or 'this boy', and a younger female by the term 'sister' or '*sisi*'. A younger person should, conversely, use the terms '*mama*' or '*tata*' (mother/elderly woman or father/elderly man). If the chairperson did not comply with these conventions, people in the audience would immediately correct him or her. In some instances, people were asked (and even physically reminded with slaps on the body) to stop speaking if they did not comply. Respectful language was also used by complainants, accused and community members when they were given the chance to speak, beginning by thanking the chairperson or the Amadlozi for listening to them. This is one of the ways in which legitimacy was conferred on the leadership. Any contravention was noticed immediately, and a community member—or, more rarely, the chairperson—would intervene and ask: 'Are you trying to undermine the Amadlozi?'

---

17 If, as often happened, cases were complicated and highly emotional, the chairperson would take firmer control over the proceedings and "guide" the exchanges to a considerable degree.

18 The term '*bhuti*' emanates from the Afrikaans word for brother: '*boetie*'.

A state courtroom conforms to dress codes and a strict spatial ar-rangement. By contrast, the absence of designated or proper places in the Amadlozi courtroom made it possible for people to shift around—voluntarily or involuntarily—between dissimilar subject positions structured by a variety of different relations. Because of the general sense of flux, one only realized who performed the different status-roles during the actual meeting. However, one particular place to the left of the chairperson (the 'space for transformation', Figure 1) was used often by accused people at a certain stage in the proceed-ings, as the following account exemplifies.

From a linked subject to a disassociated outlaw

Few distinctions between people attending the court sessions were evident at the outset. This changed during the course of a session, at times dramatically. One man was summoned to appear because he had beaten up the woman with whom he lived. The woman, who was in her thirties, had complained to the Amadlozi that the man (in his early forties) had beaten her without reason. She had visible marks on her face, and she pointed to scars on her arms and legs too. The woman was surrounded by both male and female 'family' members and neighbours. They had placed themselves to the left of the room along the wall (see Figure 1).

The man was sitting to the right of the room on the tables along the wall. He, too, was surrounded by several people, mainly age-mates and a few middle-aged women and men who were presented as 'family members'. The chairperson asked the man to rise and give his version of the story. He acknowledged that he had beaten the woman, but he claimed that he was fully entitled to do so because she needed to be disciplined. Although they were not married, they lived together and she was his woman. He pointed out that the Amadlozi had 'no right to summon him to stand here in front of young people and be ridiculed'. The situation was tense. Several people stood to shout at him: 'Don't come here and try to undermine us!'; 'How dare you come here with such an attitude?'; 'Who do you think you are?' People who appeared to be younger members of the Amadlozi intervened between the angry members of the audience and the summoned man, and it took some time to calm the situation. The chairperson reprimanded the man for abusive language and disorderly behaviour, and told people to behave and sit down so the proceedings could continue. He said it was a difficult case, one that the Amadlozi would normally deal with in private because it was a 'family matter', but he continued, 'This woman has been beaten so badly that we cannot just close our eyes'.

The chairperson then questioned both the complainant and the summoned. First, he wanted to know what the woman had done to justify the man beating her in this manner. The man began to explain that she had been 'cheeky' at home, not showing him respect, staying out late without telling him where she had gone and whom she had been visiting, and that she had stopped doing her 'housework'. He said she was 'undermining' him, and he felt that the only thing he could do was to discipline her so she learned to respect him. The audience laughed at these comments. The chairperson then turned to the woman and asked her what she had to say in response to the accusations from her partner. She shook her head and said he was lying. She was the one who was working—she had a part-time job and provided bread for the house. He (the partner) was just lazy, not working and he came to her for money so he could go to the shebeens.[19] 'What kind of man is he?' she asked the audience. The chairperson wanted to know if they had any children together, to which she answered: 'No, I got two children from my former marriage; my children are living with my mother.' The chairperson asked how long they had been together. The answer was four years. Finally, he wanted to know who owned the house. To this she responded: 'My family owns the house. He [the partner] moved in after we met. He had a job then, but now he is just drinking all my money up. Every time he is drunk, he comes and demands money and food, but

---

19 Township word for an unlicensed bar.

he is never there so I told him to leave the house because he is not my husband any more. When I told him that, he started to beat me.'

The chairperson turned to the man and asked if this was correct. After a long explanation he agreed that he had been unemployed lately, 'but that is not my fault'. The chairperson wanted to know if he had been drinking. 'Sometimes I go to the *shebeen*, but not often.' The chairman then asked if anyone in the audience knew if this was correct. Several people answered that he spent a lot of time drinking, often got into trouble when he had been drinking, and was generally known to be violent when drunk. The chairperson immediately asked the man if he was drunk when he beat the woman. When the man did not answer immediately, the chairperson walked towards him and angrily repeated the question. The man tried to say 'no', but the woman intervened and said he had been drunk. The chairperson then turned to the audience and asked for advice. He pointed out that this was a 'family matter' that should be dealt with more discreetly, but the situation required that the 'community' did not play 'hide and seek'. 'We have to take responsibility,' he said. Comments came from people of different ages. Some suggested that the man be taken out for 'punishment, because he is a criminal destroying our community'. Others said that he should be both punished and banned from the household so that the woman was not beaten further. A few elderly woman and men opted for further counselling, advice that was listened to with great attention.

The chairperson asked the beaten woman what she expected the Amadlozi to do. She responded that she wanted the Amadlozi 'to ban him (the man) from the house'. He then turned to her family members and asked what they wanted the Amadlozi to do. A person presenting himself as 'the father' responded that he did not know what to do. 'We told the man to stay away from our house,' he said, 'but the man has not respected our wishes'. They wanted him banned too, because 'he is destroying our house and name by his violent behaviour. Who knows what the next thing will be?' The chairman then turned to the people who accompanied the man and asked them for advice. Their only answer was 'not to be too harsh' because he was 'at the bottom of the heart a good person'. The problem was that he was unemployed and had started to drink. The chairperson then gathered a group of Amadlozi youths, older men and one elderly woman, by pointing them out in the room, and asked the summoned man to accompany them, together with the 'father' of the woman who had been beaten, to the house, which was situated close by. An hour later they came back. The man was directed to the area labelled 'space for transformation' on the diagram (see Figure 1). He looked as though he had been beaten up. A big plastic bag was placed next to him. The chairperson ordered him to leave the house and not come back. If he did, the Amadlozi would take charge and punish him severely. He was given the plastic bag and told to leave the room. On his way out, several community members rose from their seats at the front to lash out at him physically and many people shouted at him. After a while, his friends and family members left too. The woman and her family members remained for the rest of the session.

This is a complex case from the city outskirts, where the exercise of law and justice follows other rules than those envisaged by the Constitution. Here the Constitution has little bearing or direct impact. This particular sentencing is based on a framework of partly shared understandings of what constitutes a moral being. Within this framework there is nothing objectionable in the practice of physical or corporal punishment to discipline younger or female members of the 'community'.[20] The violent male was not expelled from the household because of violent conduct as such, but because he had been drunk and therefore 'out of his mind', thus lacking the qualities needed to show others (particularly youngsters) 'the right way'. Had he not been drunk, the case might have been discussed at a pre-meeting at most, but would never have warranted general discussion in front of the community, as public discussion of a 'family matter' is considered inappropriate.

---

20 See Buur, 2005.

Finally, it should be noted that the concept 'space for transformation' is not *emic*;[21] it is my own conceptualization. The Amadlozi do not mark out and name the space, as such, but this particular space is generally used after complaints have been raised and the accused either has had the opportunity to defend him or herself, or is brought into the court. To be placed there has consequences for a person's status as a member of the community in relation to the associated benefits: family membership, use of the court, living in the area and so on. The space is also used before people are taken out of the court for 'interrogation' or corporal punishment. Their presence in this area may either strip them of their position within the 'community' or as members of households—in that they can be subjected to banishment as well as severe physical punishment—or signify their reintegration into the community. They may be accepted back by their families as moral beings who, as a result of the (usually corporal) punishment, can now distinguish between 'good and bad'.[22] Few people enter this loosely defined space—most complaints and negotiations, for example sanctions, fines and compensation, do not require people to 'leave' the places they take up as community members. In other words, they remain with the family members and friends with whom they arrived.

Two notions of identity and relations

The arrangement and spatial structuring of the room could be interpreted as indicating that the ritually invoked/created identity formations in the Amadlozi quasi-court are constructed in contravention of the notion of rights-bearing, autonomous individuals. The Amadlozi quasi-courtroom seems to recognize a subordinated level of identity distinction, which we might call empirical. Invoked/created identity formations and identitarian discriminations are constructed according to a specific *logic of relations*. If we take the ideology of individu-

---

21 As I have explained elsewhere (Ibid.).

22 Buur, 2003; Buur, 2005.

alism first, in order to have something with which to compare the Amadlozi quasi-court, the *logic of relations* in operation can, following André Iteanu, be described as 'secondary to their poles which have precedence over them'.[23] The logic of relations can be inferred from how the *subjects* are linked by relations developed through the exchange of specific speech-acts that are transmitted in and through them. Here, subjects are treated as discrete elements that are not altered by the fact that they engage in exchanges of speech acts or form part of an elaborate system of relations. Subjects are thus considered to possess a reality higher than that assigned to the system of relations. That the system of relations is not accorded any reality separate from its elements implies that subjects are defined *a priori*. This is possible because subjects are all ontologically defined as possessing constitutionally guaranteed civic rights, securing them due process independent of what they have done or not done.

In the Amadlozi quasi-court, by contrast, the *logic of relations* cannot be described as 'secondary to their poles which have precedence over them'[24] because here relations take precedence over subjects. One implication is that a person's ontological identity as a member of the township is not defined *a priori*, but instead appears to fluctuate. As the case above exemplifies, community members are generally treated alike. Most strikingly, there is no specific order in the form of places for people when they enter the venue, and everybody participates in the same ritualized elements of the Amadlozi court: singing, prayer, reporting, greetings and so on. In the subsequent, ritualized exchanges through which the case is processed, however, community/family members are markedly distinguished from 'criminals' or 'outlaws' when the chairperson either decides upon a judgement or subjects the involved persons to further interrogation or punishment. In some instances, such differentiation is long-term and reinforced with a punishment such as expulsion. In other instances, depending on the circumstances and on further exchanges between the parties

23 Iteanu, 1990, p. 37.
24 Ibid.

(through words, gestures or corporal punishment), 'criminals' or 'out-laws' are reintegrated into the community. 'Personhood' in this sense is fluctuating; it is defined in terms of relations and is subordinated to the values that order the community. The various speech acts and the different instruments of discipline of the Amadlozi court have not only weighty consequences for the empirical status of subjects, but also the power to radically *change* their status as 'beings' so that they become either 'human beings' or 'outlaws': part of the community or outside of it. They may even be relegated to the status of 'bare-beings'—that is, beings whom one can treat as one wishes without regard for their psychological or physical well-being.[25]

The Amadlozi quasi-court invites different understandings of relations and personhood. As Marilyn Strathern has pointed out, relations can be complex in two senses. On the one hand, relations organize 'things', entities or kinds that exist in the world. On the other hand, we can look at relations as things that are created by relations. Where the first kind of relation speaks about the 'relation between things', the second kind of relation speaks about 'things as relations'.[26] The difference between the two understandings of relations is a difference between ontologies, which are themselves based on a dissimilar order of connections.[27] In the case of South Africa, the difference is that between an ontology based on the autonomous individual and one based on social constructivism, in which personhood is understood to be essentially an ongoing social construction.[28] In the first understanding of complex relations, relations are generated between persons who are always al-ready constituted. The different 'persons', in this understanding of relations, are self-contained and pre-existent because they contain the 'principles of their existence within themselves'.[29] In the sec-

---

25 See Agamben, 1998.

26 Strathern, 1995, pp. 17-19.

27 Ibid., p. 17.

28 Dumont, 1986; Comaroff and Comaroff, 2001.

29 Michel Foucault quoted in Strathern, 1995, p. 18 fn.

ond understanding of complex relations, persons are generated by relations; in other words, 'persons' became what they 'are' because of the manner in which they engaged in relations. To become a 'person' requires other elements to complete their property.[30] They were brought into existence, so to speak, by their relationships, and thus they exist within them;[31] they were made possible through a range of negotiations and exchanges connecting different identitarian entities.

The Amadlozi, in other words, operate with a different notion of personhood than that expressed in the modern ideology underpinning the South African Constitution's conception of universal citizenship. This notion can be described as fluctuating according to the different ritual contexts in which a person participates. Identity in this understanding thus appears as neither stable nor homogeneous because it is perceived from the angle of various relations. Following André Iteanu, 'the notion of 'being a relation' takes the place of our idea of 'having' relations, in the sense of possession', and it does so in two ways.[32] First, a person is known and therefore exists in relation and with reference to a whole range of 'significant others'.[33] Secondly, the identity of a person is unstable over time and is fashioned through and as part of an ongoing, often fragmentary sequence of practical encounters and activities.

It became apparent, furthermore, that the notion existed in the Amadlozi quasi-court of an undifferentiated person, maybe even a non-human, who could under certain circumstances be stripped of his/her different, relationally constituted identities. This implies that the Amadlozi to some extent stand above or subordinate other forms of identity formation, such as the type of right-leaning identity promulgated by the South African Constitution.

30 Ibid., p. 18.

31 Ibid., pp. 18-19.

32 Iteanu, 1990, p. 41.

33 Mead, 1962, pp. 67, 215-17. See also Kapferer's discussion of Mead's theory of the social self and its relationship to 'others' (Kapferer, 1991, pp. 272-4).

Township order and ritually 'making present anew'

It is important to ground the above analysis in the wider context of township order that legitimizes the interventions of the Amadlozi and functions as an important imperative for vigilantism and violence more generally. This context is intimately related to a wider universe of good and bad, and of order and disorder. When one considers the different exchange relations, the fluid organization and the manifold kinds of relations in the Amadlozi court sessions, the heavy stress on township order that runs as a sub-text through the case material above might seem strange or even contradictory. However, this is not necessarily the case if we view the Amadlozi quasi-court from the perspective of a ritual reordering or of 'making present anew'[34] a whole range of relationally constituted forms of identification and their relationship to the domain of order.

The Amadlozi explicitly connect this domain of good and bad in relation to God. The sessions usually started with the hymn, 'Lord you have no beginning or end'. Another often-used hymn was '*Jerusalem iKhaya Lam*', meaning 'Jerusalem, my home' and stressing, according to my local research assistant, that 'we're here to build a home', because the word 'Jerusalem' is a combination of two words: '*Jeru*' means 'foundation' and '*salem*' means 'peace'. '*iKhaya*' is Xhosa for 'home' (also the apartheid administrative name for the township) and '*lam*' means 'my'. That most township meetings start by singing Christian hymns speaks to the general importance of religion in South African public life, but the choice of these particular hymns is, as I see it, no coincidence. As Mary Douglas has demonstrated, most institutions need to be grounded in claims to legitimacy that are based on their pertinence to the nature of the universe.[35] In the religious universe of the South African townships, heavily imbued as they are with violence, death and social and economic misery, references to God's peaceful paradise—an order yet to come or an order

---

34 de Coppet, 1992.
35 Douglas, 1986, pp. 46, 48.

which has been disturbed—take on a special meaning. I suggest that the reference to 'otherworldly peace' becomes a commentary on the slippage between the social reality of the township and how it ideally should or could be.

This emerges from an analysis of the prayer by the chairperson (or an elderly member of the audience) that follows the hymn. Here, several themes related to the disorder of township life are addressed, along with the position and perception of the Amadlozi. Of interest, first, is the difficulty of distinguishing liars from non-liars: 'Some people who are here, some of them are liars and we don't buy their lies'. This is followed by 'We're here to stand for the truth'. This theme is repeated again and again during the prayer and the subsequent procedures of reporting, case handling and so on, and then often reiterated in comments about how to deal with worldly liars. At times, several contradictory messages are communicated at the same time, in different forms of expression, as in this statement: 'No[36] we're just inviting You to be here so that these people are coming here, and not coming here to speak lies; we don't have time to listen to lies [The 'You' refers to God]. Lord, please help these people to speak the truth and not to perceive us as people who happen to beat a lot of people. We are just here to put things into perspective and correct people, not to beat people.' Standing before the audience with eyes closed and in deep concentration, the chairperson was forcefully punching one fist into the other hand, 'emphasizing (according to my research assistant) that we[clap] are[clap] here[clap] to[clap] stand[clap] for justice[clap] not to serve somebody's interest, but to enforce justice amongst people. So he was just using that body language to correct people.' As my assistant continued, with a smile on his face, 'Jah, it's an emphatic gesture. He was using that gesture to show, even to those who cannot hear, to show them that I'm trying to put pressure on you to know what the consequences of lying

---

36 In Xhosa, one nearly always starts a sentence with a negative expression such as 'No' as a way of smoothing the following statement, for example what is stated negatively about 'other' people.

are.' Even though the room was concentrating fiercely and everyone was standing with their heads respectfully bowed, such play with two forms of language—verbal and body language—to communicate ambiguous messages of no-beating/beating often triggered nervous laughter from the audience.

Another question raised in the prayers was, 'Who it is that disturbs "peace" in the community?' This theme also recurred throughout the proceedings, with the participants stressing, 'We are here to fight crime, which makes it so difficult to live a normal life, even to trust one's neighbours. Who are you when you cannot trust your neighbours, your sons, your daughters, jah, even your own family?' This would be followed by a warning to the audience to take note that criminals do not come from outside the community; that they 'live here amongst us'. Besides common references to drinking and high levels of unemployment, the most profound problems were identified as the younger generation, which had lost direction: 'The problem is not the young kids alone, the problem is you [referring to the parents in the audience], you are failing. You do not keep order in your house; there is no discipline anymore. No respect for our culture. You have forgotten to teach your kids the right way of living [...]. We must put our house in order so that we know who is who, so that we sweep out the culprits.'

The analogue presentation of two 'worlds', one otherworldly and characterized by 'order', the other worldly and characterized by 'disorder' with the stress on the sources for 'disorder' being internal, is, as I see it, not something new. Social science literature features many references to such constructions. However, the construction warrants re-presentation, along with the analysis of similarities and differences. References in the Amadlozi quasi-courts to 'God', 'paradise' and 'peace' are based on a postulated homology between two parallel polar elements—the 'Kingdom of God' and 'life in the township'. The two elements do not look like each other; they are based on a qualitative analogy that does not express any symmetry. So, one cannot compare them; it is a conceptual similarity and not an experienced similarity, in that it is only the overall relation that is homomorphous. This implies that the otherworldly order of God cannot be corrupted by the worldly disorder, but that does not imply that the worldly cannot be made better. This, I would suggest, is at the core of the success and work of the Amadlozi.

From the point of view of communitarian order, each person may have several simultaneous, distinct identities in relation to the various ritual pre-texts in which they engage. Such forms of identitarian identification can, so to speak, be changed, remade or reshaped in the Amadlozi court, as already hinted. We can say that the persons attending the Amadlozi quasi-court are identified by the conjunction of the ritual positions they occupy, which can shift considerably or be remade during a session. Thus subjects do not possess an *'always already'* identity; their identity is instead defined as a conjunction of ritually created social relations. This, of course, is not strictly speaking correct, because each and every South African citizen does have substantial *de jure* rights, but this is not the *de facto* case for most of the lower-income groups in the South African townships and former homelands.[37] The different systems of relations are, as far as I can assess, not hierarchically ordered among themselves in any way. However entangled they may seem, many of these ritually created forms of identification were previously regulated in different ways—directly or indirectly—by the apartheid order and the various movements fighting it. With the disappearance of apartheid and the subsequent rapid changes in class composition and power relations, as well as the perceived decay of the morality of township life exemplified by the high 'crime' levels (understood broadly as explained above), no unifying mechanism for control was established to regulate township life.

The transition to democracy seems to have had the effect of leaving a power vacuum in which the Amadlozi has emerged as an exam-

---

37 From time to time, a person who has been severely interrogated by the Amadlozi and has physical disfigurements or other means of proof reports the incident to the police. There are seldom any consequences for the Amadlozi (see Buur, 2003).

ple of a local sovereign in charge of control and regulation.[38] Even though I explicitly stated above that there does not seem to be any internal hierarchical ordering of the different relations, the identity of each individual can, nonetheless—in the sense of the Amadlozi as an example for social control and regulation—be defined by its relation to something superior to it; namely the ritualized sessions of the Amadlozi group itself. This is only a momentary and instantaneous kind of ordering and "making present anew". What the Amadlozi group does is to order relations that, with the new democracy and attempts at repositioning the state as the entity for ordering social relations, have remained undefined or taken for granted. The space in which forms of identification and township order unfold is, clearly, deeply implicated in the relational involvements that define personhood.

Concluding remarks

Without accepting Marcel Mauss' whole theoretical package, what is represented in the sessions resembles what he would call a 'total social phenomenon'[39] in the limited sense that what *is* and what *ought to be* are not separated; fact (what the person has done) and value (the status of a person) belong together. What the quasi-court sessions seek to represent are actions and speech acts that attempt to make social order present anew. In this way, the ritualized acts of the sessions try to reconstitute and confirm the perceived order of the township—in all of its partial, scattered and inconsistent expressions. In reality, two ways of making social order present anew are at stake here; on the one hand, the idea of 'the community' and, on the other, various relationally constituted identity formations. The term 'the community' refers, rather nostalgically, to the time of 'pure politics' during the struggle against apartheid, when people came together and supported each other. Even though communities have been riven by violence and conflict in the past decade, a projection of past order

---

38 See Buur, 2005.

39 Mauss, 1990, p. 3; Douglas, 1990, pp. viii, ix.

is articulated repeatedly, making the longing for 'the community' extremely potent. Where, before 1994, people could rally around the struggle against apartheid, the new unifying factor is 'crime' in its various expressions and creating its own divisions and exclusions. Starting to disentangle this dimension (articulating an 'order' which has its own dynamics, power struggles and so on) could easily obscure the fact that, within the quasi-courtroom of the Amadlozi, one finds—as illustrated above—a whole range of projects for redefining and 'making present anew' the disturbed lines of authority in what is often referred to as the 'social fabric' of township life.

Paraphrasing Dumont,[40] one could say that ideally, the new democratic order should encompass its contrary by securing the rights of all the individuals that form part of the new nation-state. One aspect of this 'contrary' is that personhood is not primarily characterized by its own inherent identity or qualities, as it is in the formalized version of citizenship. As long as local forms of identity formation could be encompassed in a hierarchy of legal forms that subordinate indigenous hybrids under the citizenship style of rights and identity formation through control and regulation by the state, this difference would not as such be a problem. The encompassment of the new democracy's contrary would not differ substantially from what characterizes most multi-ethnic societies. A second aspect is the use of corporal punishment and other physical discipline techniques, intimately related to 'making present anew' the moral order of the community and yet, according to the norms of the new Constitution and the nationalized version of citizenship, unacceptable.

⚅

Agamben, G. *Homo Sacer: Sovereign Power and Bare Life*, Stanford, 1998.
Bell, C. *Ritual Theory, Ritual Practice*, New York, Oxford, 1992.
Bourdieu, P. *The Logic of Practice*, Stanford, 1990.

---

40 Dumont, 1980.

Buur, L. 'Crime and Punishment on the Margins of the Post-Apartheid State', *Anthropology and Humanism* 28(1), 2003, pp. 23-42.

—— 'The Sovereign Outsourced: Local Justice and Violence in Port Elizabeth', in *Sovereign Bodies: Citizens, Migrants, and States in the Postcolonial World*, T.B. Hansen and F. Stepputat (eds), Princeton, NJ, 2005, pp. 192-217.

—— 'Reordering Society: Vigilantism and Sovereign Expressions in Port Elizabeth's Townships', *Development and Change*, 37(4), 2006, pp. 735-57.

Comaroff, J. and J. Comaroff. 'Policing Culture, Cultural Policing: Law and Social Order in Postcolonial South Africa', *American Bar Foundation*. 29, 2004a, pp. 513–45.

—— 'On Personhood: an Anthropological Perspective from Africa', *Social Identities* 7(2), 2001, pp. 267-83.

—— 'Criminal Justice, Cultural Justice: The Limits of Liberalism and the Pragmatics of Difference in the New South Africa', *American Ethnologist* 31(2), 2004b, pp. 188-204.

de Coppet, D. 'Comparison, a Universal for Anthropology: from 'Re-presentation' to the Comparison of Hierarchies of Values', in *Conceptualizing society*, A. Kuper (ed.), London, 1992, pp. 59-74.

Douglas, M. *How Institutions Think*, Syracuse, 1986.

—— 'Foreword: No Free Gifts', in *The Gift: The Form and Reason for Exchange in Archaic Societies*, M. Mauss (ed.), Routledge, 1990, pp. vii-xviii.

Dumont, L. *Homo Hierarchicus: the Caste System and its Implications*, Chicago, 1980.

—— *Essays on Individualism: Modern Ideology in Anthropological Perspective*, Chicago and London, 1986.

Honneth, A. *The Struggle for Recognition: the Moral Grammar of Social Conflicts*, Cambridge, 1995.

Isin, E. and B.S. Turner (eds). *Citizenship Studies: An Introduction*, London, 2002.

Iteanu, A. 'The Concept of the Person and the Ritual System - an Orokaiva View', *Man* 25(1), 1990, pp. 35-53.

Janoski, T. and B. Gran. 'Political Citizenship: Foundations of Rights', in *Handbook of Citizenship Studies*, E.F. Isin and B.S. Turner (eds), London, 2002, pp. 13-53.

Kapferer, B. *A Celebration of Demons: Exorcism and the Aesthetics of Healing in Sri Lanka*, Oxford, 1991.

Mamdani, M. *Citizen and Subject: Contemporary Africa and the Legacy of Late Colonialism*, Princeton, NJ, 1996.

Mauss, M. *The Gift: The Form and Reason for Exchange in Archaic Societies*, Routledge, 1990.

Mead, G.H. *Mind, Self and Society from the Standpoint of a Social Behaviorist*, Chicago and London, 1962.

Seekings, J. 'Social Ordering and Control in the African Townships of South Africa: An Historical Overview of Extra-state Initiatives from the 1940s to the 1990s', in *The Other Law: Non-State Ordering in South Africa*, W. Schärf and D. Nina (eds), Landsowne, Cape Town, 2001, pp. 71-97.

Stepputat, F. 'Marching for Progress: Rituals of Citizenship, State and Belonging in a High Andes District', *Bulletin of Latin American Research* 23(2), 2004, pp. 244-59.

Strathern, M. *The Relation. Issues in Complexity and Scale*, Cambridge, 1995.

Wilson, F. 'Towards a Political Economy of Roads: Experiences from Peru', *Development and Change* 35(3), 2004, pp. 525-46.

7

LAW AND DISORDER IN THE PALESTINIAN WEST BANK: THE EXECUTION OF SUSPECTED COLLABORATORS UNDER ISRAELI OCCUPATION

Tobias Kelly

Throughout the second Palestinian *intifada* armed groups have increasingly appeared to be taking the 'law into their own hands', seemingly challenging the Palestinian National Authority's (PNA) monopoly in the provision of justice and the use of violence. As in the first *intifada* of the late 1980s and early 90s, *'umala* (collaborators) with the Israeli occupation have been executed by the various armed groups associated with the Palestinian nationalist movement. This chapter explores the processes behind these extra-judicial executions. It argues that the killing of collaborators should be understood in the context of the fragmentation of claims to sovereignty among West Bank Palestinians.[1] In particular, this chapter focuses on the tensions between a 'revolutionary' notion of sovereignty located in the *sha'b* (people) and an institutional notion of sovereignty located in the PNA. The history of attempts at Palestinian state-building in the West Bank has produced overlapping and multiple claims

---

1 This chapter was written before the victory of Hamas in the January 2006 Palestinian Legislative Council elections. Hamas has historically operated outside the PLO and has never recognized the Oslo Accords. Its election therefore promises to produce a new dynamics of governance, whose implications are unclear at the time of writing. The chapter also concentrates on the West Bank, rather than the Gaza Strip. The political history of the Gaza Strip has produced related but different processes.

for the right to speak in the name of the Palestinian people. It is in this context that competing networks and organizations seek to 'organise violence, retributions and entitlements'.[2] The execution of the suspected collaborator, a figure simultaneously both inside and outside the Palestinian political community, is therefore part of attempts to reproduce particular visions of what it might mean to be a Palestinian *muwatin* (citizen/national) in the face of the fragility of the Palestinian state-building project.

Capital punishment and popular sovereignty

Political regimes with claims to popular sovereignty are faced with the problem that the 'people' are a largely abstract and intangible concept. However, as Austin Sarat has argued, the taking of life in the name of the 'people' gives them a concrete presence. He writes: 'Where sovereignty is most fragile, as it always is when the locus is "the People", dramatic symbols of presence, like capital punishment, may be most important.'[3] As Foucault and many others have argued, decisions over life and death mark claims to sovereignty.[4] Such performances of sovereignty are not just found amongst authoritarian states, but also within regimes with claims to popular legitimacy. The history of many 'popular' state-building projects is shot through with violent demonstrations of claims to speak in the name of the people. It is arguably the vulnerability of these claims to popular sovereignty that makes them all the more necessary.[5] Claims to rule in the name of the people are made tangible through the taking of life in the name of the people, thereby dramatizing and confirming the location of political authority.

The work of Walter Benjamin is perhaps useful here in trying to understand the particular dynamics of violence in the name of the 'people'. Benjamin famously rejected the distinction between legiti-

---

2 Hansen, 2005.
3 Sarat, 1999, p. 5.
4 Foucault, 1977; Agamben, 1998.
5 Hansen and Stepputat, 2005.

mate and illegitimate violence as analytically, if not morally, useful categories, and instead made a distinction between 'law making' and 'law preserving' violence.[6] For Benjamin 'law making' violence founds the political order through the exercise of seemingly arbitrary force. 'Law making' violence is revolutionary, productive and arbitrary. 'Law preserving' violence on the other hand attempts to maintain the status quo, often through the deployment of seemingly more procedural force. Importantly, both forms of violence are not temporally separated, but are always present, often in the same political practices. Whether any particular act is law preserving or law making depends on the perspective on the political project at hand.

Claims to speak in the name of 'the people', and therefore to exercise violence in their name, are of course historically embedded. The category of the 'people' and the particular meanings of violence are always culturally mediated. In the West Bank, a history of fragmented state-building through the armed struggle has meant that it is far from clear who speaks in the name of the people. The Palestinian national movement is split between institutionalizing processes on the one hand and more revolutionary forms of mobilization on the other.[7] At a formal level there is a tension between the PLO, the political body claiming to present all Palestinians with the aim of creating a liberated Palestinian state, and the PNA, the bureaucratic creation of the Oslo Agreements between the PLO and the Israeli state with the specific role of providing basic services to Palestinians in the West Bank and Gaza Strip. In practice, the distinction is far from absolute as there are elements of both institutionalization and mobilization with the PLO and the PNA, and the personnel of both organisations are often one and the same. The distinction is more one of style and perspective that runs through the broader Palestinian national movement than an organisational separation. The branches of the various factions of the armed national movement are a particular example of this tension.

---

6 Benjamin, 1978 see also Hansen, 2006.

7 This is notwithstanding the history of bureaucratization within the Palestinian national movement that predates the Oslo Peace Process (Sayigh, 1997).

Although the PNA security forces were created by the Oslo Accords, they have their roots in the armed struggle of the PLO. The PNA security forces also have a very ambiguous legal definition, and overlap considerably with the armed groups. Hence there is a constant movement between 'law preserving' and 'law making' violence within the Palestinian national movement.

The practice of 'taking the law into your own hands' has often been seen as a fundamentally conservative process. As Ray Abrahams has famously argued, vigilantism is an attempt to defend a particular moral order by calling the state back to its perceived responsibilities.[8] However, in the West Bank the nature and location of the state are always in question. For West Bank Palestinians the moral and political order is in a constant state of flux, owing to the absence of a Palestinian state. The execution of suspected collaborators by the armed groups of the Palestinian national movement should therefore be seen as part of a state building process in which the very possibility and location of the state are contested. As such, collaborator killing is simultaneously an attempt to conserve particular claims to authority, and to produce a new moral and political order. It is the tensions between conservatism and change, institutionalisation and revolutionary mobilization, fragmentation and centralization that give the killing of suspected collaborators its particular shape. In a context where the feasibility of a Palestinian moral and political community is always in question, the execution of suspected collaborators is a powerful device for making claims to speak in the name of the Palestinian people and for defining its moral limits. The figure of the collaborator defines the boundaries of the Palestinian collective subject but also reveals its very weaknesses.

The collaborator in Palestinian national history

The figure of the collaborator has invoked much fear and hatred, but has had a shifting meaning in the history of the Palestinian national movement. There have historically been several sub-categories

---

8 Abrahams, 1998.

within the broader category of collaboration. Perhaps the oldest is the *samsar* (land dealer). The *samsar* is a person accused of selling land to Jews or the Israeli state. A second category of collaborator is the *wasit* (intermediary). The bureaucratic structures set up by the Israeli military in the West Bank after the 1967 occupation meant that mediating figures were often needed in order to obtain permits, passes or basic services. Closely related to the *wasit* were those Palestinians who worked directly for the Israeli administration in the West Bank. This category has included officers in the pre-Oslo police force, members of the Israeli controlled municipalities and those who worked in the Village Leagues, amongst others. Importantly, however, although Palestinians have worked for Israeli controlled institutions since 1967, it was not until the late 1980s that working for the Israeli-controlled administration in the West Bank was widely seen as collaboration.

Perhaps the most feared type of collaborator were the *jawasis* (spies) who worked for the Israeli secret service. Basic services and permits, such as permits for work in Israel or permission to build a new house, were frequently only provided in return for information to the Israeli secret service. At other times criminal charges were dropped or shortened in return for collaboration. Many *jawasis* were recruited in prison, and were asked to spy on fellow Palestinian inmates. Although the large numbers of Palestinians being held in Israeli jails represented a considerable mobilizing and educational resource in the development of Palestinian nationalism, it also represented an opportunity for the recruitment of collaborators to the Israeli security forces.

It was in the first *intifada* of the late 1980s and early 1990s that the collaborators gained particular prominence in the discourse of Palestinian nationalism. In the late 1980s an internal Fatah document defined collaborators as 'people who have lost all shame, honour and conscience … and whose interests are bound up with those of the Israeli security mechanism.'[9] However, who was and who was not a collaborator remained vague, and the label was applied across a

---

9 On file with author.

wide spectrum of behaviour from ordinary criminality to spying and selling land to Jews. Collaboration was seen as being closely linked to moral corruption, and drug dealers and prostitutes were often accused of indirect collaboration. During the first *intifada* a book known as *ad-dahiyyah taataraf* (the victim confesses) appeared across the West Bank.[10] The book sets out in detail how a Palestinian called Mazen Fahwenani recruited dozens of Palestinian men and women to work for the Israeli secret service. Fehwanani was reported to specialize in using *femme fatales* in order to take pictures of people in sexually compromising positions in order to blackmail them. Whether or not the book described real events, it was widely circulated and read, providing the dominant image of the period of collaborators as morally dubious, cynical and treacherous.

With the creation of the PNA in the mid-1990s the category of the collaborator became problematic. Many of the activities that would previously have been deemed to be collaboration, such as coordination with the Israeli military, were now being carried out by people with impeccable credentials. Jibril Rajoub, for example, a Fatah activist and a man who had spent over twenty years in Israeli jails for his nationalist activities, was appointed the head of Preventative Security (PS) in the West Bank. PS was the branch of the PNA security forces that concentrated on cracking down on Hamas and the groups opposed to the Oslo Accords, and hence liaised closely with the Israeli secret service. During the initial years of the Oslo Accords, the figure of the collaborator, as far as the dominant political discourse was concerned, fell into the background. This does not mean to say that the Israeli secret service stopped recruiting Palestinians as *jawasis* (spies), but that the language of peace with Israel that was built into the Oslo Accords made talk of collaborators politically problematic.

With the start of the second *intifada* in late September 2000 the figure of the collaborator returned to prominence. The Israeli policy of assassinating prominent nationalist activists using helicopter gun-

---

10 Fehwenani, Mazen. *ad-dahiyaah taataraf* (Arabic). Publisher and date unknown.

ships, bombs and snipers was widely seen as relying on local Palestinian collaborators on the ground and spread considerable fear, among both activists and ordinary Palestinians. It seemed that the reach of the Israeli military extended everywhere. Dozens of activists were killed in the middle of Palestinian areas otherwise out of reach of the Israeli military. As one activist after another was picked off in this way, talk of Palestinian *jawasis* (spies) became more common. They were held responsible for the ease with which the Israeli military reached into the heart of Palestinian communities. The fear of the collaborator was only temporarily surpassed by the fear of the *mustarabin* (fake Arabs). *Mustarabin* were undercover Israeli hit squads that dressed like local Palestinians in order to carry out raids on suspected militants. Throughout the first years of the *intifada*, talk of *jawasis* and *mustarabin* were all-pervasive and filled innumerable conversations as people waited for buses, sat outside cafes or met in the street.

The *jawasis* and the *mustarabin* are similar figures as they represent unknown dangers. It is impossible to tell who they are and what they might do. However, the *jawasis* provoke a stronger fear. Whilst it is possible to unmask *mustarabin* as Israeli, a *jasus* (singular for spy) comes from within the very heart of the Palestinian community. As Sharika Thiranagama has argued, figures such as the *jasus* are not an 'other' but are a distorted 'self'.[11] The *jasus* comes by definition from within the Palestinian national community. Collaborators were therefore a symbol of potential Palestinian corruption and moral weakness, and as such both hated and feared. Indeed, family members of those accused would often disown them after their death so as not to be polluted by their actions. After one accused collaborator was executed in Bethlehem in 2001, his family took out an advert in a paper saying that: '...From this day on we have no relationship or connection, whether legal, national or kin with him, owing to the treason he committed against his religion, homeland and people.'[12]

11 Sharika Thiranagama, personal communication.
12 *Al-Hayat al-Jadida*, 28 November 2001.

Such treason was commonly described as a *sarataan* (cancer) that had to be eradicated, and it was very rare to hear anyone protest against the execution of suspected collaborators.

The difficulty of knowing who was and who was not a *jasus* was made worse by the ambiguities created by the Oslo Accords. The fear created by the figure of the collaborator was a product of 'epistemic murk'.[13] The Oslo Accords created a tension between the claims of Palestinian state-building and opposition to Israeli occupation. It was far from clear who was serving the interests of the people and who was the enemy. With the creation of the PNA the Palestinian national movement was, as far as many Palestinians were concerned, itself in danger of becoming a collaborator. It was impossible to tell who was speaking in the name of the Palestinian people and who was serving the interests of the Israeli occupation.

The punishment of collaborators during the first intifada

The outbreak of the first *intifada* in the late 1980s was the first sustained attempt at Palestinian state-building in the West Bank. Not only did the PLO, based far away in distant Tunis, declare an 'independent Palestinian state', but within the West Bank, Palestinian activists began to co-ordinate an attempt to 'shake off' the Israeli occupation.[14] A United Leadership for the Uprising (UNLU), made up of representatives of the main PLO factions, began to try and organize West Bank Palestinians. At the local level popular committees (*lijnat sha'abiya*) took the lead. The make-up of these committees depended on the local balance of forces, but theyy were dominated by Yasser Arafat's Fatah faction as well as the leftist Popular Front for the Liberation of Palestine (PFLP), the Democratic Front for the Liberation of Palestine (DFLP) and the Palestinian Communist Party (PCP). Hamas, which rose to prominence during the first *intifada*, largely operated outside these structures.

---

13 Taussig, 1984.

14 Hilterman, 1991.

One of the first acts of the UNLU was to issue threats against Palestinians suspected of being collaborators. Collaborators were defined by the UNLU as those who worked openly for the Israeli administration as well as those who carried out activities for the Israeli security services. At the outset of the first *intifada*, in January 1988, the UNLU issued a communiqué which warned that 'the masses of the glorious uprising will bring to trial anyone who opposes the positions of the national consensus.'[15] The UNLU asked local *lijnat sha'abiya* (popular committees) to try suspected offenders, as well as impose sentences. Drawing on a tradition of *lijnat al-ishah* (reconciliation committees), these committees applied a mixture of *'urf* (customary law), Jordanian criminal law and PLO Revolutionary Law.[16]

As part of the attempted purge of collaborators the UNLU started by calling on collaborators to confess publicly. In May 1988, a day of repentance was called for 'all those who are flouting the will of the people.'[17] However, as the *intifada* progressed, execution was increasingly the chosen form of punishment. In February 1988, for example, the UNLU praised the killing of a suspected collaborator in the village of Qabatia, marking the start of a subsequent wave of executions.[18] By the late autumn of 1988, the UNLU was calling for the 'purging of the inside of the camp', and praised those who 'hunted the collaborators and carried out the verdict of the *intifada* and the people'.[19] Most suspected collaborators were shot on the spot. Others, however, were forced to confess publicly before being killed. In the first year of the *intifada* 20 suspected collaborators were

---

15 UNLU Circular 7, 1 April 1988.

16 The PLO Revolutionary Law dates from 1979 and was used to govern the PLO 'state within a state' in Lebanon prior to the Israeli invasion of 1982; see Sayigh, 1997.

17 UNLU Communiqué 11, 19 March 1988

18 UNLU Communiqué 9, 2 March 1988.

19 UNLU Communiqué 25, 26 September 1988 and UNLU Communiqué 28, 29 October 1988.

killed, the number rising to 100 in 1989. Between January 1988 and April 1994 the estimated number of suspected collaborators killed by other Palestinians rose to 822.[20]

The UNLU called for the execution of collaborators in the name of the Palestinian *sha'b* (people) despite the fact that various groups also claimed to be acting in the name of the Palestinian people. The actual killing of collaborators was mainly undertaken by the armed groups associated with factions of the Palestinian national movement. The largest of these armed groups was the Fatah Hawks, although Hamas, the PFLP and the DFLP all had their own armed wings. Crucially, the relationship between the UNLU and these armed groups was loose, and by the early 1990s local groups were beginning to take matters into their own hands, acting as judges and executioners. There were several groups that claimed to be linked to Fatah or the PFLP, including the Black Panthers, Red Eagles, Veiled Lions and Ninja, for instance, though these groups were constantly splitting and reforming as their members were arrested by the Israeli military.

Rather than being a coordinated armed force, therefore, the armed groups of the Palestinian national movement were *ad hoc*. They comprised overlapping coalitions, whose make-up depended on the local political context. Nevertheless, they all claimed legitimacy as part of the Palestinian state-building process. Often there was a merger of local rivalries, political disputes and the punishment of perceived offenders, as rival political factions jostled for control or sought to eliminate rivals. The punishments being handed out by the armed gangs were also becoming increasingly harsh, and by the early 1990s more Palestinians were being killed by other Palestinians than Israelis. Several people killed as alleged collaborators were widely thought to be innocent of the charges. Many of these armed groups were also seen to be blurring the line between criminal gangs and nationalism, as they operated protection rackets, demanding a 'revolutionary tax' from local merchants and businessmen.

---

20 Be'er and Abdel Jawad, 1994.

In an attempt to regain control over the armed groups operating in the name of the Palestinian national movement in the West Bank, the UNLU issued a statement in the summer of 1989 warning the armed groups not 'to eliminate even one agent without the explicit decision of the supreme leadership...'[21] At the same time there was growing criticism in the Palestinian press of the increasing number of killings. In 1992, in a coordinated attempt to rein in the armed groups the PLO and Hamas issued a joint statement calling the 'public to consider seriously the subject of the liquidation of the collaborators and to fulfil the decisions of the organisation's leadership regarding fair and mature interrogation.'[22] The criticism of the armed groups was partly that they were undermining the authority of the UNLU and the PLO, and partly that internecine Palestinian violence was benefiting the Israel occupation.

The first *intifada* therefore saw the growth in armed groups claiming to speak in the name of the Palestinian people. In a form of 'law making' violence, these groups sought to transform the status quo by punishing suspected collaborators, thereby marking the separation from Israeli occupation and the moral boundaries of the Palestinian community.

The armed groups under Oslo

In 1993 the Israeli government signed the first of the Oslo Agreements with the PLO. With the Oslo Accords many of the armed factions of the Palestinian national movement were slowly transformed into the PNA security forces. As part of the Oslo Accords the Israeli government demanded that the punishment of collaborators be stopped. However, fearful of what might happen to them following the withdrawal of the Israeli military from the main Palestinian towns, a large number of collaborators were moved by the Israeli secret service out of the West Bank, given Israeli residency cards,

---

21 UNLU Communiqué 44, 15 August 1989.
22 On file with author.

and settled in Israeli-Arab towns. In this context the activities of the armed groups and the killing of collaborators declined considerably throughout the 1990s.

In part this decline in collaborator killings can be explained by the fact that after the signing of the Oslo Accords, many of the activists in the armed factions took up positions in the various branches of the newly created PNA security forces. The number of branches of the Palestinian security forces proliferated throughout the 1990s. They included General Security (GS), Preventative Security (PS), Force 17 and Military Intelligence. Up to a dozen branches of the Palestinian security forces were reported, although their functions and chains of command were far from clear. The commanders of the local branches of the different parts of the security forces often acted independently, helped by the practice of paying wages directly into the local commander's bank account for him to redistribute. At times, these rivalries between the different branches of the security forces broke out into open gun battles, and the relationship between the GS and PS was particularly tense.

The most well-funded and trained branch of the Palestinian Security Forces was PS. This was reputedly trained by the CIA and received funds from the UK and the EU. It focused its activities on the detention of those opposed to the Oslo Peace Process in general, and Hamas activists in particular. Throughout the 1990s, it carried out widespread sweeps of suspected Hamas activists. In doing so PS operated largely outside the ordinary court system, trying people in specially created State Security Courts, applying PLO Revolutionary Law and detaining people in its own prisons.

The State Security Courts were set up under pressure from the US and Israel to try those accused of attacks on Israeli targets.[23] The judges sitting on these courts were predominantly military officers, as were the lawyers for the defence and the prosecution. Often the cases

---

23 They were also used occasionally during the 1990s in order to hear cases that Arafat wanted to be dealt with particularly quickly. These ranged from cases of paedophilia to crimes related to the provision of food.

in the State Security Courts were rushed through in a matter of days and the sentences were carried out immediately. One of the most famous cases to be heard before the State Security Courts was that of Hanoud Abu-Hanoud. Abu-Hanoud was accused by the Israeli military of being a leading figure in the military wing of Hamas, but managed to escape an attempt by the Israeli military to capture him. The Israeli raid was botched, leaving three Israeli soldiers dead, and Abu-Hanoud was able to flee to a hospital inside Nablus. After treatment Abu-Hanoud was taken into custody by the Palestinian PS. Facing demands for his extradition by the Israeli government, but unwilling to agree lest the PNA be seen as cooperating too closely with the Israeli military, Yasser Arafat quickly convened a session of the State Security Court. The trial lasted for just over an hour, during which Abu-Hanoud was charged with establishing a military organization, supplying it with weapons, and disturbing public order. Abu-Hanoud was sentenced to 12 years in prison and transferred to a prison in Nablus.[24]

It is important to note that there was considerable continuity between the new PNA police forces and the armed groups of the Palestinian nationalist movement. Part of the reason for the proliferation of branches of the security forces was to provide positions and resources for the different centres of power within the PLO. The officers of the Palestinian Liberation Army (PLA), who had been in exile with the PLO, returned to the West Bank after the Oslo Accords and became officers in the Palestinian civilian police. PS, on the other hand, was mainly made up of former activists in the *shabiba* (Fatah youth). The head of the the PS in the Gaza Strip, Muhammad Dahlan, had helped found the *shabiba* in the West Bank in the early 1980s before being deported to Jordan in 1988. The former head of PS in the West Bank, Jibril Rajoub, had spent 17 years in Israeli

---

24 Following the destruction of the Nablus prison by the Israeli military Abu-Hanoud appears to have been released. However, he was later assassinated by the Israeli Air Force. Similar trials took place in 2002 when several PFLP activists took shelter in Yasser Arafat's compound after the assassination of the Israeli Tourism Minister Rehavem Zeevi.

prisons before being deported. He acted as deputy to Abu-Jihad, the number two in Fatah, before his assassination by the Israeli military in 1988. Similarly, Amin al-Hindi, the head of GS had been a senior Fatah security officer since the 1970s.

It is also important to remember that the Oslo Accords were an interim agreement, designed to pave the way to an eventual settlement that, at the time of writing, has yet to be attained. This meant that in the interim period the PNA security forces were hanging awkwardly between being an armed movement and being the police force of an independent state. The behaviour of the PNA security forces reflected this tension of being almost, but not quite, part of a state. The different branches of the PNA security forces claimed their authority over the Palestinian residents of the West Bank both as the legal and administrative creation of the Oslo Peace Process and as part of the revolutionary state-building project of the Palestinian national movement. Many prosecutors complained that the commanders of the local branches of the security forces refused to take orders from them and often acted independently. Occasionally this resulted in direct challenges to court decisions. According to some estimates, over 95 per cent of High Court orders for the release of people detained by the Palestinian security forces were ignored, or only enforced after a considerable delay.[25]

There were tensions within the Palestinian national movement over the relationship between the PNA security forces and the Israeli state. Although Fatah, the movement that dominated the PNA, showed little opposition to the crackdown on Hamas that was launched by the PS at the behest of the Israeli military in the mid-1990s, many of its activists became increasingly disillusioned with the Oslo Peace Process. In particular, local activists who had cut their teeth during the first *intifada* came into conflict with senior Fatah leaders over their alleged corruption and acquiescence to Israeli interests. This conflict was at least in part a clash between visions of the Palestinian

---

25 PICCR, 2000. Most of these prisoners were only released after the start of the second *intifada* and the destruction of PNA prisons by the Israeli military.

national movement as a popular grassroots revolutionary process and the vision of the Palestinian national movement as represented by the bureaucratic structures and interests of the PNA and the Oslo Accords. As the Palestinian nationalist movement has tried to manage the shift from *thawra* (revolution) to *dawla* (state), the tension between popular revolutionary organizations and bureaucratic legal institutions has come to the fore.

The punishment of collaborators during the second intifada

The tension between cracking down on *Hamas* in the name of defending the Oslo Accords and punishing suspected collaborators in the name of defending the Palestinian national movement went to the heart of the dilemmas faced by those who spoke in the name of the PNA. Following the start of the second *intifada*, and the wave of assassinations of Palestinian activists by the Israeli military, the PNA started to try suspected collaborators in much greater numbers. Before the *intifada*, the State Security Courts had mainly tried those opposed to the Oslo Peace Process, but now they switched to those accused of collaborating with Israel. In late January 2001, the PNA announced a 45-day amnesty for collaborators, but nobody handed themselves in. By September 2001 the PNA was said to be holding 450 suspected collaborators in the West Bank.

The trials of suspected collaborators in the State Security Courts were usually rushed through very quickly, often lasting as little as a few hours. It has often been very difficult for those accused to find lawyers willing to represent them, and they have had to rely on court appointed lawyers, usually PNA security officers. In July 2001, for example, eight people were killed in Nablus by the Israeli Air Force and tens of thousands of people demonstrated across the West Bank. On the same day as the killing, the sentencing of those accused of aiding the Israeli military in the assassination of Thabet Thabet, a Fatah activist from Tulkarm, was brought forward in order to be announced prior to the funerals of those who had been killed in Nablus. On the days following the funerals, two other trials were held of suspected collaborators. Responding to criticism of these fast-tracked trials, the former PNA Minister of Justice Abu-Midien said that 'we are not ready to wait two or three years to punish collaborators, the street will not allow it.'[26]

Those found guilty of collaboration by the State Security Courts were usually sentenced to death, although in most cases this has not been carried out. Those executions that have taken place, however, have been conducted in public. In December 2000, for example, 'Alan Bani 'Odeh was convicted and sentenced to death by a State Security Court in Nablus for assisting in the assassination of his cousin the previous month. His hearing lasted two hours and he was shot in the courtyard of the District Governor's compound immediately. After a similar trial which also resulted in an execution, the commander of the Palestinian police, Ghazi Jabali announced that 'we have implemented the decree of God according to Islamic law.'[27]

The use of the State Security Courts took place against a background of widespread assaults by the Israeli military on the PNA security forces. Following the start of the second *intifada* in September 2000 the Israeli military accused sections of the Palestinian security forces of being involved in attacks on Israeli soldiers and civilians. The result was that it frequently bombed Palestinian police stations and prisons. This culminated in the spring of 2002 with the full scale invasion of most major Palestinian towns and cities. As part of this invasion the Israeli military arrested many Palestinian security officers and confiscated their weapons. Although the Israeli military eventually withdrew from the centre of most of the large towns, it remained on the edge and conducted frequent raids. The Palestinian security forces were forced to operate out of uniform and without guns, fearing that they would be targeted by Israeli soldiers.[28]

---

26 Al-Watan TV, 15 January 2001.

27 Ibid.

28 It was not until 2005 that some Palestinian Police began to operate more openly with uniforms and weapons, but the extent that they did so depended on the local situation.

Many Palestinians increasingly questioned the ability of the PNA to look after their basic interests, both personal and national. One common joke, playing on the Arabic spelling, claimed that there was no *sulta* (authority) only *salata* (salad). At the same time some elements of the Fatah movement feared that unless they were seen to be participating in the *intifada*, then Hamas would gain increasing influence. It was in this context that the Al-Aqsa Martyrs Brigades emerged. Although the Brigades were partly made up of local Fatah activists who had dropped out of politics in the wake of the Oslo Accords, their members also included Fatah activists who had joined the Palestinian security forces. The Brigades would play a leading role in the second *intifada* by launching attacks on Israeli soldiers and civilians. Often members of the Brigades and of the branches of the PNA security forces were the same people. However, not all branches of the Palestinian security forces took part in the armed struggle to the same degree. Members of GS and Force 17 were particularly prominent, whereas members of PS, who had previously been so prominent in the crackdown on Hamas, largely stood back. It is also important to stress that the Brigades were far from unified, but were rather a loose amalgam of local factions that used the same name.

As the *intifada* progressed, the Brigades begun to take the punishment of suspected collaborators into their own hands. Various groups, calling themselves the Revolutionary Justice Group, Al-Aqsa Brigade, Elimination Unit and Revolutionary Security System, carried out executions across the West Bank. Those accused of collaboration are often subjected to summary trials and forced to confess their crimes before being executed. The execution of accused collaborators has often taken place in public, and in several incidents the dead bodies were hung in the centre of town or village where they were killed. After the killing of a suspected collaborator in July 2001 by two men in PNA police uniforms, the Elimination Squad of Al-Aqsa Brigade claimed responsibility and issued a statement which said that 'the hand of the traitors would not have reached our heroes if it was not for those corrupt ones who sold their conscience and their religion and their dignity... We will not forgive them the blood of the martyrs that they have taken.'[29] Between 2000 and 2004, over 100 Palestinians were killed as suspected collaborators.

At times, the Brigades appeared to challenge the authority of the PNA courts. Riots broke out, for example, when a judge in Jenin requested that members of the Brigades should not carry their weapons into the courtroom. There have also been several incidents where masked men have broken into PNA courts or prisons and executed suspected collaborators. The extent to which the various armed groups and security forces challenged the PNA in general and the courts in particular depended from area to area. The Brigades were more active in the north of the West Bank, particularly in the cities of Jenin and Nablus.

However, in terms of personnel and actions, the distinction between the Brigades and the PNA security forces has often been difficult, if not impossible to make. In October 2004, 10 people in PNA police uniforms and armed with machine guns stormed into Nablus prison. They went straight to one of the cells and shot dead two men. One of the dead men had recently been found guilty of killing a member of PS. In September 2002, a hastily arranged session of the Jenin State Security sentenced three men to death for killing a PA security official, Osama Qmail. As a former activist and leading member of the Fatah Hawks in Jenin during the first *intifada*, Qmail had been involved in the killing of a member of the convicted men's family whom he had accused of collaborating with the Israeli military. With the signing of the Oslo Agreements Qmail had taken up a position with PS. During the second *intifada* family members of the man Qmail had decided to take revenge and shot Qmail. Although the court found the three men guilty of murdering Qmail, the death sentence it handed down was immediately commuted to 15 years' imprisonment as the defendants were under 18 years old at the time of the murder. Many of Qmail's colleagues in the PNA security forces and Fatah were in court to see the sentence handed down. On hearing

---

29 On file with author.

that the sentences had been commuted, the crowd in the court room turned on the convicted men and overpowered the few police officers in the building. The three men were taken to a nearby bathroom and shot dead, before being dragged out in the road.

In other incidents, PNA officials have themselves been accused of collaboration. Most often accusations of collaboration have been linked to suspected *fasad* (corruption). In 2004, there was a public scandal after it appeared that several members of the PNA cabinet had been involved in selling cement to the firms that were building the Israeli Wall across the West Bank. At other times the accusations of collaboration were linked to forms of cooperation created by the Oslo Accords. Jibril Rajoub, the former head of PS, was often accused of collaboration during the second *intifada*. In April 2002, he was accused of handing over several Hamas prisoners that he was holding in the PS prison in Baituniya to the Israeli military. More often than not these accusations of collaboration against senior PNA figures affected only their public support. At times, however, the accusations could lead to violence. In one incident, the Governor of Jenin district was kidnapped by a local Brigade faction, dragged through the streets and forced to walk barefoot through the refugee camp. He was only released on the intervention of Yasser Arafat, but was forced to leave the West Bank.

The 'law preserving' violence associated with the arrest of Hamas activists became less tenable as the Oslo Peace process dissolved into the *intifada*. Instead, the 'law making' punishment of suspected collaborators came to the fore as the PNA tried to reclaim its role as part of the revolutionary Palestinian nationalist movement. This is not to say that the armed groups were any more 'legitimate' in some abstract sense than the PNA security forces. There were widespread complaints that the factions were using the struggle against the Israeli military as a cover for their own criminal activities, protection rackets, or for killing innocent people. People routinely complained about the *fawdat as-silah* (chaos of weapons). The power and influence of the various armed groups derived from a mixture of their ability to wield coercive power, in contrast to the largely ineffective PNA, and the difficulties felt by many Palestinians in criticising groups that claimed to be acting in the name of the *watan* (nation).

Conclusions

The killing of suspected collaborators by the various groups claiming legitimacy for their actions by speaking in the name of the Palestinian 'people' was both a response to external threats to Palestinian claims to sovereignty in the West Bank and a symptom of the internal weakness of these claims. The figure of the collaborator revealed the political fragility of Palestinian claims in the West Bank. The dead bodies of suspected collaborators spoke simultaneously of these Palestinian claims to sovereignty and of the apparently all-pervading power and presence of the Israeli state in the West Bank. As Allen Feldman has written in the context of Northern Ireland, 'the corpse [is] the elemental communicative unit of political performance'.[30] In the face of its own weakness and fragmentation, the killing of suspected collaborators was a potent device giving a concrete presence to the moral boundaries of the Palestinian 'people'. The punitive nature of these responses stands in stark contrast to the claims often made about reconciliation and mediation being the dominant mode of internal Palestinian dispute resolution.[31] The collaborator was the ultimate outfielder, being a social insider who by definition could not be reintegrated into the political community. In stark contrast to the *shahid* (martyr) killed by the Israeli military, who as the archetypal Palestinian was always innocent, the collaborator was always guilty and could not be reformed.

The particular dynamics of collaborator killing must be understood in the context of tensions between claims to popular sovereignty based in the armed uprising on the one hand and claims to institutional rule based in the bureaucratic structures of the PNA on the other. This

---

30 Feldman, 1991, p. 232.
31 Bisharat, 1989.

dispersal and the tensions within the claims to punish collaborators in the name of the Palestinian 'people' arose from the contradictions inherent in the Oslo Peace Process. The PNA had been formed in the mid-1990s to serve two roles. The first was to administer basic services for Palestinians in the West Bank, while the second, at least for the most optimistic, was to pave the way eventually for a Palestinian state. In the years after the Oslo Accords, but especially after the start of the second *intifada*, it seemed increasingly unable to fulfil either role. There was a constant tension between the 'law making' violence associated with the armed struggle and the 'law preserving' violence associated with institutional structures. However, it is not simply a matter of locating the 'law preserving' violence in the PNA security forces and 'law making' violence in the armed faction of the Palestinian national movement. Both forms of violence were always present in the killing of suspected collaborators, and were always on the verge of collapsing into one another. The processes of the State Security Courts and the roadside executions by the Brigades both involved elements of what might be seen as more arbitrary productive violence, but also served to protect the interests of particular factions in the Palestinian national movement in its claim to represent the Palestinian people. The procedural violence associated with the enforcement of the Oslo Peace process seemed to call into question the future possibility of an independent Palestinian state. At the same time, the arguably more productive violence involved in the execution of collaborators in the name of the Palestinian 'people' faced the problem of tangibly locating the Palestinian 'people'.

The tension between revolutionary and procedural violence went to the heart of the dilemmas faced by the Palestinian national movement. Not able to offer a viable vision of future Palestinian liberation, but unable to defend an untenable status quo, the Palestinian national movement oscillated unstably between the two. Vigilantism is commonly seen as the outcome of a state unable unwilling to fulfil its promises to provide justice for the people it claims to represent.[32] However, the issue in the West Bank is not an attempt to call back the state to its public responsibilities—Palestinians after all have never had a state of their own—but rather is produced by contests over the very possibility of a state and a public that it would represent.

🝆

Abrahams, R. *Vigilant Citizens: Vigilantism and the State*, Cambridge, 1998.

Agamben, G. *Homo Sacer: Sovereign Power and Bare Life*, Stanford, 1998.

Be'er, Y. and S. Abdel Jawad *Collaborators in the Occupied Territories: Human Rights Abuses and Violations*, Jerusalem, 1994.

Benjamin, W. *Reflections: Essays, Aphorisms, Antobiographical Writings*, New York, 1978.

Bisharat, G.E. *Palestinian Lawyers and Israeli Rule: Law and Disorder in the West Bank*, Austin, 1989.

Feldman, A. *Formations of Violence: the Narrative of the Body and Political Terror in Northern Ireland*, Chicago and London, 1991.

Foucault, M. *Discipline and Punish: The Birth of the Prison*, London, 1977.

Goldstein, D.M. '"In our own hands": Lynching, Justice, and the Law in Bolivia', *American Ethnologist* 30(1), 2003, pp. 22-43.

Hansen, T.B. 'Sovereigns beyond the State: on Legality and Authority in Urban India', in *Sovereign Bodies: Citizens, Migrants, and States in the Postcolonial World*, T.B. Hansen and F. Stepputat (eds), Princeton, NJ, 2005, pp. 169-91.

——— 'Performers of Sovereignty. On the Privatisation of Security in Urban South Africa', *Critique of Anthropology* 26(3), 2006, 279-95.

---

32 Abrahams, 1998, p. 24; Goldstein, 2003, p. 23.

Hansen, T.B. and F. Stepputat (eds). *Sovereign Bodies: Citizens, Migrants, and States in the Postcolonial World*, Princeton, NJ, 2005.

Hilterman, J. *Behind the Intifada: Labour and Women's Movements in the Occupied Territories*, Princeton, NJ, 1991.

PICCR *Political Detention by the Palestinian National Authority During 2000*, Ramallah, 2000.

Sarat, A. 'Capital Punishment as a Fact of Legal, Political and Cultural Life: An Introduction', in *The Killing State: Capital Punishment in Law, Politics, and Culture*, A. Sarat (ed.), New York and Oxford, 1999, pp. 3-26.

Sayigh, Y.Y. *Armed Struggle and the Search for State: the Palestinian National Movement, 1949-1993*, Oxford, 1997.

Taussig, M. 'Culture of Terror, Space of Death: Roger Casement's Putumayo Report and the Explanation of Torture', *Comparative Studies in Society and History* 26(3), 1984, pp. 467-97.

8

SINGING THIEVES: HISTORY AND PRACTICE
IN NIGERIAN POPULAR JUSTICE[*]

David Pratten

Within the 'new geographies of governmentality' associated with globalization the appropriation of the means of governance by non-governmental groups has led to a crisis of 'redundancy' for the nation state.[1] In the African context Mbembe has noted the pluralization of regulatory authorities and an abrupt collapse of notions of the post-colonial state's public good. The resulting rise in the privatization of lawful violence is not a negative indicator of chaos, Mbembe states, but contains its own positivity as a sign of struggles aimed at establishing new forms of legitimate domination that restructure the existing formulas of authority.[2] One of the central features of this trend, he argues, is the '… direct link that now exists between, on the one hand, deregulation and the primacy of the market and, on the other, the rise of violence and the creation of private military, paramilitary, or jurisdictional organizations.'[3] The fracturing of the state, the increasing privatization of lawful violence and the creation

* NAE citations refer to the Nigerian National Archive, Enugu. My thanks to the ESRC, the British Academy and the Nuffield Foundation for their support of research initiatives that have contributed to this study.
1 Appadurai, 2002, p. 24.
2 Mbembe, 2001, p. 76.
3 Ibid., pp. 78-9.

of alternative jurisdictional organizations are especially pronounced features of contemporary Nigeria.

Nigerian vigilantism concerns a range of local and global dynamics beyond informal justice. By the late 1980s, in the aftermath of structural adjustment policies which saw economic opportunities dwindle at the same time as crime rates rose, the federal government encouraged local government bye-laws which legalized vigilante groups. Beyond fighting crime, these groups have spearheaded contemporary political contests between the politics of identity and citizenship, and represent divergent aspirations for Nigeria's future including Islamic reform, ethnic nationalism, and a re-calibration of the federal government structure. The return to democratic rule since 1999 has witnessed the emergence of the Bakassi Boys in the eastern states,[4] *shari'a* implementation committees (*hisba*) across the north,[5] and the maturation of the O'odua People's Congress (OPC) in the Yoruba-speaking south-west.[6]

Each of these high-profile instances points to ways in which the legitimation of vigilante activity, in its various forms, has extended beyond dissatisfaction with levels of law and order and the failings of the police. The rise to prominence of the O'odua People's Congress (OPC) in the south-west of Nigeria from the early 1990s, for instance, highlights an enduring feature of contemporary Nigerian vigilantism, the relationship between social mobilization and the politics of belonging. OPC, while operating localized vigilante operations, also champions a Yoruba 'ethnic nationalism'. Not only does this link vigilantism into national debates about ethnic marginaliza-

---

4 Baker, 2002; Ukiwo, 2002; Human Rights Watch, May 2002; Harnischfeger, 2003; Smith, 2004.

5 Human Rights Watch, September 2004; Casey, this volume; Last, forthcoming; Adamu, forthcoming.

6 Akinyele, 2001; Human Rights Watch, February 2003; Nolte, 2004. The federal government, in response, has attempted to criminalize those groups who have promoted their own or their sponsors' political agendas. The OPC was banned in 1999 and the Federal Government sought to disband the Bakassi Boys in 2002.

tion, it also implicates vigilantism into local discourses, practices and conflicts of 'indigeneity' or 'autochthony'.[7] Since 1999 opportunities for trade, employment and accommodation in Nigeria's cities have been increasingly determined by questions of identity and the practices of closure.[8]

The re-implementation of *shari'a* law across the northern states of Nigeria in 1999 and 2000, and the associated rise of *shari'a* implementation committees (*hisba*), has similarly challenged both the sovereignty and scope of federal law and how it is policed. The impetus to extend the criminal law to the jurisdiction of *shari'a* courts in the northern states has lost momentum since 2002, but the differential impact of legal codes and policing practices has nevertheless given rise to a patchwork of jurisdictional authority.

The legal sanctioning of the Bakassi Boys by south-eastern state governors from 1999 onwards has also posed fundamental questions about the constitution of the Nigerian federal state, relating to the federal or state basis for the Nigeria Police Force, with state governors arguing that the federal police are unable to police local conflicts. The federal constitution retains police authority at the centre as a form of brake on the expansion of regional or state powers, and many have seen the sponsorship of vigilante groups by the governors as a form of substitute for autonomous state-level police forces.[9]

As this brief overview suggests, it is possible to link contemporary Nigerian vigilantism to a range of regional and national-level political imperatives, and to map vigilantism onto a fracturing of the religious, ethnic, and constitutional fabric of the country. Such an analytical perspective, however, would not fully capture the historically contingent and culturally specific logics of what being a vigilante means. First, accounts that relate vigilantism to political fragmentation ignore the way in which it is a practice by which people

---

7 Meyer and Geschiere, 1999; Geschiere and Nyamnjoh, 2000.
8 Human Rights Watch, April 2006.
9 Human Rights Watch, July 2005.

actively insinuate themselves into networks of surveillance.[10] Second, to understand vigilantism as a mode of collective violence it is also necessary to take account of the moral imperatives to violence.

This chapter argues that vigilante groups and practices in Nigeria do not constitute a reflection of global trends, or a reflection of Nigeria's fractured politics; they are not entirely or satisfactorily explained as a response to crime, and as such they cannot be neatly understood as civic associations in the vanguard of popular movements to reassert autonomy and power in the face of the state. The focus here, instead, is on the cultural construction of violence, though this is not to underplay the significance of police under-resourcing and corruption or the way these factors contribute materially to the emergence and continuing legitimacy of vigilantes as they provide protection from the 'life-choking dangers' of armed robbers and thieves.[11] While vigilantes provide a compelling but interpretively layered script within popular Nigerian discourse, their practices need to be related to cultural logics and social imperatives as both counterpoint and complement to the 'police-failure' thesis.

Comparatively, contemporary vigilantism across Nigeria represents the articulation of claims to a set of rights based on the historical and spiritual legitimacy of young powerful men, 'sons of the soil', defending the community under local religious injunction and protection. Throughout the country, vigilantes draw upon familiar modes of social action in which young men of the community protect and punish. In this context vigilantism is as much a set of practices concerning the symbolic construction of community as it is a question of combating criminality. In northern Nigerian states these groups represent a grassroots response to the failures of the judicial system and to the inequalities experienced by young men who

---

10 De Certeau, 1984, p. 96.

11 Ekeh, A Review of HRW'S and Cleen's Report 'The Bakassi Boys: The Legitimization of Murder and Torture' on State Sponsored Vigilante Groups in Nigeria, http://www.africaresource.com/index2.php?option=com_content&do_ pdf=1&id=35, Date accessed: 31 May 2006.

invoke piety as a political act and join vigilante groups to enforce the *shari'a* code. Last, for instance, points to the way in which vigilantism forms part of a quest for modes of citizenship beyond that of the nation.[12] In this reading the rationale for vigilantism in northern Nigeria is linked to a widespread anxiety over the identity and activities of strangers within the Muslim community (*jama'a*), which has provided the groundswell for an impulse and imperative of 'renewal'. The enforcement of *shari'a* and the role of *hisba* are therefore the result of a 'new piety' in which the proper order of public interaction among Muslims is reconstituted.

In a parallel recent example Nolte's analysis of youth politics in the Yoruba-speaking southwest illustrates that the mobilization and vigilantism of Nigerian youth draw on a repertoire of practices and cultural logics linked to the ideology and practices of pre-colonial initiatory societies.[13] Once charged with executing criminals and protecting against witchcraft, the Oro society's responsibilities also included punishing those who challenged town unity. This role proved of particular political salience during the nationalist period and was manifest in violent attacks on northern migrants during the 1950s and 1960s. The legitimacy of vigilante groups formed from the 1980s onwards was derived, in part, from the close association between young men disenfranchized and disempowered by the post-oil boom economic downturn and the Oro society. As Nolte describes, 'While vigilante and Oro groups did not become identical, many young men were either members of both organisations or were content to cooperate with the other group. Thus, many of the young men involved in vigilante activities used charms of Oro origin for their spiritual protection.'[14] These appropriated Oro practices, including a secret language unintelligible to non-initiates, were taken up by members of the Oodua People's Congress which was formed in 1994, in the light of the annulled 1993 election, to protect

---

12 Last, forthcoming and echoed in Casey's chapter in this volume.
13 Nolte, 2004.
14 Ibid., p. 71.

Yoruba ethnic interests through lobbying support for traditional authorities, 'protecting' community interests against non-indigenes, and night patrols.

In both these examples the historical understanding of the ideology and practices associated with Nigerian vigilantism and its legitimization are central. This chapter similarly argues for the historically contingent and culturally specific logics of what being an Annang vigilante means in south-eastern Nigeria, and points to the need to take account of the moral imperatives to violence.[15] Two main points are argued. First, that vigilantism should be perceived historically as a contested site of judicial authority which captures a broad range of economic and political strategies, especially for the political category of youth. Second, that vigilantism should be seen in the context of the semiotic frameworks and conceptions of personhood that shape it.

From secret societies to vigilantes

This first section traces a historical trajectory from secret societies to vigilantes and outlines the ways in which contemporary vigilantes occupy a familiar, if contested, space within the Annang social fabric. Within this decentralized political economy there has always been a plurality of judicial fora in which hierarchies of chieftaincy power (of the patrilineal clan, the village and the lineage itself) combined with the seasonally shifting roles, rights and responsibilities of initiatory secret societies. In this setting judging cases was always an index of power and a contested resource.

Perhaps the most direct historical trajectory in community security is the link between pre-colonial night-guards (*ufok usung*) and contemporary vigilantes. Surveillance (*ukpeme idung*, to watch the village) was organized by lineage heads who picked small groups of young men to monitor paths and plots from palm-leaf constructed hides (*ufok usung*—road house). In Annang the protection of produce

---

15 The ethnography discussed here is based in Annang-speaking communities in Ukanafun Local Government Area, Akwa Ibom State. During the colonial period this region fell under the Abak District of Calabar Province.

was paramount,[16] and the theft of seed yams or cassava stems—for the following year's harvest—was considered abhorrent. These guards would parade thieves they had caught around the village and the market (*etak ino*—to parade a thief). In addition to courts (*esop*) held by lineage, village and clan heads, the Annang political landscape was differentiated by the men's secret societies: *awie owo* (*ekong*), the warrior cult, *ekpo*, the ancestral masquerade, and *ekpe*, the leopard society.[17] In the southern Annang area *ekpe* was the executive arm of village government and implemented judicial decisions in tandem with lineage heads and village chiefs. Any thief who was caught would be paraded through the market, beaten and either sold or killed at the execution grove (*ukang ino*—place, thief). The fate of those executed was related to their relatives by the phrase the leopard had 'eaten' them (*ekpe omum enye ata*—'leopard caught person chew'). Combined with their rights to recover debts and catch and kill stray livestock on crop land, the lucrative privileges of status that membership of the leopard society conferred led to the saying that 'the leopard is food' (*ekpe edi udia*).

Contemporary vigilantes claim, or have assumed, many of the functions of pre-colonial *ufok usung* and the secret societies like *ekpe*. Parallels are evident in the opportunities they offer for social recognition outside the lineage, especially to younger men, and in continuities of social practices ranging from oaths of secrecy and innocence, singing shaming songs, and modes of parading and punishing thieves. Pre-colonial modes of youth mobilization and initiatory societies therefore offer not only a model of organization, but also modes for the transmission of social practice. To illustrate the continuities in vigilante practice, however, it is necessary not only to identify inflections of the past in current practice but also to trace a narrative history of the relationship between alternative judicial fora, chieftaincy and the state as shaped through the colonial and post-colonial periods.

---

16 Cf. Austen, 1986 p.385.

17 Messenger, 1957; Offiong, 1984; Ottenberg and Knudsen, 1985.

181

In many senses the history of colonial law in south-eastern Nigeria can be read as a series of tactics designed to subvert the formal impositions of a colonial judiciary. Popular reaction to the unfamiliar prominence accorded to the chiefs during this period, with the institution of the Warrant Chief and Native Courts, was met with overt and covert responses from the elders of the secret societies. These included imitating colonial paraphernalia in the establishment of 'parallel' warrant chiefs, the continued sittings of illegal weekly village tribunals, and the 'revival' of secret societies and their powers of punishment over thieves.[18] Evidence of secret society activities during the First World War years, for example, illustrates that they were inspired by particular grievances with the Native Court system. Reports appeared in 1916, for instance, that *ekpe* societies throughout Ikot Ekpene Division, including the Annang villages of Abak District, had revived its former judicial functions. In January, representatives of the *ekpe* society had been called to meet at Obo market.[19] There they agreed to revive the rule that intruders should be apprehended and killed by the society. The witness statement of Akpan Ekoreko living at Ikot Ama, given during the ensuing investigation, exposes the clandestine details of its activities:

The first meetings of the Ekpe Society in connection with the new law was at Ikot Akpan Essiet in the compound of Chief Ebok Idiang (Ikot Ama Court). There an oath was sworn that no one should report what was arranged to the DO [District Officer]. It was then arranged that any[one] caught stealing should be killed and not taken to the DO. Another meeting was held at Ntaw Akpa Oko in the compound of Akpan Nwoko (Ikot Ama Court). Mbiam was again sworn and the same law proclaimed. An order was passed that every town should give their Court Member a goat and 100 manillas because it was their business to get the matter settled if the DO came to hear of it. After that there was a big general meeting at Edet Akpan Efiong. At this meeting 1200 manillas was subscribed to act as a fund to bribe the police if any one should be killed, and if the family tried to complain to the DO they were to be flogged and turned back. Their townspeople

---

18 Afigbo, 1972; Pratten, 2007.

19 DO Ikot Ekpene to Resident, Calabar Province, 25 August 1916, NAE: CALPROF 4/5/42.

would then deal with them. ... Since then several people have been killed under this law. About 9 days ago a man stole 1 manilla in Etim market and he was seized by the Ekpe people. I can't say if he has been killed, but the matter was not reported to any of the Courts. This law was made because the Native Court could not give them sufficient punishment. This law could never have been made without the Native Court Chiefs who were all present at the meetings.[20]

The Native Courts were unpopular because of their procedures and their punishments. The courts lacked effective sanctions in calling witnesses, judges were frequently bribed and the review process collapsed under the weight of demand. Reinterpretations of customary law during the early colonial period outlawed 'repugnant' practices, so that recourse to oaths (*mbiam*) and ordeals (*ukang*) was made illegal and investigative procedures, oath-swearing on testimony in the Native Courts, became a parody of traditional practice. In addition, Native Court punishments were insufficient to act as deterrents. Punishment for theft became a standing grievance, especially when the penalty was reduced from two years' to six months' imprisonment in 1914. Imprisonment was roundly rejected since it carried less social stigma than being publicly shamed in a market. Secret societies and village tribunals, in contrast, had many merits which were absent in the Native Courts since there was little or no delay, there was no writ of summons, no journey to a distant venue, no fear of adjournment, less fear of bribery, and parties were guaranteed to be heard out in full.[21]

While such 'revivals' continued during the 1930s and 1940s, these decades were characterized by a concern over another form of subversion—clandestine courts. There was a rapid multiplication of formal courts after the introduction of reforms in 1933, but the popularity of the justice they offered, as indicated by litigation rates, declined sharply. In part the decline was linked to the cash crisis during the depression, but the unpopularity of the government-approved courts

20 Statement of Akpan Ekereke of Ikot Esukpon, 25 June 1916, NAE: CALPROF 4/5/42.
21 Nigeria, 1953 p.12.

in civil matters also led litigants back to alternative village tribunals, and it was claimed that 'The extraordinary low figures point to the setting up of one or more illegal courts.'[22] The question of illegal courts was extensively revisited during the 1930s since it was apparent that courts representing various constituencies were being held clandestinely:[23]

Clan courts not recognised by Government still assemble from time to time in some areas. Their proceedings are kept in the dark, because the fines and fees which they collect are the perquisites of the judges.[24]

Ironically, it was also recognized that the clandestine courts, along with a broad range of informal tribunals at lineage, village and clan level and among the initiatory societies, were essential to the operation of the colonial legal system. They acted as an effective filter so that most civil matters appearing before the Native Courts were, in effect, appeals arising from decisions given by village elders.[25] Without pre-screening of cases the already overloaded system would collapse:

Without such multitudinous and sometimes petty societies with their heads and their powers of trying certain cases the village or Native Courts would be full to overflowing with trivial cases; in fact, without them, life would be impossible.[26]

The 1940s and 1950s witnessed various forms of secret society revival, and debates over customary forms of dealing with crime. Various apparent incitements to mob violence came on top of instances in Abak and Ikot Ekpene Districts in which communities resorted to vigilante justice:

---

22 'Annual Report, Abak Division', 1930, NAE: CALPROF 2/11/10.

23 Report on the Eastern Provinces by the Secretary for Native Affairs (S. M. Grier), 1922, RH: 723.12.v.43 (12).

24 'Annual Report, Calabar Province', 1930, NAE: CSE 1/86/188.

25 Ibid.

26 Marshall, 1932. 'Obong Village Group, Abak District', NAE: CSE 1/85/4905A.

I constantly receive complaints from persons who have been assaulted and even made to dance in markets without trial on allegations that they are thieves. They are frequently persons who have been seized by the gangs of men appointed to guard farms. I am of the opinion that these gangs often seize innocent persons with the intention of extorting money by threats. ... A case has just been reported of a woman who hanged herself after being publicly disgraced by being paraded openly in markets as a thief. Lawless elements are taking part in organised blackmail ...[27]

These organized gangs who were appointed to catch thieves were the *ufok usung*, men chosen by lineage or village heads to mount road-blocks and act as night guards. As with the secret societies during this period, the government opposed the *ufok usung* on the grounds that they had '... developed into an organisation for demanding money with menaces.'[28] It was believed that the use of the guards proved a fruitful source of revenue for village chiefs who held illegal trials in which persons arrested by the *ufok usung* were forced to confess their crimes. Sometimes, after the thief had been shamed by being rubbed with charcoal and paraded around the market they were taken to the Native Court, tried and sentenced again.[29] As a result of similar reports *ufok usung* were banned in certain Annang communities.[30]

In the light of new crime threats in the 1950s, however, calls for official recognition of night guards re-emerged, and in 1951 the Ikot Ekpene County Council argued that the continued activities of the *ufok usung* patrols demonstrated a genuine need for more protection than was being provided by the Nigeria Police.[31] Despite the long-running government opposition to the night watchmen the state-sanctioning of vigilante patrols saw their fortunes reversed in 1952:

---

27 D.O. Abak to Resident, Calabar, 1941, CALPROF 3/1/1956.

28 Acting Resident, Calabar to Secretary, Eastern Provinces, 1941-57, CALPROF 3/1/1957.

29 Ibid.

30 Native Authority Ordinance (No. 43), 1933, CALPROF 3/1/1957.

31 Secretary, Eastern Provinces to Chairman, Ikot Ekpene County Council, 14 August 1951, NAE: CALPROF 3/1/1957.

An interesting development in the Ikot Ekpene Division has been the establishment of a system of Rural Police Patrols. Small, uniformed bicycle patrols now visit outlying villages at regular intervals in order to collect information and to maintain contact with the people. Side by side with these patrols there exists the traditional system of village guards which again became active during the crime wave which was reported in 1951. With a view to regulating these institutions, and to co-ordinate their activities with those of the Nigerian Police, an embryo 'Watch Committee' has been set up consisting of representatives of the County Council and the Local Police Authority. It is an informal body.[32]

By the 1960s and early 1970s, with extensive migration of young men to the cities and the debilitating effects of the civil war, *ufok usung* declined. Shortly after the civil war, however, as a result of unemployment and demobilization Nigeria witnessed a rapid increase in armed robbery incidents. Armed robbery, known as '*amauke!*' ('your money or your life!') had first been reported in this region as an outbreak as the 'menace of a secret society of criminals' in Uyo in 1959.[33] In response the federal government of General Gowon promulgated the Armed Robbery and Firearms Decree of 1971. Locally such measures had limited effect and the mode of popular justice in Ibibio-speaking communities continued. In Nsit Atai during 1979, for instance, a celebrated armed robber 'disappeared' on the order of *ekpo ndem isong*, the *ekpo*-led village council whose judgements were carried out clandestinely.[34] Indeed, vigilante action, based directly on secret society revivals or drawing indirectly upon the idiom of the secret society, has been a common response to crime since the Civil War.

More recent trends of devolved and privatized security have to be seen within the context of moves on the part of the Federal Government in the 1980s to improve the image of the police, to respond to the notorious Anini case,[35] and to embrace policies of 'community

---

32 Annual Report, Calabar Province, (C.J. Mayne), 1952, RH: MSS Afr. S.1505.6.

33 Udoma, 1987, p. 495.

34 Offiong, 1989, p. 45.

35 Marenin, 1987.

policing' which were promoted internationally.[36] From that point until today there has been an official tolerance and, at times, promotion of vigilante groups, especially during the well-publicized 'crime-waves' of the 1990s. In 1991 the Divisional Police Officer in Ukanafun called on villages to form vigilante groups before the Christmas rush. This request echoed that of the Paramount Ruler of Ukanafun Local Government who had proposed a resolution in the Traditional Rulers' Council in August 1996 that each village should be responsible for the formation of a vigilante committee.[37] The Akwa Ibom State Administrator's concern at the increasing rate of armed robbery in the state led him to remind traditional rulers in April 1997 to report any suspected criminals or 'strange faces' in their domains,[38] and as a result of renewed 'underworld activity' in 1998, the State Police Commissioner criticized local government councils for failing to fund the local police effectively, and called on communities to mount vigilante patrols.[39]

Vigilantes like the youth association Mboho Ade Uforo Ikot Akpa Nkuk (MUKAN—'Unity for progress') in the Annang village of Ikot Akpa Nkuk formed security patrols called 'vanguards' to counter a rise in armed robbery from the late 1980s onwards. MUKAN imposed an all-night curfew and mounted roadblocks on the bush paths leading to the village. Their responsibilities were defined as follows:

1. Every member of the Association is empowered to arrest and interrogate anybody caught stealing or suspected to have stolen and report them straight to the Police.
2. Mount routine patrols at markets to check for suspects and stolen goods.
3. Those caught buying stolen goods will be reported to the village council and to the Police.

---

36 Fourchard, forthcoming.

37 Minutes of the Ukanafun Traditional Rulers Council meeting, 20 September 1996.

38 *Punch*, 28 April 1997.

39 *Post Express*, 3 November 1998

4. Mount roadblocks at night in some streets in the village to trap thieves.[40]

By 1997 MUKAN recorded 23 cases of apprehending and parading thieves, and 18 cases in which suspects caught by the vigilante group were later convicted in the Magistrates' Court. When it was first formed the vigilante force constituted around a dozen night guards each of whom was a powerful man (*okposong owo*), a local category of person defined by an ability to suppress a rival's power. This exclusive basis for recruitment to the vigilante group shifted to an inclusive principle in response to a crime wave in 2000. Then any young man who had lived in the village for at least two years had to register as a youth/vigilante group member. As a result the vigilante group grew substantially with up to one hundred vigilantes guarding the village each night. Active membership of the vigilante group therefore came to constitute both a marker of youth and the basis of local citizenship.

Despite public statements in their support the Police and the local chieftaincy tended to reach rather uneasy accommodations with local vigilante groups in practice. The provision of effective justice constitutes an overriding performative criteria for contemporary Annang village chiefs. Chiefs are under pressure by youths to endorse vigilante patrols and are frequently subjected to accusations of complicity with criminals, especially of releasing thieves on receipt of bribes. During the 1990s therefore, as chieftaincy underwent a national crisis of legitimacy under successive military regimes, chiefs co-operated with vigilantes so that they might gain respect from both the Police and their villages for handing over thieves to the authorities, thereby increasing their authority by gaining influence over a clandestine police force.[41] Chiefs who apparently fail to fulfil these judicial responsibilities face considerable opposition. The nomination of the village head of Ikot Akpan Ebo in Adat Ifang clan was revoked, for example,

---

40 Mukan Memorandum, 9 December 1988.
41 Comparatively see Heald, 1986a.

when it emerged that the chosen candidate was unable to handle the village's 'crime-wave'.[42]

Relations with the Nigeria Police have been similarly fraught. When the vigilantes in Ikot Akpa Nkuk first took thieves to the Police the officers demanded bribes for taking the cases. While there is considerable everyday cooperation between vigilantes and police, the former nevertheless occupy a precarious legal position. This was exposed in June 2004 when the vigilante group leaders were arrested for being in possession of illegal weapons. A local politician intervened to release the vigilantes on bail and an arrangement was subsequently brokered by which the vigilantes were able to retain weapons effectively licensed to them by the village council, and were issued with ID cards authorized by the Police who kept a register of vigilante members.

In addition to inserting themselves into these judicial niches, contemporary vigilante groups should also be located within a broad range of economic and political strategies. The following press report illustrates something of the range of expectations which contemporary vigilantes confront:

Vigilante group responsibilities include: checking the anti-social behaviour of hoodlums, protection of community-based projects; and preventing the vandalization of public infrastructure and social amenities. It also includes guarding against border clashes, communal hostilities and infiltration of those considered security risks.[43]

As this list indicates Nigerian vigilantism and the actions of youth associations more generally have to be configured in a wider mode of 'civic vigilance' or 'civic vigilanteism'.[44] Annang youth groups contest power through complex and ambiguous conceptions of accountability. Youth-led vigilante groups draw on a rhetoric of public accountability that is based upon localized understandings of the rights and

---

42 Minutes of the Ukanafun Traditional Rulers Council meeting, 28 February 1992.

43 *The Pioneer*, 29 March 1999.

44 Pratten, 2006; Watts, 2004.

roles of youth and how an Annang youth (*akparawa*) is distinguished by representing community interests (*atang iko otu*—to speak words in public). These young men maintain a vigilance towards community affairs covering a range of issues including judging cases, intervening in domestic affairs and claiming rights on behalf of the community. Positions within the vigilante associations have therefore become important career paths within the local political hierarchy. Youth leaders have graduated to take up places alongside the lineage elders on the village council, and in Ikot Akpa Nkuk, for instance, the former youth chairman sits on the village council, the current secretary of the vigilante group is clerk to the village council and the current youth chairman sits as chairman of his lineage assembly.

Vigilantes not only bring criminals to book but also deal with domestic matters. In establishing themselves as informal tribunals they hear minor cases and domestic disputes. Meeting most evenings after work the youth tribunal in the village of Ikot Akpa Nkuk has become a popular forum for the settlement of cases and hears accusations of witchcraft, land disputes, and physical assault. Their judgements are quick and decisive, their costs minimal, and their authority widely recognized. Often vigilante group members are also called upon by parents to discipline stubborn children (*nchong iwuo*—strong head) by 'strokes of the cane' (for persistent truancy, for example) in similar ways to secret societies, *ekpo* in particular, who were 'hired' to intimidate disobedient children. Youth-led vigilante groups also contest and enforce economic rights. In Ikot Akpa Nkuk a new taskforce was established in 2002 whose main function was to seize goats that strayed into people's farmland. The owner of the goat would then pay the vigilantes a N1,200 fine to release the animal. Indeed, the current vigilante group has developed an effective debt-collection system by which items of property are seized from debtors on behalf of those owed. Though precursors of these animal husbandry and debt recovery practices are not explicitly recalled, these initiatives are remarkably reminiscent of the roles assumed by Annang secret societies.

Vigilance towards the state and business interests takes two main forms—accountability and extraversion. Regarding the first, a discourse on corruption is apparent in the trajectories of Annang collective action during the twentieth century in which improvement unions and their elite leaders have sought ethical probity in public office-holders. In the second instance, modes of extraversion and brokerage are employed to assert rights over scarce inward investments. Within the Niger Delta these overlapping discourses give rise to a now well-established tension between oil companies, youth and chiefs.[45] Elsewhere the youth associations 'welcome' contractors to their communities with demands for 'settlement'. Here, for instance, the Ikot Akpa Nkuk vigilante group outlined its demands to a contractor who was erecting a mobile telephone mast on the site of local government headquarters:

To the Contractor
Site II, Ikot Akpa Nkuk
Ukanafun LGA
2 July 2003
Dear Contractor
Youth Demands

We, the Vigilantic group of Ikot Akpa Nkuk in Ukanafun LGA welcomes [sic] you into our community mostly for giving us the due recognition by making yourself available in our midst, once again we say—you are welcome.

For your information sir, with due respect, we are demanding that the following positions be sub-contracted to us in order to make the work easier for you.
They are:
1. All supplying of sand and gravel
2. Excavation for fencing
3. Employment of labourers
4. Moulding of Blocks
5. Building/Dressing of the fence
6. Consultation fee of N50,000.00

---

45 Human Rights Watch, 1999; Watts, 2003.

Sir, we are fully ready to co-operate with you here till the work is over if you are with us. We wish you a job well done.

Thanks.

Signed

Evidence from contemporary Annang vigilantes suggests that in these circumstances justice at the margins of the state is not simply a matter of 'folk' notions of law and justice versus state sanctioned ideas of justice—rather, that they are enmeshed in one another. Hence, while vigilantes may claim to be based outside and in opposition to an ineffectual state, they are nevertheless engaged in practices and discourses presented within 'languages of stateness'.[46] The vigilante groups discussed here therefore need to be set against a broader regional dynamic that considers how a rhetoric of accountability is dispersed throughout southern Nigeria. As Mbembe suggests, areas below the state sphere are where new forms of belonging and social incorporation gestate.[47] These are not necessarily overtly political movements but they do constitute visible, if ambiguous, sites where new normative systems, new common languages, and the constitution of new regimes of governance are being negotiated. This section has illustrated that these contemporary regimes of governance are nevertheless informed and inflected by a long historical trajectory of popular justice and its modes of social mobilization organisation, especially initiatory societies and, as the following section outlines, by notions of practice and personhood with which they are associated.

Singing thieves

'Popular' violence tends to obey moral imperatives and is often structured in terms of 'legitimate' targets and appropriate punishments. These imperatives produce notions of justice and law with different kinds of imaginaries from those available in the official sites and

---

46 Hansen and Stepputat, 2001.

47 Mbembe, 2001, p. 93.

representations of justice and law.[48] These views of justice are often 'retrospective vision[s] of a world restored to its proper order', but this is not to say that they are based on unchanging notions of cultural norms and practice.[49] Rather, the complexity of lived experience inflects both past and imagined futures into an ambiguous, dynamic and very powerful notion of the moral order and of the routines by which it should be upheld.

Annang vigilance concerns the making of cognitive, temporal and spatial boundaries. This section explores the ways in which vigilante practices are shaped by cultural values and the representation of deviant types. Contrary to a thesis which stresses the current salience of flexible categorisations of the person necessitated by the economic precautions of neo-liberalism,[50] this evidence points to an inherent inflexibility concerning the concept of the thief and an imperative to punishment. Crime in this context means not simply the commission of any single offence but also being a 'bad lot', a moral evaluation of character often seen as a set of dispositional attributes that are 'inherent, unalterable and irremediable'.[51] Annang conceptions of criminals, thieves in particular, are delineated, with a petty thief (or 'cassava' thief) considered less menacing than an armed robber whose status is on a par with murderers and the most malevolent of witches. The diabolization of the category of 'armed robber' is both a local and national register. This press report relating to the crime trends in Akwa Ibom State gives a broad sense of the awe with which armed robbers are perceived:

There was a period in 2000 when rural areas were passing through very terrible conditions of insecurity. People slept in the bush or in churches. The armed robbers usually wrote to villagers giving the date and time they would strike. Now there is a resurgence. Armed robbers are engaging in house to house operations. Some villagers have risen to the challenge by setting up

---

48 Das and Poole, 2004, p. 22.
49 Spencer, 2003, p. 1570.
50 Goldstein, this volume.
51 Heald, 1986b, p. 76.

vigilante groups to ward off robber attacks. ... The bandits have generally disregarded the efforts of the vigilante groups in view of their superior guns and dangerous weapons. Some people have suggested the introduction of the Bakassi Boys to help rid Akwa Ibom of these robbers. ... The police should permit vigilante groups formed by villages or neighbourhoods to be properly armed with guns to be able to tackle armed robbers.[52]

Brazen 'house to house' operations which 'disregarded' vigilante responses must be read not only in terms of arrogance and armaments, but also as an interpretation of their spiritual power and protection. To foretell a robbery in the way described here, by writing to warn villagers of the date and time of their arrival, indicates an ability to prognosticate and threaten common to practices of ritual murder. Witches are believed to determine a victim's exact date and time of death, and writing down the name of an enemy along with the date and time for their murder is a key element in the manufacturing of both a ritual murder and the zombification of a victim who enriches their attacker by vomiting money (*afia ifot*—white witch).[53] The armed robber is therefore conceived in Annang society in ways analogous to familiar representations of malevolent forces, non-human ancestral spirits and witches,[54] and the imperative to combat the scourge of armed robbery as expressed clearly here extends to a widespread legitimacy of vigilantes as evidenced in the popular regional legitimacy of the notorious Bakassi Boys.

Annang concepts of personhood and evaluations of a thief's character are captured in the routine performances of contemporary vigilantes when they catch a thief. Once apprehended, or found guilty by an ordeal or by the vigilante's tribunal, the thief is stripped and rubbed with a mixture of charcoal and palm oil. The thief is then tied at the waist with the rope of a palm-wine tapper and paraded around

---

52 *The Pioneer*, 4 February 2002.

53 See also Smith, 2001, p. 818.

54 For the police too, it is reported that for those individuals labelled 'armed robbers' there is often an automatic presumption of guilt which, human rights observers and others suggest, has served as a justification for unlawful detention, torture and execution (Human Rights Watch, July 2005).

the village, usually to the market and the village head's compound. On the way both the thief and the gathered crowd will sing.

ino adat ino aka udia, ino adat ino aka udua
thief, take thief to market
woooo ino
shame you thief
wooo ino adia nnok
the thief is eating shame.

The thief carries an item on their head to demonstrate what they have stolen. In this song the thief carries a basket of cassava on their head:

iwa ayaya-o, iwa ayaya-o, iwa ayaya-o, sa ama oduk idem
cassava is good, cassava is good, cassava is good, because it has produced big ones.

For their part the thief will be made to sing verses of remorse such as this:

naka isinam abah oh-oh
I will not do it again

After 'turning him around the village' and 'playing for the chief' a thief is taken to the Police or to his father's compound (in less serious cases).

Shaming through this public performance should be seen against a range of social control mechanisms, oath-taking and songs, which are associated with the secret societies. Societies and masquerades, known generically by a single term *obobom*, shared a repertoire of songs.[55] These performances resonate with the symbolic oppositions of cleanliness and impurity. These oppositions are especially clear in the performance of the women's 'yam' society, *ebre*. *Ebre* played an important role in the public attribution of character within the village by parading and singing shaming songs (*ikuo owo*—to sing person). These songs were directed against thieves (*ino*), prostitutes (*akpara*), murderers (*awot owo*) and witches and poisoners (*ifot*). The

---

55 Jeffreys, 1951 Messenger, 1962; Scheinberg, 1977.

main *ebre* performance on *ofiɔŋ* market day involved dancing around a yam basket (*akpan ebre*). The dancers rotated by the right-hand side to demonstrate that they were women of straight and true character (*nnen nnen owo aŋwaan*). This performance was an ordeal for the audience and various deviant categories—including thieves, men who had not been initiated into *ekpo*, and women who had had an abortion—who were apprehended, paraded and shamed if caught watching. *Ebre* songs shaming thieves included:

akohe udehe ino kat ubok ise
if you are not a thief, open your hand and let us see

and:

Anwan Akpan Akpe ade okporoko nisok ntie afot iba nkop eneye ita nkwoho aba
Anwan Akpan Akpe is a stockfish thief in the market. I will sit down with both buttocks and hear her. I have sung myself, because I sing with the mouth of the truth

Vigilantes are also linked to a range of practices and ordeals that establish truth and character. In the Adat Ifang clan, on *Obo* market day wives prepare food, invite their parents and friends from their natal villages, and dance for the vigilantes. This is the ordeal of cleanliness (*ukaŋ akee sana*) and is held to test and celebrate the character of women married into the village. The type of food a woman produces proves that she works hard in the farm and has no reason to steal. The woman's innocence, cleanliness and beauty are designated by wearing a palm frond (*eyei*) on her right hand. She will sing '*mmenyong ukaŋ, ukaŋ akee sana*'—'I went to ordeal, ordeal found me clean'. Here again the concept of cleanliness (*sana*) is an idea of personhood and character which contrasts with the dirty or ugly character (*mbubiam ilo*).

Key elements of these performances are not only informed by a long historical trajectory of parading and shaming thieves, they are also clues to the legitimacy of vigilante action. Both types of thief, cassava thieves and armed robbers, are coded within a common semiotic framework. The visual representation of the thief in the village parade re-embodies the symbolism of masquerade performance.

The aesthetic representation of Annang personhood is captured at its most figurative in the ancestral masquerade (*ekpo*) and in its use of beautiful and ugly masks. At harvest time each year the ancestors return to their lineages in the form of the *ekpo* masquerade. *Ekpo* is indigenous to the Ibibio-speaking language cluster and in its simulation of ancestral presence represents Annang cosmology writ large. Members of the society wear carved wooden masks which become possessed by the spirits of the ancestors. Beautiful masks are worn in the opening and closing performances of the masquerade in the market, and are painted white or yellow to represent good spirits (*mfon ekpo*). Beautiful masks portray the face in a human form and stress fertility, often with a series of smaller, children's faces carved upon the forehead. Ugly masks, in contrast, are darkly painted with exaggerated and distorted features representing malevolent, wandering spirits (*idiok ekpo*). They are usually smaller with non-human features such as jagged teeth and sometimes represent disfigurement and diseases such as gangosa.[56]

Malevolent ancestral spirits, those invoked by enemies or provoked by disregard, are potent, dangerous and unpredictable. During the *ekpo* performance there is, consequently, a strong emphasis on the control of the fiercest spirits represented by the masks. The most awesome and dangerous of the masks is that of the spirit of the ghosts (*ekpo ndem*). Wearing this mask is a form of ordeal and only a descendant of the society's founder can don it without suffering misfortune. Its highly ambiguous source of power contributes to *ekpo ndem's* status. The initiate who wears the *ekpo ndem* mask sleeps for seven nights in the forest (*akai*) where he must not eat food cooked by a woman. He will pour libations on the graves of seven 'wicked' people (*idiok ilo*—ugly character), and he will consume roots known as *adung abasi* (root of god) that make him feel like he is flying. His seclusion, invocations and consumptions each contribute to an enhanced state of malignant possession which is demonstrated in various symbolic forms, including the way the masked performer is tied

---

56 Simmons, 1957. See also Messenger, 1973, pp. 121-3.

at the waist with palm-tapper rope to prevent him from attacking onlookers, and the way he circulates around the market clockwise, by the left-hand side thereby demonstrating his malicious intent.

Like malevolent spirits thieves are paraded with a rope at the waist and are painted black with charcoal and oil. The use of palm oil, in fact, is a common signifier of transformation—of raw into cooked and of nature into culture—in Annang society.[57] For both men and women palm oil was symbolically associated with an aesthetic of health and beauty, but significantly the embodiment of oil's symbolic values was associated with key moments of transforming the self, especially in rites of initiation. The use of palm oil on the thief similarly designates the shift of status from human to non-human. Overall, therefore, these aesthetics of alterity captured in vigilante performance exaggerate difference on the basis of symbolic oppositions: thief/vigilante; dirty/clean; left/right; lie/truth; ugly/beautiful; sterile/fertile; and guilty/innocent. These oppositions map onto conceptions of the person which distinguish between those of good spirits (*eti owo*) and those of bad (*idiok owo*), and in turn between those whose infractions can be forgiven and reformed, and those who are 'natural blood criminals', whose crimes demand retribution. 'We don't regard a bad soul' one vigilante told me, 'When we catch a criminal like that we tell them that they are a dead somebody, look very well, as of now you are a dead somebody because we will kill you out.' Within this cultural construction of vigilante violence the classifications of purity and impurity, good and bad, are constituted by cosmology:

It is concerned with the ordering and reordering of social and political categories, with the defining of self in distinction to other, with good and evil. ... concerned with the reconstitution of a moral order of the world.[58]

---

57 Pratten, 2007.
58 Malkki, 1995, pp. 55-6.

This is not to reduce violence to a bodily and spatial symbolic repertoire. These embodied practices do not represent or memorize the past, they enact the past, bringing it back to life.[59]

Indeed, this interpretation of the logics of vigilante violence is based on an ongoing internal discourse over the proper way in which to handle thieves. While these practices of shaming and parading inscribe signs of power and deviance on the body, the link with masquerade performance is both embodied and discursive. Indeed, there continues to be a lively debate about whether the practice should be continued. A former vigilante leader, for instance, stated that the MUKAN group almost stopped this method of crime prevention 'because it looked outdated and primitive.' While the Police disapproved of the practice, so did some of the village elders who drew attention to the particularly rough treatment of a woman who was stripped naked, beaten and hauled through the market bound by a rope. By 1997, the MUKAN vigilantes were under pressure from the chieftaincy to counteract excesses and take a thief to the village head before proceeding to parade and shame them. This discourse echoes current debate about the continued salience of the practice and a concern with whether the shaming of thieves in this manner looks like 'playing masquerade'. In 2004 members of the vigilante group said that 'Ekpo are the ones to use [charcoal] ashes—they mix it with oil. We decided to stop rubbing thieves—because it resembles masquerade—it is somehow playful. If you happen to paint criminal now it is a masquerade, it means we are playing masquerade.' Vigilantes, therefore, recognized that their coding of a thief was like 'playing masquerade', and the practice continues despite the critical voices of those who think it undermines their standing because it associates the forces of order and progress with something playful and traditional that is banned by the authorities.[60]

---

59 Bourdieu, 1990, p.73.

60 Comparatively on the ambivalence of the concept of 'playing' masquerade in the context of violence see Moran, 1995, p. 80.

Conclusion

In Annang-speaking communities of southern Nigeria youth are organizing around idioms which draw on longstanding traditions of solidarity such as initiatory and masquerade cults which are rich repositories of ideas of initiation, modes of collective covert action, and the aesthetics of violence. Unlike recent studies, the purpose of this chapter is not to expose a hidden, non-discursive history of pre-colonial practice in the post-colonial present, but rather to trace a historical trajectory from secret societies to vigilantes in discourse and practice.[61] Like the emergent Mande hunter associations along the Guinea coast in West Africa, Nigerian vigilante movements also have an ambiguous relationship with the state—while they some-times (in their state-sponsored guise) defend against insurgency, they are also actively part of these insurgent processes. In both com-parative instances hunter associations and vigilantes confound simple oppositional categories of pre-modern and modern, pre-colonial and post-colonial, esoteric and rational.[62] These recent forms of insurgent violence and protection have been dismissed as 'random misfits', yet both provide a lens on a microcosm of contemporary trends in inse-curity and the failings of the state, and on the nature of citizenship. Local ways of making sense of disorder, and of justifying violence, rest on an ontology and semiotics that are relevant precisely because of the privatization and deregulation of security that are key features of our times, not in spite of them.

This chapter highlights the localized meanings and imperatives of vigilantism in southern Nigeria. The cultural and historical reper-toires that inform Nigerian vigilantism, it should be emphasized, do not constitute a 're-traditionalization'[63] of cultural forms, nor a 'per-version' of social institutions.[64] To dismiss as neo-traditional, reac-

---

61 Shaw, 2002; Ferme, 2001; Argenti, 2006.
62 Leach, 2004 p.xv.
63 Chabal and Daloz, 1999.
64 Ikelegbe, 2001.

tionary or dysfunctional the cultural and social frameworks through which vigilantism is made meaningful for vigilantes and the communities in which they operate is to obscure the activities that take place within these associational forms and obscure the trajectories of routine and histories of knowledge and accountability that enable us to understand popular responses to disorder.

🎕

Adamu, F.L. 'Gender, Hisbah and the Enforcement of Morality in Northern Nigeria', *Africa* forthcoming.

Afigbo, A.E. *The Warrant Chiefs: Indirect Rule in South-Eastern Nigeria, 1891-1929*, London, 1972.

Akinyele, R.T. 'Ethnic Militancy and National Stability in Nigeria: A Case Study of the Oodua People's Congress', *African Affairs* 100(401), 2001, pp. 623-40.

Appadurai, A. 'Deep Democracy: Urban Governmentality and the Horizon of Politics', *Public Culture* 14(1), 2002, pp. 21-47.

Argenti, N. 'Remembering the Future: Slavery, Youth and Masking in the Cameroon Grassfields', *Social Anthropology* 14(1), 2006, pp. 49-69.

Austen, R.A. 'Criminals and the African Cultural Imagination: Normative and Deviant Heroism in Pre-colonial and Modern Narratives', *Africa* 56(4), 1986, pp. 385-98.

Baker, B. 'When the Bakassi Boys Came: Eastern Nigeria Confronts Vigilantism', *Journal of Contemporary African Studies* 20(2), 2002, pp. 223-44.

Bourdieu, P. *The Logic of Practice*, Stanford, 1990.

Buur, L. and S. Jensen. 'Introduction: Vigilantism and the Policing of Everyday Life in South Africa', *African Studies* 63(2), 2004, pp. 139-52.

Chabal, P. and J.-P. Daloz. *Africa Works: The Political Instrumentalization of Disorder*, London, 1999.

Das, V. and D. Poole. 'Introduction', in *Anthropology in the Margins of the State*, V. Das and D. Poole (eds), Oxford, 2004, pp. 2-32.

De Certeau, M. *The Practice of Everyday Life*, Berkeley, 1984.

Ekeh, P.P. 'A Review of HRW'S and Cleen's Report "The Bakassi Boys: The Legitimization of Murder and Torture" on State Sponsored Vigilante Groups in Nigeria', http://www.africaresource.com/index2.php?option=com_content&do_pdf=1&id=35, Date accessed: 31 May 2006.

Ferme, M.C. *The Underneath of Things: Violence, History, and the Everyday in Sierra Leone*, Berkeley, 2001.

Fourchard, L. 'A New Name for an Old Practice: Vigilante in Southwestern Nigeria', *Africa*, forthcoming.

Geschiere, P. and F. Nyamnjoh. 'Capitalism and Autochthony: The Seesaw of Mobility and Belonging', *Public Culture* 12(2), 2000, pp. 423-52.

Hansen, T.B. and F. Stepputat. 'Introduction', in *States of Imagination*, T.B. Hansen and F. Stepputat (eds), Durham, 2001, pp. 1-38.

Harnischfeger, J. 'The Bakassi Boys: Fighting Crime in Nigeria', *Journal of Modern African Studies* 41(1), 2003, pp. 23-49.

Heald, S. 'Mafias in Africa: the Rise of Drinking Companies and Vigilante Groups in Bugisu, Uganda', *Africa* 56(4), 1986a, pp. 446-67.

—— 'Witches and Thieves: Deviant Motivations in Gisu Society', *Man* 21(1), 1986b, pp. 65-78.

Human Rights Watch, 'Bakassi Boys: The Legitimization of Murder and Torture', Vol. 14 No 5. (A), May 2002.

—— 'Political Shari'a'? Human Rights and Islamic Law in Northern Nigeria', Vol. 16 No 9 (A), September 2004.

—— '"Rest in Pieces" Police Torture and Deaths in Custody in Nigeria', Vol. 17, No. 11(A), July 2005.

—— 'The O'odua People's Congress: Fighting Violence with Violence', Vol. 15 No. 4, February 2003.

—— *The Price of Oil: Corporate Responsibility and Human Rights Violations in Nigeria's Oil Producing Communities*, Human Rights Watch, 1999.

—— '"They Do Not Own This Place": Government Discrimination Against "Non-Indigenes" in Nigeria', Vol 18, No. 3(A), April 2006.

Ikelegbe, A. 'The Perverse Manifestation of Civil Society: Evidence from Nigeria', *Journal of Modern African Studies* 39(1), 2001, pp. 1-24.

Jeffreys, M.D.W. 'The Ekong Players', *Eastern Anthropologist* 5(1), 1951, pp. 41-7.

Last, M. 'The Search for Security in Muslim Northern Nigeria', *Africa*, forthcoming.

Leach, M. 'Introduction to Special Issue: Security, Socioecology, Polity: Mande Hunters, Civil Society, and Nation-States in Contemporary West Africa.' *Africa Today* 50(4), 2004, pp. vii-xvi.

Malkki, L.H. *Purity and Exile: Violence, Memory, and National Cosmology among Hutu Refugees in Tanzania*, Chicago, 1995.

Marenin, O. 'The Anini Saga: Armed Robbery and the Reproduction of Ideology in Nigeria', *Journal of Modern African Studies* 25(2), 1987, pp. 259-81.

Mbembe, A. *On the Postcolony*, Berkeley 2001.

Messenger, J.C. 'Anang Acculturation: A Study of Shifting Cultural Focus,' PhD thesis, University of Michigan Microfilms, Ann Arbor, 1957.

—— 'Anang Art, Drama and Social Control', *African Studies Bulletin* 5(2), 1962, pp. 29-35.

—— 'The Carver in Anang Society', in *The Traditional Artist in African Society*, W.L.d. Azeredo (ed.), Bloomington, 1973, pp. 101-27.

Meyer, B. and P. Geschiere (eds) *Globalization and Identity: Dialectics of Flow and Closure*, Oxford, 1999.

Moran, M. 'Warriors or Soldiers? Masculinity and Ritual Transvestism in the Liberian Civil War', in *Feminism, Nationalism, and Militarism*, C.R. Sutton (ed.), Arlington, VA, 1995, pp. 73-88.

Nigeria, 'Report of the Native Courts (Eastern Region) Commission of Inquiry', 1953.

Nolte, I. 'Identity and Violence: the Politics of Youth in Ijebu-Remo, Nigeria', *Journal of Modern African Studies* 42(1), 2004, pp. 61-89.

Offiong, D.A. 'The Functions of the Ekpo Society of the Ibibio of Nigeria', *African Studies Review* 27, 1984, pp. 77-92.

—— *Continuity and Change among the Traditional Associations of Nigeria*, Zaria, 1989.

Ottenberg, S. and L. Knudsen 'Leopard Society Masquerades –Symbolism and Diffusion', *African Arts* 18(2), 1985, pp. 37-44 & 93.

Pioneer, 'Curbing the resurgence of robbery in Akwa Ibom', 4 February 2002.

——, 'Vigilante Groups', 29 March 1999.

Post Express, 'Akwa Ibom State Police Commissioner criticises local government councils for failing to fund the local police', 3 November 1998.

Pratten, D. 'The Politics of Vigilance in South-eastern Nigeria', *Development and Change* 37(4), 2006, pp. 707-34.

—— *The Man-Leopard Murders: History and Society in Colonial Nigeria*, Edinburgh and Indiana, 2007.

Punch, 'Akwa Ibom State Administrator's concern at the increasing rate of armed robbery', 28 April 1997.

Scheinberg, A.L. *Ekon Society Puppets: Sculptures for Social Criticism*, New York, 1977.

Shaw, R. *Memories of the Slave Trade: Ritual and the Historical Imagination in Sierra Leone*, Chicago, 2002.

Simmons, D.C. 'The Depiction of Gangosa on Efik-Ibibio Masks', *Man* 57, 1957, pp. 17-20.

Smith, D.J. 'Ritual Killing, 419, and Fast Wealth: Inequality and the Popular Imagination in Southeastern Nigeria', *American Ethnologist* 28(4), 2001, pp. 803-26.

—— 'The Bakassi Boys: Vigilantism, Violence and Political Imagination in Nigeria', *Current Anthropology* 19(3), 2004, pp. 429-56.

Spencer, J. 'Collective Violence', in *Oxford India Companion to Sociology and Social Anthropology*, V. Das (ed.), Delhi, 2003, pp. 1564-80.

Udoma, U. *The Story of the Ibibio State Union*, Ibadan, 1987.

Ukiwo, U. 'Deus ex Machina or Frankenstein Monster: the Changing Roles of Bakassi Boys in Eastern Nigeria', *Democracy and Development: A Journal of West African Affairs* 3(1), 2002, pp. 39-51.

Watts, M. 'Development and Governmentality', *Singapore Journal of Tropical Geography* 24(1), 2003, pp. 6-34.

—— 'Resource Curse?: Governmentality, Oil and Power in the Niger Delta, Nigeria', *Geopolitics* 9(1), 2004, pp. 50-80.

9

'YOU KNOW AMERICA HAS DRIVE-BY SHOOTINGS? IN CREGGAN, WE HAVE DRIVE-BY BEATINGS.' CONTINUING INTRACOMMUNITY VIGILANTISM IN URBAN NORTHERN IRELAND*

Rosellen Roche

Introduction

You know America has drive by shootings? In Creggan, we have drive by beatings. Let's get out, let's get shot by the 'Provos' [Provisional Irish Republican Army]. Let's get scared fucking shitless. /.../[1]

My aunt took the two wains [children or babies] over the shop to get them ice pops, the 'Provos' pulled up in the car, get out and beat the Christ out of him [a friend]. My two wee cousins were just standing there squealing.

I was all, 'Fuck up. Get her into that shop!'

Our Maureen was all, 'Where did our Mary go?'

---

* This article was written while a Postdoctoral Fellow of the ESRC, Award Reference PTA-026-27-0865.
1 All speech used here has been transcribed from original tape recordings or field notes taken between 1999-2001 and 2002-2005. The symbols /.../ and /IA/ appearing in the text indicate, respectively, that material has been edited out and that material was inaudible at that point on the tape for transcription.

Our Mary was standing beside them. Like as far away from me to you, watching them. A four year old wain watching somebody getting the biggest hiding [beating] of their life with a crowd of about four older men beating the fuck out of him. /.../

Like she was four years of age and she was shouting, 'Ma there's the "Provos!"'

Four words—'Jack is getting done.'

Emer, 17, Catholic[2]

On a wet, very windy afternoon in Northern Ireland's second largest city, Derry/Londonderry,[3] Emer and I settled in for another chat. As the rain pounded against the window, Emer and I talked frankly about some of the punishment routines conducted by the local para-militaries. It was not something we had planned to do, but it came up in conversation just as easily as Emer's desire to move to Dublin or her taste for her Grandmother's cooking. For Emer, this type of 'punishment beating' was not startling or unexpected in any way. Shrugging her shoulders, she would tell me there were lots of reasons why punishment beatings happened in her area: vandalism and graffiti, selling drugs when you were not allowed to sell them (some people could, but it depended on the drug, and of course, who you were), or generally just 'acting the maggot'.[4]

---

2 All names have been changed from their original. However, the subjects' age and community affiliation are original.

3 In the 17th century the place known by its Irish Gaelic name 'Dóire' (meaning 'oak grove') was officially named 'Londonderry' because of the London Livery Companies' financial interests in the city. Community factions still argue over the official naming of the city; however, colloquially, the city is often referred to as 'Derry' by both Protestant and Catholic citizens who hail from the city. The city's district council areas are referred to as the Derry District Council areas (DCCD) and this expression is most commonly used in this piece. The name remains an important symbol of division between the communities, earning the city the title of 'Stroke City' by BBC Radio Foyle's popular presenter Gerry Anderson.

4 Emer intends 'acting the maggot' to infer generally behaving badly in any way.

Equally for Emer, the perpetrators of these punishments are not unusual either. Emer's uncle is in the 'Provos', and she too has been warned and punished on a few occasions. And Emer is not alone. Many young people whom I have come to know have had their own personal experiences with paramilitaries in their housing estates, while others related experiences of paramilitary policing activity within their family circles.[5] Referring to the 'Provos' in her area as 'the boys in blue'—using a common American slang expression for police—Emer sums up by relating that the patrols in her area are people in the community, who on the one hand, 'scare the fuck out of people who never done fuck all wrong' and on the other hand, 'are good all right, they do punishment beatings and shit like that there.'

For over four decades, young people growing up in urban, working class housing areas in Northern Ireland have been raised within the context of community endorsed systems of intracommunity vigilantism and retributive justice.[6] Drawing from over five years of

---

5 Exclusively qualitative fieldwork was carried out between 1999 and 2001 with over 190 young people in deprived areas of the Derry City Council District areas between the ages of 16 and 21. 52 young people were involved in lengthy tape-recorded discussions which often spanned over several sessions. The tape-recorded sessions were split evenly between gender and communities (26 Catholic/26 Protestant, 26 males/26 females). Funding for that initial project was provided in the main from Peterhouse College at the University of Cambridge and the Harry Frank Guggenheim Foundation, Washington DC. Subsequent qualitative and quantitative research was undertaken in 2002-2005 by me as Head of Project for a separately funded project entitled the Towards Reconciliation and Inclusion Project (TRIPROJECT) hosted by the charity Derry Youth and Community Workshop. Over 900 young people between the ages of 15 and 25 participated in the programme. This programme was funded in the main by the European Union's Peace II Funds/ Programme for Peace and Reconciliation facilitated by the Community Foundation for Northern Ireland. Other funders also included the Community Relations Council for Northern Ireland, the Derry City Council, the Policing Board for Northern Ireland, the Ireland Funds and the Honourable the Irish Society. The opportunity for this article to be written was while I was a Postdoctoral Fellow for Economic and Social Research Council (ESRC) of the United Kingdom at the School of Anthropological Studies at Queen's University of Belfast. For further information cf. Roche, 2005; Roche, 2003.

6 This paper addresses situations of paramilitary vigilantism exclusively within

qualitative and quantitative research within Northern Ireland, this paper focuses on the understanding of the unwritten social 'rules' that dictate and maintain vigilantism inside both Nationalist/Republican Catholic (Republican) and Unionist/Loyalist Protestant (Loyalist) ethnonationalist[7] enclaves in the face of changing state security procedures and a social push for peace. In particular, this paper focuses on the punishment of youth by their local paramilitary authorities who often take charge of the intracommunity punishment procedures to resolve 'antisocial behaviour'[8] within their communities.

Following a brief overview of the historical and cultural context of such measures, illustrating the differences yet drawing out the growing commonalities between communities, this examination then explores the unwritten 'rules' concerning such punishments. Two examples then follow. Drawn from dozens of such testimonies, these two case studies are used to illustrate the commonality between the two communities concerning incidents of punishment as well as the

---

their own communities. These forms of punishment are referred to here as 'paramilitary punishment' or 'punishment beatings' throughout this article. Although, as Kennedy mentions, this does infer a type of morality to the beatings, i.e. the victims deserve such harsh 'punishment', I use these terms because they are what those in the communities use to refer to these types of vigilantism and community correction. Cf. Kennedy, 1994. This essay does not cover sectarian retribution, vigilantism that goes into the opposite community, or what Rosenbaum and Sederberg would consider falling into the remit of 'social group control vigilantism'. Cf. Rosenbaum and Sederberg, 1974. An example of such would be where a Catholic individual is punished for stealing cars from a Protestant area by Loyalist paramilitaries, bringing into question whether the attack is retributive policing or sectarian (or both) in nature. Cf. 'They Are Lower Than Animals', *News Letter*, 5 Nov. 2002.

7 Coulter, 1999, pp. 61-100.

8 'Antisocial behaviour' is a loose term that is used as a blanket expression to cover activities that community members find annoying or troublesome. Some antisocial activities are considered illegal by the state while others would be considered disruptive to a particular community. Some of the activities included in this encompassing term could be under-age drinking, drinking in public spaces, general reckless behaviour, and joyriding. This term, however, can be extended to encompass anything that community members (or paramilitary members) find upsetting, and is therefore often subject to personal interpretation.

intricate and often intimate nature of the relationships between those who are punished and those who are applying these punishments.[9] Understanding and expecting the mechanisms used to control anti-social behaviour, these young people discuss the personal relationships as well as the social nuances and understandings that affect how and when this type of behaviour control is enacted.

By focusing on everyday subjects such as young people, those 'who are commonly situated on the edge of the state and at the bottom of the political heap',[10] rather than the paramilitaries who carry out such justice regimes, vigilantism is seen, as Abrahams suggests, as a 'frontier' phenomenon[11] straddling state and communal concepts of law and illegality with an element of security of its citizens at its core.[12] Equally, vigilantism is viewed here as something which frequently surfaces among communities where, at the very least, there is dissatisfaction with the state, and quite often is emergent in communities which see the state as corrupt, or which refuse altogether to recognize the state.[13] Finally, as many authors discuss, vigilantism is seen in this context as a group phenomenon.[14] Beyond this, however, I posit that vigilantism in the current Northern Irish case should not be considered merely a group phenomenon; it is a set of actions performed by groups of people, but it can also be considered a system of unwritten but agreed cultural 'rules'—a tacit understanding shared

---

9 Most direct quotations related here are taken from conversations with young people in the Derry City Council areas, although one individual also relates experiences from Belfast. Recent research from 2006 in Belfaast and the DCCD areas illustrate strong similarities between the two cities regarding paramilitary punishment.

10 Abrahams, 1998, p. 3.

11 Ibid.

12 Cf. also Abrahams, 1987; Brown, 1975; Brown, 1963; Johnston, 1996; Johnston, 1992; Silke, 1999; Rosenbaum and Sederberg, 1976; Rosenbaum and Sederberg, 1974; Sluka, 2000; Sluka, 1989 for interesting variations regarding the nuances of vigilantism.

13 Ibid.

14 Ibid.

between the paramilitaries, those that use these punishment procedures and those that get punished. In this sense, whether a vigilante act is perpetrated alone or with many is irrelevant. It is the social comprehension of the unwritten 'rules' of such an occurrence that keeps it squarely within the realm of a group phenomenon and in this way expands our understanding of collective violence and social violence.[15] By focusing on everyday citizens who sanction and experience this community control, instead of the vigilantes and their political paramilitarism,[16] I aim to illustrate that rather than falling into previously dichotomized categories of paramilitary behaviour,[17] or even changing into Mafioso categories as their commitment to illicit and legitimate trades increases,[18] when viewed from the perspective of those involved in such punishment vigilantism currently remains very close[19] to what it has been for decades in the everyday life of

---

15 Particularly Tambiah, 1996. Cf. also Das, 1995; Das, Kleinman, Ramphele and Reynolds, 2000; Farmer, 1997; Kleinman, Das and Lock, 1997.

16 Cf. Rosenbaum and Sederberg, 1974 where the authors discuss this form of vigilantism as 'social group control'. Much emphasis has been given to this type of retributive justice in Northern Ireland as well as the 'hit men' and the assassinations that were associated with the height of the 'Troubles'. Cf. Alexander and O'Day, 1984; Crawford, 2003; Crawford, 1999; Feldman, 1991; O'Brien, 1993; Silke, 2003; Silke, 1998 Sluka, 2000; Whittaker, 2001.

17 In particular, Feldman, 1991, pp. 46-59.

18 Cf. Abrahams, 1998; Gambetta, 1993; Heald, 1997; Hess, 1973; Hobsbawm, 1959; Jacobs, Friel and Radick, 1999; Sterling, 1994.

19 Elsewhere, both Colin Knox and I touch on issues of masquerading or what could be thought of as a type of paramilitary identity theft, where individuals are assaulted by men who may be wearing balaclavas and other sorts of 'paramilitary-type' gear but the victim is unsure whether they are truly part of a paramilitary vigilante group. Indeed, the expression 'paramilitary-type' is often used by the media, governmental bodies and ordinary people alike in describing shootings and beatings where the assault follows the patterns of a paramilitary assault or could be considered to be connected to a particular paramilitary group. While most beatings and shootings are directly related to the paramilitary members of each community, occasionally this sort of identity theft can happen. This opens up a new avenue for discussion regarding whether the communal legitimacy of the historical process for community policing will continue. I hope to address this question, as well as other important blurred areas of community control

citizens in Northern Ireland's working class housing estates—a process that is both a useful mechanism for community protection and an historically embedded process of internal community management.

Background to a beating: differences and similarities

The opinion of many in the community seemed to point towards the belief that violence was needed to curb violence, with one participant believing that drug dealers should be dealt with in the old fashioned way and 'put in a hole'. …This opinion was shared by many, and one woman agreed with the gun when it came to 'constant troublemakers or those disturbing old people'. Another person remarked that it was 'the only language they know.'

'Heated Exchanges as Creggan Debates', *Derry Journal*, 7 October 2005

After the onset of the recent 'Troubles' in Northern Ireland in and following 1968,[20] the consolidation of security apparatuses within the mid seventies[21] led to increased paramilitary initiatives in both Republican and Loyalist communities. Here I outline some of the differences between intra-communal vigilantism within the two communities, but also seek to show how current trends bring these two agendas closer together. To begin, the Republican movement and its major paramilitary representation, the Irish Republican Army (IRA),[22] have assumed a role of community policing since the beginnings of the 'Troubles'. This policing procedure was enforced because of what the Republican movement saw and still sees as a corrupt and absent police force,[23] and has been integral to the ethos of modern Republicanism to defend and serve their communities. Within this

---

in a forthcoming article. For reference to these subjects cf. Knox, 2003 Roche, 2003.

20 Bew and Gillespie, 1999.

21 Ellison and Smyth, 2000.

22 The IRA is also referred to as the 'Provisional IRA', the name of the dominant faction after a split in the historic organization in 1970, and is colloquially referred to as the 'Provos', the 'Provies' or the 'RA'.

23 Ellison and Smyth, 2000 and Ní Aoláin, 2000.

remit, the Republican paramilitaries enforced and continue to enforce communal behavioural rules and curfews for residents within local housing areas[24] while punishing what they or their community members believe to be inappropriate or antisocial behaviour. Not excluded from this justice scheme were children and young people, who were and still are punished for (and on occasion directed to commit) acts of destructive or antisocial behaviour.[25]

These paramilitary policing practices, while condoned by many in Republican communities, can be just as easily condemned. As early as Burton's anthropological research conducted within a 'solidly working-class Catholic community' that he calls 'Anro', throughout 1972–73 complaints were reported regarding the rules and discretionary practices of paramilitary action within that community.[26] Twenty years later, testimony from O'Connor's[27] more popularized inquiry into the Catholic community in Northern Ireland in 1992-93 noted this same ambivalence towards what is and what is not acceptable Republican community control and policing. Other authors, such as Kennedy[28] and O'Doherty,[29] also note, to one degree or another, that the creation of community support through these practices is the result of both the power and the terror that these forces hold over their communities.

---

24 Roche, 2003.

25 This is a yet another complicated variation on the issue of community control. At times, paramilitaries in each community have been documented as having 'encouraged' or directed youths to participate in some antisocial behaviour, particularly rioting. Throughout my fieldwork this practice was well known in both Republican and Loyalist areas. Most recently, rioting in Loyalist areas in Belfast in September 2005 was reported to have been coordinated and encouraged. Cf. Independent Monitoring Commission, *Seventh Report*, London, 2005, p. 29.

26 Burton, 1978, pp. 87-9.

27 O'Connor, 1993, pp. 127-9.

28 Kennedy, 1994, pp. 67-80.

29 O'Doherty, 1998, p. 11.

Loyalist paramilitary nuances are neither less fraught nor uncomplicated. However, Loyalist community punishment and policing were subject, at least in their inception, to different concerns from their Republican counterpart. First, this is due to the separation of Loyalist paramilitary factions in many Unionist housing areas. Loyalist housing areas are subject to a variety of predominating Loyalist factions in their areas, such as the Ulster Defence Association (UDA), the Ulster Volunteer Force (UVF) and the Loyalist Volunteer Force (LVF). Second, the political agenda and the nuances of Loyalist paramilitaries differ from their Republican counterparts. Indeed, the security apparatuses of the state are recognized within Loyalism/Unionism, and the forces of the state and the forces of Loyalist paramilitaries are not in 'open conflict'.[30] Thus the impetuses for some Loyalist communities to support paramilitary squads are more complicated and illustrate a lack of confidence among Loyalists in the government's ability to purge the province of its Republican threat. Conway,[31] investigating Loyalist punishment attacks, stresses that Loyalist organizations have been more involved in policing their own organizations and punishing their own members for undesirable conduct. He continues by reporting that rather than youths being punished for antisocial behaviour, they are persuaded to join-up or at least contribute part of the takings of any illegal activity resulting in economic substance for the paramilitaries.[32]

Recent research, however, begins to amend some of these differences, bringing the socio-political reasons for punishment beatings in both Republican and Loyalist enclaves dispositionally closer together. First, changing (or finally recognized and discussed)[33] feel-

---

30 Silke, 1999, p. 3.

31 Conway, 1997.

32 Ibid.

33 McVeigh's research on harassment among those aged 17-28, published in 1994, noted that the social identity of most of those identifying harassment was based on class rather than religion, illustrating a 'hidden factor' in harassment. McVeigh, 1994.

ings of the lack of confidence in state policing procedures in Loyalist areas are coming to the fore. O'Mahony *et al.*,[34] writing on the results of the Northern Ireland Community Crime Survey, show very high dissatisfaction in Loyalist working class areas in the abilities of the police, while my recent survey work with young school leavers in the Derry City Council District (DCCD) areas[35] finds that young disaffected Protestants are some of the most discontented with police performance, and are more in favour of paramilitaries 'looking out' for their own communities than their Catholic counterparts. Equally, my earlier and strictly qualitative work in the same area indicates that Loyalist paramilitary punishment of youths and children outside their own units and within their controlled housing areas is prevalent and predictable in the Loyalist enclaves included in that study.[36]

Second, while illicit activities such as illegal trade in alcohol, cigarettes and fuel has been something in which paramilitary organizations in both communities historically have been involved, the trafficking and use of illicit drugs in Northern Ireland and its intimate connection with post-ceasefire paramilitary activity cannot be ignored. Opening with the words 'Northern Ireland has a drugs problem' in 1999, the 'Drugs Strategy for Northern Ireland 1999' document stridently made a point to address the growing concern in the province. Focusing on this use, Higgins, Percy and McCrystal[37] note trends in substance use, pre- and post-ceasefire, pointing out that trends concerning drug use in Northern Ireland have increased since the mid-1990s, the rise coinciding with the peace process. In an earlier article, Higgins and McElrath also note:

...the state of transformation in which Northern Ireland finds itself presents a future with a range of previously unknown opportunities as well as potentially major concerns. These range from greater mixing across communities, greater inward migration, and enhanced association with the Republic of

---

34 O'Mahoney, Geary, McEvoy and Morison, 2000.

35 Roche, 2005.

36 Roche, 2003.

37 Higgins, Percy and McCrystal, 2004.

Ireland to the growth of a club scene in post-ceasefire Northern Ireland. Of concern is the army of paramilitaries with differing drug ideologies, looking for a fresh role as well as the possibility of increased demand for and supply of drugs associated with the demographic and cultural shifts.[38]

The tangle between pre- and post-ceasefire years and drug use and distribution in Northern Ireland is a complex one. Higgins and McElrath comment that as early as 1996 the Northern Irish Affairs Committee highlighted community perceptions of the relationship between paramilitaries and drugs.[39] Although, historically, the IRA is reputed to have held some of the most conservative views on the trafficking and use of drugs within its own communities,[40] there is evidence of splinter Republican groups earning profits from the sale of illicit drugs and even meeting Loyalist paramilitaries to demarcate particular areas in Belfast where each community could traffic its drugs.[41] Furthermore, my recent work illustrates changing communal understandings regarding the rules and agendas within Republican enclaves about the paramilitary involvement in the 'who', the 'what', and the 'how much' of the current operations: who sells what kind of drug to whom and for what price. When these rules are transgressed, vigilante paramilitary punishment was known to follow.[42] Owing to the varied and decentralized organizational structure of Loyalist paramilitarism, and its political "pro-state" agenda,[43] Loyalist paramilitaries historically have been reported as 'ethically' and economically more involved in some particular illicit activities.[44] Prominent authorities on Loyalist involvement in the drug trade,

---

38 Higgins and McElrath, 2000, p.55.
39 Ibid., p. 32.
40 Ibid.
41 Holland and McDonald, 1994.
42 Roche, 2003.
43 Wilkinson, 1986.
44 Higgins and McElrath, 2000.

such as Bruce[45] and McKittrick,[46] note that, in a way not unlike recent Republican reprimands,[47] while Loyalist magazines fervently tout the cessation of Loyalist involvement in the trafficking and sale of drugs, the involvement continues. Finally, my recent survey work undertaken with disaffected young people echoes this activity and highlights the involvement of both communities' paramilitaries in the trafficking of drugs in the DCCD and nearby areas.[48]

Blueprint to a beating: the escalation of threat, with what, and who gets it

They usually do it in an order ye know. Like, warn ye and shite like that there. /.../ They, themins that are doin' it, they just then come and get ye if you're about doing it again. They come and get ye and they batter [beat] ye. It just happens so it does. All the time like. Everyone knows about, so they do.

Edward, 24, Protestant

Concerning the practicalities and the semantics of a paramilitary member making a threat, performing a beating, performing a shooting or kneecapping,[49] or ordering an expulsion of a community

---

45 Bruce, 1994.

46 McKittrick, 1994.

47 I am referring here to the recent statements from the IRA on the destruction of all weapons on 26 September 2005 and its cessation of subsequent illegal activities. Cf. 'IRA 'Has Destroyed All Its Arms',' BBC News Northern Ireland, 26 Sept. 2005; 'IRA Progress Signs 'Encouraging',' BBC News Northern Ireland 19 Oct. 2005. Also, all reports of the Independent Monitoring Commission, Belfast.

48 Roche, 2005, pp. 156-7. In this study there was some variation in how young people noted that they obtained their drugs. More Catholic users stated that they obtained illicit substances from 'a dealer' (39 per cent) compared to Protestant users (25 per cent), while more Protestant users stated that they obtained illicit substances from 'several dealers' (34 per cent) compared to Catholic users (28 per cent). These results pattern the common 'street knowledge' that, owing to more divisions among the paramilitaries and their prolonged involvement in drug trafficking within Protestant enclaves, there would be more dealers available.

49 Exiling is the process of 'asking' particularly bothersome individuals in the

member,[50] the communal 'rules' are recognized and well known. As Edward states above in the introductory quotation: 'They usually do it in an order ... Everyone knows about it, so they do.' However, the eventual actions taken by the paramilitaries carrying out such beatings can depend on a number of factors. These factors include who is involved in the antisocial behaviour, their relationship to the paramilitaries involved and the type of 'crime' committed.

To begin with, the paramilitaries in the area come to learn about the incident. Either during or after an incident, a person in the community will alert the paramilitaries, or the paramilitaries are annoyed somehow by the incident themselves. Just one of the young people who provided a glimpse into this stage[51] was Dympna, a 17-year-old Catholic. Briefly, she notes how the paramilitary members and families are contacted by telephone and the personal relationships with those that carry out the warnings and punishments:

We, my daddy, I just . . . I know people. People used te phone us out at four or five in the morning because say their husbands or their boyfriends came home blocked [drunk and/or high] and hit them. And they wanted something done or whatever.

After an 'investigation' concerning the accused has been undertaken by community members (paramilitary or otherwise), some of the factors that would influence their/her/his punishment(s) would depend on the severity of the offence, if the offence was repeated, how the offence was brought to the attention of the paramilitaries and who was troubled by the offence.[52] If an offender repeats a crime,

---

community to leave. Usually the exiled person is given a 24 to 48 hours to leave and a set amount of time (six months, one year and so on) before permission is granted for return. There is further explanation of the frequency of this practice included in this section.

50 Kneecapping is the process of punishment where the 'culprit' is shot anywhere in the legs. I have also heard the term used by young people to mean being whacked in the front of the knee, shattering the kneecap, with a baseball bat or pipe.

51 Roche, 2003.

52 It is important to also remember that identification of crimes committed

it is usually accepted that the punishment will increase in scale or intensity. Logically, Dympna continues:

The way they see it is … so what, ye get hit but then ye get over that. But, naw I don't hear nothing really bad. The boys that give Jack [boyfriend] the hidin' [beating], apparently they were put out of Derry [exiled by the Provos]. They're like, really bad.

Following Dympna, if an offender is 'really bad', an example of such a scale of punishment would be that a first offence would lead to a verbal warning. This could be accomplished by an anonymous telephone call, through personal channels or in person. A second offence would lead again to a verbal warning or a warning that could include shots to the person's residence or, on occasion, their place of work. At this time, some possible physical contact could occur. If physical contact is inevitable, verbal punishment sessions and beatings can occur with a range of possibilities: beating with fists only/possible expulsion/beating with weaponry/possible expulsion/kneecapping. Unwritten too in this unwritten 'rule' book are standards. Simon, a 22-year-old Protestant (also sometimes involved in this activity), attempted to make it clearer to me:

Look, there's a limit, like. A limit to it. Everybody gets, em, knows the limits like. The limits to it. It's sort of what ye are doin' at the time. How much you do do it. /…/ You're not gonny get done if your just out drinkin' like, 'causing a disturbance. But ye can get done if ye steal, or ye do a wile [very] lot of bad things. Even rowin' in front of everyone (in public). My mate got done for that, so he did. But he did it all the time, so he did. Everyone just got sick of his mouth [arguing].

While there is no *absolute* pattern regarding appropriate vigilante punishment in either community, these unwritten rules about appropriate punishments to fit the crime and the escalation of these punishments are well recognized and implicit in both communities.

---

and their eventual punishment are often subject to a considerable amount of personal discretion depending on, for example, how the offender is related to the paramilitaries, or how the victim is related to them. Cf. Knox, 2003; Knox, 2001b; Knox, 2001a; Knox and Monaghan, 2002.

Equally, there is an understood range of weaponry used in threats and attacks.[53] Some of these objects are everyday items anyone could find in their workrooms or kitchens. Some are weaponry such as guns, while still others are even more gruesome, developed over the decades of punishment beatings and made specifically for that purpose. Some of the typical tactics and weapons used in punishment threats and attacks that were related to me included: threatening letters, bullets sent in envelopes addressed to the perpetrator, shots fired at a residence or workplace, cigarettes for burns or a threatening flame, paint, petrol, oil, tar, tar and feathers, baseball bats, Hurley sticks, pieces of wood, pieces of wood with nails through them (to inflict puncture wounds), knives, iron bars, golf clubs, hammers, meat tenderizers, drills, and guns.

Official governmental agencies such as police services, hospital reports and the more recent Independent Monitoring Commission (IMC), the paramilitary watchdog headed by the Canadian General John de Chastelain, give some insight into reports of certain incidents such as assaults and shootings connected to paramilitary punishments. Looking back a decade ago, the Royal Ulster Constabulary (RUC)[54] records indicate that between 1995 and 2000, over 1,000 people received paramilitary punishments or shootings from both Republican and Loyalist paramilitaries.[55] In the recent context, the reports concerning these types of attack show similar statistics, though figures suffer from some ups and downs. The Seventh Report of the IMC, released in October 2005, notes that from 1 September

---

53 Knox 2001a, Knox 2001b, and Knox and Monaghan 2002.

54 On 1 November 2001 Northern Ireland's well-known police force, the Royal Ulster Constabulary, became the Police Service of Northern Ireland (PSNI) as a result of state security changes and the need for more equal community representation in the force following the Good Friday Agreement signed in April 1998.

55 Michael Hall (series ed.), 'Restoring Relationships: A Community Exploration of Anti-Social Behaviour, Punishment Beatings and Restorative Justice' in *Farset Community Think Tank Projects* [*Pamphlet 29*]. Newtownabbey, 2000, p. 3.

2004 to 31 August 2005 there were 193 'paramilitary-style' attacks (which include both shootings and assaults).[56]

However, it is important to remember that many incidents also involving paramilitary threat, assault, expulsion or even shooting never come to be reported through governmental channels. As one official working for the Northern Ireland Association for the Care and Resettlement of Offenders (NIACRO), a non-governmental interagency supported organization, stated in January 2006: 'The reports from the PSNI (Police Service for Northern Ireland), the IMC, for shootings, they are probably pretty accurate as they get their information from hospitals. But when it comes to being beat, some people just take the beatings and just go home, if you know what I mean.'

Looking back again, while RUC figures for 1999, for example, listed 206 cases of paramilitary punishments, the NIACRO Youth Justice Unit received 624 referrals during that same year.[57] In the more recent context, in 2001, NIACRO expanded its 'Base2' initiative, an organization dealing with families under paramilitary threat, to include the Community Re-Integration Project (CRIP), a project that deals with young people seeking reintegration into their communities after being under threat as a result of their offending behaviour. In the period between April 2002 and March 2003, CRIP reported 75 referrals between the ages of under 16 and 24, with 39 completing the programme, returning to the community of exile or being integrated in an alternative community.[58] The IMC also notes

---

56 *Seventh Report of the Independent Monitoring Commission*, London, 2005, p. 55. There are different progress reports in this area since the ceasefire in 1994. Currently, while assaults have decreased in Republican areas, they have increased in Loyalist areas. Cf. Ibid. For years after the ceasefire, however, punishments overall were on the rise and at rates higher than ever before. Cf. Knox, 2003; Knox, 2001b; Knox, 2001a; Knox and Monaghan, 2002.

57 Cf. Hall (2000:3 [Pamphlet 29]). Hall also notes on the same page: 'Even allowing for the fact that an actual threat was found to exist in only 74% of (the 624) cases, it still indicates a largely hidden problem.'

58 Community Re-Integration Project (CRIP), 2003.

that its mapping of paramilitary violence can only be produced if a 'valid postcode (for the location of the attack) is associated with the incident'; thus there could be gaps in analysis if postcodes were denied or fictionalized.

Finally, Kennedy notes that the majority of paramilitary punishments are enacted on young people, predominantly males, under thirty years of age.[59] Although there has been reported reluctance within Republican communities to physically attack and to shoot young women,[60] this is not universally true as young women from both communities can be targets for attacks if they have engaged in antisocial behaviour.[61] Whatever the gender of the target, highlighting the allegiance of communities towards this form of punishment, Knox and Monaghan state that: '(t)hese individuals are identified as the 'type of person' who is likely to be involved in 'hooding' (antisocial) behaviour and therefore a 'deserving' victim of paramilitary violence. The result is that the culpability of the paramilitaries as perpetrators of violence is significantly reduced through their role as community protectors.'[62]

Two views to a beating

Previously, anthropologists examining the phenomenon of violence in relation to paramilitaries in Northern Ireland, such as Feldman,[63] have categorized activities referring to the 'masked' men in Northern Ireland in terms of one thing ('hardman') or another ('gunman'). Feldman states:

Comparisons of violence are encoded in the oppositional figures of the "hardman" and the "gunman." "Gunman" refers to the paramilitaries irrespective of political affiliations. The "hardman" was the local bare-fisted

---

59 Kennedy, 2001, p. 100.
60 Morrissey and Pease, 1982, p. 164.
61 Cf. Knox and Monaghan, 2002, pp. 31-8; Roche, 2005; Roche, 2003.
62 Knox and Monaghan, 2002, p. 62.
63 Feldman, 2000; Feldman, 1991.

street fighter intimately associated with specific neighbourhoods though often enjoying a city-wide reputation.[64]

For the keepers of local tradition, old-timers, and paramilitaries, the violence of the hardman and the violence of the gunman summarise different periods, forms, techniques and intensities of violent practice.[65]

While these interpretations can be quite accurate, particularly when discussed by those in the 'masks' themselves, what of the everyday tacit knowledge of the community members? What of those people, young people, who most frequently experience this type of punishment?

Many young people provide invaluable insight when they are consulted. Sharon, for example, a 17-year-old Protestant, explains a punishment beating that she witnessed in her own home. This assault happened to her brother, Ryan. Ryan works in a local meat factory near the city and it was there that Sharon feels the rumour started about Ryan 'slaggin' off the UDA or UVF or whatever'. Ryan knew the individuals, 'a whole pile of them', who worked in the factory and understood who was affiliated to either the UDA or the UVF. It was those individuals who accused Ryan of wrong doing, 'carried it onto their street', and eventually got a group of individuals of one paramilitary organization to go to Ryan's home.

Sharon explains the sequence of events that led up to the incident, beginning, '(t)here was a telephone call telling my brother te watch himself. But he didn't take no notice of it. And then there, a fella next door gave, says te him, 'Ryan, watch yourself!' He (the neighbour) was doin' that te be nice. But know, he couldn't say much more. Know, 'cause and then he would've got it. But he was, know, he just warned him. And then ah, there was two shots at the house then one night.'

---

64 Feldman, 1991, p. 46.
65 Ibid. p.47.

And whenever I was up in my room, there was a knock at the door and I was goin' down, gonny go down and answer it, but then I thought, 'Naw. My brother will answer it.'

And he answered the door and there was four of them standin' at the front door, know, all in black? They just went te him, 'Get him!' Threw him te the ground and started hittin' him. Three wi' baseball bats and wan wi' a claw hammer. And I heard him, and I went on in te the landing and know, he was shoutin', 'Shar, help me!'

And em, they must've seen me like, but I climbed out of my bedroom window. Know, we have an extension built? And ye can climb on te the kitchen roof. And I climbed down and in te the back yard. And I ran 'round, and when I ran 'round he wasn't there, I thought they might've took him wi' them or something. Know, like I must've scared them off because know they saw me, so they did. /.../

He'd four stitches te the head, they hit him wi' a claw hammer. Six in each knee, four on one shin and five on the other. And then ah, he'd a chunk took out of him on the leg. And he'd eight stitches in it, five inside.

They just left him lying and they walked. Know, he staggered down te my granda's. He said if somebody had of seen him know, they would've thought he was plastered (drunk) or something. /.../

Em, but the, know we didn't think then that they'd knock at the house. But my ma's worried because they say know, the first is the wan, that warnin', then there's a shot, then there's a beatin', and then there's a bullet te the head or the knees done or whatever. So my ma, that's why she's, know she's worried. /.../

And there's a man /.../ And he brought my ma as much information that he could. Know, he told her that, know it's all over and done wi' and there shouldn't be nothing else happen. And if there is, know, it's not them doin' it. So that's why my ma has calmed down a bit now.

Because of her brother's beating Sharon thinks Ryan has 'grown up a wee bit' and understands better 'the way it has te be, just.' She states: 'Ye come to know the way it works, like.'

Emer, speaking in the opening quotation, witnessed and experienced threats and punishment situations herself. In a situation involving Emer and her friend Petey, she relates an incident of community policing that was intended to control some antisocial behaviour Emer and her friend were committing, as well as to serve as warning about using illicit drugs in the area. Recognizing one of the men as her uncle, she described an incident involving several local men.

He didn't know that I seen him that day running around in his fucking suit and there he is pullin' me and Petey out of the car 'cause we were up joyriding up the back roads.

We where speeding about, taken a hand out of each other.[66] I kept blind folding him and going, 'Go! Drive!'

And he was all, 'You're a fucking dickhead, wee girl!'

And all we seen was the car coming flying out behind us and we thought, 'We're dead. We're fucking dead.'

I was all, 'We're dead. Look who's car it is! Jesus, it's our Declan! Put your foot down!' [Explaining to me] Our Declan's a big chucky boy.[67]

They sped up behind us and we were driving around for about fifteen minutes, speeding around all the corners and beatin' all over the place. They didn't know that I knew who it was like, but we ran out of petrol [laughter] so we just swung the doors open and jumped and let the car roll on down the hill and we ran like fuck and all I heard was ahhhhhhh behind us. 'We're going to die! Run!' [Laughter]. I was all, 'I'm too young to die, I'm only fucking sixteen.' /.../

66 'Take the hand' or to 'take the hand out of' someone means to tease or to taunt.

67 'Chuck boy' refers generally to someone who supports Sinn Féin or the IRA. It can also mean a member of the IRA. The expression stems from 'Tiocfaith Ar Lá' (pronounced 'chucky ar la'), an Irish Gaelic expression used by Republicans meaning 'Our Day Will Come'.

They put our hands behind our backs and made us kneel down on the grass and it soaking too. /.../ They just, they were up the back roads to see if they're any hoods hanging about, up joyriding in the car, see if they could get anybody that they were looking for, at that time they were after Petey 'cause he was up to shit, he had been up stealing car visors and stuff as usual. Me and him decided then, right, 'Fuck this',

They were all, 'What's your name?'

(Petey answers), 'George'.

(They reply), 'Your name's not George. You're Petey McCloskey!'

And he was all, 'Up yours!'

(They reply), 'Put your hands behind your back. Did we tell you to speak? No!'

I started crying then 'cause I seen the blood coming out of my head from whatever way I fell. Wan of the boys came around the front of me, I don't know who it was but he came 'round. I think it was Mal. He came around the front of me and he goes, 'Hold your head up!'

And I go, 'Naw!'

He goes, 'Hold your head up!'

And I put my head my head down, (explaining) like my chin was in my chest.

He goes, 'You hold your head up!'

And I go, 'Naw!'

And he goes, 'Don't crack up with me!'

Petey goes, 'Emer, hold your head up!'

And I go, 'Naw!'

And he (the paramilitary) kicked Petey and goes, 'Did I tell you to speak?'

And I go, 'Fuck it in you dickheads!'

They were all, 'Do you know who we are?'

And I was all, 'Do I look as if I give a fuck?'

'Ahh, so you're another wee hard ticket running around this town are ye? So we're going to have to watch out for you dealing Es now as well?'

I was all, 'I don't deal drugs, naw!'

(They reply), 'But we know you take them! Aye right. We've seen you plenty of nights in Fusion (a local night club), girl!'

Declan turns 'round and goes, 'You!'

All I heard was the big deep voice and I thought, 'Ah Jesus, I'm going to die. He's going to batter me.'

He was all, 'You!'

I go, 'What?'

(He replies) 'Get up!'

And I go, 'Naw!'

He goes, 'Get up now!'

And I go, 'Naw! I don't take orders from you!'

He goes, 'Get up!' And all I heard was . . . [makes the noise of a trigger being pulled back] and I was, 'Oh Jesus Christ'.

Petey looked at me and goes, 'Get up!'

And I go, 'Naw!'

And he started laying into Petey again for talking.

They beat the Christ out of him. They never battered me. They wouldn't lay a hand on me 'cause I wasn't doing nothing, at that time. Well I don't do anything wrong anyway know what I mean, all right, I take a couple of Es at the weekend and smoke a bit of pot but that's it. If I was to do coke and stuff like that there they wouldn't know about it, but. / . . . /

I mind going into the house and our Bernadette turned 'round and goes to me, 'What the fuck happened you? Your trousers are soaking. Our Declan was on the phone there now.'

(Emer replies), 'What did he say?' [Laughter]

(Bernadette replies), 'He was just asking for you.'

(Emer responds), 'Was he . . . Aye. Bastard.'

Privy to a beating: concluding

Communal opinions concerning paramilitary punishment beatings, whether Republican or Loyalist, suffer from what I would term a 'consensus of misconsensus'—where ordinary everyday community members 'miss' each other in consensus of opinion concerning the results of such punishment regimes, but come together in agreement regarding the continuing debate surrounding the topic, tacitly allowing and relying upon the practice to continue. The intra-community paramilitary policing and vigilantism in both communities consequently should be considered to suffer from a circular conundrum where many community members often feel punishment is too harsh or unjustified, but similarly support the efforts in both abstract and actual terms, out of a lack of confidence in the police service, a perceived personal need, a perceived community loyalty, or plainly fear.

Although it could be argued at the height of assassinations and bombings ' . . . the individuation and personal visibility of the hardman are contrasted to the effaced persona of the gunman,'[68] here in situations such as Emer's, for example, to disconnect the two 'personas' would be an error. For Emer, her uncle is a family member, a 'hard bastard', as well as a paramilitary. The balaclava does little to hide his relationship to Emer and in situations such as these there is little care for the 'recodification of the human face'[69] or the wearing of balaclavas.

For the young people, the face behind the balaclava is far from hidden or removed from their everyday context of life. Acting alone,

---

68 Feldman, 1991, p. 53.

69 Ibid. Feldman is stressing the ethical change from hardman to gunman, particularly throughout the height of the 'Troubles'. Here he emphasizes the visual propaganda of the paramilitaries of that time and the use of the balaclava, gun and victim as assisting with a cultural shift from hardman to gunman, so that for the men of that era '(t)here is no such thing as a hardman now. . . ' (Ibid., p. 47).

these individuals are fathers, uncles, aunts, brothers, cousins, neighbours or even peers.[70] Together they are the familiarly known 'boys'.[71] Neighbourhood, social, personal and even familial connections are evident. And beyond the physicality of those who attack, the rules of engagement are understood. Sharon knows the men who attacked her brother for they work in the same factory. The man next door, who is also connected, warned her family it was coming. It was Emer's uncle who threatened and beat her. She recognized him by his car and his trousers. Dympna, after her boyfriend was brutally attacked outside a nightclub and went to hospital for weeks, knew who was sent out of the city and when they were sent out 'just for bein' bad'. While finally, Dympna's father had to opt out of service after being wakened for months to punish spousal abuse in their local neighbourhood: 'It just got too much', he had to 'take a break', she told me. Too many people were calling him to sort out their problems.

While the distinction of 'neighbour' or 'father' from 'paramilitary' may have been important for some in the community when paramilitary personnel have been involved in political bombings and shootings outside of the realm of community punishment, in the contemporary cases of community enforced and allowed punishment procedures it is important that we do not overlook what is implicit to those that know and experience this type of vigilantism. For the young people and the other ordinary citizens involved in these occurrences, those that hand out the warnings, beatings, kneecappings, expulsions and shootings are not individuals very far away from their understanding, hidden behind a balaclava and unknown. Rather, they are part of a common tacit system in which many people 'know the way it has to be', 'just take the beating and go home', and understand the 'limits' of how and when a person 'gets done'. An acceptable and predictable knowledge network in which 'Ma's worried because they say, know,

---

70 These are the relations that were noted to me as being involved in some form of community policing throughout conversations with the young people.

71 For more information on this idea, cf. Roche, 2003, pp. 170-8.

the first is that warnin', then there's a shot, then there's a beatin', and then there's a bullet te the head or the knees done or whatever.'

With such a system briefly laid bare, these networks have the potential to expand the growing dialogue surrounding collective, or communal, violence. Tambiah[72] for example, discusses three perspectives on collective violence, describing forms of collective violence as 'eruptive', 'semiotic and performative' and 'chronic'. Tambiah describes the third 'chronic' perspective 'less as eruptions' and more as a 'force or agency that has attained its own autonomy'.[73] While words like 'communal' linked with 'violence' call to mind great groups of individuals gathered together under one cause engaged in violence, I suggest that the term may equally apply to areas where tit-for-tat violence and knowledge networks concerning social rules of violent engagement have become collectively owned. In the case of punishment beatings in the current context, because the community members understand the rules in a long-standing societal context, and these 'rules' follow a certain order and have 'limits', these threats and beatings are merely part of a continued tradition within their areas despite changes in the paramilitary activities surrounding them. Indeed, from an economic assessment alone, growing paramilitary involvement in Northern Ireland in both illicit and legitimate business ventures could be seen to bring them definitionally closer to the Mafiosi. Importantly, however, the classification of Mafia is inextricably linked to economics—protection of those involved in its business enterprises is secondary.[74] In the case of paramilitary community vigilantism in Northern Ireland, while business is booming, the community element in this type of activity remains something to

---

72 Tambiah, 1996, pp. 221-43.

73 Ibid.

74 Cf. Abrahams, 1998; Gambetta, 1993; Heald, 1997; Hess, 1973; Hobsbawm, 1959; Jacobs, Friel and Radick, 1999; Sterling, 1994. Cf. also Moore, 2003, for an interesting commentary of Mafia/Northern Irish connections as established by the famous fraudster Colin Lees.

which the people inside of these communities relate to as a continued and historic community control.

What remains to be seen is if this perception and understanding of paramilitary punishment beatings changes in the light of the paramilitaries' growing economic involvement in illicit and legitimate trades, or if pressurized by further state security initiatives stemming from the ongoing peace process. What this contemporary perception and understanding can do, however, is lend us precious insight into—and allow us outsiders to be privy to—the expectations and unwritten 'rules' of shared communal knowledge networks; the understandings and complexities of what people perceive as effective vigilante control and the nuances concerning the ultimate sanctioning of that control.

Abrahams, R. 'Sungusungu: Village Vigilante Groups in Tanzania', *African Affairs* 86(343), 1987, pp. 179-96.

—— *Vigilant Citizens: Vigilantism and the State*, Cambridge, 1998.

Alexander, Y. and A. O'Day. *Terrorism in Ireland*, London, 1984.

Bew, P. and G. Gillespie. *Northern Ireland: a Chronology of the Troubles, 1968-1999*, Dublin, 1999.

Brown, R.M. *The South Carolina Regulators*, Cambridge, Mass., 1963.

—— *Strain of Violence: Historical Studies of American Violence and Vigilantism*, New York, 1975.

Bruce, S. *The Edge of the Union: the Ulster Loyalist Political Vision*, Oxford, 1994.

Burton, F. *The Politics of Legitimacy: Struggles in a Belfast Community*, London, 1978.

Community Re-Integration Project (CRIP). *Annual Report*, Belfast, 2003.

Conway, P. 'A Response to Paramilitary Policing in Northern Ireland', *Critical Criminology* 8(1), 1997, pp. 109-21.

Coulter, C. *Contemporary Northern Irish Society: an Introduction*, London, 1999.

Crawford, C. *Defenders or Criminals?: Loyalist Prisoners and Criminalisation*, Belfast, 1999.

—— *Inside the UDA: Volunteers and Violence*, London, 2003.

Das, V. *Critical Events: an Anthropological Perspective on Contemporary India*, Oxford, 1995.

Das, V., A. Kleinman, M. Ramphele and P. Reynolds (eds). *Violence and Subjectivity*, Berkeley, 2000.

Ellison, G. and J. Smyth. *The Crowned Harp: Policing Northern Ireland*, London Sterling, Va., 2000.

Farmer, P. 'On Suffering and Social Violence', in *Social Suffering*, A. Kleinman, V. Das and M.M. Lock (eds), Berkeley, 1997, pp. 261-84.

Feldman, A. *Formations of violence: the narrative of the body and political terror in Northern Ireland*, Chicago and London, 1991.

—— 'Violence and Vision: The Prosthetics and Aesthetics of Terror', in *Violence and Subjectivity*, V. Das, A. Kleinman, M. Ramphele and P. Reynolds (eds), Berkeley, 2000, pp. 46-78.

Gambetta, D. *The Sicilian Mafia: the Business of Private Protection*, London, 1993.

Heald, S. *Controlling Anger: The Sociology of Gisu Violence*, Ohio, 1997.

Hess, H. *Mafia and Mafiosi: the Structure of Power*, Lexington, Mass., 1973.

Higgins, K. and K. McElrath. 'The Trouble with Peace—The Ceasefires and their Impact on Drug Use among Youth in Northern Ireland', *Youth & Society* 32(1), 2000, pp. 29-59.

Higgins, K., A. Percy and P. McCrystal. 'Secular Trends in Substance Use: The Conflict and Young People in Northern Ireland', *Journal of Social Issues* 60(3), 2004, pp. 485-506.

Hobsbawm, E. *Primitive Rebels: Studies in Archaic Forms of Social Movement in the 19th and 20th Centuries*, Manchester, 1959.

Holland, J. and H. McDonald. *INLA: Deadly Divisions*, Dublin, 1994.

Jacobs, J.B., C. Friel and R. Radick. *Gotham Unbound: how New York City was Liberated from the Grip of Organized Crime*, New York, 1999.

Johnston, L. *The Rebirth of Private Policing*, London, 1992.

—— 'What is Vigilantism?' *British Journal of Criminology* 36(2), 1996, pp. 220-36.

Kennedy, L. 'Nightmares within Nightmares: Paramilitary Repression in Working-Class Communities', in *Crime and Punishment in West Belfast*, L. Kennedy (ed.), Belfast, 1994, pp. 67-80.

—— *An Analysis of the Age and Gender of Victims of Paramilitary "Punishment in Northern Ireland"*, Ireland Affairs Comittee—Relocation Following Paramilitary Intimidaion. Belfast, 2001.

Kleinman, A., V. Das and M.M. Lock. 'Introduction', in *Social Suffering*, A. Kleinman, V. Das and M.M. Lock (eds), Berkeley, 1997, pp. ix-xxvii.

Knox, C. 'The 'Deserving' Victims of Political Violence: "Punishment" Attacks in Northern Ireland', *Criminal Justice* 1(2), 2001a, pp. 181-99.

—— '"See no Evil, Hear no Evil'. Insidious Paramilitary Violence in Northern Ireland', *British Journal of Criminology* 42(1), 2001b, pp. 164-85.

—— 'Joined-up' Government: an Integrated Response to Communal Violence in Northern Ireland?' *Policy and Politics* 31(1), 2003, pp. 19-35.

Knox, C. and R. Monaghan. *Informal Justice in Divided Societies: Northern Ireland and South Africa*, Basingstoke, 2002.

McKittrick, D. *Endgame: the Search for Peace in Northern Ireland*, Belfast, 1994.

McVeigh, R. *"It's Part of Life Here ...": the Security Forces and Harassment in Northern Ireland*, Belfast, 1994.

Moore, C. *The Bankrupt, the Conman, the Mafia and the Irish Connection*, Dublin, 2003.

Morrissey, M. and K. Pease. 'The Black Criminal Justice System in West Belfast', *The Howard Journal* 21, 1982, pp. 159-66.

Ní Aoláin, F. *The Politics of Force: Conflict Management and State Violence in Northern Ireland*, Belfast, 2000.

O'Brien, B. *The Long War: the IRA and Sinn Féin*, Syracuse, 1993.

O'Connor, F. *In Search of a State: Catholics in Northern Ireland*, Belfast, 1993.

O'Doherty, M. *The Trouble with Guns: Republican Strategy and the Provisional IRA*, Belfast, 1998.

O'Mahoney, D., R. Geary, K. McEvoy and J. Morison. *Crime Community and Locale: The Northern Ireland Communities Crime Survey*, 2000.

Roche, R. 'The Inheritors: An Ethnographic Exploration of Stress, Threat, Violence, Guts, Fear and Fun Among Young People in Contemporary Londonderry, Northern Ireland,' Unpublished Doctoral Dissertation, University of Cambridge, 2003.

—— *Something to Say: The Complete TRIPROJECT Report on the Views of Young School Leavers in the Derry City Council District Areas*, Belfast, 2005.

Rosenbaum, H. and P. Sederberg. 'Vigilantism—Analysis of Establishment Violence', *Comparative Politics* 6(4), 1974, pp. 541-70.

—— (eds). *Vigilante Politics*, Philadelphia, 1976.

Silke, A. 'The Lords of Discipline: The Methods and Motives of Paramilitary Vigilantism in Northern Ireland', *Low Intensity Conflict and Law Enforcement* 7(2), 1998, pp. 121-56.

—— 'Ragged Justice: Loyalist Vigilantism in Northern Ireland', *Terrorism and Political Violence* 11(3), 1999, pp. 1-31.

—— (ed.) *Terrorists, Victims and Society: Psychological Perspectives on Terrorism and its Consequences*, Chichester, 2003.

Sluka, J.A. *Hearts and Minds, Water and Fish: Support for the IRA and INLA in a Northern Irish Ghetto*, Greenwich, 1989.

—— (ed.) *Death Squad: the Anthropology of State Terror*, Philadelphia, 2000.

Sterling, C. *Crime without Frontiers: the Worldwide Expansion of Organised Crime and the Pax Mafiosa*, London, 1994.

Tambiah, S.J. *Leveling Crowds: Ethnonationalist Conflicts and Collective Violence in South Asia*, Berkeley, 1996.

Whittaker, D.J. (ed.) *The Terrorism Reader*, New York, 2001.

Wilkinson, P. *Terrorism and the Liberal State*, New York, 1986.

PROTECTION AND POLITICS

FLEXIBLE JUSTICE: NEOLIBERAL VIOLENCE AND 'SELF-HELP' SECURITY IN BOLIVIA[1]

Daniel M. Goldstein

In the second week of October 2003, a week that marked the anniversaries of both the Columbian 'discovery' of the New World and 21 years of Bolivian democracy, the Bolivian state killed 62 people in violent confrontations in and around the nation's capital, La Paz, and neighbouring El Alto.[2] The massacres occurred in the context of the so-called 'Gas War', a massive social protest joined by peasant groups, trade unions, coca farmers, and the urban poor, against the Bolivian government's plans to export natural gas through a Chilean port for sale to the United States. Fearing that once again, as has happened so many times in the neoliberal era, a vital component of the Bolivian 'national patrimony' was to be expropriated by foreign interests, this loose coalition of indigenous and labour groups took to the streets, demanding cancellation of the gas sale and the

1 A longer version of this chapter was originally published in *Critique of Anthropology* (2005, 25 pp. 389-411). Funding for this research was provided by a Grant for Research and Writing from the John D. and Catherine T. MacArthur Foundation. For help and feedback on this work, I thank Juan Manuel Arbona, Jennifer Burrell, Philip Coyle, Angelique Haugerud, Billie Jean Isbell, Benjamin Kohl, Kathryn Ledebur, Sally Engle Merry, Shannon Speed and the anonymous reviewers, as well as the editors of this volume. Special thanks to Rose Marie Achá, Eric Hinojosa, and Theo Roncken for help with research and reflection on these ideas.

2 *Opinión*, 'Tensa calma y total parálisis en ciudades de La Paz y El Alto', p. A1. Cochabamba, 13 October 2003.

DANIEL M. GOLDSTEIN

resignation of Bolivia's president, Gonzalo Sanchez de Lozada. The bloodiest confrontation between protestors and the state occurred on 12 October, when heavily armed police and military units attempting to escort petrol tankers past a blockade in El Alto fired live ammunition into a crowd of people challenging this action. In response to these killings, protestors' calls for the president's resignation escalated, while blockades, marches, and demonstrations gained momentum throughout the country. Despite international support, the president's ruling coalition crumbled in the face of continued domestic unrest, and Sanchez de Lozada fled the country a few days later.

As human rights scholars and activists have discovered,[3] democratic governance does not automatically produce the rule of law and respect for human rights, a fact that has become painfully clear to Bolivians and students of the Bolivian sociopolitical landscape in recent years.[4] Though officially a democracy since 1982, Bolivia has struggled to implement democratic political and legal reform while contending with the requirements of neoliberal structural adjustment and the globalization of capital. The Bolivian state, a star pupil of the neoliberal school, has diligently complied with the demands of international lending agencies and foreign nations (especially the United States), restructuring its economy to provide a more favourable climate for multinational investment, privatizing national industries and slashing state payrolls and programmes, while watching unemployment rise and poverty worsen for the majority of the national population.[5] State efforts to impose these political and economic mandates have sometimes been accompanied by violence, both by and against the state and its representatives. Indeed, as the violence of the Gas War reveals, Bolivian society today, though formally democratic, is

---

3 E.g. Godoy, 2002.

4 The election of Evo Morales as Bolivian president in December 2005 on an anti-liberal platform raises important and, at the time of this writing, unanswerable questions about the future relationship between state and civil society in Bolivia.

5 Kohl, 2002.

240

more violent than ever; according to the Bolivian Permanent Human Rights Assembly, more Bolivians were killed by the state in 2003 than during any year of the military dictatorships.

These violent events and continued unrest have their roots in the Bolivian state's efforts to comply with foreign pressures and structural adjustment programmes encoded in transnational strategies of political and economic reorganization, and thus represent forms of 'neoliberal violence'.[6] Neoliberal violence is at once structural and undeniably physical; it entails an inequitable distribution of resources within a rigidly hierarchical society, which ultimately must be implemented and maintained by state violence, and which in turn engenders violent responses. This violence is quotidian—it marks the everyday lives of poor, marginalized (and, in Bolivia, indigenous) people, creating a profound sense of insecurity, an anxious and fearful 'structure of feeling'[7] that colours every aspect of daily existence—and in moments of rupture like the Gas War, it can be shockingly bloody. It also transcends the geographical and ideological space of the nation-state, being motivated by and pursuant to the demands of a transnational political-economic regime that reconfigures national policies and programmes according to its own logic of privatization, 'responsibilization' and 'flexibility'.[8] In the economic restructuring that underlies it and the reduced capacity of the state to provide services that this restructuring creates, neoliberal violence produces violations not only of the political and civil rights of individuals, but of their social and economic rights as well.

I put forth the idea of neoliberal violence because I want to use it as a frame for interpreting yet another kind of violence currently ongoing in Bolivia, one that I think must be viewed within this same, broader context of neoliberalism and the rights violations it engenders if it is to be properly understood. I am referring to the vigilante lynching of thieves by groups of residents in many urban neighbour-

---

6 Auyero, 2000.

7 Williams, 1977.

8 Harvey, 1991; Ong, 1999.

hoods throughout Bolivia, but particularly centred in the southern zone of Cochabamba, Bolivia's third largest city. While exact numbers are difficult to come by, my own research, supplemented by that of Acción Andina, has documented hundreds of such incidents in and around Cochabamba over the last five years.[9] As I discuss below, lynching has proliferated in Cochabamba and elsewhere in Bolivia in conjunction with the nation's overall economic decline, and as people's vulnerability to violence, official corruption, and criminal predation has escalated.

My attempt in this chapter to understand lynching violence should not be misconstrued as an effort to rationalize or justify it. Without a doubt, lynching represents an indefensible form of violence, a violation of the most basic rights of human beings. And yet, what I want to suggest here is that these lynchings should be understood not in isolation from the ongoing violence produced by the Bolivian state, but in concert with it. The spate of lynchings occurring in Cochabamba and other locations across Bolivia is generated by and in reaction to transnational violence that is at once structural, physical, and all-pervasive in Bolivia today. Far from the spontaneous expressions of an innately primitive and anti-democratic nature (a common interpretation of lynching, as I will discuss in more detail below), lynchings are collective expressions of rage and despair in a context of total vulnerability, not only to crime but to the ravages of a political-economic order that has a disproportionate and prejudicial impact on poor and indigenous people. Facing mounting violence and crime, unemployment and a sense of powerlessness to confront a sociopolitical order that ignores their demands for economic, legal, and social justice, these people respond with violence, in a futile effort to control crime and as a response to the nation-state's neglect of their own rights to justice and security in their communities.

At the same time, the form and the logic of vigilante justice in Bolivia today are profoundly shaped by and expressive of certain basic

---

9 Goldstein, 2003; Acción Andina, 2003, http://www.cedib.org/accionandina/index.php.

principles of neoliberalism itself. In particular, the 'privatization' of justice reflects key organizational—indeed, cultural—themes of neoliberal political economy, and rather than working to reduce lynching violence, the national state and its transnational underwriters, as principal proponents of the logic of flexibilization and privatization, can actually be viewed as co-conspirators in its elaboration. I thus suggest that lynchings in Bolivia today be understood as a kind of neoliberal violence, produced both by the scarcities and deficiencies of the kind of 'sclerotic state'[10] that neoliberalism precipitates, and by the logic of transnational capitalism itself, which has saturated civil society and public culture.[11]

In the next section of this chapter, I provide a summary description of lynching in Cochabamba, with reference to the larger discursive frameworks within which it is typically interpreted. I then go on to suggest that lynching should be understood as part of a larger practice of violence that pervades neoliberal society, and in fact partakes of the fundamental logic of 'flexibility' that lies at its heart. The next section of the chapter discusses other forms of 'privatization of justice' in Bolivia, including police corruption and private police firms, suggesting further linkages between neoliberal economic logic and the provision of security in the contemporary Bolivian city. In the conclusion, I analyze these various forms of violence and security provision within the broader context of neoliberal capitalism, with

---

10 Speed and Reyes, 2002.

11 In this analysis, I follow Aihwa Ong in understanding globalization as the flow not only of capital, information, and people across national borders, but of the cultural logics that underpin post-Fordist capitalism and have a profound impact on, and are negotiated by, local populations. This approach aims to integrate, rather than bifurcate, the local and the global, the cultural and the political-economic. 'Only by weaving the analysis of cultural politics and political economy into a single framework,' Ong says, 'can we hope to provide a nuanced delineation of the complex relations between transnational phenomena, national regimes, and cultural practices in late modernity...An understanding of political economy remains central as capitalism...has become even more deeply embroiled in the ways different cultural logics give meanings to our dreams, actions, goals, and sense of how we are to conduct ourselves in the world.' Ong, 1999, p. 16.

suggestions for how this discussion can affect our understandings of global and local linkages in contemporary society.

Lynching violence in Bolivia

The vigilante lynching of criminal suspects has become a common practice in the marginal *barrios* of Bolivian cities, with the majority of such incidents being reported in the southern zone of Cochabamba. As I have described elsewhere,[12] one of the first of these lynchings occurred in one such *barrio* (Villa Sebastián Pagador) in 1995, when I was there doing fieldwork. In that event, three individuals were caught red-handed robbing a home in broad daylight, and were nearly lynched by a crowd of angry residents. When the police finally arrived, dressed in riot gear, to disrupt the lynching, people attacked the advancing police cordon with stones until they were dispersed. This near-lynching, as it turns out, was an early forerunner of what has since become a common practice of collective violence by the residents of marginal *barrios* all around Cochabamba. According to reports that I have collected from police sources, social service agencies, and local newspapers, literally hundreds of lynchings or attempted lynchings have occurred in Cochabamba during the last six years. Indeed, events of this kind have occurred with such frequency in the popular *barrios* of Cochabamba and elsewhere that, according to a recent report, Bolivia ranks second in the world (behind Guatemala) in the number of lynchings that have taken place.[13]

Lynchings have occurred with such frequency in Cochabamba that they have become routinized, and unfold according to their own ritual schema. Typically in these incidents, a criminal suspect (usually a supposed thief, child molester, or some other kind of felon or petty criminal) is apprehended by a group of local residents, who

---

12 Goldstein, 2003; Goldstein, 2004.

13 *Opinión* 14 July 2003, 'Bolivia ocupa el segundo lugar en el mundo en casos de linchamientos', p. 4A. Cochabamba. For considerations of lynching in other Latin American contexts, see Burrell, 2002; Castillo Claudett, 2000; Godoy, 2006; Guerrero, 2001; Fuentes Díaz and Binford, 2001; Vilas, 2001.

are quickly joined by other inhabitants of the zone. This group ties up the suspect and subjects him (or sometimes her) to verbal and physical abuse, which can include beating, hair cutting, and stoning. Sometimes these tortures lead to death, as the suspect is doused with petrol and set on fire by the angry mob. More often than not, however, the police arrive to rescue the lynching victims or otherwise disrupt the event. In most cases, both the victims and the perpetrators of lynching violence are of indigenous origin (Quechua and/or Aymara) and belong to the poorest, most marginal sectors of Bolivian society. As the next section of this chapter discusses in more detail, lynch mob participants in Cochabamba typically justify their violence as a response to rising crime in their neighbourhoods and the apparent inability or unwillingness of the authorities to police their communities effectively.[14]

The sudden upsurge in lynchings since 2000 is not, I would argue, coincidental. Popular discontent with the neoliberal state, brewing since the implementation of the New Economic Policy (state decree 21060) in 1985, began to crystallize and find expression around the turn of the millennium. Significantly, 2000 was the year the 'Water War' erupted in Cochabamba.[15] A large-scale popular uprising in response to the Bolivian state's attempt to privatize the water supply system in that city, the Water War forced the cancellation of the state's contract with the multinational Bechtel corporation, an event that was internationally hailed as a popular victory in the struggle against globalization.[16] Several economic shocks may also have contributed to the rising tide of popular violence in Cochabamba at around this same time. The relatively successful coca-eradication programme (the so-called *Plan Dignidad*) initiated in 1997 dur-

---

14 Other similar incidents in more rural contexts include the executions of suspected cattle thieves in the Cochabamba valley, and the execution of the mayor of Ayo Ayo, an Aymara community on the Bolivian altiplano. This latter incident, though initially described as a lynching, later proved to be more of a mob-style execution, enacted by rival gangs in this town.

15 Farthing and Kohl, 2001.

16 Finnegan, 2002.

DANIEL M. GOLDSTEIN

ing the presidency of General Hugo Banzer had by 2000 begun to severely affect the regional economy of Cochabamba, as many families lost a longstanding source of informal income. Additionally, the Argentine economic crisis negatively affected the Cochabamba economy, as thousands of migrants were forced to return home and families dependent on foreign remittances lost a considerable portion of their income. By 2000, people in Cochabamba had become poorer and increasingly frustrated with a privatizing state whose promises of greater prosperity for all had clearly failed to materialize.[17]

Despite its many connections to contemporary political economy, local media accounts typically frame the lynching violence on Cochabamba's south side as acts of savagery, committed by people who lack a basic respect for democracy and civilized society. Bolivian newspaper commentaries frequently denounce lynching as 'an attack on social institutions'[18] that threatens to unravel the fabric binding the human community together. Lynchings are described as 'primitive and cruel', an embarrassment for a nation striving for modernity and progress: 'The lynchings make Bolivia one of the most backward countries on earth', remarks one editorial writer.[19] 'The image of Bolivia, of all of us, should not be marked by the primitive conduct of certain groups of people.' Another columnist characterizes lynchings as acts of 'primitive barbarism', asserting that they are symptoms of 'social degradation' indicating that Bolivian society 'is losing the fundamental values that are needed to build a democratic society.'[20] Lynchings are described as a brake on national progress and an obstacle to democratic advancement. From the perspective of analysts who produce the formal public discourse about the meaning of lynchings

---

17 My thanks to Ben Kohl for his thoughts on these subjects.

18 *Los Tiempos*, 30 March 2001, 'Linchamiento: Atacan a instituciones sociales', p. B-3. Cochabamba.

19 *Opinión*, 21 June 2002, 'Los linchamientos se repiten porque las autoridades no hacen nada para evitarlos', p. A1. Cochabamba.

20 *Opinión*, 29 July 2003, 'El linchamiento tiene hermanas siamesas: La pobreza y violencia', pp. 10-11A. Cochabamba.

in Bolivia, it is the lynchings themselves that are the cause, rather than an expression, of the failure of democracy in Bolivia today. By labelling lynching a survival of some bygone era whose practitioners themselves are retrograde, the practice and its perpetrators are made to stand as representatives of a pre-democratic past that now serves as an anchor weighing on national political development.[21]

In reading such accusations, however, the fact cannot be overlooked that those being so characterized are indigenous Quechua and Aymara people, and that indigenous people in the Andes have long been depicted in terms similar to those being used to describe lynchings and lynch mobs in Bolivia today—as retrograde and primitive, threats to orderly urban life and to civilization itself. Since the colonial era, the very presence of indigenous Andeans in the urban landscape has been considered a violation of the nation's 'racialized imaginative geography',[22] which locates 'Indians' properly in the countryside, 'white' or '*mestizo*' populations in the city.[23] In a similar fashion, indigenous rural-to-urban migrants in Cochabamba have long been perceived by the city's white middle class (and by the institutions of media, government, and commerce that they control) as invaders, threats to the longstanding social and political order of the city.[24] These people's poverty has been characterized as bearing disease and contamination into the city;[25] their patterns of land invasion and spontaneous settlement have been viewed as attacks on

---

21 This problem is also apparent in arguments (offered by some lynch mob participants seeking to justify their actions by an appeal to 'tradition') that theorize lynching to be some sort of holdover from the rural past, a contemporary expression of older forms of traditional law (*derecho consuetudinario*). While physical forms of punishment were not unknown in rural Andean contexts, contemporary urban lynchings represent distinct forms of violence that must be understood (I argue) within the current context of neoliberal reform.

22 Radcliffe and Westwood, 1996.

23 Weismantel, 2001.

24 Goldstein, 2004.

25 See Colloredo-Mansfeld, 1998; Douglas, 1966.

the 'rational' and orderly growth of the city itself.[26] Accusations of 'barbarism' and antagonism towards democracy ascribed to lynching intersect with this enduring racist critique of indigenous urbanites, demonizing the actors without attempting to understand the context that makes their violence possible and predictable.

Instead, I argue that lynching should be understood in the context of neoliberal structural reform, within which it is embedded and from which it derives its logic and, in the minds of its perpetrators, its legitimacy. Lynching, in a sense, fulfils the highest mandates of neoliberal rationality; it represents the privatization of justice, the assumption by individuals of a service ordinarily provided by the state, and so points to the increasing importance of 'flexibility' as a personal and communal survival strategy in neoliberal society. Lynching fills the gap left by the withdrawal of the state from the delivery of official justice, as citizens themselves take on the responsibility of creating security when the state will not. Given the state's orientation towards responsibilization—the transfer of state functions to citizens and informal or non-governmental associations—lynching is the logical and indeed predictable response of people required to be flexible in providing for their own needs.

Neoliberalism and the crisis of security

Neoliberal economic reforms accompanying democratization throughout most of the 'developing world' were intended to create a more productive environment for transnational capitalism by removing barriers to trade and creating a 'flexible' workforce that could provide cheap labour to transnational industries.[27] Flexibility is a critical dimension of late capitalism, part of the post-Fordist logic that allows corporations to maximize the turnover rate of capital by eschewing fixed production facilities and their associated labour costs, replacing these older, inflexible relations of production with

---

26 Solares Serrano, 1986.
27 Harvey, 2001.

strategies of 'outsourcing', labour reorganization, and geographical mobility as part of a regime of 'flexible accumulation'.[28] Promising a more efficient economy that would create more and better jobs for national workers while curtailing state involvement in both market regulation and the social reproduction of labour, neoliberalism has thoroughly displaced the developmentalist model that had for decades been the dominant approach to economic policymaking, shifting the emphasis in public discourse from national development to global competitiveness and efficiency. Whereas in the earlier economic model the state was a major player in promoting national development by controlling market forces and guaranteeing (at least rhetorically) jobs and social welfare for the poor, in the neoliberal era the state encourages the development of 'self-help' social and economic mechanisms, devolving responsibility for the maintenance of workers from the private sector and the state to local communities, non-governmental organizations, families, and individuals.[29] These reforms have resulted in a measurable increase in economic inequality and a dramatic decline in the standard of living for the rural and urban poor, as ownership of land and other resources has become further concentrated, peasants have been dispossessed, and public-sector jobs have disappeared.[30] Today at least 260 million people in Latin America live in poverty.[31]

Within Latin America, Bolivia has been one of the most aggressive implementers of the neoliberal model. Since 1985, the Bolivian state has promoted policies that have withdrawn the state from direct participation in the national economy, privileging private sector firms as the engines of development and encouraging self-generation of employment for displaced workers.[32] Virtually all nationally owned industries have been privatized (or 'capitalized', in the language of

---

28 Harvey, 1990; Inda, 2000.

29 Gill, 2000.

30 Gwynne and Kay, 2000; Lustig, 1995; Petras and Veltmeyer, 1999.

31 Aiyer, 2001; Bulmer-Thomas, 1996; Chossudovsky, 1997.

32 Benería, 1996; ILO, 2002.

the system[33]), the political potential of trade unions has been de-fused,[34] state programmes and jobs have been cut, and the state itself has been 'decentralized', with the transfer of federal responsibilities to municipalities and non-governmental organizations.[35] In the realm of labour policy, Bolivia has emphasized a programme of la-bour flexibilization ('*flexibilización laboral*'), a mainstay of Bolivian economic policy since 1985. Being flexible in the Bolivian context means being willing to work on short-term contracts, in home-based industries, and, increasingly, in the informal economy, creating one's own income-generating opportunities when the regular economy fails to provide work. Flexibility also means caring for oneself and one's family by working without a net, that is, through self-employ-ment without benefit of public provision of social security. In the language of Bolivian neoliberalism, these forms of *flexibilización* and *responsibilización* of individuals represent what sociologist Ulrich Beck has identified as 'a generalization of employment insecurity' within post-Fordist capitalism,[36] compounded by a complete sun-dering of the social reciprocity that capital and the state historically provided to labour.

Flexibility and individual responsibility, then, are the watchwords of Bolivian society today, and the state has pursued specific policies that put these principles into practice. For example, the Bolivian state is a major proponent of privately owned micro-enterprises, small-scale business interests intended to promote 'economic democracy' by generating new forms of employment, thereby providing market integration for the poor and marginalized.[37] Micro-enterprise pro-motion positions the state as taking an active role in providing for its citizens, part of the state's own attempt to stabilize neoliberalism through highly visible public policy initiatives intended to demon-

---

33 Kohl, 2002.
34 García Linera, 1999.
35 Kohl, 2003; Medeiros, 2001; Postero, 2000.
36 Beck, 1992, p. 143.
37 Rhyne, 2001.

strate its commitment to strengthening the domestic economy. But, as Arbona points out, micro-enterprises in fact require very little investment or oversight on the part of the state, and serve to transfer social-welfare responsibilities from the state to the working poor themselves.[38] Micro-enterprises fulfil the demands of international lenders in that they do not require the state to participate directly in the national economy, while promoting 'individual responsibility as the only possibility for securing welfare'.[39] In the words of a presidential decree on the subject of micro-enterprises, the Bolivian workforce is encouraged to be 'flexible', and to demonstrate 'responsibility, creativity, and adaptability'[40] in generating employment in the face of the ongoing economic crisis. But the state offers no concrete alternatives when such enterprises fail, nor any material support to ensure that they do not.

The economic insecurity created by neoliberal reforms is complemented by a physical insecurity resulting from rising crime rates that have accompanied structural adjustment, compounded by the deficiencies of an unreliable and inequitable system of official justice. For the upper class, police and judicial services are at least nominally available to investigate crimes, respond to grievances, and resolve conflicts. But for the majority of crime victims, who are typically poor and marginalized, honest and reliable police protection or recourse to the law is simply nonexistent. Instead, the poor themselves are often criminalized in public discourse and in police practice, and experience heightened police violence, as states adopt more repressive and violent measures in the name of crime control.[41] Even in the absence of direct experience of crime, the fear of criminal and state violence, perpetuated by 'talk of crime', ratchets up the levels of insecurity people confront and the extremes to which they are willing

---

38 Arbona, n.d.

39 Ibid., p. 13.

40 Presidencia de la República de Bolivia, 1998; cited in ibid.

41 Davis, 2003; Frühling, 2003; Méndez, O'Donnell and Pinheiro, 1999; Pereira and Davis, 2000; Schneider and Amar, 2003; Ungar, 2002.

to go to attain security.[42] Especially in urban areas, a general feeling of fear and insecurity may seem all-encompassing and inescapable, part of the *habitus* of daily life.[43] Facing widespread police corruption and violence, compounded by a generalized and apparently endless economic 'crisis', urban residents experience an overwhelming sense of 'ontological insecurity', a pervasive sense of despair and uncertainty that Anthony Giddens has identified as one of the defining conditions of late modernity.[44]

While neoliberal economic policy has become ubiquitous throughout Latin America since the mid 1980s, the hegemony of neoliberal philosophy has been far from absolute, the promised benefits of democratic and economic reform being contradicted by the escalating poverty and violence of neoliberal society. Nevertheless, the themes of flexibility, privatization, and self-help individualism, so prominent within liberal capitalism, emerge as profound cultural forces that shape the behaviour of national subjects, and in turn are shaped by them. As the ethnographic discussion in the next section of this chapter explores, this is particularly true in efforts initiated by poor urban Bolivians to establish 'security' in their communities. Abandoned and victimized by the state and its policing and judicial apparatus, for many citizens the only viable option for obtaining security appears to be 'self-help' justice-making (for the most part, through lynching) to create some semblance of order in their community (though this strategy tends to perpetuate the cycle of violence within which poor communities are already ensnared). Rather than rely on the empty promises of the state and its official justice system, many residents of Cochabamba's marginal *barrios* recognize the need to be 'flexible', to use 'responsibility, creativity, and adaptability' in pursuing 'justice' by other means. If the state will not provide work, people must create their own employment opportunities; similarly,

---

42 Caldeira, 2000; Dammert and Malone, 2003; Elbert, 1998; Rotker and Goldman, 2002.

43 Garland, 2001; Merry, 1981.

44 Giddens, 1990.

if the state will not provide justice, punishing criminals becomes an individual responsibility. Taking the law 'into one's own hands' has a very different resonance when understood in light of these larger, official discourses and practices, as the next section explores.

'There is no justice in Bolivia': police inadequacy and vigilantism

The failure of the state to provide adequate security and an accessible justice system to its people has been one of the key sources of state delegitimation in Bolivia today, and pertains directly to the neoliberal restructuring of the nation so visibly denounced in the Gas War. Even as the national crime rate quadrupled between 1993 and 1999, the overall budget for the Bolivian national police force shrank; most of that budget was allocated toward purchasing equipment rather than hiring or training police officers. In 1999, the police budget was reduced by 25 per cent, and in each year since it has been cut by an equal or greater percentage of the remaining total.[45] The lack of police protection is particularly evident in urban areas, which have expanded rapidly over the last few decades, again in response to neoliberal reforms that closed the nationally owned mining sector and otherwise jeopardized rural livelihoods, propelling people to the cities. In Cochabamba, for example, fewer than 1,000 police officers are assigned to protect a population of nearly 800,000 residents;[46] fewer than a dozen police vehicles are deployed in the city, while a fleet of police motorcycles sits idle, the department lacking funds to buy petrol to run them. The investigative capacity of the Cochabamba branch of the national police force is similarly weak; police lack the training and material resources to collect and preserve evidence, and to follow up leads effectively. The police morgue is a veritable house of horrors, with the cadavers of crime victims left to decompose in

---

45 Ungar, 2003, p. 34.

46 In contrast, for example, New York City has approximately one police officer for every 200 people (http://www.nyc.gov/html/nypd/home.html).

the open air for periods of up to three weeks, the authorities lacking refrigeration facilities and medical personnel to perform prompt autopsies. Forensics departments are understaffed, and lack even the most basic equipment (including rubber gloves and surgical instruments) to go about their work in a manner that guarantees the validity of evidence obtained.[47]

Officially, crime rates in Bolivia increased 140 per cent per year between 1995 and 2002,[48] though most crimes still go unreported owing to citizens' complete lack of faith in the police institution's ability to investigate and arrest criminal suspects. People of all social classes in Cochabamba attribute this failure to the deep and extensive corruption that permeates the Bolivian police and legal professions, a result of the poor salaries paid to justice professionals (a street officer earns under $1,300 a year) and the ever-present temptation to profit from one's contacts with criminal networks.[49] Human rights activists argue that corruption actually serves to maintain the police force as an institution; in the absence of adequate public funding, the force relies on the money its officers skim or extort from the criminals they apprehend to allow them to purchase such mundane necessities as petrol.

The fear of police corruption came through clearly in interviews I conducted with groups of residents from different social classes, genders and occupations in marginal neighbourhoods of Cochabamba city. Many people asserted that the police were inept and corrupt, and that the administration of justice favoured the rich over the poor and the middle class. 'The police are terrible,' reported one woman, a coordinator of an artisan's group in the city.[50] 'There is no justice in Bolivia. At least for the poor there isn't. You have to have money to get justice.' Many people contend that the police will not investigate

47 G. Herrera, 'Médicos forenses están abandonados a su suerte,' *Los Tiempos*, 20 July 2003, p. C3. Cochabamba.

48 G. Conte, 'Para un especialista, el delito es 'regulado' en Bolivia por la policía.' *Desarme.org*. La Paz 2003.

49 Ungar, 2003.

50 All translations of interviews and other texts are my own.

unless the complainant pays them to. People report that the police demand money to pay for the costs of routine investigations:

The first thing they ask for in the PTJ [*Policía Técnica Judicial*] is money. My niece was murdered and when we went to the police so that they would investigate, the first thing they asked us for was $100 to begin the investigation. Imagine how much they would want to complete the investigation! Because we didn't have money, we had to leave it at that. She was killed, she was buried, but nothing.

Another artisan recounted her own experience of being robbed, and going to report the crime to the police:

I go into the PTJ, which at that time was operating out of the main plaza, I go in and, 'Yes, I recognize him, there he is.' They have photos of those offenders (*malhechores*) all over the place in there, and I go, 'That's him,' I say… 'Ahh! Of course that's him, *señora*, tomorrow we'll go and recover [the money]. But only half.' 'Okay,' I said, 'half.' I accepted, no? Such blackmail! But I accepted, half. And to this day I haven't got my half.

The sense of powerlessness that people derive from their encounters with police colours their view of official justice more generally, and shapes their understanding of their own subordination within the broader sociopolitical arena. In the words of another artisan:

It seems to me that our hands are tied, that we can't do anything, we don't have the power, those that are in power, yes, they can do and undo things… but society can't do anything because we don't have the power, we don't have the political power, we don't have the economic power, so if we protest it is all in vain…

Many people confronting this situation of vulnerability and powerlessness see a direct link between police corruption and neglect and the impulse to take the law into their own hands. In Villa Sebastián Pagador, on Cochabamba's far southeastern fringe, a group of women described what happened after a crime was committed in the *barrio* in 1995. Here, lynching is described as the direct result of police inaction and corruption:

Señora 1: There is a denunciation, the police come, they take notes, notes, that's it, then the thing is forgotten. If you don't put down any money, there is no investigation.

Señora 2: That's why we make justice with our own hands, too, sometimes we tie him up, like that time when the residents here...

Señora 1: They burned him.

The extortion committed against crime victims and their families by the national police represents another form of Bolivian privatization, in this case the privatization of public functions by the very personnel charged with their execution. Police corruption converts the public administration of justice into a private resource that maintains both individual police officers and, ironically, the police institution itself. Corrupt officers turn the police investigation into a form of prospecting (what economists call 'rent-seeking behaviour'[51]) using their authority to pursue individual profit, while paying kickbacks to officers higher up the ladder who naturally turn a blind eye to such proceedings. The police department further encourages this 'entrepreneurial' behaviour, both to cover its institutional costs and to turn a profit for its operatives. Encounters between private citizens and public officials like those described above thus constitute a double victimization for those who report crimes to the police—first at the hands of criminals, and then at those of the police themselves, all of whom operate according to a code of profit maximization at the expense of the poor. A 1999 study of the Bolivian national police issued by an external review panel (composed of officers and representatives of the Colombian police force) described the police institution as 'a bunker whose operation is concentrated to a large degree, in attending to individual interests related to illicit enrichment, the granting of favours to groups from outside the institution, and the obtaining of a higher social position through the ranks of the police hierar-

---

51 Kohl, 2004; Krueger, 1974.

chy.'[52] For poor *cochabambinos*, this state of affairs translates directly into individual responsibility and an impulse to take matters into their own hands. Said another Cochabamba resident: 'I also have this attitude of lynching, because I don't see any other way, that the laws, that the judicial organizations don't offer a real solution to handling delinquents... Especially, there is no solution within the justice [organizations], each person has to make his own justice.'

The police themselves generally concur with the assessment that they are unable to control crime or police the *barrios*. Privately, individual police officers confess a certain sympathy for the lynchings, which commonly occur in *barrios* where they themselves reside. My friend Fausto Huanca, for example, a low-ranking street officer in the national police force and a resident of Villa Pagador, is deeply ashamed of the corruption reported among the police, and considers it a black mark on an otherwise decent profession. At the same time, Don Fausto is a member of a force deeply stratified along class and racial lines. For the most part, members of the officer corps tend to be classified as 'white' in the national racial hierarchy, a distinction that generally correlates with a middle- or upper-class income, background, and lifestyle. Ordinary police officers of the lower ranks like Don Fausto, on the other hand, tend to be categorized as indigenous and poor. Like Don Fausto, they live in the *barrios* rather than in the city centre or the better suburbs, and so are themselves vulnerable to the same kinds of criminal predation as their neighbours. Trained in the service of a police force that is both nationalistic and resolutely masculine, men like Don Fausto espouse a rhetoric of law that places the exercise of control and violence solely in the hands of the 'legally constituted authorities'. But they also recognize that these authorities are themselves corrupt, and as *barrio* residents they share the critique of the police made by the majority of their neighbours. The low-level policemen recognize that they are underpaid and typically called upon to do the dirtiest jobs of repression and control, but they

---

52 'Policía Boliviana, búnker del enriquecimiento' *Los Tiempos* 3 November 2003, p. B-2. Cochabamba.

also embrace this work as their duty as citizens and as men.[53] They thus regard lynching as a problem and an inevitability. Don Fausto, for example, condemns lynching as a crime, an inappropriate exercise of force that must be prosecuted to the fullest extent of the law. On the other hand, he is highly sympathetic towards the lynch mob and its aims, and is reluctant to criticize the actions of people who are, in matter of fact, his friends, relatives, and neighbours.

Other private forms of policing and law enforcement have also emerged in recent years, which put a prettier face on vigilante justice while participating in the same logic and similar techniques as the lynching. In Cochabamba today, more than 100 private security firms have been created to provide private police services to all those willing to pay. Though originally confined to the wealthier neighbourhoods, today these security firms can be found in most parts of Cochabamba, filling in for the absent state in poor *barrios* throughout the city. In Villa Pagador, for example, residents of a *barrio* sector known as Segundo Grupo contribute one boliviano (approximately 15 US cents) per day to pay for a security patrol on the main avenue running through their zone. Private security firms like this one are often founded and managed by retired military or police officers, entrepreneurs schooled in violence and corruption who take advantage of the need for their services created by deficiencies in the very institutions they formerly served. Firms exploit the general climate of fear and insecurity created by rising crime and state inadequacy to generate business for themselves. On the street where I live in Cochabamba, for example, the local security provider (a firm with the witty English-language name Bolivian Pest Control) puts out a monthly newsletter in which it reports on various cases of police inadequacy in Cochabamba, citing newspaper articles to that effect; it also offers its clients suggestions on how to improve home security, including such helpful tips as 'Every time you enter or leave your dwelling, secure the door with two turns of the lock and put on the security chain and if you have another lock use that one, too,' and

---

53 Compare with Gill's study of the Bolivian military (Gill, 2000).

'Women and young ladies should avoid drying their underwear in visible places and should not wear scanty clothing on balconies or in front of windows, in case a sex maniac is watching.' Fear-mongering of this sort represents yet another kind of structural violence, one generated by the neoliberal state and exploited by private firms that have arisen in its absence.

Conclusion

Neoliberal violence, including physical violence produced by the military, police personnel, private security guards, and lynch mobs, and the structural violence of poverty and insecurity, are all grounded in the reforms of the neoliberal state and the cultural logic of privatization, flexibility, and self-help that accompanies them. The Bolivian state's response to the lynching phenomenon is a further indication of this relationship. Even as it has formally denounced lynching as a threat to democratic society, the Bolivian state (in keeping with its broad neoliberal stance celebrating individual enterprise as an alternative to state involvement) has acted to encourage private and citizen's groups to further adopt responsibility for justice administration. For example, just a few weeks prior to his forced resignation in 2003, President Sanchez de Lozada responded to increasingly strident calls for improved 'citizen security' in Bolivia by announcing a plan (never implemented) to create 'anti-crime gangs' (*pandillas anticrimen*) in various Bolivian cities. These gangs, officially known as 'youth citizen security brigades' (*brigadas juveniles de seguridad ciudadana*), would have consisted of young people who would patrol certain zones of the city, confronting other, criminal youth gangs and somehow preventing them from committing crimes. Decried by critics and human rights defenders as unleashing 'a new war against society',[54] the president's proposal was steeped in the logic of the liberal citizen, in which 'good' people would act independently and without state supervision to deter 'bad' people from committing antisocial acts. This same logic

54 G. Conte, 'Bolivia y sus "pandillas anticrimen": Una nueva forma de guerra contra la sociedad,' *Desarme.org*. La Paz, Bolivia 2003.

DANIEL M. GOLDSTEIN

provides the foundation for the lynch mob, whose members view themselves as filling in for the absent state, pursuing '*delincuentes*' and '*malhechores*' who prey on the good people of society. Lost in this good/bad distinction is the fact that *delincuentes* and *linchadores* (lynch-mob participants) alike are poor people of indigenous origin, engaged in an escalating cycle of violence whose end is not currently in sight. The state's embrace of this logic amounts to an endorsement of vigilantism as a mode of securing justice, which likewise requires no state supervision or state financing to execute.

Neoliberalism, like the classical liberalism from which it is descended, has at its base a claim to promote individual freedom, a promise to liberate the individual from the inherently oppressive power of government.[55] The authors of 20th-century liberal capitalism, economists like F.A. Hayek and Milton Friedman,[56] believed that only by restricting the state's involvement in economic planning and management could the state's coercive power be effectively limited. Economic regulation, in this view, imposes constraints on the basic liberty of the individual (said to be the cornerstone of Western civilization), thus requiring the separation of the economic from the political to create a freer and more democratic society. At the same time as it mandates the state's withdrawal from the national economy, however, liberalism assumes that the state will provide the broader social and civic institutions within which capitalism can function unfettered and individual liberty can be attained. This task includes the establishment and maintenance of democratic rule of law, to create a safe and stable society within which capital markets can flourish and individual potential can be achieved. Key to the entire system is respect for individual rights and freedoms: according to liberalism's proponents, by granting rights to individuals, and by respecting popular sovereignty and maintaining the rule of law to guarantee these rights, the state recognizes human dignity and promotes individual

55 Anderson, 1992.
56 Hayek, 1944; Friedman, 1962.

liberty.[57] In the name of such noble ideals, neoliberalism has become the dominant paradigm of 21st-century global political economy.

But the contradiction between liberalism's promise and its reality in Bolivia is manifest in the lives of people living under its domin- ion. Like police officers who at once condemn and sympathize with lynching violence in the *barrios* of Cochabamba, ordinary citizens demonstrate a contradictory consciousness when facing the insecu- rity of daily life in a neoliberal democracy. As the protests by mem- bers of the so-called 'popular classes' in both the Water War and the Gas War clearly indicate (and as the 2005 election of Evo Morales as Bolivian president underscores), people in Bolivia recognize that their poverty has its roots in transnational capitalism, and that the forces of privatization and the open market have had negative im- pacts on their employment opportunities, standard of living, and access to basic services. Protestors who reject the privatization and expropriation of natural resources are articulating a critique of global political economy that accurately perceives the role of transnational forces in restructuring Bolivian social life, forces that are ultimately responsible for their diminishing economic and personal security.

As I have suggested in this chapter, however, at the same time as they stridently and publicly reject neoliberalism, in their communi- ties ordinary Bolivians have adopted practices that clearly express and enact neoliberal rationality. The same cultural logic of individual responsibility, flexibility, and self-help that informs both Bolivian labour policy and the state's approach to justice administration has pervaded civil society and its base communities, whose members privatize justice when the state refuses to treat it as a public good. This is the double-sided nature of what I have identified as neolib- eral violence. Not merely an expression of the state's commitment to protecting and defending the interests of capital, neoliberal violence is also structural violence, an inherent component of the neoliberal project and its associated cultural values, which underlie the general condition of insecurity that is both cause and result of popular vio-

---

57 Fukuyama, 1992.

DANIEL M. GOLDSTEIN

lence. The Gas War nakedly revealed the Bolivian state's fundamental disregard for the rights of individuals when they challenge the state's neoliberal schemes; the insecurity of daily life is a less visible, though equally destructive, form of violence, and as a source of social disarticulation it precipitates other forms of violence in their turn.

※

Aiyer, A. 'Hemispheric Solutions? Neoliberal Crisis, Criminality and "Democracy" in the Americas', *Urban Anthropology and Studies of Cultural Systems and World Economic Development* Summer-Fall, 2001, pp. 239-52.

Anderson, P. *A Zone of Engagement*, London, 1992.

Arbona, J.M. *Restructuring the Informal Economy: the State and the Promotion of Micro-enterprises in Bolivia*, n.d.

Auyero, J. 'The Hyper-shantytown: Neo-liberal Violence(s) in the Argentine Slum', *Ethnography* 1(1), 2000, pp. 93-116.

Beck, U. *Risk Society: Towards a New Modernity*, London, 1992.

Benería, L. 'The Foreign Debt Crisis and the Social Cost of Adjustment in Latin America', in *Emergences: Women's Struggles for Livelihood in Latin America*, J. Friedmann, R. Abers and L. Autler (eds), Los Angeles, 1996, pp. 11-27.

Bulmer-Thomas, V. *The New Economic Model in Latin America and its Impact on Income Distribution and Poverty*, London, 1996.

Burrell, J. 'Intimate Violence: After lynching in Todos Santos Cuchumatán.' Paper presented at the 101st annual meeting of the American Anthropological Association, New Orleans, 21 November 2002.

Caldeira, T.P.R. *City of Walls: Crime, Segregation, and Citizenship in São Paulo*, Berkeley, 2000.

Castillo Claudett, E. 'La justicia en tiempos de la ira: Linchamientos populares urbanos en América Latina', *Ecuador Debate* 51, 2000, pp. 207-26.

Chossudovsky, M. *The Globalization of Poverty: Impacts of IMF and World Bank Reforms*, London, 1997.

Colloredo-Mansfeld, R. '"Dirty Indians", Radical *Indígenas*, and the Political Economy of Social Difference in Modern Ecuador', *Bulletin of Latin American Research* 17(2), 1998, pp. 185-205.

Dammert, L. and M.F.T. Malone 'Fear of Crime or Fear of Life? Public Insecurities in Chile', *Bulletin of Latin American Research* 22(1), 2003, pp. 79-101.

Davis, D.E. 'Law Enforcement in Mexico City: Not yet under Control', *NACLA Report on the Americas* 37(2), 2003, pp. 17-24.

Douglas, M. *Purity and Danger: an Analysis of Concepts of Pollution and Taboo*, London, 1966.

Elbert, C.A. 'Ideología, corrupción y excesos policiales', *Pena y Estado: Revista Latinoamericana de Política Criminal* 3(3), 1998, pp. 63-80.

Farthing, L. and B. Kohl. 'Bolivia's New Wave of Protest', *NACLA Report on the Americas* 34(5), 2001, pp. 8-11.

Finnegan, W. 'Leasing the Rain', *The New Yorker*, 2002.

Friedman, M. *Capitalism and Freedom*, Chicago, 1962.

Frühling, H. 'Police Reform and the Process of Democratization', in *Crime and Violence in Latin America: Citizen Security, Democracy, and the State*, H. Frühling, J.S. Tulchin and H.A. Golding (eds), Washington, 2003, pp. 15-44.

Fuentes Díaz, A. and L. Binford. 'Linchamientos en Mexico: Una respuesta a Carlos Vilas', *Bajo el Volcán* 2(3), 2001, pp. 143-56.

Fukuyama, F. *The End of History and the Last Man*, New York, 1992.

García Linera, A. *Reproletarización: Nueva clase obrera y desarollo del capital industrial en Bolivia (1952-1998)*, La Paz, 1999.

Garland, D. *The Culture of Control: Crime and Social Order in Contemporary Society*, Chicago, 2001.

Giddens, A. *The Consequences of Modernity*, Cambridge, 1990.

Gill, L. *Teetering on the Rim: Global Restructuring, Daily Life, and the Armed Retreat of the Bolivian State*, New York, 2000.

Godoy, A.S. 'Lynchings and the Democratization of Terror in Postwar Guatemala: Implications for Human Rights', *Human Rights Quarterly* 24(3), 2002, pp. 640-61.

—— *Popular Injustice: Violence, Community and the Law in Latin America*. Stanford, 2006.

Goldstein, D.M. '"In our own Hands": Lynching, Justice, and the Law in Bolivia', *American Ethnologist* 30(1), 2003, pp. 22-43.

—— *The Spectacular City: Violence and Performance in Urban Bolivia*, Durham and London, 2004.

Guerrero, A. 'Los linchamientos en las comunidades indígenas: ¿La política perversa de una modernidad marginal?' *Ecuador Debate* 53, 2001, pp. 197-226.

Gwynne, R.N. and C. Kay. 'Views from the Periphery: Futures of Neoliberalism in Latin America', *Third World Quarterly* 21(1), 2000, pp. 141-56.

Harvey, D. *The Condition of Postmodernity: an Enquiry into the Origins of Cultural Change*, Oxford, 1990.

—— 'Flexibility—Threat or Opportunity', *Socialist Review* 21(1), 1991, pp. 65-77.

—— *Spaces of Capital: towards a Critical Geography*, Edinburgh, 2001.

Hayek, F.A. *The Road to Serfdom*, Chicago, 1944.

ILO. *Women and Men in the Informal Economy: A Statistical Picture*, Geneva, 2002.

Inda, J.X. 'A Flexible World: Capitalism, Citizenship, and Postnational Zones', *PoLAR: Political and Legal Anthropology Review* 23(1), 2000, pp. 86-102.

Kohl, B. 'Stabilizing Neoliberalism in Bolivia: Popular Participation and Privatization', *Political Geography* 21(4), 2002, pp. 449-72.

—— 'Restructuring Citizenship in Bolivia: El Plan de Todos', *International Journal of Urban and Regional Research* 27(2), 2003, pp. 337-51.

—— 'Privatization Bolivian Style: a Cautionary Tale', *International Journal of Urban and Regional Research* 28(4), 2004, pp. 893-908.

Krueger, A.O. 'The Political Economy of the Rent Seeking Society', *American Economic Review* 64(June), 1974, pp. 291-303.

Lustig, N. *Coping with Austerity: Poverty and Inequality in Latin America*, Washington, DC, 1995.

Medeiros, C. 'Civilizing the Popular? The Law of Popular Participation and the Design of a New Civil Society in 1990s Bolivia', *Critique of Anthropology* 21(4), 2001, pp. 401-25.

Méndez, J.E., G.A. O'Donnell and P.S. Pinheiro (eds). *The (un)Rule of Law and the Underprivileged in Latin America*, Notre Dame, 1999.

Merry, S.E. *Urban Danger: Life in a Neighborhood of Strangers*, Philadelphia, 1981.

Ong, A. *Flexible Citizenship: The Cultural Logics of Transnationality*, Durham and London, 1999.

Pereira, A.W. and D.E. Davis. 'New Patterns of Militarized Violence and Coercion in the Americas - Introduction', *Latin American Perspectives* 27(2), 2000, pp. 3-17.

Petras, J. and H. Veltmeyer. 'Latin America at the End of the Millennium', *Monthly Review* 51(3), 1999, pp. 31-52.

Postero, N. 'Bolivia's Indígena Citizen: Multiculturalism in a Neoliberal Age.' Paper presented at the Meeting of the Latin American Studies Association, Miami, Florida, 2000.

Radcliffe, S.A. and S. Westwood. *Remaking the Nation: Place, Identity and Politics in Latin America*, London, 1996.

Rhyne, E. *Mainstreaming Microfinance: How Lending to the Poor Began, Grew, and Came of Age in Bolivia*, Bloomfield, CT, 2001.

Rotker, S. and K. Goldman (eds). *Citizens of Fear: Urban Violence in Latin America*, New Brunswick, NJ, 2002.

Schneider, C. and P.E. Amar. 'The Rise of Crime, Disorder and Authoritarian Policing: An Introductory Essay', *NACLA Report on the Americas* 37(2), 2003, pp. 12-16.

Solares Serrano, H. *Movimientos Urbanos en Cochabamba*, Cochabamba, Bolivia, 1986.

Speed, S. and A. Reyes. '"In our own Defense": Rights and Resistance in Chiapas', *PoLAR: Political and Legal Anthropology Review* 25(1), 2002, pp. 69-89.

Ungar, M. *Elusive Reform: Democracy and the Rule of Law in Latin America*, Boulder, CO, 2002.

—— 'Contested Battlefields: Policing in Caracas and La Paz', *NACLA Report on the Americas* 37(2), 2003, pp. 30-36.

Vilas, C.M. '(In)justicia por mano propia: Linchamientos en el México contemporáneo', *Revista Mexicana de Sociología* 63(1), 2001, pp. 131-60.

Weismantel, M.J. *Cholas and Pishtacos: Stories of Race and Sex in the Andes*, Chicago, 2001.

Williams, R. *Marxism and Literature*, Oxford, 1977.

11

PRIVATE SECURITY AND PUBLIC INSECURITY:

OUTSOURCED VIGILANTISM IN MODERN RUSSIA

Mark Galeotti

Fourteen years after its dissolution, the KGB has returned to Russia. The initials which once stood for the Committee of State Security (*Komitet gosudarstvennoi bezopasnosti*) now mean Civil Security Complex (*Kompleks grazhdanskoi bezopasnosti*), a volunteer militia acting as both a neighbourhood watch service and, according to reports, a dispenser of summary, vigilante justice.[1] Likewise in 2005, when the inhabitants of a village outside Nizhny Novgorod caught a gang of burglars, instead of turning them over to the police, they kept them in a jerry-built cage, subjecting them to regular beatings.[2]

Today's Russia is in the midst of a number of often contradictory processes: the centre's bid to assert its right and ability to govern; the consolidation of a new elite, drawn largely from the old, and defined by access to one or more of three key resources (money, political power, coercion); and a fragmentation of effective political authority and national identity. One manifestation of this crisis is the multiplication of the state's coercive forces such as new paramilitary police forces, local security units and ministerial guard forces.[3] This has been accompanied by the rise of a private security industry which ranges from well-trained and professional branches of international compa-

---

1 *AFP news service*, 10 Oct. 2005.

2 *The Scotsman*, 29 July 2005.

3 For more on this see Galeotti, 1997b.

267

nies through to the paramilitary arms of extremist political groups.[4] In the main cities of Russia, private security is ever-present, from the camouflage-fatigued armed guards at banks and shops to the pervasive network of commercial intelligence and counter-intelligence operatives. Generally better paid and equipped than the regular security apparatus, they are also widely regarded as more efficient.

At the same time there is an extensive underground market in security and coercion, largely supplied by the Russian *mafiya* (Russians use the word, and it is rendered here in transliterated form to distinguish it from its Italian counterpart).[5] Organized crime has thrived, and while no longer operating so overtly as in the 'Wild 90s' when drive-by-shootings and car-bombings were almost commonplace, it is nonetheless ubiquitous and powerful.

The rise of the private security industry and its companion phenomenon, the spread of the *mafiya*, is both cause and symptom of a continuing crisis of the post-Soviet Russian state. Hence, this is not simply to decry the police's failings or to note an interesting aspect of the marketization of modern Russia. The ability to protect its citizens' lives, rights, and property, and a direct or indirect monopoly over coercion, are central to the modern state.[6] Indeed, despite the best efforts of the Soviet and now the Russian state, a tradition of turning to separate, informal channels for security, punishment and restitution has not been eliminated so much as given new form. To

---

4 For a general studies of the Russia security industry, see 'Russia: Private Security', *Oxford Analytica East European Daily Brief*, 15 Aug. 1995; Galeotti, 1997a; Varese, 2001 pp.59-68; Volkov, 2002 pp.134-54.

5 Diego Gambetta has written cogently on the role of mafias as non-state providers of protection, and this thesis has been applied to Russia by Federico Varese (Gambetta, 1993; Varese, 2001). Vadim Volkov has also explored the 'violent entrepreneurs' who use their capacity to wield organized force for profit (Volkov, 2002 p.27). For general English-language overviews of the Russian *mafiya*, see the contributions in Galeotti, 2002.

6 A direct monopoly exists when only the state's own agents may use force. In the case of an indirect monopoly, others, such as private guards, may also use force, but only as and when the state allows them to, and always subject to the state's authority

be glib, where once a Russian might take the law into his own hands or those of his community, he now outsources the job to professionals. This is often in preference to the state, which is regarded as just one more provider in a crowded security and enforcement market, and an often ineffective and uncompetitive one at that.

Vigilantism past

Russia is heir to a long and strong tradition of vigilantism, above all the widespread rural culture of *samosud*, 'self-judging'.[7] While often characterized as lynch law, this was a surprisingly complex and consistent way of maintaining order and mainstream cultural values within the pre-revolutionary peasant commune and deterring crimes from without. Its foundations were built on an assessment of harm and a show of restitution. Crimes which damaged the commune's coherence and chances of survival were punished most severely, but in most cases the aim was to create a settlement which not only left the victim satisfied and potential future criminals deterred but also avoided depriving the community of a worker. Thus, punishment was often through humiliation and restitution, returning stolen goods or providing other compensation, a shaming charivari through the village and then the purchase of vodka for the village elders and victim to cement the perpetrator's reintegration into the community. Outsiders, on the other hand, were of no long-term value to the community, could be punished without fear of alienating their family and friends, and needed to be deterred. As a result they were typically treated rather more brutally, with the most violent punishments being reserved for arsonists and horse thieves.[8] A horse, for example, represented a source of muscle-power, more horses and, eventually, meat to eat and bone and sinew to use. In the marginal life of a Russian village, the loss of one could have a catastrophic impact. Thus

7 For key studies of *samosud*, see Frank, 1999, and Frierson, 1987.
8 See Frierson, 1997, pp. 115-18; Worobec, 1987.

horse thieves were almost always killed, their bodies left at a nearby crossroads as a warning to others.

The Tsarist state had little understanding of or sympathy for *samosud*, regarding it as arbitrary mob violence. This attitude was compounded by exasperation with a peasant moral economy that saw nothing wrong with poaching from crown forests (they felt that the Tsar had enough trees to spare them some firewood) yet unleashed violent punishment on those who perpetrated other crimes. However, there was little it could practically do, not least because its relatively small police forces were concentrated in the cities. In the countryside, the balance of local coercion often lay with the village or the gentry instead. A typical local constable would have a 'beat' of up to 1,800 square miles to patrol, with only the help of a few half-trained auxiliaries.[9] The local landowner, by contrast, might have a dozen Cossacks and other armed retainers at his beck and call. Within a few days or a week, the constable's appeal for help could have a unit from a local army garrison in the area, but for immediate assistance he had to work with rather than against local interests. The result was that the agents of the state were often forced to participate in or accede to the separate (and often contradictory) vigilante practices of the landowners or the peasant communities. Even after the Emancipation of the Serfs in 1861, the new courts were generally dominated by the gentry at the top and the traditional village elders at the bottom, so that little changed in practice. If anything, the dying years of the Tsarist order saw 'popular vigilantism [grow] to fill the vacuum left by waning institutional controls.'[10]

The police were more heavily represented within the cities, but different modes of vigilantism were still evident there. Those with money or political power maintained their own protectors, not least in the *dvorniki* (doormen) of apartment blocks, often used as thuggish enforcers rather than mere guardians of property.[11] Meanwhile,

---

9 Weissman, 1985, p. 49.

10 Burds, 1998, p.206.

11 Neuberger, 1993, pp. 50-1.

rapid urbanization in the late nineteenth century brought about an influx of impoverished peasants, often coming to the city on a seasonal basis. Their squalid, overcrowded and dangerous slums were dangerous and difficult to police, and most Tsarist officials chose not to bother.[12] In the slums, what 'justice' there was, and it was little, was often meted out by vigilante gangs who transferred the peasant *samosud* to new conditions.[13] The broken bodies of thieves and murderers were left in the streets or heaved into a convenient river. Even in more law-abiding areas, vigilantism was widely seen as an acceptable, even necessary, response to police weakness and incompetence. For example, in the midst of social unrest and so-called 'hooliganism' in 1905-6, workers in St Petersburg organised neighbourhood watches, with the blessing of the city council.[14]

Vigilantism and Bolshevism

For all its rhetoric, the Bolshevik state soon abandoned any faith in the moral economies of its workers and peasants. *Samosud* was suppressed, especially after a number of incidents in which Bolshevik agitators had been lynched by conservative villagers.[15] Over time, and especially with Stalin's collectivization campaign, the countryside was brought more firmly into the grip of the state. In the mid-1920s, peasant unease about a perceived leniency shown by the courts led to a resurgence of rural vigilantism,[16] but although incidents persisted, by the 1930s the distinctive phenomenon of *samosud* appeared quashed.

Nonetheless, Russians have proven to have an extraordinary ability to distort or evade the will of their state in their own interests, and

---

12 Brower, 1990, pp. 193-6.

13 Eklof and Frank, 1990, pp. 95-6.

14 Neuberger, 1993, pp. 92-3.

15 See, for example, Kuromiya, 1998, p. 86.

16 This finding from Jeremy Smith's research into secret police documents (1922-29) is reported at: http://www.esrcsocietytoday.ac.uk/ESRCInfoCentre/Plain_English_Summaries/econ_performance_and_development/economic_growth/index260.aspx

arguably *samosud* and other forms of non-state protection and enforcement persisted throughout the Soviet era. The increased power and ubiquity of the new order meant that these phenomena had to manifest themselves covertly, within the formal organs and practices of the state. After all, the imposition of a Party monopoly over coercion and protection in theory proved only too pliable in fact. Arguably, the new elite dispensed with the Cossacks and personal retainers of the tsarist nobility only to replace them with state-sanctioned and -funded counterparts. Certainly, there were numerous instances in which such officers' loyalties were clearly to their patrons rather than to the impersonal forces of state and law. This was not just a personal but also an institutional process, as a wide range of security agencies emerged which reported to local managers and authorities and were responsible for protecting industrial enterprises, collective farms and ministries. While it was beyond the resources of an ordinary citizen to maintain his or her own private enforcers, they could in effect hire them. Private security as such was banned until the 1980s, but the endemic corruption of the Soviet police was notorious and meant that immunity and protection were both for sale.[17]

This was not always a matter of personal venality. In the chaotic years of the 1920s and 1930s, when virtual civil war was raging across the Russian countryside, rural officials often took it upon themselves to dispense arbitrary justice, sometimes with the sanction, or at the request, of the local community.[18] In this respect, they replaced the elders of the pre-revolutionary commune in managing *samosud*. In the cities of the post-war era, 'Comrades' Courts' allowed housing communities to fine, shame and admonish those of their number causing a nuisance or distress.[19] The community acquired even greater opportunities for self-policing through subversion of the

---

17 Officers who refused to accept bribes were sometimes punished by group or individual vigilantism for this failure to honour the mainstream social contract! (Chalidze, 1977, p. 105).

18 Fitzpatrick, 1994, p. 236.

19 Gorlizki, 1998.

institution of 'district inspectors.' These officers lived in and policed the sprawling housing estates. The intention was to improve policing by embedding officers within the community, but in practice they found themselves having to balance their institutional responsibilities with the practical consideration that those they were policing were also their neighbours. Instead of being the state's eyes and ears in the community, they tended to favour community loyalties. Under constant pressure to keep reported crime figures low, many would deal with petty crimes committed by locals informally. Sometimes, this involved simple restitution, or the so-called *kulachnoe pravo*, the 'law of the fist'. This philosophy, usually endorsed by the community, was captured by a retired police officer who reminisced, 'Send a boy to prison and he comes back a thief; give him a few smacks with a truncheon, though, and he becomes a man.'[20] Outsiders caught committing crimes in the estate, however, were dealt with harshly and typically also saddled with sundry other unsolved local offences.[21] In short, the district inspectors reproduced the moral economy embedded within *samosud*, and in return could expect favours and gifts along with a degree of local cooperation when dealing with crimes which transgressed the generally-accepted norms.[22]

On one level, these phenomena are common to any society. Even the most disciplined and dutiful police force will shelter some corrupt officers, just as those who are rich, powerful and well-connected can arrange matters to their own advantage. However, the extent to which this was institutionalized in the USSR would have a significant impact on developments after the collapse of the Soviet state in 1991.

---

20 Personal conversation, 2004.

21 This is based on discussions with serving and retired Russian police officers, through the 1990s.

22 Much the same happened with the *druzhiny*, volunteer police auxiliaries, who often placed loyalty to their community over the abstract demands of the law and interests of the state (Favarel-Garrigues and Huérou, 2004, p. 15).

Rival providers: the private security industry and the mafiya

One of the basic features of the modern state is its monopoly over legal coercion and, by extension, its ability to use this to provide an acceptable minimum level of protection to individuals and society as a whole. In Russia today, few believe that the state can do this.[23] With the authorities perceived to be unable to provide an adequate level of protection, many turned instead to private providers. The police became just one more competitor in a rich and complex market which emerged in protection and coercion, and which was fuelled by the commonplace use of violence to take over businesses and eliminate potential rivals in the 'wild 90s'. Furthermore, in the light of the inability of the court system to provide quick, effective and reliable redress, alternative methods of resolving disputes and recovering debts became a necessity. Bodyguards and the other trappings of private security became an integral part of Russian business culture, and by 2004 this had become a $2 billion industry, which is growing at a rate of 40 per cent annually.[24]

As Russians have looked elsewhere for their protection, the private security industry has expanded. The economic liberalization introduced by Gorbachev in the late 1980s, especially the new opportunities to create cooperatives and small businesses, led to the rise of a private security industry, albeit initially on a very small scale.[25] Many of the first non-state but also non-*mafiya* security businesses were founded by Afghan war veterans.[26] Indeed, most of the first private security providers were 'voluntary associations' which also included martial arts clubs, Cossack revivalists and even the Young Communist League. Most of these firms are business organizations now, but others, such as the Cossack associations, are arms of political groups

---

23 For a useful analysis of businesspeople's attitudes, see Radaev, 2000.

24 *Moscow Times*, 7 February 2005.

25 *Izvestiya*, 17 September 1990.

26 *Pobratim* (newspaper of the SVA, the Union of Veterans of Afghanistan), 10 (1991); *Krasnaya zvezda*, 9 Aug. 1991; Galeotti, 1995 p.61; *Christian Science Monitor*, 12 Oct. 2000.

formed either to raise funds or to provide a pretext for maintaining paramilitary forces.[27] Cossacks, whose culture has become associated with extreme nationalism, racism, an intolerance of alternate life-styles and rough-and-ready summary justice, have been recruited by, amongst others, Moscow's mayor to patrol some of the city's railway stations and market places.[28]

More pernicious still has been the rise of organized crime as a competitive force within this marketplace. While Russia has been heir to a long tradition of organized criminality, from the horse thief gangs of the nineteenth-century countryside to the heavily-tattooed 'thieves within code'[29] who lorded it over Stalin's Gulag prison camps, this was largely kept controlled by a state unwilling to accept any overt challenges to its authority. From being the weakest partner in an unholy trinity along with black-market entrepreneurs and corrupt Party bosses, they benefited greatly from the Soviet collapse and instead emerged as a ruthless, powerful and increasingly autonomous force.

Organized crime has penetrated deeply into the legal economy. While many criminal gangs are purely parasitic, only offering 'protection' against the threat they themselves represent, others will actively extend protection—a 'roof' (*krysha*) in Russian jargon—against tangible threats from criminals as well as the less obvious problems caused by excessive red tape, competitors and the like. The quest is thus not so much to avoid paying protection money so much as to find reliable and effective criminal protectors; as explored by Varese and others, a 'good' *krysha* is considered a much more honest, efficient and market-responsive form of protection than the state.[30]

---

27 These groups also include the neo-fascist Russian National Unity organisation (RNE), whose commercial activities are seen by many as little more than a front to allow them the right to acquire weapons. See Jackson, 1999.

28 *Nezavisimaya gazeta - Nezavisimoe voennoe obozrenie* supplement, 8-14 Feb. 1997; Grau, 1993 and updated version http://fmso.leavenworth.army. mil/documents/cossack/cossack.htm; Robert Parsons, 'Cossack revival gathers momentum', *RFE/RL*, 5 May 2005.

29 *Vory v zakone*, literally 'thieves within the law'.

30 Varese, 2001. See also Gradosel'skaia, 2000.

The state as private provider

In Russia, serving law-enforcement officers are openly available for hire. While it is not unknown in the West for commercial enterprises to sponsor or support their local police, often in return for privileged treatment, it is a question of degree. How far do controls exist to ensure the primacy of the police's role as an arm of the state and society? Most police commands include a department known as the Extra-Departmental Guard (VO—*Vnevedomstvennaya okhrana*) precisely to offer such services. In some cases, this is provided by regular police attached to the unit (and thus not available for 'proper' police work), in others by officers in effect moonlighting on their own time, but on behalf of their employer. Other agencies also market such services, from army garrisons to border troops.

This further blurs the boundaries between private and public, and ensures that the best security goes to the highest bidder. It takes officers away from their primary duties at a time when the police are already under strength. One study in St Petersburg found that of all mobile police patrols in the city during business hours, half of them were actually earmarked for the VO. As a result, emergency calls from businesses protected by private security firms with contracts with the VO were answered on average in 65 per cent of the time it took police to reach the unfortunate others.[31] More significant have been the questions raised about how this affects the professionalism and priorities of the police, especially in the light of certain high-profile embarrassments. In 1996, for example, a corruption scandal broke in Moscow over the security arrangements of a Russian-German joint venture called *Malkom*. Its facilities were guarded by a heavily-armed police unit specially formed for the purpose. When questions were raised as to the propriety of spending public funds maintaining such a unit, it was transferred to the VO. This meant that the unit could continue to flout the restrictions on weapons even though the po-

---

31 Internal St Petersburg Main Internal Affairs Directorate Report, January 1999.

lice unit was attached to *Malkom* full-time. The local elite rallied round *Malkom*, which also subsidized a local school and allegedly provided generous gifts to grandees including the region's police chief.[32] Similarly, when Vasili 'Naum' Naumov, alleged head of the *Koptevskaya* gang, was murdered in January 1997, it emerged that his 19 bodyguards were all members of *Saturn*, an elite police commando team.[33] While initial press speculation concentrated on juicy tales of undercover operations or *mafiya* corruption of the police, the truth was more prosaic: he had simply hired them through the VO.[34] One senior officer subsequently commented, 'I didn't know whether to be more embarrassed that our boys had been hired to protect a *mafiya* boss or that they had failed.'[35]

Vigilantism and out-sourced security

How this proliferation of providers of violence, threat and security connects with vigilantism is a remaining puzzle. Vigilantism essentially springs from two associated problems. The first is a refusal by citizens to rely exclusively on the agents of the state to meet their needs for protection and justice; this protection may be from overt threats, such as violence or a failure to meet contractual obligations, or from perceived social threats. The second requirement is that the state, or elements within it, is either unable or unwilling to prevent vigilante actions. It may be that it regards them as a useful exercise in extralegal coercion, a convenient exercise in scapegoating, a release of building pressures, or it may simply share the vigilantes' beliefs. Alternatively, the state may lack the resources to prevent vigilantism, or at least to be able to do so without diverting efforts from higher priorities.

---

32 *Rossiiskaya gazeta*, 22 June 1996.
33 *Kommersant-daily*, 13 March 1997.
34 *International Herald Tribune*, 14 May 1997.
35 Personal conversation, April 1997.

The traditional model of the vigilante is the individual or the group taking the law into their own hands, delivering what they consider justice to those who transgress social boundaries. *Samosud* was an unusually institutionalized form but one which nonetheless very clearly fitted this pattern. However, where do the (self-)righteous passions fuelling vigilantism go when the state is, on the one hand, sufficiently organized and brutal to crack down on overt displays of extrajudicial violence, but on the other, professing ideals and priorities at odds with the moral economy of the masses, or else unable to provide the security they require?

The answer would appear to be that the vigilante impulse becomes sublimated into new and often more pernicious compounds. Russia has always had a market economy. Behind the drab uniformity of the Soviet planned system thrived a bustling underground economy in goods and favours, one which at once both subverted and supported the official economy. Everything was for sale, from goods to jobs, and justice was no exception. This helps to explain the degree of corruption within the modern Russian police and judiciary but also the way that the same vigilantism is now so commonly 'outsourced' to specialists. Outsourcing is easier, safer and more cost-effective. There is still scope for the old-fashioned vigilante, whether the 'lone wolf' or the group, though these are more likely to be acting out personal pathologies than being the enforcers of collective morality. Rather, and more generally, vigilantism takes place through institutions and private providers of coercion. Many of the cultural bases which contribute to the vigilante mindset are still strong in Russia, even if their roots can be traced back through centuries of Tsarist authoritarianism and decades of Soviet misrule.

There are three main reasons why contemporary vigilantism in Russia is legitimized. First, a fragmenting social dynamic demands that Russian citizens and corporations respond to disorder by looking beyond the law and the state. Secondly, these activities are a direct response to documented mistrust of the authorities' abilities or intentions. And thirdly, they are legitimated against a background of widespread support for violent self-defence, summary justice and capital punishment.

Beyond the law: kinship and community

As Vladimir Shlapentokh has observed, 'in contemporary Russia, as well as in medieval Europe, personal relationships are often more important than relationships based on the formal roles in political, social and economic structures.'[36] This applies equally well to protection—whether from crime, breaches in contracts or even arbitrary and predatory treatment from officials themselves. Time and again, the institutions of the new Russia have proved wanting. The overall result is a fragmentation of society into smaller units—regions, ethnic groups, companies, townships, families. These are often in direct competition and as a result seek to guarantee their own security as a symbol of their political autonomy. When the police or other agencies of the state can do so effectively, then they will turn to them. However, there is a wide range of other mechanisms and agencies available to meet this demand when they cannot. Ordinary Russians may look to their personal and community resources: fitting new locks on apartment doors, for example, learning martial arts for self-defence or organizing mutual watch groups. In Omsk, for example, Favarel-Garrigues and Le Huéron found the local tyre factory encouraging its workers and plant security officers to operate as unofficial local vigilante groups by night.[37] Those with the resources or inclination may go further, hiring the private security firms or illegal providers of security.

Major public figures and organizations are no longer content to rely on the state. While most Western companies have some kind of security arm, in Russia this can literally mean private armies. The gas monopoly Gazprom, for example, has extremely close links with the government (indeed, its chairman, Dmitri Medvedev, was also head

---

36 Shlapentokh, 1996, p. 66.
37 Favarel-Garrigues and Huérou, 2004, p. 18.

of Putin's presidential administration from 2003 and was appointed First Deputy Prime Minister in 2005). This means that a Federal Security Service team is attached to its Security Service, just as FAPSI, the government communications security agency, was known to advise it.[38] This is clearly not enough: it also maintains a force of anything between 10,000 and 20,000 security officers.[39] Even government agencies, ministries and public figures have sought to establish their own, autonomous security agencies. These not only ensure the protection of their principals and their families, but engage in lobbying, gathering information on potential rivals and even launching smear campaigns against them.[40] Likewise, given that President Putin's centralizing impulses have blocked attempts to create locally-accountable police forces, many city and regional authorities have hired or established private security forces as substitutes. There is clearly a deeply-rooted malaise not only in the state's legitimacy but its very ability to assert its authority. 'Violent entrepreneurship' is more than just an alternative form of economic organization, implicitly it is also laying down the rules for the most primal questions of who has effective power and social authority.

Mistrusting authorities' abilities and intentions

Almost a decade and a half since the collapse of the Soviet regime, most Russians still mistrust and fear the police. Successive opinion polls show low levels of trust in the police, sometimes as low as 4 per cent,[41] while a series of surveys conducted by Yakov Gilinsky found almost three quarters of crimes going unreported; the most common

---

38 *Nezavisimaya gazeta*, 6 Feb. 1997.

39 *Nezavisimaya gazeta*, 6 Feb. 1997 gives the 20,000 figure; 10,500 security staff was given in a 1995 report. 'Russia's mafia: no problem too big', http://www.msnbc.com/news/127833.asp.

40 For example, Aleksandr Korzhakov, Boris Yeltsin's security chief, makes it clear that a central part of his work was digging up *kompromat*, compromising materials, on his principal's rivals (Korzhakov, 1997).

41 *MosNews*, 3 Oct. 2005.

reason for this was that 'nothing would be done'.[42] The extent to which crimes are under-reported or dealt with by alternative means of retribution and restitution is an important index of the community's assessment of the authorities' value as protectors. The authorities may be seen as efficient but hostile, which means that the penalties in attracting their attention outweigh the benefits, or else that they would be unwilling to devote their resources to addressing the citizen's needs. This is often the case for marginalized communities with special reasons to fear the authorities. Alternatively, the authorities may be considered incompetent or otherwise unable to carry out their duties. In Russia, both views appear prevalent.

If anything, the state is often regarded as predator rather than protector. This was perhaps best exemplified by the paramilitary Tax Police, which operated between 1993 and 2004. They were funded through a 'bounty' system: the government only covered a fraction of their operating costs, and otherwise they had to rely on a cut of 10 per cent from the revenues they collected.[43] An unfortunate side-effect was a tendency to operate as extortionists. The Tax Police would raid a firm and threaten a complete audit (which, given the complex and often contradictory nature of the tax code, would almost certainly uncover some misdemeanour).[44] Faced with the disruption and costs of an audit, the firm would often admit some spurious tax liability to end the raid.[45] On one level an innovative experiment in raising tax which brought vitally-needed revenue into state coffers, this practice relied on the tactics of the racketeer, and was seen as such by many Russians.

---

42 Gilinsky, 2005, p. 339.

43 *Argumenty i fakty*, no. 25, 1998.

44 'Russia: Tax Policing', *Oxford Analytica East Europe Daily Brief*, 18 Aug. 1998.

45 Based on an unscientific trawl of such cases in Moscow in 1999-2000, there seemed to be an unofficial benchmark figure that the Tax Police expected to be bought off for about 5 per cent of the firm's annual profit.

If the state itself begins to move into moral equivalency with organized crime, its only saving grace will be if it is *better*. All states ultimately acquire authority and legitimacy because they can offer a competitive, reliable and effective 'roof' for their citizens, whether expressed in the form of police on the streets or of welfare provisions to protect against unemployment or ill-health. However, if the state is perceived as a fairly uncompetitive supplier in a competitive market for security, then it has lost an essential attribute of statehood.

Thus, corruption and the acquisition of a criminal *krysha* become rational and even legitimate business decisions. To take an example drawn from personal consultancy experience, it became increasingly clear to one European firm operating in Moscow that its security agency was padding invoices; an audit revealed that substantial sums were being drawn in cash for unexplained purposes. When confronted, the Russian private security firm freely admitted that it was paying off a powerful local gang. It presented this as the best option, as the payments were far cheaper than the costs of upgrading the firm's security to meet the gang's threat or bribing the local police to deal with it.[46]

Supporting violent self-defence, summary justice and capital punishment

In general, Russian culture is still marked by impatience with the legal niceties of due process and law, over swift and summary justice. The distinction between the two is even embodied in its language. There are, for example, two fundamental words for crime: *prestuplenie*, the technical term, which implies a breach of the law as defined by the state, and *zlodeyanie*, often translated inelegantly as 'wickedness', meaning a transgression of the mainstream moral economy which may, or may not, also mean breaking the law. Likewise, in his insightful study of the wider lessons in Russian crime fiction,

---

46 Details have been removed to maintain commercial confidentiality, but this took place in 1995.

Anthony Olcott observes 'one of the fundamental tensions of the *detektiv* genre, that between *zakon*, or "law", and *spravedlivost*, which usually is translated as "justice" but which etymologically might better be rendered as "righteousness".'[47]

This tension is evident in the high level of support for summary and capital justice, which often informs public policy. Many legislators even advocate public gun ownership because the state cannot protect its citizens.[48] In 2002, for example, the State Duma passed amendments to the Criminal Code substantially expanding the citizen's rights in self-defence, up to and including the use of deadly force. This was a popular move, but was passed disregarding the concerns of the police.[49] Likewise, although President Yeltsin introduced a moratorium on the death penalty in 1997, in order to comply with the requirements of the Council of Europe, there is little evidence that this represents a general and genuine abandonment of Russia's traditional enthusiasm for state killing. His successor Putin has, for example, sanctioned the assassination of Chechen rebels abroad and boasted that rebels not laying down their arms would be 'wiped out, even in the outhouses.' In this, he has considerable levels of public support: in 2003, the State Duma passed a non-binding resolution to abandon the moratorium by 266 votes to 85, and in 2005, 65 per cent of Russians polled supported the resumption of the death penalty.[50]

---

47 Olcott, 2001, p. 96.

48 For example Anatoly Luychenko, a Parliamentary aide and one of the drafters of the 1997 Law on Weapons, admitted a direct connection: 'There was no need to own guns before, because under the Soviet Union there was virtually no crime. The situation has changed radically. The state absolutely cannot provide for the protection of its people.' *Austin American-Statesman*, 17 November 1997.

49 *Pravda*, 8 February 2002.

50 *BBC News*, 15 Feb. 2002; *MosNews*, 6 July 2005. In fairness, the 65 per cent figure is unexpectedly high—in a similar poll in 2004, 42 per cent backed the death penalty for terrorists (*Pravda*, 21 Feb. 2004), but even so this demonstrates significant public support for judicial execution. For a wider exploration of Russian attitudes see Mikhlin, 1998.

Indeed, the runaway success of the violent films *Brat* ('Brother') and *Brat-2*, whose hero turns vigilante when his brother is threatened by criminals and his friend is killed by the American mafia, as well as the popularity of the ultra-violent crime-fighting novels known as *boyeviki* ('fighters'), attest to a strong constituency in support of summary retribution.[51] On a less gratuitous level, the film *Okraina* ('Outskirts') follows a peasant community as they track down the corrupt officials who sold their farm to an oil firm, beating and torturing their oppressors on the way. Many of the accolades it received were not so much for its artistic merits as for the moral of the tale.[52]

However, it is important to appreciate that this is not simply a matter of personal and state security. Russians retain in the main a belief that the defence of their interests ought to be a responsibility of the state. It is simply that, with the state unable or unwilling to do the job, they need to look for alternatives. Nor is this simply a matter of punishment. For example, the city of Yekaterinburg, one of the most thoroughly criminalized in Russia, gave birth to the 'City without Drugs' movement, which advocates beating dealers and imprisoning addicts in makeshift lockups to force them through 'cold turkey'.[53]

The new vigilantism

Nonetheless, overt vigilantism is rare in modern Russia. The explanation appears to be that Russians have come to understand that they can still punish those they feel deserve it and secure their own lives, property and interests outside the state system, without putting themselves directly in harm's way. Russians make cost-benefit analyses of whether it is worth turning to the authorities in a variety of situations. Where the structures of the state appear useful, effective and in

---

51 The *boyeviki* genre emerged in the 1990s, and is represented by violent 'heroes' more than adequately described by their nicknames, such as 'Savage'.

52 *New York Times*, 2 April 2004.

53 *Chicago Tribune*, 23 Apr. 2000; *Sunday Times*, 17 June 2001; Wolfe and Malinowska-Sempruch, 2004 p.43.

tune with their own moral economy, they will use them to the fullest. Indeed, one of the key 'administrative resources' in today's Russia is precisely the ability, through financial support, personal connections or political clout, to induce and empower the legitimate law-enforcement authorities to provide protection. This operates at every level, from the individual turning to a friend on the police force to talk to a noisy neighbour to the corporation calling on the commisioner to warn off *mafiya* racketeers. Conversely, Russians appear to have few qualms in turning to other 'violent entrepreneurs'. This assumption of personal and collective responsibility for protecting their interests and values is, ultimately, the essence of vigilantism. In this respect, Russians are simply 'outsourcing' expressions of a vigilante impulse that was once expressed by direct personal or community action.

What is different about contemporary vigilantism is that it has lost much of its social and redemptive character. It is dominated by threat and violence, with few counterparts to the charivaris of *samosud* (beyond quite widely-held views that drug-dealers and addicts deserve public humiliation).[54] This is because the very concept of 'community' in modern Russia has fragmented. Gone are the old small, closed social worlds, which placed a premium on maintaining long-term connections and members of the community. Now, Russians live in overlapping and fluid communities each in turn competing and interacting with numerous others. Thus, vigilantism is now not about reintegration, but prevention, deterrence and retribution.

It is also about direct individual and community interest. Beyond the hate crimes of a minority of bigots, modern vigilantism is not generally directed against any perceived outsider community or moral transgressors, as once it was against Jews, radicals, homosexuals and the like. The closest has been the persecution of Chechens and others from the Caucasus following such high-profile terrorist incidents as the 2002 Moscow theatre siege. However, this is at least in part because, with Chechens now attacking civilian targets (including a school, a theatre and a hospital), there was a generalized

---

54 Ibid., pp. 42-43.

sense of threat—Russians were not persecuting a community enemy so much as one they thought might strike at them personally. By the same token there has not emerged any counterpart to the Latin American *justiceiros* ('justice makers'), moonlighting police officers who murder criminals who appear untouchable by the law, primarily out of a sense of cleansing society rather than because the victims have threatened them or their allies' interests.[55]

In their foreword to *Vigilante Politics*, Rosenbaum and Sederberg raised a key question: 'Are new types of vigilantism likely to evolve?'[56] Russia's situation makes it clear that they are. There are countries and situations in which it will still erupt in its traditional forms, the lone avenger or angry lynch mob delivering summary 'justice' to those seen to have defied popular morality. However, the same impulses and processes can also take new and more subtle forms. Sharp and Wilson's imaginative study of the extent to which a private security operation in the British town of Doncaster plumbed the vigilante impulse has demonstrated that this is not a uniquely Eurasian matter.[57] However, the richness of its vigilante tradition and the failure of its state institutions mean that Russia offers a particularly vivid example of the new 'outsourced vigilantism', and of the way that the vigilante impulse can clothe itself in the agencies and institutions of contemporary life.

✦

Brower, D.R. *The Russian City between Tradition and Modernity, 1850-1900*, Berkeley, 1990.

Burds, J. *Peasant Dreams and Market Politics: Labor Migration and the Russian Village, 1861-1905*, Pittsburgh, 1998.

Chalidze, V.I. *Criminal Russia: Essays on Crime in the Soviet Union*, New York, 1977.

---

55 Huggins, 1991, p. 4.

56 Rosenbaum and Sederberg, 1976, p. 29.

57 Sharp and Wilson, 2000.

Eklof, B. and S. Frank (eds), *The World of the Russian Peasant: Post-emancipation Culture and Society*, Winchester, 1990.

Favarel-Garrigues, G. and A.L. Huérou. 'State and the Multilateralization of Policing in Post-Soviet Russia', *Policing & Society* 14(1), 2004, pp. 13-30.

Fitzpatrick, S. *Stalin's Peasants: Resistance and Survival in the Russian Village after Collectivization*, Oxford, 1994.

Frank, S. *Crime, Cultural Conflict, and Justice in Rural Russia, 1856-1914*, Berkeley, Calif.; London, 1999.

Frierson, C. 'Crime and Punishment in the Russian Village—Rural Concepts of Criminality at the End of the 19th Century', *Slavic Review* 46(1), 1987, pp. 55-69.

—— 'Of Red Roosters, Revenge and the Search for Justice: Rural Arson in European Russia in the Late Imperial Era', in *Reforming Justice in Russia, 1864-1996: Power, Culture, and the Limits of Legal Order*, P.H. Solomon (ed.), Armonk, 1997, pp. 115-18.

Galeotti, M. *Afghanistan: the Soviet Union's last War*, London, 1995.

—— 'Boom Time for the Russian "Protectors"', *Jane's Intelligence Review*, 9 (8), 1997a.

—— 'Policing Russia', *Jane's Intelligence Review*, Special report No. 15, 1997b.

—— (ed.). *Russian and post-Soviet Organised Crime*, London, 2002.

Gambetta, D. *The Sicilian Mafia: the Business of Private Protection*, London, 1993.

Gilinsky, Y. 'Police and the Community in Russia', *Police Practice & Research* 6(4), 2005, pp. 331-46.

Gorlizki, Y. 'De-legalization in Russia: Soviet Comrades Courts in Retrospect', *American Journal of Comparative Law* 46(3), 1998, pp. 403-26.

Gradosel'skaia, G. 'Tenevoe nalogooblozhenie v legal'noi ekonomike (po materialam issledovaniya v Moskve i Volgograde)', in *Konkurentsiya za nalogoplatel'shchika: Issledovaniya po fiskal'noi sotsiologii*, Moscow, 2000, pp. 49-58.

Grau, L. 'The Cossack Brotherhood Reborn', *Low Intensity Conflict & Law Enforcement* 2(3), 1993.

Huggins, M.K. (ed.). *Vigilantism and the State in Modern Latin America: Essays on Extralegal Violence*, New York, 1991.

Jackson, W.D. 'Fascism, Vigilantism, and the State—The Russian National Unity movement', *Problems of Post-Communism* 46(1), 1999, pp. 34-42.

Korzhakov, A. *Boris El'tsin: ot rassveta do zakata*, Moscow, 1997.

Kuromiya, H. *Freedom and Terror in the Donbas: a Ukrainian-Russian Borderland, 1870s-1990s*, Cambridge, 1998.

Mikhlin, A.S. *The Death Penalty in Russia*, New York, 1998.

Neuberger, J. *Hooliganism: Crime, Culture, and Power in St. Petersburg, 1900-1914*, Berkeley, 1993.

Olcott, A. *Russian Pulp: the "Detektiv" and the Russian Way of Crime*, Oxford, 2001.

Radaev, V. 'Corruption and Violence in Russian Business in the Late 90s', in *Economic Crime in Russia*, A.V. Ledeneva and M. Kurkchiyan (eds), Berlin, 2000, pp. 63-82.

Rosenbaum, H. and P. Sederberg (eds.). *Vigilante Politics*, Philadelphia, 1976.

Sharp, D. and D. Wilson. '"Household Security": Private Policing and Vigilantism in Doncaster', *Howard Journal of Criminal Justice* 39(2), 2000, pp. 113-25.

Shlapentokh, V. 'Russia: Privatization and Illegalization of Social and Political Life', *The Washington Quarterly* 19(1), 1996, pp. 65-85.

Varese, F. *The Russian Mafia: Private Protection in a New Market Economy*, Oxford, 2001.

Volkov, V. *Violent Entrepreneurs: the Use of Force in the Making of Russian Capitalism*, Ithaca, NY, 2002.

Weissman, N. 'Regular Police in Tsarist Russia, 1900-1914', *Russian Review* 44(1), 1985, pp. 45-68.

Wolfe, D. and K. Malinowska-Sempruch. *Illicit Drug Policies and the Global HIV Epidemic: effects of UN and National Government Approaches*, New York, 2004.

Worobec, C. 'Horsethieves and Peasant Justice in Post-Emancipation Russia', *Journal of Social History* 21(2), 1987, pp. 281-93.

I2
MARKETS OF PROTECTION: THE MAOIST
COMMUNIST CENTRE AND THE STATE
IN JHARKHAND, INDIA.[1]

Alpa Shah

Introduction

When Jharkhand separated from Bihar within the Indian Union in
2000 one cause for hope reiterated by many was that decentralization
of the state would strengthen the fight against the terrorism of growing left-wing extremism. After a violent outbreak against landlords
by a tribal peasantry who forcibly occupied land, burned records and
cancelled old debts in 1967 in Naxalbari, West Bengal, this so called
extremism caught the imagination of many people internationally
as the Naxalite movement—an armed peasant and worker uprising
against landlords and capitalists, inspired by Marx, Lenin and Mao

1 I have worked in Jharkhand since January 1999. The ESRC Postdoctoral
Fellowship and Postgraduate Research Studentship supported much of my
fieldwork and writing. Thanks to participants in workshops where earlier drafts
were presented: a joint workshop of the Goldsmiths College Anthropology
Department and the LSE Development Studies Centre and a Global Vigilante
Workshop at the University of Sussex. This paper also appears in Kelly and Shah,
forthcoming, thanks are due to *Critique of Anthropology* and Sage publications
for permission to reprint here. Special thanks to Chris Fuller, Rob Higham,
Toby Kelly, Jonathan Parry and David Pratten for comments on earlier drafts.
Most of all I am grateful to the people of Bero, whose names I cannot reveal, for
the insights they have given me into their lives.

Tse-tung.[2] Since 1967, official histories show the movement to have declined and factionalised along ideological, organizational and geographical lines.[3] But after 1984, when the Yadav caste supporters of one branch, the Maoist Communist Centre (MCC), brutally killed 42 Rajputs in the Aurangabad and Gaya districts, Bihar state banned the Naxalites and they increasingly became identified as an extremist or terrorist problem. The Naxalite goal was seen as the creation of a liberated territory from Nepal to Andhra Pradesh, and in the late nineties Jharkhand became a crucial territorial link.

The MCC itself declared that its protest in Jharkhand was against 'bourgeois state oppression' and for the tribal poor, with an overall goal of forming a parallel administration in a 'liberated zone'. In this region the MCC would disable interference from the state. Indeed, between January 2001 and February 2002, the major MCC strikes in Jharkhand were against the police.[4]

In 2001, within a few months of taking power, the new Bharatya Janata Party (BJP)-led Jharkhand government declared extremism or terrorism as its major inherited problem and launched an 'Operation' against it. It proclaimed 10 of its 22 districts as terrorist infested 'red' zones and legitimized a large budgetary allocation for police 'modernization', acquisition of Border Security Forces, Central Reserve Police, Para Military Forces and the creation of armed camps in 'red' areas. The agenda appeared to be in line with the BJP-led central government in New Delhi which in December 2001, feeding off global anxiety after September 11th, sharpened its terrorism crack-down

---

2 The early Naxalites acknowledged their inspiration from the Chinese revolution and the first Naxalite party, the Communist Party of India (Marxist-Leninist) (CPI(ML)) had Chinese approval. For brief histories see Banerjee, 1980 and Singh, 1995.

3 For summaries on the emergence of different branches of the Naxalite Movement in Bihar see Bhatia, 2000, pp. 46-63; in Andhra Pradesh see Sinha, 1989, and for Maoists in Nepal see Gellner, 2002.

4 Police reports claim that 74 police lives were lost (cf *Hindustan Times*, Ranchi, p. 2. 1 November 2001).

by introducing the controversial Prevention of Terrorism Ordinance, soon after made into a Parliamentary Act (POTA).

Under POTA the MCC and other main Naxalite factions in Jharkhand, the Party Unity faction and the Peoples War Group, were identified as terrorists. By March 2004, according to the Union Home Ministry, Jharkhand saw the largest number of arrests under POTA. From the formation of the new state, 234 people were arrested, more than 650 people had cases pending against them and more than 3,200 people were named as involved in terrorist activities. Naxalism was increasingly defined not only as a major law-and-order problem but also a 'national security' issue creating 'red' terror in the country.

Establishing the Naxalites as terrorists, the Jharkhand state juxtaposed the alleged rationality and legitimacy of its government to the irrationality and violence of the 'extremists', claiming to combat the threat of a dark age of chaotic Hobbesian violence taking over its vulnerable rural tribal heartlands. The 'final solution' called for an increase in state security in the name of protection of its citizens.

Abrams suggests that the state is a triumph of concealment, to be approached as the reification of an idea that masks real power relations by legitimizing them under the guise of public interest.[5] In light of the recent American and British 'war against terror' fought in the name of 'protecting' the West from terrorist threats, Abrams' call to demystify the idea of the state, to understand how that idea works, seems still pertinent. One way of exploring this idea—to support Taussig's suggestion of writing back against terror—is to look behind the mask that protects a state by hiding its own violence, thereby questioning the boundary between the state and the terrorist.[6]

Leach was among the first anthropologists critically to consider the continuity between the state and the 'terrorist', pointing out that history provides striking examples of how the 'legitimate' actions of the state become the criminal acts of the 'enemy': the deviant

---

5 Abrams, 1988, p. 82.
6 Taussig, 1986, p. 4.

characteristics of the hero [the state] and the criminal [terrorist] are essentially the same.[7] Others have since argued that 'the major form of terrorism in the world today is that practised by states and their agents and allies'.[8] In Northern Ireland, the direct input of the British military in the sectarian campaign against the Catholics is exposed.[9] While in Latin America, attention is drawn to death squads appearing in states receiving military assistance from the US,[10] and to how the Venezuelan state constructs a drama against alleged subversives in order to re-enact its own civilizing myths.[11]

In this chapter I question the boundaries between the 'terrorist' extreme-left armed guerrilla Maoist Communist Centre (MCC) and the local state in Jharkhand, eastern India. I question the received wisdom that the MCC is a poor people's movement against the state. I show not only that the MCC's spread in rural Jharkhand is dependent on a rural elite intimately connected with the state but also that, on occasion, it is used by and worked in collaboration with state officials. But continuities in people are not the only basis for focusing on the similarities between the MCC and the local state. As representatives of the state had previously done, the MCC sells protection in return for support.

This protection is, as Tilly famously argues, an ambiguous commodity, calling up 'images of shelter against danger provided by a powerful friend' or evoking 'the racket in which a local strong man forces merchants to pay tribute in order to avoid damage—damage the strong man himself threatens to deliver'.[12] Showing state makers as entrepreneurs selling protection, Tilly crucially points out that, 'if protection rackets represent organised crime at its smoothest, then war making and state making—quintessential protection rackets

---

7 Leach, 1977, p. 27.
8 Sluka, 2000, p. 1.
9 Ibid.
10 Chomsky and Herman, 1979.
11 Coronil and Skurski, 1991.
12 Tilly, 1985, p. 170.

with the advantage of legitimacy—qualify as our largest examples of organised crime'.[13] Terrorism, banditry, piracy, gangland rivalry and state making all belong on the same continuum selling protection. In Jharkhand, the MCC is selling protection both for access to the informal economy of the state and for security against the threat of its own violence.

As Gambetta explains of the Sicilian mafia, the commodity with which the MCC has been most closely associated is protection.[14] The MCC grassroots support is not based on a shared ideology, nor on violence alone, but on having greater control over what can be termed a *market of protection*. In selling protection, the MCC competes in a market previously controlled by parts of the local state. This chapter shows that in Jharkhand violence becomes deployed in selling protection to bargain for power and material benefits, and as such extends Elwert's concept of 'markets of violence'.[15] Unveiling this market of protection is thus central to an exploration of the boundaries between the state and its alleged enemies, the terrorists, in rural Jharkhand.

Drawing attention to the continuities between the state and the terrorist, the ethnography of the MCC allows commentary on Abrahams' ideal types of vigilantes, mafiosi, guerrillas and resistance movements. Abrahams argues that the mafia trades protection for business and is, unlike vigilantes, primarily concerned with economic profit making for itself and does not necessarily get involved in a substitute law and order maintenance system as vigilantes do.[16] As this chapter shows, in rural Jharkhand, the MCC appears both like the mafia (as its spread is dependent on control over a market of protection for supporters to profit from access to the informal economy of the state) and like the vigilante (in that it gets involved in local

---

13 Ibid., p. 169.

14 Gambetta, 1993. Gambetta's important work deconstructs the popular stereotype of the mafia as mere criminals.

15 Elwert, 1999.

16 Abrahams, 1998 pp. 164-9.

dispute resolution). Abrahams also argues that ideal types of guerrilla and revolutionary movements, unlike vigilantes, typically engage in covert organized resistance against an 'occupying power'. While this is true to some extent of the MCC, as this chapter shows, in addition to such attacks, the MCC also establishes itself through classic vigilante activity of the resolution of local disputes, although this is not usually crime control. Is the MCC then state, terrorist, vigilante, mafia or a revolutionary movement? It seems that the MCC's successful spread is partly dependent on the flexibility with which it is able to appear as all of these ideal forms in different ways at different points and to different people.

A party of the poor?

My stories begin in Tapu village, Bero Block, Ranchi District, Jharkhand.[17] An hour's walk from the administrative and market town of Bero, about 50 kilometres from Jharkhand's capital Ranchi, Tapu's 550 people live in mud houses without electricity or running water. Government census statistics show the area to have a Scheduled Tribe population of about 60 per cent with non-tribals forming the rest. However, given the persistent problems of defining people as tribal,[18] a more useful socio-economic distinction in the area is between an economic and political elite and a poorer tribal peasantry. The elite consists mainly of descendants of ex-*zamindari* (landlord) families, who are usually higher caste Hindus, though some are of middle caste and Scheduled Tribe origin. They own sufficient land to grow a market surplus, hire farm labour, often run small businesses, and are generally educated. The tribal peasants, in contrast, are mostly illiterate and earn their livelihood from agriculture and hard manual labour. The majority of villagers are the ex-tenant de-

17 Tapu, like most names of people and some places, is a pseudonym. India's State administration divides federal states into districts which are in turn divided into several blocks consisting of many villages—Bero Block had 114 villages.

18 For a short critical review of tribals being considered a radically distinct group see Corbridge, 2000.

scendants of *zamindars* and mainly fall into the Indian government categories of Scheduled Tribes, and some Scheduled Castes, as well as other lower castes.

Just before I arrived to live there in November 2000 the MCC had massacred nine people in a nearby village and the areas to the immediate west of Bero Block were said to be Naxalite strongholds. The organization wanted to expand further east and it did not take much imagination to see that the forest around Tapu was attractive. I began reconstructing the mode of this expansion through personal narratives such as that of one of my closest friends, Shiv Ahir, and his friend Khand Oraon. Although Shiv was not a *zamindar* descendant, the tenant descendants I lived with regarded him like the *zamindars* because he shared their Yadav caste, was educated and made a good living from farming. Khand owned a line-hotel, a food and night stop, in Bero.

In the midst of wedding celebrations in February 2001, Khand arrived at Shiv's house with three strangers and a few bottles of rum. After several shots, the men revealed their identity, saying they need-ed a good worker like Shiv to build an MCC base in Tapu, introduce the movement and eventually hold meetings and solve village disputes.[19] Shiv was informed that the MCC expanded in the following way. Men like Khand, who knew the local terrain, became MCC in-formers. They introduced the MCC to strategically selected people, like Shiv, who would share their knowledge of the geographical and social structure of a village and welcome them to live in their houses whilst an MCC base was established in the forest. If the police came, the villagers would disguise the MCC as 'guests'.

Subsequently, the MCC introduced itself to the villagers and gained their support through the 'resolution' of village disputes in 'people's courts'. While there was some history of local disputes reso-lution by local leaders in both inter- and intra-village courts (called the *parha*) that had been revived in the 1960s by the Congress party

---

19 Later, two of the three men became identified as Chandra and Anil Ganjhu —a surname given by the Maharajah to families who became *zamindars*.

Member of Legislative Assembly (MLA) and then in the 1990s by the Jharkhand Mukti Morcha (JMM) MLA, it was clear that MCC involvement in dispute resolution also entailed the creation or careful manipulation of pre-existing village tensions that might not otherwise have become disputes and that MCC men would adjudicate the courts. If dispute resolution did not enable greater MCC dominance, it was clear that the MCC would resort to more coercive means to bring the village under its control. When all the villagers had come under the fold of the MCC, a few youths would be recruited for MCC bases in other places to be trained and armed as members of 'squads' that form their underground red guerrilla army. Those who had helped the MCC gain access to the village could be sent to neighbouring areas as Area Commanders, to spread the organization further. And so, in this network fashion, the organization planned and implemented expansion.

As Shiv recounted these plans, it became evident that this MCC expansion challenged at least one conventional notion of the socio-economic basis of its grassroots support. For the central Bihar region Bhatia has argued that 'for the first time, on a sustained basis, after 1947 the poor can turn to their [Naxalite comrades] in the time of injustice and know that there is somebody who will stand up for them against oppressive and exploitative forces, whether it be upper castes-classes or the state.'[20] More recently, Stuart Corbridge has described the new state's failure to pay attention to its tribal communities as accompanying a 'rising tide of Naxalism', and argues that this is no coincidence—that turning to the Naxalites represents a more reasonable choice for poor tribal people given their opposition to the state (2002: 56, 69).[21] This perspective leads Corbridge and Harriss to argue that, 'In this Hobbesian world the empowerment of the poor and the poorest is often in defiance of the state and its officers.'[22] Moreover, drawing on Bhatia, they attribute the MCC's

20 Bhatia, 2000, p. 79.
21 Corbridge, 2002, pp. 56, 69.
22 Corbridge and Harriss, 2000, p. 206.

success to its ability to contest 'the power of established politician-contractor groupings,' represented by others too as the first target of elimination for the MCC.[23] The new BJP Jharkhand government also attributes the Naxal problem to its poor rural populations who know no better than to join, implying that these are undeveloped masses it inherited from the failed modernizing mission of the last government. Whether Jharkhand State, MCC or academic, the conventional rhetoric reproduced is that the MCC's main support base is the rural poor and that it is aligned against the local elites who are intimately connected with the state.

While this received wisdom may ring true for central Bihar or for the later spread of the MCC, the evidence from the Bero area shows that the MCC's initial grassroots support in Jharkhand is not among the poorest population but among an already established rural elite. Shiv, Khand and their friends were educated men from the wealthiest village families which included both heirs of an older elite status from a *zamindari* lineage and a newer, educated (and often Scheduled Tribe) elite. The majority of villagers, such as the families I lived with in Tapu, are descendants of ex-tenants of the landlords. During my fieldwork the poorest villagers had not heard about the MCC, and those that had believed the organization only existed elsewhere. Indeed, when I pushed my Tapu family and relatives on who the MCC might be, most had the ambiguous idea that it was a group that moved around committing violence. With parallels to their desire to keep away from what they consider a dangerous and alien state, they wanted no involvement with this foreign group and certainly had no idea that the MCC had come to their village.[24]

---

23 Ibid. See also Bhatia, 1988 and *Frontline*, 24 May 2002, p. 39.

24 Shah, 2007. There are no doubt similarities with 'revolutionary' movements in other parts of the world—some have argued that peasants in the Peruvian Maoist insurgency of the Shining Path were only won by imposition as the movement was one of intellectuals and disillusioned, educated young people (Degregori quoted in Bourque and Warren, 1989, p. 19; Starn, 1999; Stern, 1998).

ALPA SHAH

The village problems resolved by the MCC, including pre-marital sex, adultery and alcohol consumption, further reflect the movement's bias towards a rural elite. This is evident for instance in the MCC reprimanding those involved in pre- and post-marital sexual affairs. Of the five cases that the MCC resolved in nearby 'captured' villages, three concerned such affairs, each of which resulted in the accused lover being beaten. Whilst such affairs are common amongst both the rural elite and the poorer peasantry, their moral policing among the poor is of concern to an elite who sought to reproduce a purer image of a less sexually promiscuous tribal population.[25] A bias towards a rural elite is also evident in the MCC's campaign against alcohol consumption. Following the pasting of anti-drinking posters on Bero buildings in 2000, uniformed MCC men broke the pots of tribal peasants who were selling village-brewed rice beer and alcohol distilled from the *mahua* flower in markets west of Tapu.

There are several points to note about this campaign. The first is that the attacks on local brews do not threaten sellers of elite status, the *zamindar* descendants, who sell the 'English' variety of alcohol, whisky, rum, gin and beer, in their line-hotels or shops. The second is that while drinking home-made brew is a part of poor village peasant market and ritual culture where men and women of different generations openly drink together, village elites have Sanskritized and Brahminicized and therefore claim the higher caste values that alcohol consumption is morally wrong and ritually impure. In practice, of course, although the MCC bans alcohol consumption, a central part of its networking with the village elite is drinking and meat-eating sessions behind curtains. On these occasions, 'English' alcohol is preferred, as local brews are considered distasteful. The third point is that, like the reprimanding of post-marital and pre-marital sexual affairs, this anti-drinking campaign had been promoted by the political party JMM—Jharkhand Mukti Morcha or Jharkhand Liberation Front—in earlier years: a point to which I will return.

---

25 Shah, 2006.

MCC propaganda maintains that the Naxalites are a 'people's movement' of the poor and exploited, and that their struggle focuses on land redistribution, better terms for sharecroppers, minimum wages, access to common property resources, basic social rights, respect for lower castes, and effective policing of criminal gangs.[26]At least in this part of Jharkhand in the initial stages, however, there is little commitment to the movement's ideological underpinnings among MCC supporters. Comparatively, a deviation from revolutionary socialist ideologies within the Naxalite movement is not so surprising. Stoll, for instance, argues that when people joined the revolutionary movement in Ixil in Guatemala that did not mean that they took the revolution's ideological message to heart.[27] And with the recent resurgence of the Naxalites too, it is recognized that it is unusual for grassroots supporters to understand their mobilization in terms of a Marxist-Leninist vision of armed struggle by peasants and labourers against landlords and capitalists.[28] For the elite, however, the Jharkhand evidence suggests that MCC supporters embrace an alternative vision of modernity and morality in which their superiority is reinforced over the rural peasantry who are to be sexually and socially disciplined. This vision promotes a higher caste notion of better citizenship, which, while not always practised by the elite themselves, is nevertheless repressive towards tribal peasants.

Two roads: contracts, corruption and protection

Beyond their own elevation within this social hierarchy, however, there are other more pressing motives for village elite support for the MCC. The abolition of *zamindari* in the early fifties meant that these elites, who faced a gradual impoverishment, increasingly attempted to sustain their lifestyles by accessing state-related resources directly (for example through government jobs) or indirectly (for instance

---

26 Bhatia, 2000.

27 Stoll, 1993.

28 Dalit critics of the Naxalite movement have accused it of being *'Brahminwadi'* (Bhatia, 2000 p.162).

through government contracts). They maintained (in the case of the *zamindar* descendants) or created (in the case of the newer elite) their position by cultivating extensive links with the state. They became entrepreneurs who maintained their financial position relative to the tribal peasantry in large part because of their participation in the informal economy of state schemes. As a result of their intimate connections to state officials they were particularly effective in siphoning off money from the state.

The expansion of the MCC is intimately linked to the politics of access to this economy of state patronage. In return for their co-operation in harbouring and fostering the movement, recruits in areas under MCC control are offered privileged and protected access to state resources. Hence, when the MCC arrived in Tapu, it promised Shiv contracts from the Block Development Office (BDO) schemes of the Ministry of Rural Development. Most BDO schemes involve infrastructural construction projects such as roads, dams and community buildings which require a villager to act as the contractor. The funds for these projects are paid in the form of cheques addressed directly to the contractors, who are assumed to siphon off up-to 10 per cent of the total project money for themselves. For those attempting to diversify their incomes the stakes of becoming a contractor are very high.

BDO contracts are, however, limited in number and competition is fierce. To obtain a contract, one needs a 'source', a powerful person who has leverage over state officers sanctioning contracts. Moreover, one needs supporters who will both threaten competitors and offer protection. In effect the MCC guaranteed Shiv a contract and the subsequent protection to siphon off illicit money from state schemes. Thus the MCC entered a pre-existing market to sell protection, engaging in activities that were already established in the area. In his study of Santhali involvement in the Midnapore Naxalite uprising, Duyker argues that the movement was successful in areas where people had already participated in local mass-movements.[29] Indeed,

---

29 Duyker, 1987, p. 104.

the Bero scenario shows that the MCC's expansion pattern reflects a pre-existing history of people who were connected by their participation in the earlier campaigns of the JMM.

These continuities are illustrated in Shiv's story. Shiv met Khand in the early nineties when Khand led the Bero branch of a more militant wing of the JMM. Then, Shiv was frustrated that, despite his college education, there seemed little prospect of a better life other than that offered by Tapu's mud huts. For several years Shiv had delivered some of his buffalo milk to Akshay Roy's line-hotel in Bero. Akshay, a descendent of neighbouring village *zamindars*, was Khand's brother-in-law. He was also known as the 'right-hand man' of Vishwanath Bhagat, an Oraon tribe man, who had been the Bero Block JMM president and candidate in 1995 for election as Member of Legislative Assembly (MLA) to the State legislature.[30] Through Akshay, Shiv became involved in Vishwanath's election campaign. While there were other reasons, Shiv was primarily attracted to the JMM cause by the promise that if Vishwanath was elected his workers and supporters would receive contracts to implement BDO schemes.[31]

Vishwanath held considerable leverage over the distribution of BDO resources by the head of the office, the Block Development Officer, because as MLA he could influence the officer's transfer to a new post every three years.[32] To secure his own transfer, the officer in turn maintained a good relationship with the local MLA by, for example, awarding construction projects to the MLA's workers. Knowing that not every MLA candidate's promises would be kept, and despite competition from the ex-*zamindar* elite of Tapu, Shiv felt he would secure a contract because of his long relationship with

---

30 India is a federal union. The Vidhan Sabhas are directly elected bodies for the administration of the government in the states. MLAs are elected to the Vidhan Sabha at five-year intervals from constituencies that are single-member and territorial with the population in each constituency being more or less the same.

31 Shah, November 2005.

32 Robert Wade's model of the corruption-transfer mechanism outlines how this dependency works in Andhra Pradesh (Wade, 1985).

Akshay. In 1996, following Vishwanath's election success, Shiv did obtain Tapu's first BDO contract to build a track to the village. In order to acquire the contract Shiv received support from Akshay, Khand and Vishwanath who protected him in various ways from the growing attentions of the *zamindar* descendant faction. For instance, when one night a group of men from the *zamindar* lineages, armed with axes, knives and sticks, woke Shiv throwing a clay pot full of their urine and faeces at his door, Shiv scared them away by flashing a gun that Khand had given him. More generally, it became known that Shiv was supported by Vishwanath and his workers who, backed by state officials, had the reputation of beating up those who came in their way, and whom Tapu *ex-zamindars* feared. Hence, as MLA Vishwanath offered protection to his supporters, including aspiring entrepreneurs like Shiv, in order to glean illicit resources from the local state. On the one hand he offered protection from competing entrepreneurs, and on the other hand, by having leverage over, and colluding with local state officials who were also implicated in the corruption, Vishwanath shielded Shiv and his other supporters from the scrunity and sanctions of the state apparatus.

When the MCC came to Tapu, it marketed a very similar kind of protection to that which Vishwanath had offered his workers in the past. To Shiv, the MCC became one among other actors, such as the MLAs and certain state officers, who protected entrepreneurs to access illicit state resources. In fact, as the MCC gained greater support in the area, the boundaries between the local state and the MCC became ever more porous as state officers themselves sought MCC protection. By cultivating a web of associations with each other the MCC and the state enjoy a degree of interdependency which is demonstrated by a second story.

As Shiv was being introduced to the MCC in 2001, and about five years after he had built the dirt road to Tapu, Vishwanath, whose MLA days were over, lodged a proposal to the Ministry of Rural Development to build another road between two villages neighbouring Tapu. Being a large project, the road involved substantial commissions. When the road was given the go-ahead, the Ranchi District Commissioner ordered a block official, not a villager, to be the scheme's contractor. The BDO did not tell Vishwanath that the project had been given the go-ahead, and meanwhile selected his favoured block official, Khasi, as the contractor. The BDO feared that if Vishwanath knew of the go-ahead, he would impose his preferred block official and the money from the scheme would go into Vishwanath's pockets, rather than his own. The BDO appointed Khasi because he had a reputation for being feeble and could easily be manipulated.

In order to ensure that the work was completed, the BDO also asked for the involvement of a man named Bhavesh. Although he could easily have been mistaken for one, Bhavesh was not a state official. He was reputed to be an excellent engineer and knew the local terrain so well that, in exchange for an illicit cut, Block officers relied on him to complete large projects: Bhavesh was an unofficial engineer for almost all large Block Office schemes.

One day a Block Office clerk leaked to Vishwanath the news that the road agent had been appointed. No longer having powers over the BDO as his MLA days were over, Vishwanath called Khasi to his house, told him to take his fixed percentage, but said that Vishwanath would construct the road. Khasi and the BDO turned to Bhavesh for assistance as he had MCC contacts in Bharno, west of Bero. Bhavesh asked the MCC to protect Khasi in exchange for 5 per cent of the total price of the road. The MCC, in any case wanting to expand in the concerned area, agreed. A few days later Vishwanath and Akshay were called to Bharno and threatened. Scared of the MCC, they backed off and Khasi began the work on the road. The story of the second road project illustrates a number of points of connection and interdependence between the state and the MCC. First, the state officers bought protection from the MCC to exploit state resources.[33] Khasi and the official from the BDO called on the

---

33 The mafia in Southern Italy operates within a similar set of relationships with state officials and politicians (Gambetta, 1993).

MCC for protection from a rival claim being made by the former elected representative (Vishwanath) to ensure that they would make illicit profits from the construction of a state project. Second, the threat of violence towards contending contract bidders was a familiar strategy that as MLA Vishwanath had himself employed in the past. In this way, by guaranteeing contract awards through violence and intimidation the MCC assumed a familiar position once played by state officials.

What made entrepreneurs and state officials alike turn to the MCC rather than the likes of Vishwanath? Let us return to Shiv's story and, in particular, to what happened after the MCC's visit.

Selling protection: the role of fear

After he was approached in 2001 Shiv neither agreed nor disagreed to help the MCC. Building the 1996 track had been life-threatening as the *zamindar* descendants had threatened to kill him, and Shiv now wanted to stick to income from his cattle and his fields. However, he realized that evading them would not be easy and decided to maintain a marginal position as a silent observer, hoping to acquire enough information to know when to avoid them. As the year passed and more men like Akshay were wining and dining the MCC, Khand and the others pressurised Shiv to specify a day for an MCC Tapu visit. Shiv spent days with relatives in other villages and when in Tapu feigned illness while his father delivered the milk. Away from Bero, he could avoid Khand and Chandra. However, in February 2002, they caught up with him and insisted that in ten days, eight men would come for a night picnic. Shiv immediately left Jharkhand on a three-day journey to Maharashtra to escape and work in a factory.

Two years later when I returned to Tapu, Akshay and Khand's brother both reported that Shiv had recently visited his family but returned to Maharashtra. I was surprised then when I spotted Shiv in the Bero market. His grandmother's death and brother's separation from the joint family meant he now had to stay in Tapu. He had been there two months but was keeping a 'low profile' because he still lived in fear that Khand and Akshay would pressurize him to support the MCC. As for Khand, his line-hotel was locked and empty. I was told that he would occasionally visit after dark. There were rumours that Vishwanath and the then MLA were also competing for protection from the Naxalites for votes in the next elections. Although the tenant descendants still thought that the MCC was not in their area, the movement had slowly increased its influence among the rural elite.

The MCC's success appeared to be based on its increasingly coercive control of the area, which meant that village elites not only felt that co-operation would afford them protection to continue their involvement in the informal economy of the state, but also came to fear the consequences of non-co-operation. In fact one striking aspect of Shiv's story is the fear that the MCC could induce among its grassroots targets like him. Shiv took the drastic decision to leave Jharkhand because he feared the consequences of his failure to co-operate with the MCC. As with Spencer's friend in a Sri Lankan Sinhala village, Shiv's movements exemplified how, within this dominant frame of fear, it is not easy to find individuals who actively resist involvement in violence.[34] Members of the local elite in Tapu repeatedly told me they felt compelled to support the MCC for their 'suraksha'. Suraksha is Hindi for protection. It was clear that what was meant by suraksha was not simply protection from competing factions but also protection from the MCC itself, which threatened those who were not its supporters.

The sense of the need to comply, at least to some degree, with the agenda of the MCC in return for protection from the MCC itself was exacerbated by a fear of the organization. This fear of the MCC is linked not only to knowledge of those individuals who are involved in the MCC's grassroots operations, nor just to stories of its massacres, but also to a fear of the invisible qualities of the MCC as a very powerful, almost mythical and mystical organization. As both Taussig and Mitchell suggest, fear is often stronger in the absence of

---

34 Spencer, 2000.

the thing that causes it than in its presence.[35] The idea of an immense power behind the MCC is perpetuated in several 'invisible' ways. First, it is created through an *idea* that the MCC is a highly centralized and hierarchical organization in which each region is divided into zones, sub-zones, areas, and villages. This combines to give the sense of a movement whose overall purpose is to create a Maoist belt from Nepal to Andhra. Second, the image of the MCC's power is perpetuated through the clandestine nature of its operations, and the movement of opaque secrets and hidden resources. False names are used, for instance, and people recruited at the local level have only vague ideas about who else is actually involved in the hierarchy above their Area Commander or among the membership of geographically adjoining units.[36] The village elites understand that this veiled structure is strategically constructed so that if one member is caught, they will only be able to reveal a very limited amount about the organization.

This cloud of secrecy generates uncertainty about the size and spread of the organization. An idea is generated that the MCC could be anywhere and everywhere. Although this idea is dependent on secrecy, as in Parry's discussion of corruption, it is also perpetuated by the apparent breach of secrecy. Selective leaks include reports that the MCC has arrived in particular villages or is planning certain operations, and are reinforced by taking a journalist or a foreign anthropologist to an MCC 'hideout'.[37] Such tactical breaches of secrecy enhance the idea of the MCC as a powerful organisation, making people fear the consequences of not supporting it and thus accelerating its expansion. In areas of new expansion it is easy for someone to suspect that another person, perhaps everyone, could be involved, and this creates pressures to join.[38]

---

35 Taussig, 1984; Mitchell, 2002.

36 Kunnath, 2004.

37 Parry, 2000.

38 The reverse could become the case in MCC-controlled areas where people suspect each other of betraying the MCC. In Bihar, Kunnath was struck by the

Third, rumours of state complicity with MCC add to the myth of its power and scope. I was constantly told by people in Bero that the MCC has supporters among block officials, forest officials, and the police. In fact when I returned to Bero in January 2004, one of the most frequent rumours circulating was that when the Bero police were about to arrest an MCC collaborator, the Speaker of the Jharkhand Assembly intervened and the young man was released. The point being made was that like all politicians, the Speaker too profited from MCC protection. And in Ranchi circles the gossip was that the MCC was in bed with many government functionaries and political party leaders, and even that the Jharkhand's Land Reforms and Revenue Minister was an ex-Naxalite squad commander.[39] Such rumours created the idea that the MCC is so powerful that it is increasingly infiltrating the state.

These 'invisible' qualities of the MCC combine with stories of its capacity for violence to reproduce the myth of its power. Media reports spread chilling news of the MCC's notorious violence elsewhere. The threat of violence is perpetuated by the MCC's strategy of disarming those areas in which it aims to expand. Between April and June 1999, when I was conducting fieldwork in Bero, the MCC demanded and collected all registered civilian rifles and guns, which were usually in the possession of the old *zamindari*-descended elites. These weapons were no doubt reused by the MCC underground cells. At the local level fear is then linked to the power of an armed organization operating within a disarmed area. The MCC sold protection to its supporters by spreading the idea of its increasing coercive control of the area and by creating a fear of itself. For its grassroots supporters, an idea of the MCC's power is thus created not only through meeting its members, its everyday functions, its grassroots campaigns, but also through its more invisible qualities.

---

degree to which people suspected those around them to be police informers or working for rival Naxal groups, and the degree to which he was constantly living in a state of fear: Kunnath, 2004.

39 *Hindustan Times*, Ranchi, 6 December 2001, p. 11.

Conclusion

In this chapter I have sought to question some of the boundaries between the state and the 'terrorist' in the context of the MCC in Jharkhand State, India. There is a disjunction between popular media and academic perception of MCC activity and the evidence at the village level. In Jharkhand, the MCC's initial grassroots support was among a rural elite including entrepreneurs who tried to maintain their dominance through their connection with an informal economy of the state. The primary reasons they supported the MCC were not ideological but because connection with the MCC held the promise of protection to capture state resources through corrupt contract practices.

In exploring the MCC's grassroots expansion in Jharkhand, I have unveiled the continuity between the operation of the MCC and parts of the local state as control over a market of protection. The MCC is operating in a market of protection in which its competitors and collaborators were parts of the local state. This protection is, as Tilly argues, a 'double-edged' commodity.[40] It is both protection against competitors for access to the informal economy of the local state, and also protection from the possibilities of its own violence. The markets of protection work in similar ways to those Taussig identifies for the state in Latin America—by creating enchantment with the state's power, but also a fear of the protector.[41] In rural Jharkhand the MCC is successfully competing with political and bureaucratic networks in this market of protection, fragmenting the local coercive control and thus winning over the support of the village elite. This is made possible by the success of the MCC in presenting itself as a dual structure: a visible one and an invisible one. Like the sublime and profane qualities that Hansen suggests mark the way the state is imagined, the visible powers of the MCC encompass its involvement in local politics, its embodiment through local people and its

---

40 Tilly, 1985, p. 170.
41 Taussig, 1997.

everyday activities, while the invisible powers of the MCC involve its opaque secrets, its vast hidden resources and higher authorities, and its capacity for violence.[42]

As the MCC expands in the Jharkhandi area, one is left wondering about the nature of the Indian state. It appears that the monopoly of state protection in the Jharkhandi rural landscape is beginning to disintegrate. The MCC's visible and invisible qualities seem more pervasive than those of the state in producing the myth of its power and authority, and in inducing notions of fear among its grassroots targets. There is indeed a great deal of continuity between the activities of the state and the MCC in the Jharkhandi area—not only did the state remain the major source of resources, both rural elites and state officials who once gave support to local politicians were now supporting the MCC. The people who represented the MCC are the same as those who also represented the state. Indeed, local politicians too are now seeking the protection of the MCC. Looking at these continuities raises the question of whether at the grassroots the MCC and the state have begun to look very similar.

While at one level the state and the MCC work in tandem, at another they publicly declare and perform a war against each other. What does this discrepancy tells us about the production and creation of both? Heyman and Smart suggest that states and illegal practices, whether terrorism, black marketing or illegal immigration, enjoy some sort of co-existence.[43] The point is not simply that this is a symbiosis of default, that the boundaries produced by one enable the definition of the other, but rather that states often tolerate, or even foster, forbidden activities. My suggestion is that a mutually beneficial relationship may develop from a rhetoric positing the MCC against the state. In the case of the state, for example, an anti-extremist, anti-terror campaign enabled the BJP-led Jharkhand government to demand more resources from the central government to perform its protective capacity by making arrests under the Prevention of Ter-

---

42 Hansen, 2001, p. 35.
43 Heyman and Smart, 1999.

rorism Act. This was perhaps important in a context where the new government had little credibility amongst those who had fought for independence and who felt that Jharkhand's autonomy had far more to do with political bargains between a restricted number of elite actors than with pressures from below, and who feared that the tribal poor would not be protected by this Hindu government. Through action against terrorism, the state is able not only to enhance the terror and power of the MCC, but also to promote the power of the state itself. In Andhra Pradesh, Sinha argues that 'in many places the first direct contact which the people have had with the state machinery has been through the Maoist movement and the state's reaction to it'.[44] One suggestion is that to some degree, in Jharkhand, the state and the anti-state or 'terrorist' may enjoy another kind of symbiotic relationship: a theatrical rhetoric of one against the other that actually promotes the idea of both. Perhaps to some extent, and at least for some time, in order to promote the idea of itself, it is in the interest of the new Jharkhand state to have a competing notion of the enemy state within.

Abrahams, R. *Vigilant Citizens: Vigilantism and the State*, Cambridge, 1998.

Abrams, P. 'Notes on the Difficulty of Studying the State', *Journal of Historical Sociology* 1(1), 1988, pp. 58-89.

Banerjee, S. *In the Wake of Naxalbari: a History of the Naxalite Movement in India*, Calcutta, 1980.

Bhatia, B. 'Rethinking Revolution in Bihar', *Seminar* 464, 1988, pp. 27-31.

———— 'The Naxalite Movement in Central Bihar', PhD Thesis, University of Cambridge, 2000.

---

44 Sinha, 1989, p. 317.

Bourque, S.C. and K.B. Warren. 'Democracy without Peace: The Cultural Politics of Terror in Peru', *Latin American Research Review* 24(1), 1989, pp. 7-34.

Chomsky, N. and E.S. Herman. *The Washington Connection and Third World Fascism*, Boston, 1979.

Corbridge, S. 'Competing Inequalities: The Scheduled Tribes and the Reservations System in India's Jharkhand', *Journal of Asian Studies* 59(1), 2000, pp. 62-85.

—— 'The Continuing Struggle for India's Jharkhand: Democracy, Decentralisation and the Politics of Names and Numbers', *Commonwealth and Comparative Politics* 40(3), 2002, pp. 55-71.

Corbridge, S. and J. Harriss. *Reinventing India: Liberalization, Hindu Nationalism, and Popular Democracy*, Cambridge, 2000.

Coronil, F. and J. Skurski. 'Dismembering and Remembering the Nation—the Semantics of Political Violence in Venezuela', *Comparative Studies in Society and History* 33(2), 1991, pp. 288-337.

Duyker, E. *Tribal Guerrillas: the Santals of West Bengal and the Naxalite Movement*, Delhi, 1987.

Elwert, G. 'Markets of Violence', in *Dynamics of Violence: Processes of Escalation and De-escalation in Violent Group Conflicts*, G. Elwert, S. Feuchtwang and D. Neubert (eds), Berlin, 1999, pp. 85-102.

Gambetta, D. *The Sicilian Mafia: the Business of Private Protection*, London, 1993.

Gellner, D.N. *Resistance and the state: Nepalese experiences*, New Delhi, 2002.

Hansen, T.B. 'Governance and Myths of the State in Mumbai', in *The Everyday State and Society in Modern India*, C.J. Fuller and V. Bénéï (eds), London, 2001, pp. 31-67.

Heyman, J. and A. Smart. 'States and Illegal Practices: An Overview', in *States and Illegal Practices*, J.M. Heyman (ed.), Oxford, 1999, pp. 1-24.

Kelly, T. and A. Shah. 'A Double Edged Sword: State Protection and Violence', *Critique of Anthropology*, forthcoming.

Kunnath, G. 'Under the Shadow of Guns. Negotiating the Flaming Fields of Caste/Class War in Bihar, India ', *Anthropology Matters* 6(2), 2004, http://www.anthropologymatters.com/journal/2004-2/Kunnath_2004_under.htm, accessed May 2006.

Leach, E. *Custom, Law and Terrorist Violence*, Edinburgh, 1977.

Mitchell, T. *Rule of Experts: Egypt, Techno-politics, Modernity*, Berkeley, 2002.

Parry, J. "The 'Crisis of Corruption' and the 'Idea of India': A Worm's Eye View", in *Morals of Legitimacy: between Agency and System*, I. Pardo (ed.), New York, 2000, pp. 27-55.

Shah, A. 'The Labour of Love: Seasonal Migration from Jharkhand to the Brick Kilns of Other States in India', *Contributions to Indian Sociology (n.s.)* 40(1), 2006, pp. 91-118.

—— 'Keeping the State Away: Democracy, Politics and Imaginations of the State in India's Jharkhandi', *Journal of Royal Anthropological Institute*, 13 (1), 2007, pp. 129-45.

—— 'Beyond 'Combatting Corruption' - Morality and the State: Insights from Jharkhand, Eastern India.' Paper presented at the Manchester University Anthropology and Moral Change Workshop, November 2005.

Singh, P. *The Naxalite Movement in India*, New Delhi, 1995.

Sinha, S. *Maoists in Andhra Pradesh*, New Delhi, 1989.

Sluka, J.A. (ed.) *Death Squad: the Anthropology of State Terror*, Philadelphia, 2000.

Spencer, J. 'On not Becoming a 'Terrorist': Problems of Memory, Agency and Community in the Sri Lankan Conflict', in *Violence and Subjectivity*, V. Das, A. Kleinman, M. Ramphele and P. Reynolds (eds), Berkeley, 2000, pp. 120-40.

Stoll, D. *Between Two Armies in the Ixil Towns of Guatemala*, New York, 1993.

Taussig, M. 'Culture of Terror, Space of Death: Roger Casement's Putumayo Report and the Explanation of Torture', *Comparative Studies in Society and History* 26(3), 1984, pp. 467-97.

Taussig, M.T. *Shamanism, Colonialism, and the Wild Man: a Study in Terror and Healing*, Chicago, 1986.

—— *The Magic of the State*, New York, London, 1997.

Tilly, C. 'War Making and State Making as Organized Crime', in *Bringing the State Back in*, P.B. Evans, D. Rueschemeyer and T. Skocpol (eds), Cambridge, 1985, pp. 169-91

Wade, R. 'The Market for Public Office—Why the Indian State Is Not Better at Development', *World Development* 13(4), 1985, pp. 467-97.

TRAJECTORIES AND TRANSISTIONS

13

VIGILANTISM, TRANSITION AND LEGITIMACY: INFORMAL POLICING IN NORTHERN IRELAND

Neil Jarman

Introduction

The declarations of ceasefire by the main paramilitary groupings in Northern Ireland in 1994 threw into stark relief the role that these organizations played in forms of 'policing' within the residential areas that they dominated. Where the previous focus had been on paramilitary activities directed at the state and the security forces, now greater attention was paid to the role of the paramilitaries in responding to crime, anti-social behaviour and forms of indiscipline, and on the use of 'punishment' beatings and shootings, which left the victims with broken and bruised limbs and bodies, to enforce their sense of order on their communities. From one perspective such attacks highlighted the cruelty and viciousness of the paramilitary groups and their continued need to impose their authority on reluctant communities, while from another it highlighted both the lack of legitimacy of the state and the police in many working class areas and the demand for some degree of order and justice in the absence of an acceptable police force.

The trajectory of the peace process since 1994 has included on the one hand a wide ranging reform of the Royal Ulster Constabulary (it became the Police Service of Northern Ireland in 2001) and the criminal justice system,[1] and on the other hand attempts to address the continued role of paramilitary organizations as active agents in the arena of policing and justice. The police reform process placed a prominent emphasis on the need for the PSNI to engage more openly and effectively with the communities that they police and for greater levels of accountability both at a regional level and to the local communities. But in contrast to South Africa, which those involved in the Northern Irish transition kept in constant view, there was no option for former members of armed groups to be incorporated within the state structures. Instead the debate focused on the necessity for the decommissioning and demilitarization of paramilitary weapons and structures as part of the transition to a peaceful and democratic society. Although there was some acknowledgement that paramilitary prisoners had acted out of political conviction, the role of paramilitary groups in policing their communities was considered to be no more than vigilantism, and could therefore have no role in future models of policing.

The exclusion of paramilitary activists from participation in the policing and criminal justice system was not challenged by the broad movements of which the armed groups were a part.[2] There was no

---

1 As part of the Belfast/Good Friday peace agreement of 1998 the British government established a review of policing and the criminal justice systems. The two reports *A New Beginning: Policing in Northern Ireland. The Report of the Independent Commission on Policing in Northern Ireland*, Belfast, 1999 (widely known as the Patten Report) and *The Review of the Criminal Justice System in Northern Ireland*, Belfast 2000, have served as the basis for ongoing and wide-ranging reforms.

2 The two main communities in Northern Ireland are the Catholics and Protestants. Catholics generally favour Northern Ireland's incorporation into a single Irish state, and are also known as nationalists. The militant form of nationalism is known as Republicanism. The Republican movement includes a paramilitary wing, the IRA, and a political wing, Sinn Féin. Protestants generally favour the retention of links with the United Kingdom and are known as Unionists. The militant form of Unionism is known as Loyalism. This movement includes two main paramilitary groups, the Ulster Defence Association and the Ulster Volunteer Force, which is linked to the small Progressive Unionist Party.

demand by Republicans or Loyalists that their members should be eligible to join the police. Even though the political movements linked to the paramilitary groups accepted the in-principle legitimacy of a radically reformed police service and acknowledged the state monopoly over policing, all the paramilitary groups continued to carry out 'punishment' attacks in their areas[3]. Furthermore, over recent years the two broad movements have extended their work in imposing and sustaining a form of order within their communities through the creation of a number of restorative justice projects and the development of community-policing activities to monitor sectarian rioting and anti-social behaviour.

This chapter discusses the main forms of informal policing and justice-related activities that have emerged in Northern Ireland in the context of developing a greater understanding of the boundaries of contemporary vigilante activity. The use of punishment violence is a classic form of retributive vigilante activity, but the development of restorative justice projects and community policing patrols suggests a desire to move beyond such shadowy activities and implies a willingness among those associated with Republicanism and Loyalism to accept a more formal involvement in policing and justice matters. To some extent this desire has been acknowledged and reciprocated by the state. This chapter explores some of the issues that emerge at the interface between formal and informal policing and justice.

Vigilantism, force and autonomy

Recent discussions of vigilantism have highlighted the diverse and ambiguous nature of activities covered by the term.[4] Although it ap-

---

3 The use of paramilitary punishments has steadily been reduced by all groups. In July 2005 the IRA decommissioned and demilitarised their organisation and in January 2007 Sinn Féin recommended support for the new policing structures as a part of the process for re-establishing devolved governement in Northern Ireland.

4 The most prominent considerations have been from anthropology by Abrahams, 1996; Abrahams, 1998, and criminology Johnston, 1992; Johnston, 1996.

pears to be a relatively straightforward and commonly understood activity, discussions of vigilantism acknowledge that it involves actions that can be characterized both as forms of policing and as forms of justice. Some vigilante activities are primarily a response to a perceived failure of the criminal justice system to suitably punish offenders and are therefore described as a form of popular or informal justice. In other cases vigilantism involves more public forms of policing activities that are designed to act as a deterrent or to prevent something happening. Whereas vigilante justice is readily assumed to involve the use of violence, vigilante policing may involve a much less obviously threatening range of activities. This broad understanding helps to explain why, although vigilantism has historically been viewed as activities that take place beyond the bounds of the rule of law, recent work by Ray Abrahams and Les Johnston have noted that it is not necessarily illegal or unlawful, nor is it carried out as a challenge to the state or the formal criminal justice system. Instead both authors highlight the fact that vigilantism involves activities carried out because of a real or perceived failure of the state to deliver on its claims to hold a monopoly in managing law and order and delivering justice. Abrahams identifies vigilantism as a form of frontier activity that is undertaken in the absence of the agents of the state (and thus follows on from earlier studies of this theme which focused on vigilante activity in the context of white settler expansion across the USA[5]). But he also retains a very broad view of the types of activity that should be incorporated within the notion of vigilantism. Johnston on the other hand argues for a narrower view in his description of vigilantism as 'autonomous' activity. He excludes a range of policing and justice activities, such as the role of state agents acting on their own volition, private policing activity and forms of 'responsible citizenship' from his classification of vigilantism. But he does set out six key characteristics of vigilante activity that provide a useful framework for consideration of the subject. Johnston argues that vigilantism involves private (but not commercial) voluntary ac-

---

5 Brown, 1975; Rosenbaum and Sederberg, 1976.

tivity, encompassing planning and organization that is autonomous from the state, and that vigilantes use or threaten force in response to crime or deviancy to increase collective safety or security.[6]

The key elements that appear to distinguish vigilantism from other forms of activity that aim to increase a collective sense of safety and security are the use of force and the autonomy of those involved in the activity. Johnston's definition of force, in which he includes both actual use of force and threatened use of force, is very broad. For example, he classifies the American Guardian Angels as a vigilante group as their activity 'certainly involves the potential to use or threaten the use of force—albeit for defensive purposes,'[7] and because Angels' members are trained in martial arts and the use of non-lethal restraining holds while their operational philosophy does not exclude the use of defensive force. This broad categorization of the concept of use of force, which includes merely the possibility of its use for defensive purposes, effectively ensures that almost any form of autonomous or non-state activity aimed at improving levels of safety and security would probably have to be classified as vigilantism. Indeed, few examples of active citizenship are specifically predicated on a formal adoption of non-violence.

The potential use of force is also the factor that brings vigilante activity into conflict with the state, as the state's monopoly over the legitimate use of force remains one of the defining characteristics of modern democratic societies. Vigilante activity may not challenge the state in the sense that revolutionary groups do, but it does undermine the authority of the state, in so far as it emerges in response to the failure of the state to carry out its responsibilities.

In contrast to the broad definition of the use of force, the concept of autonomous citizenship is relatively narrowly defined in Johnston's classification. Autonomous activity is defined as private voluntary activity carried out without the support or authority of the state. It is contrasted primarily with 'responsible activity', which is also carried

---

6 Johnston, 1996.
7 Ibid., pp. 227-8.

out by private citizens with the backing of the state but necessarily excludes forms of activity that might involve or threaten force. Autonomous citizenship also excludes commercial or profit making activity, and thus all forms of private security activities, which are designed to increase safety or security, are excluded from this classification of vigilantism. One is thus left with a concept of vigilantism that exists in tension with other forms of public activity that aim to ensure that public order is maintained. It is contrasted to the work of the police because vigilantism does not seek the authorization of the state. But it is also distinctive from forms of commercial security because vigilantism is not carried out for profit, and it is contrasted with 'responsible' citizenship because it does not espouse the use of force nor engage with the state.

The broad definition of use of force and the narrow definition of autonomy effectively mean that much informal or community-based activity that aims to improve local levels of safety or security will necessarily be classified as vigilantism, with all the pejorative connotations that come with the term, whereas similar forms of commercial activity are not defined in such negative terms. But, while community-based crime and order management initiatives are poorly documented, they are probably more widespread than is assumed.[8] Furthermore the relationship between such autonomous activities and the state and its formal criminal justice system may not be as fixed nor as antagonistic as Johnston's perspective suggests. The remainder of this chapter explores recent developments in Northern Ireland in relation to informal systems of justice and policing, the issues of autonomy and use of force and the relationship with the state.

Conflict and Northern Ireland

British influence in Ireland dates from the twelfth century, but in the seventeenth century extensive settlements from England and Scotland, which were encouraged to impose greater levels of order and

---

8 See Jarman, forthcoming.

control, had a permanent impact on the island. The native Catholic Irish were increasingly marginalized, demographically, economically and politically, by the Protestant settlers, while the victory of the Protestant King William III at the Battle of the Boyne in 1690 not only secured the English throne for his religion, but also confirmed the Protestant domination of Ireland. British rule in Ireland was challenged by armed uprisings on numerous occasions before the 1916 Easter Rising triggered events that led to the withdrawal of Britain from the larger part of Ireland. Although Catholics favoured independence, the majority Protestant population of the north-east opposed separation from Britain, and in 1921 Ireland was divided into two political entities, the Free State, with its capital in Dublin, and Northern Ireland, which remained part of the United Kingdom.

Northern Ireland was a divided and contested state. Between 1921 and 1972 the Protestant majority dominated all aspects of the political and economic spheres, while Catholics experienced extensive discrimination. Many Catholics did not recognize the state and favoured the reunification of Ireland. The Irish Republican Army (IRA), which had been formed after the Easter Rising, maintained a presence in some Catholic areas and occasionally carried out military attacks. Emergency laws remained in force throughout the period and the overwhelmingly Protestant Royal Ulster Constabulary (RUC), which was heavily militarized, was used to control any expression of Catholic opposition. Catholics were thus hostile to the police, which they considered to be primarily focused on keeping them 'in their place'.

In the 1960s the Northern Ireland Civil Rights Movement began to actively challenge discrimination against Catholics, but its demands were resisted by the government. Civil rights protests and demonstrations were closely managed by the police and countered, sometimes violently, by many within the Protestant community. As tensions increased Catholics became more militant in their challenge to the Unionist state. In 1969 Catholic opposition to a parade by the Protestant Apprentice Boys in Derry led to rioting. As violence spread to Belfast the RUC lost control of the situation and the British government sent in troops to restore order. This marked the beginning of what is known locally as the Troubles, a period of armed conflict in which the IRA challenged the continued union with Britain. It fought a military campaign in which its opponents were the RUC, the British army, and the Loyalist paramilitary groups, which had been set up to defend the interests of the Protestant community. The Troubles led to an increasing segregation of working class communities in Northern Ireland. Residential areas became increasingly defined as Protestant or Catholic, and the armed paramilitary groups had a prominent role in defending 'their' territories from attack. In the early 1970s many Catholic areas were effectively no-go areas for the state forces and, although they eventually re-established some level of control, the police and the army were regarded as hostile forces and 'legitimate targets' for the IRA. Similarly, as the state sought to confront armed groups in Protestant areas, they too became estranged from the security forces. The Troubles thus left a vacuum in the provision of law and order in many working class areas.

Paramilitary policing and justice

From the early years of the Troubles paramilitary organizations on both sides of the sectarian divide have been involved in a range of activities that have been variously interpreted as forms of policing, as acts of 'alternative' or 'informal' justice, or as means of imposing control over sections of the local population.[9] These activities became known as paramilitary 'punishments'. The punishments have involved an escalating scale of actions that begin with the issuing of threats and warnings, but lead on to beatings, shootings, expelling people from their home areas or forcing them to leave Northern Ireland. The vast majority of victims have been young men. The paramilitaries targeted people who were, or who were accused of being, involved in crime and anti-social behaviour, people who had been acting as

---

9 Bell, 1996; Conway, 1997; Human Rights Watch, 1997; Kennedy, 1994; Morrissey and Pease, 1982 . Munck, 1988; Silke and Taylor, 2000; Thompson and Mulholland, 1994. Winston, 1997.

informants and (particularly in the early days of the conflict) people who were considered to have been fraternizing with the enemy. Violence was also used to punish members of paramilitary groups who had broken internal rules or discipline. Forms of paramilitary violence are only used to discipline people from the same community as the particular group carrying out the attack. They have not therefore been considered as part of the conflict *per se*, but rather as a matter of internal social control.

Although it might be considered understandable for organizations which considered themselves at war to deal with recalcitrant members and informants, the adoption of a more formal role in responding to crime and threats to local order appears to have been something that was undertaken, in part at least, under pressure from the local community. The origins of paramilitary policing activity in the early 1970s are poorly documented, but they appear in large part to be a response to the absence of state policing. The nationalist population had long been hostile to the predominantly Protestant RUC, but the sustained conflict also created tensions between Loyalists and the police, and in working class areas there was increasingly a deficit in authority, which was filled to some extent by the paramilitary groups. With little or no formal police presence on the ground members of the local resident communities began to contact local members of the paramilitary organizations to identify individuals responsible for criminal activities or 'joy riding' and demand that the organizations punish those involved. It is still frequently asserted that paramilitary involvement in the 'punishment' of crime and anti-social behaviour is due to pressure from members of local communities who demand 'justice' that is both swift and sharp.

Although there were some attempts to establish a more formalized system of 'alternative' justice in Republican areas through the creation of 'people's courts',[10] paramilitary policing was soon limited to the use of force as a means of 'punishing' those who were considered guilty of some form of deviance. Throughout the Troubles these

---

10 Munck, 1988.

activities were popularly known by the generic term of 'kneecap-ping', the practice of shooting the victim in the leg, usually through the flesh rather than through the knee itself, or being beaten with wooden staves or iron bars. It is generally accepted that there was something of a formalized tariff system which structured the form of the punishment being delivered. An individual who was identi-fied as a 'hood'[11] might be warned or threatened a number of times before being shot, and depending on the seriousness of the 'offence' the victim might be shot in one or both legs, or in the legs, ankles, wrists and elbows. Individuals might also be kneecapped on more than one occasion for persistent 'offences'. There was also a potential escalation of punishment involving the exiling of individuals from Northern Ireland or shooting them dead. Despite the brutality of the violence many people in working class areas appeared to regard kneecapping as an acceptable and necessary form of deterrent and retribution. The annual number of attacks fluctuated over the course of the Troubles, but punishment violence has remained a prominent form of paramilitary activity.

Between 1973 and the declaration of paramilitary ceasefires in 1994 there were 1,997 recorded punishment shootings, while the po-lice recorded 619 such beatings between 1982 (when they first began to record such attacks) and 1994[12]. While the ceasefires signalled an end to the military campaign against the state and to attacks between the rival communities, they did not lead to an end to punishment attacks. In fact, the average annual figures increased. Between April 1995 and the end of March 2005 the police recorded a total of 2,646 punishment beatings and shootings.[13] There was a reduction in the

---

11 The term 'hood' is used to describe someone involved in non-political crime or violence. It has subsequently been appropriated as a term of identity by young people. Graffiti proclaiming 'UTH' (up the hoods) are widespread in both Protestant and Catholic areas as marks of defiance against the paramilitary authorities.

12 Monaghan, 2004.

13 PSNI, *Statistical Report: 1st April 2004–31st March 2005*, Belfast, 2005, pp. 45-6.

number of shootings after 1994, as the use of guns was considered a potential breach of the ceasefires, and instead beatings became the dominant form of attack, but there was also an increase in the severity of the beatings.[14] A number of people suffered multiple fractures to the bones, while in two of the worst cases individuals were hung upside down on railings and nailed to a fence in a form of crucifixion after they had been beaten.

These forms of paramilitary violence most clearly fall within both the popular understanding of vigilante activity and the characteristics of vigilantism as defined by Abrahams and Johnston. Whether they are regarded as attempts to establish a system of alternative 'justice' or as a means of maintaining an acceptable level of order within the local communities, extreme violence has frequently been used as an act of retribution and a response to the perceived or actual demands of local people. Paramilitary punishment violence has been condemned by the government and by those political parties not associated with paramilitary groups, but people within the Republican and Loyalist movements have rationalized it, if often in an apologetic way, as a necessary response both to the conflict and to the absence of a policing system that is acceptable to many in working class communities[15].

One reason that the attacks have continued is that few people have any sympathy for the victims of the violence.[16] These victims are usually young men on the margins of society who are alienated from, and hostile to, dominant forms of authority, whether the state, the paramilitaries or the local community. The continuation of these attacks indicates that there is still a lack of belief in the state police and

---

14 See for example the reports on attacks in 1999 and 2001: http://news.bbc.co.uk/1/hi/uk/300521.stm and http://news.bbc.co.uk/1/hi/northern_ireland/1503496.stm

15 For discussions of the history of policing in Northern Ireland and the relationships between working class communities and the police see Ellison and Smyth, 2000; McGarry and O'Leary, 1999 Mulcahy, 2006; Weitzer, 1995; Wright and Bryett, 2000 .

16 Knox, 2001.

the criminal justice system, which cannot deliver the desired form of swift and appropriate 'justice' that is demanded by some within the local communities. The persistence of the attacks also suggests that the paramilitary organizations, and the wider movements with which they are associated, believe they have a role, and even a responsibility, to play in imposing order within their areas. This remains the case even though the IRA acknowledged the need to move away from the use of force when its command ordered an end to its armed campaign and moved to decommission its weapons in July 2005. The eighth report of the International Monitoring Commission (IMC), published in February 2006, noted that in the six months following this statement IRA members had not carried out any authorized paramilitary attacks. However, the report also noted that the organization 'has used other methods of exercising community control' and that there were signs that it was an 'organisation which wants to maintain its traditional role within its communities.'[17] In particular, the IMC report highlighted the growing advocacy of community-based restorative justice as a means by which paramilitary structures might continue to try to exert influence within their communities.

From punitive to restorative justice

The broad Republican and Loyalist political constituencies have always argued that the persistence of paramilitary 'punishment' violence is a matter of responding to the continued tensions between their communities and the police, which discourage people from reporting crime. It is also claimed to be a response to ongoing demands from within their communities that something must be done to try to reduce the levels of crime and disorder. Although the violence has continued through the period of political transition both the Republican movement and sections of the Loyalist community (particularly

---

17 International Monitoring Commission, *Eighth Report*, London, 2006 pp. 18-19. The International Monitoring Commission was established in 2003 to monitor all forms of paramilitary activity. It normally issues reports every six months.

those associated with the Ulster Volunteer Force) began to consider whether alternative forms of 'community based justice' might remove the rationale behind violent paramilitary punishment and provide an effective response to the problems of crime and disorder. This approach links the emergent thinking of the wider constituencies with the early analysis of paramilitary punishments as a form of 'alternative justice' which it was not possible to develop or implement effectively within a context of urban warfare that existed in the early 1970s.[18] The Republican movement, for example, views itself as the legitimate inheritors of the independence movement of the early twentieth century and of the first Irish government proclaimed in 1916; there is therefore a logic to its willingness to 'police' its communities and to impose forms of 'justice' on criminals and other recalcitrants. In both Loyalist and Republican areas the paramilitary organizations have claimed a legitimate status and also a social responsibility to help in the maintenance of forms of order; under the peace process there has been a practical and conceptual space to translate this from a simple use of brute force to the development of more widely acceptable forms of localized social control.

The Loyalist and Republican constituencies have followed separate paths in exploring ideas for providing an alternative community-based response to crime and disorder, but they each decided that a system of restorative justice should be developed to replace the existing system of punitive justice. The principles of restorative justice are based on the view that crimes create breakdowns in relationships between offender and victim and between offender and the wider community, and these fractured relationships need an appropriate response if the impact of the crime is to be addressed. Whereas the formal state approaches to justice are based, at least in part, on seeking retribution through punishment, restorative approaches aim to rebuild the networks of relationships and to reincorporate the perpetrators of crimes into the community rather than exclude and stigmatize them. Both constituencies claimed that restorative

---

18 Morrissey and Pease, 1982; Munck, 1988.

approaches drew on long-established practices among native peoples in New Zealand and North America, while it was also asserted that the model proposed in the Republican community drew upon an indigenous Irish history of communal justice from the time of the Brehon Laws of the eighth century through to the colonial period.[19] But concepts of restorative justice have come to be widely analyzed, supported and promoted over recent years,[20] and by 1998 the concept had received political support from Sinn Féin and the Progressive Unionist Party, and the Community Restorative Justice and the Greater Shankill Alternatives projects had been set up to develop the work in the Catholic and Protestant communities respectively.[21] Each group has subsequently established restorative justice programmes in a number of locations.

The restorative justice projects involve a mix of people; some may have a paramilitary background but many do not, some are volunteers, others are paid staff. The projects work predominantly with young males who have been accused of acts of crime or anti-social behaviour (precisely the group targeted in punishment attacks). In each community the restorative justice projects investigate complaints, they may organize mediation between victims and offenders, and they agree appropriate restitution or reparative work. The perpetrators are usually referred to the programme by people from within the community or from paramilitary groups; many of those who are referred will be under threat from a paramilitary group, but participation in a programme is voluntary—some prefer to opt for the formal criminal justice system, others are simply prepared to accept a paramilitary punishment.

Participants undergo a process that involves coming to terms with their activities and agreeing a process of personal change. This may

---

19 Auld, Gormally, McEvoy and Ritchie, 1997 pp.13-15; Bell, 1996, pp. 146-50.

20 See for example McEvoy and Newburn, 2003; Zehr and Toews, 2004.

21 See Greater Shankill Alternatives, n.d., and Auld, Gormally, McEvoy and Ritchie, 1997.

involve stopping criminal behaviour, coming off drugs and stopping drinking. The programme may involve forms of education or training, as well of forms of community reparation, which may involve working as a volunteer to help local groups, clean up the area or assist in communal activities. For example, the Alternatives project is working with a young man who has been using drugs heavily and supporting this through forms of criminal activity. Having been referred to Alternatives because of a threat by the paramilitaries he has agreed to participate in the programme. The first stage involved coming to an understanding of how he was seen by others and how he might hope to change, and defining goals for himself. He then worked with the youth worker at Alternatives to develop a programme focusing on physical fitness and education activities, and exploring options for work, while at the same time is helping to keep the local community centre lean and tidy. To fulfil the programme he must complete 30 units of activity lasting between 50 and 70 hours in total. This will be spread over a period of up to a year. The programme is thus formally structured and the participants are mentored and supported by the project staff for the duration. Furthermore their behaviour is monitored for a period of up to twelve months after completing the programme by project workers, family members and people within the wider local community. While the programmes can only be undertaken with the consent of the perpetrators, the incentive is that the perpetrators avoid both the formal criminal justice system and the informal system of paramilitary punishment, and also end up with more positive personal goals and a better relationship with their local community.

Although the two approaches are broadly similar, there is one significant difference regarding their relationships with the police. The Community Restorative Justice projects working in Catholic areas refuse to engage with the police in any way, while the Loyalist Alternatives project works closely with the PSNI. These contrasting approaches are a direct outcome of the broader Republican and Loyalist attitudes to the police, but this situation will presumably change when the police reform process is considered acceptable to Sinn Féin and it takes up its positions on the various policing accountability bodies.

The restorative justice projects have been considered a relative success in working with perpetrators in their respective areas. The number of projects has steadily increased and both Community Restorative Justice and Alternatives are seeking funding that will allow a consolidation and extension of their work. Nevertheless, many outside the Republican and Loyalist constituencies remain suspicious of the community based restorative justice projects, even though the principles of restorative justice have been accepted by the state and adapted by the PSNI.[22] The main concerns are due to the close links between the projects and the wider Republican and Loyalist movements; Mark Durcan, leader of the Social Democratic and Labour Party, for example, encapsulated many of the concerns when he argued, 'We can't have local warlords turning into local law lords'.[23] The leaders of many of the political parties without links to a paramilitary group have questioned whether those participating in community restorative justice programmes have any real choice if the alternative is a punishment beating by the paramilitaries. Thus, although the community restorative justice projects have sought to become a legitimate element of a responsive system of justice, they are still frequently condemned as simply another form of vigilantism. This attitude came to the fore in late 2005 when the British government issued a consultation document designed to consider how the various community restorative justice projects should relate to the criminal justice system.[24] The document accepted that community-based restorative justice schemes had a legitimate role to play as long as they worked within a basic set of guidelines that would be framed by principles of human rights and accountability. It was initially pro-

---

22 Criminal Justice Review, 2000; Dignan and Lowey, 2000; O'Mahoney, Chapman and Doak, 2002.

23 *Belfast Telegraph*, 19 October 2005.

24 Northern Ireland Office, 2005.

posed, however, that the schemes would not have to engage formally with the police, although they would be expected to engage with the criminal justice system via the Probation Board or the Youth Justice Agency. It was generally interpreted in the media that this was an important phase in mainstreaming community-based restorative justice and providing a framework for its future funding by the state, and this would mean that such schemes would be part of the formal criminal justice system. But, the proposals provoked strong reactions from many politicians and within the media as the proposed guidelines allowed the restorative projects to avoid any contact with the police, and this was regarded as nothing more than a means of legitimizing a form of vigilante activity.[25]

This approach raises interesting issues for the theoretical consideration of vigilantism. Johnston's analysis argues that the mere possibility of the use of force requires extra-state activity to be classified as vigilantism, and therefore the close relations between those involved in restorative justice projects and paramilitarism suggests that there remained an implicit threat of violence if someone resisted the invitation to follow the restorative programme. This is the view of the opponents of the government proposals. But, once the state appears willing to support, and thus legitimize, such activities, subject to appropriate guidelines and a framework of accountability, should they still be considered as forms of vigilante activity? This would appear to represent a loss of the critical element of autonomy from the state, and may be part of the process of incorporation of formerly autonomous activities into the formal criminal justice system—an objection voiced by some within the wider Republican community.[26] In a study of 'community police patrols' in the USA, Gary Marx and Dane Archer identified four types of relationship between such patrols and the police, defined by whether the patrols were supple-

---

25 See for example Garret Fitzgerald 'Vigilante Groups may be given control of law', *Irish Times*, 21 Jan 2006 and 'North's justice scheme threatens democracy' *Irish Times*, 4 February 2006.
26 McEvoy and Mika, 2002.

---

mental or adversarial to the police, and whether they were supported or opposed by the police.[27] They suggest that the police tended to co-opt those patrols which saw themselves as supplemental to the police, while those that were adversarial tended to develop more hostile relationships, resisted engagement with the police and eventually became subject to police surveillance and investigation. In contrast, in Northern Ireland the government seems to be adopting an approach that is attempting to neutralize the impulse towards autonomy and the potential for continued use of extra-state violence, and to incorporate the erstwhile vigilantes into the formal justice system. This type of approach undermines any sense of an absolute gulf between vigilantism and state justice, but rather appears to acknowledge that they are taking different routes to similar objectives.

Community patrols

The third community-based policing initiative involving people who have been associated with paramilitarism is the mobilization of networks of activists to maintain a physical presence on the streets, to monitor potential flashpoint locations and events. This is effectively a form of community policing patrol. These networks draw upon diverse groups of people, and while some may have a paramilitary history, others have a base in faith groups, political work or community activity, and while there may be some individuals involved in both the community networks and the restorative justice projects, the two activities are otherwise completely separate. The monitoring or policing activity, which may be initiated for political reasons, in response to crime or disorder, because of a lack of appropriate policing, or because of a combination of all of these factors, has only occasionally been documented but may be more widespread than at first thought.[28] The small number of existing studies of community

---

27 Marx and Archer, 1976.

28 See for example: Sagar, 2005 for a discussion of patrols in Britain; Cullinan, 1999, discusses patrols in South Africa, as does Baker, 2002. See also Abrahams, 1996 for patrols in Tanzania, and the papers by Pratten and Jensen this volume.

patrols draw upon a variety of approaches to the phenomenon but reach similar conclusions. Marx and Archer discuss numerous examples in the 1960s and 70s USA, and situate their analysis within the context of vigilantism. They conclude that in the absence of police resources, the patrols may be a necessary response to some situations. More recent discussions of community patrols in Australia describe the phenomenon as a means of 'self-policing' and argue that while the patrols do not fit within mainstream approaches to policing, nevertheless they should be considered as a legitimate means of providing security and increasing safety in some contexts.[29] The development of such patrols in Australia, South Africa and the USA has been in a context of ethnic or racial tensions, and within working class or marginalized communities. Whilst community patrols may be a practical counterbalance to the growth of private policing in wealthy residential areas, concerns have been raised that such activities may be little more than a form of second-class policing and serve to legitimize an avoidance of responsibility by the state.[30] There is therefore a degree of ambivalence about how far such autonomous policing patrols should be welcomed.

In Northern Ireland, the community patrols have been initiated in a context of recurrent outbreaks of public disorder, sectarian tensions and continuing mistrust of the police, and as an attempt to reduce violence and conflict. There are two main potential sources of disorder, the numerous parades organized by the Orange Order and similar organizations, and the boundaries or interfaces between Protestant and Catholic working-class residential areas.[31] The tensest period is during the summer 'marching season' when parades passing close to interface areas are frequently challenged by protestors and readily erupt into violence. These events may in turn set off a spiral of exchange attacks, which may last for weeks or longer. In 1996, protests over one parade in Portadown sparked a week of riots across Northern

---

29 Marx and Archer, 1976; Blagg and Valuri, 2004a; Blagg and Valuri, 2004b.
30 Marx and Archer, 1976, p. 155; Sagar, 2005, pp. 109-10.
31 Bryan, 2000; Jarman, 1997.

Ireland, while the inter-communal tensions, which are sustained in part by parades, in North Belfast, the most heavily divided and contested part of the city resulted in 376 riots and 1,014 disturbances in the eight years between 1996 and 2004.[32] The 'culture of violence'[33] is such in Northern Ireland that exchanges of verbal abuse can rapidly escalate into rioting, which includes the throwing of stones, bottles, fireworks, petrol bombs and blast bombs, and on occasion to the use of live fire. In response the police have a variety of weaponry including batons, plastic bullets, water cannons and live ammunition.

Following the extensive violence in July 1996, community workers in North Belfast co-ordinated grassroots activists into localized networks and provided them with mobile telephones (a new and expensive technology at the time) to ensure that all members of the networks could keep in touch with each other at all times.[34] The phones enabled the members of the networks to monitor the main flashpoints, and to coordinate responses to the mobilization of crowds or outbreaks of disorder. For example, on one occasion crowds of youths were throwing missiles at each other from their bases on either side of the Crumlin Road in North Belfast. Neither side was willing to give way and stop its attacks while the other side was still a threat. The two communities' activists could see each other, although they could not speak face to face because of the violence. However, they could speak by phone and thus were able to synchronize a de-escalation of the violence. Youths on each side were persuaded to move back, and the participants could in turn see their counterparts on the other side moving back. The activists were thus able to bring the trouble under control without recourse to police intervention.

In other situations the phones have enabled people to respond quickly to rumours and to counter claims of attacks or provocations. On one occasion at the Torrens interface people on the Catholic side could hear Loyalist music and could see smoke rising over the

32 Jarman, 2004.

33 Ibid., p. 435.

34 Jarman, 2003; Jarman, 2005.

barrier; rumours spread that people on the other side had attacked a house and were gathering a crowd for further trouble. Phone calls between members of the network were able to confirm that it was only young people burning wood on a bonfire and there was no threat to the neighbours; however, the young people were also encouraged to move away from the interface and the music was stopped. In this case the rumour was undermined and the good faith and standing of the members of the phone network as 'being able to sort things out' was enhanced.

As the members of the networks have became more confident and people on each side have developed trust in their counterparts in the other community, the phone links have increasingly enabled them to synchronize their responses and coordinate attempts to defuse tensions. As well as monitoring tensions at interfaces, the localized networks have often mobilized much larger numbers of people to help manage crowds at parades. In some areas the community activists marshal those protesting against the parades; in others they have been involved in marshalling people supporting the parades. In both cases members of the wider Republican and Loyalist movements have been prominently represented on the ground.

Over recent years, the community patrols at interface areas have become an established feature of community activity and have been one of the key factors in reducing the scale of the violence in such areas. Members of the local networks readily acknowledge that they are often at their most effective when they have the involvement or support of the main paramilitary organizations. However, this appears to be not so much due to the threat of force, as to a wider communal desire to prevent disorder. The paramilitaries can actively foment disorder and they can actively work to prevent disorder, but they can also take a neutral position where their non-intervention can give scope for others to take a lead. We have noted that an essential element of vigilante activity is a willingness to use force or violence, even if only for defensive purposes, and although the community networks in Northern Ireland aim to prevent violence and disorder,

there is a certain vagueness about the limits of their restraint. On occasions people have been accused of not making a serious attempt to
stop acts of violence from within their own community, and a small
number of individuals have been accused of active involvement in
rioting. Some of those involved in co-ordinating the peaceful management of interfaces have also said that they would not stop people
who responded aggressively to an attack from the other side, as this
would be an understandable reaction to an external threat. There is
thus a diverse range of views about how and when it is appropriate
and reasonable to use force or violence, and attitudes to the use of
violence are never clear-cut.

Furthermore, once the IRA announced that its members would
no longer engage in any acts of violence, it became clear that it no
longer had the same capacity to control a crowd in some situations.
Protests against two parades in North Belfast in June and July 2005
erupted in serious violence as many young men ignored the remon-
strations of senior Republicans and attacked the marchers and the
police with a range of missiles and weapons. This raises two key issues. First, it suggests that at least some of the capacity to control
crowds and prevent disorder derives from the status and or presence
of key individuals, and that this presence might impute a potential
threat of violent retribution against anyone who challenged their
authority. Second, it indicates something of a possible sea-change
in the status of the political actors associated with paramilitarism
within some communities, and thus the potential for communal self-
policing. In recent years the presence of certain prominent politicians
has been an important element in attempts to manage public order,
and events in 2005 suggest that their capacity to control crowds may
well be diminished without the underlying threat of force. These two
points together highlight the uncertainty of how far the effectiveness
of forms of community policing is associated with the 'authority' of
the actors and the process of policing, and how far it is due to an
underlying potential threat of the use of violence against those that
challenge local structures of authority. This issue remains unresolved

and the ambivalence over the possible use of force perhaps serves as a potential factor that helps minimize the actual need to use force.

Despite the underlying potential for the use of force by community activists, many senior police officers have come to acknowledge the value of the role they have played in managing disorder. When the community-based policing networks were first established very limited contacts were maintained with the police. The local police commander was informed of the initiative and some contacts were maintained with neighbourhood police among activists from the Loyalist communities. However, over the years senior officers in many areas have come to recognize the benefits of having local networks willing to try to reduce trouble. The police are now often willing to wait until the members of the community networks have attempted to intervene before they send police officers in riot gear into a situation, and in some cases police officers have telephoned activists at home to ask them to intervene when they can see people beginning to gather at flashpoints. This recognition of the potential of community activists has in turn led to complaints that the police are expecting too much. One activist recalled how he had been woken in the early hours by a call from the police asking him to sort out some trouble in his area. He told them they would have to sort it out themselves as he was on holiday in another country! Similarly, although Republican activists will not liaise directly with the police, chains of communication have been established to enable messages to be sent to the police to ask them to withdraw or to allow the activists more time to intervene. Both the police and the activists know that there are times when the police will have to intervene, but both also know that police intervention can all too readily serve to escalate a situation on the ground. The community networks thus remain autonomous from the police but work together informally to achieve mutually desirable aims. Furthermore, most if not all community-based projects receive funding from the state for staffing, for project costs or to pay for mobile phones. Like the restorative justice projects, therefore, they have to an extent been brought into the ambit of the formal criminal justice system.

In more recent developments in some Catholic areas the community policing activity has been extended and expanded through the establishment of several Community Watch programmes. These involve similar patrolling activities that are designed to respond to problems of public disorder such as anti-social behaviour, noise, alcohol consumption and joy-riding, but whereas the community interface networks aim to reduce disorder between Protestant and Catholic communities, the Community Watch projects deal with disorder within the Catholic community. While there has been a general expansion of community policing activities, there is some debate within the Republican community about whether they should be acting as 'the police' and whether they will want to police their areas in the longer term. This suggests that the future will perhaps be similar to the situation discussed by Marx and Archer, who found that maintaining autonomy over a longer term was difficult and that most community patrols were either incorporated into formal policing systems or disbanded once the immediate crisis context had passed.[35]

Conclusions

This chapter discusses three forms of community-based activity that respond to the concerns of local communities with crime and disorder in Northern Ireland. Over the course of a sustained conflict and a period of political transition, the two political-paramilitary constituencies of Republicanism and Loyalism have developed a varied and interconnected network of informal forms of policing and justice. Each of the three activities, 'punishment' attacks, restorative justice projects and community policing networks, can be considered as forms of vigilante activity, primarily on account of their autonomy from the state and their attitudes towards the use of force. However, classifying the activities as vigilantism has become increasingly prob-

---

35 Marx and Archer, 1976 pp.136-7.

lematical in relation to Johnston's definition for two reasons. First, the activities in Northern Ireland retain an ambiguous relationship with the potential use of force and second, both the active participants and the state have sought to reach forms of accommodation with each other and this raises issues about the autonomy of the non-state actors.

The issue of the scope for use of force is problematic because Johnston regards even the potential use of force by non-state autonomous actors as crossing the bounds into vigilante activity. In Northern Ireland the punishment activity clearly falls within this classification system, but in the case of the restorative justice projects and the community policing networks, violence has not been used and has in fact been disavowed specifically by those involved in restorative justice. But because individuals with paramilitary backgrounds are involved in both activities there remains, certainly in the minds of some commentators and possibly in the minds of some within the community concerned, a potential for the use of force for those who refuse to respond to the requests of the community activists. It is difficult to see how this ambiguity will be dissipated except over time and through experience. Yet it also raises questions about the value of retaining 'potential for use of force' as a factor in classifying autonomous activity as vigilantism. The potential use of force concerns the work of bouncers and some forms of private security workers as much as autonomous policing actors.[36] This suggests that we need to give further consideration to our understanding of vigilantism and view it as part of a wider continuum of policing activities, rather than as something beyond the bounds of legitimacy.

This understanding of vigilantism as an activity that exists as part of a continuum and which is adaptive and adaptable appears to have been acknowledged by some state actors in Northern Ireland, and this has challenged the status of the erstwhile autonomous activists. The paramilitary forces have essentially agreed to stop their recourse to retributive punishments and the state has developed working rela-

---

36 Hobbs, Hadfield, Lister and Winlow, 2003, chapter 7.

tionships with the restorative justice projects and the community policing patrols. The state has thus legitimized much of the autonomous activity, while at the same time attempting to incorporate it, formally or informally, into the orbit of the wider criminal justice system. For their part the proponents of the informal activities have been willing to work with the state, but at the same time are trying to maintain their autonomy. This process is ongoing and the outcome is far from clear, but it marks a departure from normative state responses to vigilantism. This may in part be due to the specific context of Northern Ireland, as a society in a political transition and with well-established patterns of community activism, though similar experimental approaches to policing and justice have been developed in South Africa.[37] The explorations between erstwhile vigilantes and the state may well be a factor of the conflict transformation process, and the need to explore a wider range of order management processes as part of the period of transition, rather than having any wider significance.

However, it is also a fact that in all societies elements of public order and low level crime are managed informally, by families or kin groups, local communities, peer groups and other informal structures of authority, without the involvement of institutional police agencies. But there is also a growing recognition of the need to involve a broader range of groups and organizations in the management of public order and control of anti-social behaviour. Recent developments across the United Kingdom include the use of community support officers and neighbourhood wardens to patrol estates and residential areas, and of stewards to control crowds at sports events, door supervisors to manage the night-time economy, and private security patrols to monitor wealthier residential areas and shopping centres. Increasingly the police are but one of a wide range of agencies with a responsibility for the management of order in public space. The evidence from Northern Ireland suggests that there is a growing (although by no means universal) acknowledgement of the

---

37 Brogden and Shearing, 1993, pp. 130-65; Scharf and Nina, 2001; Sekhonyane and Louw, 2002.

valuable work that can be done by informal and autonomous groups in responding to violence and crime. It remains to be seen whether such activities will continue, whether they will retain their autonomy or whether they will be more fully incorporated as the actions of responsible citizens.

✻

Abrahams, R. 'Vigilantism: Order and disorder on the frontiers of the state', in *Inside and Outside the Law: Anthropological Studies of Authority and Ambiguity*, H. Olivia (ed.), London, 1996, pp. 41-55.

—— *Vigilant citizens: vigilantism and the state*, Cambridge, 1998.

Auld, J., B. Gormally, K. McEvoy & M. Ritchie *Designing a System of Community Restorative Justice in Northern Ireland: A Discussion Document*, Belfast, 1997.

Baker, B. *Taking the law into their own hands: lawless law enforcers in Africa*, Aldershot, 2002.

Bell, C. 'Alternative Justice in Ireland', in *One hundred and fifty years of Irish law*, N. Dawson, D.S. Greer & P. Ingram (eds.), Belfast, 1996, pp. 145-67.

Blagg, H. & G. Valuri 'Aboriginal Community Patrols in Australia: Self-policing, Self-determination and Security', *Policing and Society* 14(4), 2004a, pp. 313-28.

—— 'Self-policing and Community Safety: the Work of Aboriginal Community Patrols in Australia', *Current Issues in Criminal Justice* 15(3), 2004b, pp. 1-15.

Brogden, M. & C. Shearing *Policing For A New South Africa*, London, 1993.

Brown, R.M. *Strain of violence: historical studies of American violence and vigilantism*, New York, 1975.

Bryan, D. *Orange parades: the politics of ritual, tradition, and control*, London, 2000.

Conway, P. 'A Response to Paramilitary Policing in Northern Ireland', *Critical Criminology* 8(1), 1997, pp. 109-21.

Criminal Justice Review *Review of the Criminal Justice System in Northern Ireland*, Belfast, 2000.

Cullinan, K. 'Nights in 'Gangster Mecca'', *SIYAYA!* 5, 1999, pp. 18-27.

Dignan, J. & K. Lowey *Restorative justice options for Northern Ireland: a comparative review*, Belfast, 2000.

Ellison, G. & J. Smyth *The crowned harp: policing Northern Ireland*, London Sterling, Va., 2000.

Greater Shankill Alternatives *The Story*, Belfast, n.d.

Hobbs, D., P. Hadfield, S. Lister & S. Winlow *Bouncers: Violence and Governance in the Night-time Economy*, Oxford, 2003.

Human Rights Watch *To serve without favour: policing, human rights and accountability in Northern Ireland*, New York, 1997.

Jarman, N. *Material conflicts: parades and visual displays in Northern Ireland*, Oxford, 1997.

—— 'Managing Disorder: Responses to Interface Violence in North Belfast', in *Researching the troubles: social science perspectives on the Northern Ireland conflict*, O. Hargie & D. Dickson (eds.), Edinburgh, 2003, pp. 227-44.

—— 'From War to Peace? Changing patterns of Violence in Northern Ireland, 1990-2003', *Terrorism and Political Violence* 16(3), 2004, pp. 420-38.

—— 'Managing Conflicts by Phone: The Mobile Phone Networks in Northern Ireland', in *People building peace II: successful stories of civil society*, P.v. Tongeren, M. Brink, M. Hellema & J. Verhoeven (eds.), Boulder, 2005, pp. 435-40.

—— 'Responsible Citizens or Dangerous Vigilantes? Community-based Policing and the Management of Public Order', *Critique of Anthropology*, forthcoming.

Johnston, L. *The rebirth of private policing*, London, 1992.

—— 'What is vigilantism?' *British Journal of Criminology* 36(2), 1996, pp. 220-36.

Kennedy, L. 'Nightmares within Nightmares: Paramilitary Repression in Working-Class Communities', in *Crime and punish-*

ment in West Belfast, L. Kennedy (ed.), Belfast, 1994, pp. 67-80.

Knox, C. 'The Deserving Victims of Political Violence: Punishment Attacks in Northern Ireland', *Criminal Justice* 1(2), 2001, pp. 181-99.

Marx, G.T. & D. Archer 'Community Police Patrols and Vigilantism', in *Vigilante Politics*, H. Rosenbaum & P. Sederberg (eds.), Philadelphia, 1976, pp. 129-57.

McEvoy, K. & H. Mika 'Restorative Justice and the Critique of Informalism in Northern Ireland', *British Journal of Criminology* 42, 2002, pp. 534-62.

McEvoy, K. & T. Newburn (eds) *Criminology, Conflict Resolution and Restorative Justice*, Basingstoke, 2003.

McGarry, J. & B. O'Leary *Policing Northern Ireland: Proposals for a New Start*, Belfast, 1999.

Monaghan, R. "An Imperfect Peace': Paramilitary 'Punishments' in Northern Ireland', *Terrorism and Political Violence* 16(3), 2004, pp. 439-61.

Morrissey, M. & K. Pease. 'The Black Criminal Justice System in West Belfast', *The Howard Journal* 21, 1982, pp. 159-66.

Mulcahy, A. *Policing Northern Ireland: Conflict, Legitimacy and Reform*, Cullompton, 2006.

Munck, R. 'The Lads and the Hoods: Alternative Justice in an Irish Context', in *Whose law & order?: aspects of crime and social control in Irish society*, M. Tomlinson, T. Varley & C. McCullagh (eds.), Belfast, 1988, pp. 41-53.

Northern Ireland Office *Consultation on draft guidelines for community-based restorative justice schemes*, Belfast, 2005.

O'Mahoney, D., T. Chapman & J. Doak *Restorative cautioning: a study of police based restorative cautioning pilots in Northern Ireland*, Belfast, 2002.

Rosenbaum, H. & P. Sederberg (eds) *Vigilante politics*, Philadelphia, 1976.

Sagar, T. 'Street Watch: Concept and Practice: Civilian Participation in Street Prostitution Control', *Br J Criminol* 45(1), 2005, pp. 98-112.

Scharf, W. & D. Nina (eds) *The Other Law: Non-State Ordering in South Africa*, Lansdowne, 2001.

Sekhonyane, M. & A. Louw *Violent Justice: Vigilantism and the State's Response*, Pretoria, 2002.

Silke, A. & M. Taylor 'War Without End: Comparing IRA and Loyalist Vigilantism in Northern Ireland', *Howard Journal of Criminal Justice* 39(3), 2000, pp. 249-66.

Thompson, W. & B. Mulholland 'Paramilitary Punishments and Young people in West Belfast: Psychological Effects and the Implications for Education', in *Crime and punishment in West Belfast*, L. Kennedy (ed.), Belfast, 1994, pp. 51-66.

Weitzer, R. *Policing Under Fire: Ethnic Conflict and Police-Community Relations in Northern Ireland*, Albany, 1995.

Winston, T. 'Alternatives to Punishment Beatings and Shootings in a Loyalist Community in Belfast', *Critical Criminology* 8(1), 1997, pp. 122-8.

Wright, J. & K. Bryett *Policing and Conflict in Northern Ireland*, Basingstoke, 2000.

Zehr, H. & B. Toews (eds) *Critical Issues in Restorative Justice* Monsey, N.J., 2004.

14

WHEN VIGILANTES TURN BAD: GANGS, VIOLENCE, AND SOCIAL CHANGE IN URBAN NICARAGUA

Dennis Rodgers

Introduction

On 12 February 2002, I returned for the first time in almost five years to *barrio* Luis Fanor Hernández,[1] a poor neighbourhood in Managua, the capital city of Nicaragua, where I had previously carried out research on youth gang violence.[2] I was revisiting in order to 'update' my original study, a process that I have to admit I conceived less as a 'realist' cataloguing of social change than as a 'constructivist reconstruction' of my initial interpretations, to use the terminology of Burawoy's theory of 'reflexive ethnography'.[3] As I followed Nicaragua from afar, little seemed to have changed since my initial study, and I thought that my revisit would therefore mainly involve rethinking the processes I had uncovered previously from new theoretical viewpoints. This rather naïve notion was completely shattered on my first day back in the *barrio* when I met Ronnie, who as a nine-year-old member of the local gang had been an important informant

---

1 This name is a pseudonym, as are all the names mentioned in this chapter.

2 See Rodgers, 2000. This first period of fieldwork was carried out between July 1996 and July 1997. The second period described in this chapter was conducted between February and March 2002 as part of the London School of Economics Crisis States Programme (see http://www.crisisstates.com).

3 Burawoy, 2003.

DENNIS RODGERS

in 1996-97. He greeted me with an enthusiastic '*Oye*, Dennis, what's up?', and followed this up with a rapid-fire patter of questions:

'How are you, *hombre*, where have you been, it's been a while since we've seen you around here. What's new, you look like you've really changed... *¡Te pusiste gordo, maje!* (You've become fat, mate!).'

'Hi Ronnie, nice to see you too!', I answered. 'I'm doing OK, sorry it took me so long to come back, all sorts of things have happened, my life's completely different now. But hey, you've changed as well, man! You were just a kid last time I was here and look at you now—you're so big! What are you now, 14, 15, no? How are you doing? What are you up to? Are you still a *pandillero* (gang member)?'

'Nah, I'm no longer with the *pandilla* (gang), all that's changed, *maje*. So much has changed here—you won't recognise the *barrio* (neighbourhood), I tell you. The gang's not the same as when you were here, it's got a different *onda* (ethos) now and no longer looks after the neighbourhood any more but does its own thing instead. ...The whole *barrio* is completely different to when you were here before, Dennis. Everything's fucked up now, especially the gang, which has turned bad...'

It came as a surprise to hear that Ronnie was no longer a gang member, as he was not yet of an age to have 'matured out' of the youth gang, as inevitably happened to all members at some point between the ages of 18 and 23 years old (youth not being an eternal condition). At the same time, my prior research had shown that *pandillero* trajectories are difficult to predict, and several 14-15-year-olds had left the gang during my fieldwork in 1996-97. It was, however, a complete shock to hear that the gang had 'turned bad', as Ronnie put it. The main finding of my previous research had been that contrary to received wisdom, the *pandilla* had provided a significant measure of stability and order to the local neighbourhood in a wider Nicaraguan context of crisis, insecurity, and state and social breakdown. I could see no reason why the gang might have 'turned bad' considering the country's continuing dismal predicament, but it rapidly became clear that Ronnie was not wrong in his assessment of the *pandilla*'s changed dynamics, to the extent that during the course of my revisit I sometimes felt as if I was re-investigating a completely different phenomenon.

This chapter explores how and why Nicaraguan *pandillerismo* (youth gangsterism) changed so radically between 1997 and 2002. It begins by tracing the major differences between the 1996-97 manifestation of the *barrio* Luis Fanor Hernández gang that I initially studied, on the one hand, and its 2002 avatar on the other, highlighting in particular the divergences relating to the gang's violent social practices and attitudes towards the local neighbourhood community. Drawing on the theoretical lens of vigilantism, it characterizes the variation between the two manifestations of the *barrio* Luis Fanor Hernández gang as resulting from the inherent 'lability' of vigilante practices, and considers what this tells us about the nature of the gang's evolution, but also what it does not tell us. It then explores the actual details of the process of the gang's transformation between 1997 and 2002 in order to properly understand this 'lability', before concluding with some general considerations about processes of institutional change.

Pandillerismo in barrio Luis Fanor Hernández, 1997–2002

In 1996-97, the *barrio* Luis Fanor Hernández *pandilla* was made up of about 100 male youths aged between 7 and 22 years old, who engaged in a variety of violent activities ranging from petty delinquency to gang warfare. These all complied with a cardinal 'golden rule', however, which was not to prey on local neighbourhood inhabitants. The victims of the local gang were always outsiders, and gang members in fact went out of their way to protect local neighbourhood inhabitants from outside criminals and *pandilleros*. Even what at first glance seemed to be an unmitigatedly destructive form of *pandilla* violence, gang warfare, was, it could be argued, fundamentally socially constitutive. Conflicts followed set of rules of behaviour—attacking certain opposing gang members rather than others, defending local neighbourhood inhabitants, fighting in particular ways—that played important roles in the construction of the individual gang member self, for example. Gang wars also contributed to the constitution of the gang as a group, reaffirming the collective unit by emphasizing the primordial distinction between 'us' and 'them'. But gang warfare was, arguably, also about a broader form of social construction that related to the local community. Indeed, the *pandilleros* qualified their wars as being motivated by their 'love' for the neighbourhood, portraying their fighting against other gangs as 'acts of love'.[4] As a gang member called Julio put it:

'You show the neighbourhood that you love it by putting yourself in danger for people, by protecting them from other *pandillas*... You look after the neighbourhood; you help them, keep them safe...'

This is by no means implausible. Gang warfare was semi-ritualized, and followed set patterns. The first battle of a *pandilla* war involved fighting with sticks, stones and bare hands, but each new battle involved an escalation of weaponry, first to knives and broken bottles, then to (handmade) mortars, and eventually to guns, AK-47s, and fragmentation grenades. Although the rate of escalation could vary, its sequence never did and *pandillas* did not begin their wars immediately with firearms. This ritualized escalation arguably constituted both a restraining mechanism—escalation is a positive constitutive process in which each stage calls for a greater but definite intensity of action and is therefore always under the actors' control—and an 'early warning system' for local neighbourhood inhabitants. Although gang wars often had negative consequences for the local community—people were sometimes caught in the cross-fire of gang wars, and infrastructural damage was common—these were arguably indirect insofar as gangs never directly victimized the local population of their own neighbourhood. The threat to local neighbourhood populations stemmed from other gangs, whom the local gang would

---

4 Parallels can be made with the notion of the 'love for the people' that Ernesto 'Che' Guevara (Guevara, 1969, p. 398) saw as being the mark of 'the true revolutionary'. This is perhaps particularly appropriate considering the strong associations that exist between Nicaraguan *Sandinismo* and the 'Cult of Che' (see Lancaster, 1988, pp. 132, 85).

engage with in a prescribed manner, thereby limiting 'the all-pervading unpredictability of violence'[5] and locally creating a predictable and relative 'safe haven' in its own neighbourhood.

In a wider context of chronic insecurity, this function was arguably socially positive, and certainly local neighbourhood inhabitants very much recognized it as such, never calling the police during gang wars, nor ever denouncing gang members.[6] Although there was some ambivalence towards the gang phenomenon—the parents of gang members frequently worried about their offspring, and would often publicly berate their *pandillero* sons—there was no fear of the local gang in the neighbourhood, and it was generally viewed positively. As *Don* Sergio put it during an interview in 1997:

'The *pandilla* looks after the neighbourhood and screws others; it protects us and allows us to feel a little bit safer, to live our lives a little bit more easily... Gangs are not a good thing, and it's their fault that we have to live with all this insecurity, but that's a problem of *pandillerismo* in general, not of our gang here in the *barrio*. They protect us, help us—without them, things would be much worse for us.'

This view of the gang stemmed not only from the fact that the *pandilla* was the purveyor of security but also from its position as the only social institution in the neighbourhood that displayed any sort of 'community spirit'. Indeed, the gang's violent 'care' for the *barrio* stood in sharp contrast to the wider atomization and social breakdown, and arguably provided the only concrete institutional medium through which an otherwise absent form of '*communitas*'[7] was enacted in *barrio* Luis Fanor Hernández. Neighbourhood inhabitants who otherwise shunned each other—to avoid entangling themselves into webs of reciprocal obligations—would avidly seek each other out to swap stories about the gang, exchanging eye-witness accounts,

---

5 Arendt, 1969, p. 5.

6 At the same time, the police were not a visible presence in the neighbourhood in 1996-97, partly because gangs out-gunned them, which obviously made patrolling and control difficult (Nicaragua Network News, 2001).

7 Turner, 1969.

spreading rumours, and re-telling incidents, thereby converting the *pandilla* into the primary symbolic index of community, in a manner that bears comparison with Bloch's classic description of the development of a 'communal aesthetic pleasure' among the Merina and Zafimaniry of Madagascar as a result of local youth violence.[8]

However, it became rapidly apparent on my return to *barrio* Luis Fanor Hernández in 2002 that the gang had changed radically by comparison with 1996-97. It was now made up of just 18 youths aged 17 to 23 years. Although all had belonged to the gang in 1996-97, the gang's practices and attitudes had evolved. Gang warfare had disappeared, levels of intra-neighbourhood gang-related violence had increased, and the gang was now intimately connected to a thriving local crack cocaine-based drug economy.[9] The *pandilleros* were now a threatening presence, no longer imbued with an ethos of 'loving' the *barrio*, as a *pandillero* called Roger made clear:

'We couldn't give a fuck about the *barrio* inhabitants any more… If they get attacked, if they're robbed, if they have problems, who cares? We don't lift a finger to help them any more, we just laugh instead, hell, we even applaud those who are robbing them… Why should we do anything for them? Now we just hang out in the streets, smoke crack, and rob, and nothing else!'

This was very visibly related in part to crack consumption. Although drug consumption had been widespread within the gang in 1996-97, the main drug consumed at the time had been marijuana, which has very different neurological and psychiatric effects to crack. Crack makes users extremely violent, as a gang member called Chucki emphasized:

'This drug, crack, it makes you really violent, I tell you… when I smoke up and somebody insults me, I immediately want to kill them, to get a machete and do them in, to defend myself… I don't stop and think, talk to them, ask

---

8 Bloch, 1996, p. 216.

9 Although cocaine and crack were available in Managua in the mid-1990s, they were not widespread and only became prevalent from 1999 onwards. For a detailed explanation of the growth of the cocaine trade in Nicaragua see Rodgers, 2004.

them why or whatever... I don't even recognize them, all I want to do is kill them... it's the drug, I tell you, that's where the violence comes from...'

There were very obviously many more acts of spontaneous, unpredictable public violence occurring in *barrio* Luis Fanor Hernández in 2002 compared to 1996-97, and the majority could be linked to crack consumption. Furthermore, most incidents seemed to involve gang members. Although they were by no means the only crack users in the neighbourhood, the gang clearly constituted a privileged site of crack consumption, and all the *pandilleros* were crack addicts. Consequently, it was extremely common to see drugged *pandilleros* stopping local inhabitants in the streets and asking for money for another fix. If ignored or refused, they would almost invariably lash out.

At the same time, although crack consumption was an important factor behind this changed behaviour pattern and the consequent rise in insecurity, to a larger extent this was arguably the result of the gang's intimate association with drug trafficking. Cocaine began to be traded in the *barrio* around mid-1999, initially on a small scale by just one individual but rapidly expanding into a three-tiered pyramidal drug economy by mid-2000. At the top of the pyramid was the '*narco*' who brought cocaine into the neighbourhood. The *narco* wholesaled his goods to, among others, half a dozen '*púsheres*' (*sic*) in the neighbourhood. *Púsheres* resold this cocaine in smaller quantities or converted it into crack which they sold from their houses, mainly to a regular clientele which included the '*muleros*', who were the bottom rung of the drug dealing pyramid, selling small doses of crack to all comers on *barrio* street corners. There were 19 *muleros* in *barrio* Luis Fanor Hernández, 16 of whom were *pandilleros*.[10] The rewards of such small-scale dealing were substantial: an individual *mulero* could make US$350-600 per month, equivalent to three to five times the

---

10 All of the various actors of the drugs trade were in fact linked to the *barrio* Luis Fanor Hernández *pandilla* in one way or another. The *narco* was an ex-gang member from the early 1990s and all the *púsheres* were either ex-*pandilleros* from the mid-1990s or else closely related to ex-*pandilleros*, and the three non-*pandillero muleros* were former gang members.

average Nicaraguan wage. At the same time, although gang member *muleros* conducted their drug dealing transactions individually, the gang as a group acted to ensure the proper functioning and protection of the *barrio* drug economy in general, providing security services to the *narco* and to *púsheres*, and making certain that transactions proceeded smoothly. *Pandilleros* would enforce contracts, roughing up recalcitrant clients if the *narco* or *púsheres* asked them to, as well as guarding drug shipments as they moved both within and outside the *barrio*.

The gang would also make sure that clients could enter the neighbourhood unmolested by either the local population or outsiders, and the ritualized wars of the past with other gangs had completely disappeared as a result, presumably because they would have made it difficult for potential clients to come safely into the *barrio*, and were therefore detrimental to the gang's changed drug dealing preoccupations. Violent confrontations with other gangs did still occur, but in a different way. For example, in early 2001 a group of *muleros* from the nearby *barrio* Nosara gang occupied one of the entrances to *barrio* Luis Fanor Hernández in order to intercept crack clients. When they realized what had happened, the *barrio* Luis Fanor Hernández *pandilla* attacked them instantly with guns and shot two dead and left three critically injured. The gang had furthermore also instituted a veritable regime of terror at the level of the neighbourhood. *Pandilleros* would strut about the streets, menacingly displaying guns and machetes, and verbally warn *barrio* inhabitants of potential retribution should they denounce them or others involved in the local drugs trade.[11] They would moreover frequently back these threats with acts of arbitrary violence as *Doña* Yolanda described:

---

11 Although there were more police patrols in the neighbourhood than five years previously, these were clearly token in nature, and tended simply to drive down one street of the *barrio*, turn around, and drive back up a parallel street—generally past the *muleros* on their street corners. There were sporadic police raids on *barrio púsheres*—although never on the *narco*—but these tended to turn up little of suspicion, as the *púsher* would have generally received a tip-off from a corrupt policeman (as one told me after being raided). When the police did,

'Five years ago, you could trust the *pandilleros*, but not any more... They've become corrupted due to this drug crack... They threaten and attack people from the *barrio* now, rob them of whatever they have, whoever they are... They never did that before... They used to protect us, look out for us, but now they don't care, they only look out for themselves, for their illegal business ('*bisnes*')... People are scared, you've got to be careful what you say or what you do, because otherwise they'll attack you... Even if you say nothing, they might still come and rob you, come into your home, steal a chair, food, some clothes, whatever they can find... They often do, you know it's them, but you can't blame them, otherwise they'll come and burn your house down... It's their way of telling you to be careful... If you say anything to them, if you do anything, if you denounce them, then they'll come at night and wreak their vengeance... We live in terror here in the *barrio*, you have to be scared or else you're sure to be sorry... It's not like it used to be when you were here last time, Dennis, when the *pandilleros* were kids we could be proud of because of what they did for us and for the *barrio*... They're like strangers to us now, they just do things for themselves and never for the good of the community like before...'

Mutatis mutandis: gangs, violence, and vigilantism

I have argued elsewhere that *pandillas* and their violence can clearly be seen as primary forms of social structuration in contemporary urban Nicaragua, rather than the unmitigated source of chaos and disorder that they are generally perceived to be.[12] In particular, I contend that they can be conceived as examples of 'social sovereignty' that organically establish localized but variable regimes of political order within the wider conditions of social and state breakdown, constrained economic circumstances, insecurity and uncertainty that characterize post-revolutionary Nicaraguan society. This is something that came out particularly strongly in interviews I conducted with ex-*pandilleros*.

---

occasionally, find evidence, it only affected reputedly ambitious *púsheres* who were potential rivals to the *narco*, which supported the consensus in the *barrio* that the police had been 'bought' by the *narco* and that he used them to get rid of his enemies. It seems likely that the *narco* may have been reluctant to use the *pandilleros* for this purpose owing to their close links with the *púsheres*, who were all ex-*pandilleros*.

12 Rodgers, 2006.

Although gangs in Nicaragua can be traced back to the 1940s, by all accounts they were small-scale and relatively innocuous youth aggregations until the early 1990s, when their numbers increased massively and they became significantly violent. This development was clearly linked to the end of the civil war which affected Nicaragua for much of the 1980s, as many of the new gang members were 16- to 20-year-old youths, freshly demobilized from the Sandinista Popular Army or the Contra forces. Gang members from this period whom I interviewed all mentioned that becoming *pandilleros* had seemed a natural continuation of their previous roles as conscripts or guerrillas, that is to say as 'defenders of the Nation' or as 'freedom fighters'. The early 1990s were highly uncertain times in Nicaragua, as 'social conflicts …reached a new level of barely restrained anarchy',[13] partly due to a widespread process of 'state disintegration'.[14] Ex-*pandilleros* recalled feeling a sense of responsibility for their friends, families, and local communities in the face of this insecurity, and joining or constituting a gang had been a means of 'serving' and 'protecting' them more effectively than doing so individually.

To this extent, a parallel can clearly be made with notions of vigilantism, which Abrahams has classically described as including a range of violent social practices that emerge from the efforts of communities 'to make sense of their lives and maintain some sort of order in their world', particularly 'in "frontier" zones where the state is viewed as ineffective or corrupt'.[15] Indeed, the association between youth gangsterism and vigilantism is not new. Suttles, for example, famously analyzed gangs in inner city Chicago neighbourhoods as 'vigilante peer groups' policing and defending 'warrior societies' in the face of 'the failure of …public institutions'.[16] Although Abrahams cautions against assimilating 'autonomous "informal sector" groupings' such as gangs with vigilantism, on the grounds that the

---

13 Lancaster, 1992, p. 293.
14 Isbester, 1996.
15 Abrahams, 1998, pp. 3, 9.
16 Suttles, 1972, p. 191.

former tend to break 'first- rather than second-order legal rules',[17] this is in many ways a moot point in contexts where legal rules to all intents and purposes hardly apply. Indeed, this is something that Abrahams implicitly recognizes when he discusses the way vigilantism 'occupies an awkward borderland between law and illegality',[18] insofar as it is formally illegal but informally accepted. As a result, vigilante practices are frequently legitimized through 'commonsense' notions of 'decent, independent, law-abiding citizens, anxious to live and work in peace, and ready to defend their right to do so if the state fails them',[19] despite the fact that they do not actually have any formal right to do so.[20]

Ultimately, both gangs and vigilantism can be characterized as highly ambivalent social phenomena. At the same time, however, this ambivalence arguably derives less from the fact that they emerge in a legal twilight zone than from the fact that they are 'rather labile ...manifestations [that] are relatively short-lived, and ...always capable of slipping and sliding in one direction or another'.[21] This 'lability' means that social practices such as vigilantism or Nicaraguan *pandillerismo* that might at first glance seem in some way normatively positive—insofar as they create order in contexts of chaos—have the potential to rapidly become socially negative. This is something that is particularly well illustrated by the evolutionary trajectory of the *barrio* Luis Fanor Hernández *pandilla* between 1997 and 2002, whereby it mutated from being a vigilante-style social form that promoted a solidaristic sense of local community in the face of wider processes

---

17 Abrahams, 1998, p. 163.

18 Ibid., p. 7.

19 Ibid., p. 3.

20 The discourse that emerged in the mid-1990s justifying the *barrio* Luis Fanor Hernández gang's violent activities as 'acts of love' for the neighbourhood arguably similarly provided the institution of *pandillerismo* with a localized legitimacy, as was evidenced by *Don* Sergio's 1997 testimony, as well as *Doña* Yolanda's remark five years later that 'the *pandilleros* were kids we could be proud of because of what they did for us and for the *barrio*'.

21 Abrahams, 1998, p. 7.

of social breakdown—something that could plausibly be spun as normatively positive—to a more exclusive and predatory institution focused on promoting a limited form of capital accumulation based on the exploitative control of a particular resource: something more difficult to support and justify in social terms.

At the same time, though, while thinking about the transformation of *pandillerismo* in terms of changes in the institution's normative form and function makes a good deal of sense, it arguably tells us little about the specific processes through which change occurs. As Cohen has pointed out, this is important insofar as it is necessary to go beyond simply describing either the function or the form of an institution in order to properly understand it, particularly when considering this institution over time.[22] Although there is obviously a relationship between form and function, neither form nor function is inherent to any given institution, and neither continuity nor change in either necessarily entails continuity or change in the other, since different forms can achieve a specific function, while conversely, a particular form can fulfil different functions. From this perspective, in order to really understand the 'lability' of Nicaraguan vigilante gangs, it is important not only to have a picture of what is common and what is different between the two manifestations of the *barrio* Luis Fanor Hernández *pandilla* described above, but also to have a sense of the actual process of transformation it underwent, as it is this that will provide us with a real understanding of how and why Nicaraguan *pandillerismo* changed.

Tracing the transformation of the barrio Luis Fanor Hernández pandilla

It would be tempting to link the differences between the *barrio* Luis Fanor Hernández *pandilla* in 1997 and 2002 to crack cocaine. Certainly, this is what Ronnie intimated during our conversation on the

---

22 Cohen, 1969, p. 219.

first day of my return to the neighbourhood. When pressed as to why the gang had 'turned bad' he suggested:

'Because of all sorts of shit, *maje*, because of all sorts of shit... But most of all because of *la droga* (drugs)...'

'Drugs? What do you mean, marijuana?'

'No, of course not, *maje*, that stuff's *nitua* (cool), you know what it's like, there's nothing harmful about marijuana. No, *maje*, what I'm talking about is *la piedra* (the stone), crack cocaine. Marijuana is nothing compared to that shit, I tell you. Crack's changed everything...'

At the same time, the emergence of drugs only goes so far in explaining why *pandillerismo* in Nicaragua underwent such a wholesale transformation, particularly when one considers that all the testimonies I gathered in *barrio* Luis Fanor Hernández tended to suggest that the gang was already in the process of changing when cocaine made its appearance in the neighbourhood in 1999.

Indeed, the gang's mutation seems to have begun as early as the end of 1997. The *barrio* Luis Fanor Hernández *pandilla* had until then been divided into distinct age and geographical subgroups: there were three age cohorts—the 7 to 12 years olds, the 13 to 17 years olds, and those 18 years old and over—and three geographical subgroups, respectively associated with the central area of the neighbourhood, the '*abajo*' (or west) side of the neighbourhood, and the '*arriba*' (or east) side of the neighbourhood. The different geographical subgroups had distinct names, respectively '*los de la Calle Ocho*' (named after the alleyway where this group tended to congregate), '*los Cancheros*' (because of a '*cancha*', or playing field—if only in name, because all it was in fact was a stretch of relatively un-potholed road—on that side of the *barrio*) and '*los Dragones*' (because all its members had a dragon tattoo). These different subgroups generally operated separately, except in the context of gang warfare, when they would come together in order to defend the neighbourhood or attack another. At the same time, even if the different groups were very autonomous, the individual gang members always presented

361

themselves as members of a generic *barrio* Luis Fanor Hernández *pandilla*, and none of the subgroups, whether determined by age or geography, ever fought each other, although fights did occasionally break out between individuals.

Around November 1997, the *Calle Ocho pandilla* subgroup fell apart because its entire elder age cohort 'matured out' of the gang simultaneously. This seems to have been precipitated by the departure from the neighbourhood of a prominent member of that age cohort a few months previously and the sudden death of another. The younger members of the subgroup were absorbed into the two other *barrio pandilla* subgroups and the *Calle Ocho* subgroup ceased to exist. This polarization of the gang into two subgroups had important consequences for the gang's internal dynamics. The tripartite structure of the gang had constituted a stable system, with each subgroup effectively holding the others in a balance of power. Binary structures, however, are inherently oppositional, and by all accounts there rapidly developed a strong sense of rivalry between the two remaining subgroups. This was reflected in the development of a heightened sense of subgroup territoriality that culminated in areas of the *barrio* dominated by one group becoming no-go areas for the other and vice-versa, something that was unprecedented compared to past internal *barrio* Luis Fanor Hernández gang dynamics.

Tension was further heightened towards the end of 1998 when the *Cancheros* subgroup changed its name to '*Los Killers*', because members of the subgroup were involved in a series of murders. Around Easter 1999, this tension erupted into a full-fledged conflict between the *Killers* and the *Dragones* subgroups. Ronnie, who had then been a member of the *Dragones*, explained the situation in the following way:

The conflict was inevitable. They [the *Killers*] believed they were the masters, you understand. They believed they were better than us. But here, in the *pandilla*, everybody's equal, you can't have a situation where some are better than others, we're all equal, you understand, nobody is better than anybody else. In the *pandillero* language, we say that they were shitting bigger than their arses ('*se la tiraban aquí del culo*'), that they were getting too big for their boots. They were trying to put one up on us, which wasn't right, you understand, and so we had to make them respect us, to make them understand ... We had to make them respect what we call the law of ice ('*la ley del hielo*'). What this means is that when somebody tries to put one up on you, if they try to dominate you, then you have to give it to them, you've got to hit them, slash them, beat them up real good, you know, smash their head against the wall until they're covered in blood, defeated, dead, perhaps, at any rate so that they'll never defy you again. That's what you have to do to make them respect the law of ice, as we say here in Nicaragua, so that's why the conflict between us was inevitable.'

The inevitable conflict was sparked off when a family with four youths belonging to the *Killers* moved from the west side of the *barrio*, which was the *Killers*' side, to the east side, the *Dragones*' side. The *Dragones* wanted nothing to do with the four *Killers pandilleros*, but at the same time gave them an ultimatum to either leave the *Killers* or leave their side of the *barrio*. Refusing the *Dragones*' demands, the *Killers* decided to take pre-emptive action and attack the *Dragones* by surprise one evening. This was unprecedented behaviour insofar as it was the first time one *barrio* Luis Fanor Hernández *pandilla* subgroup attacked another. The *Dragones* had—fortuitously for them—been planning a surprise attack on a neighbouring *pandilla* later that night and so had their weapons at hand, and the fight quickly escalated into a raging gun battle that had little in the way of the customary ritualized nature of gang warfare. The gang subgroups fought each other for several hours, causing widespread damage to *barrio* houses, and almost one hundred neighbourhood inhabitants were injured, although somewhat miraculously there were no deaths. The *Dragones* eventually acquired the upper hand and went on a rampage, hunting down and beating up *Killers* gang members—in one gruesome case cutting the ear off one (while the *pandillero*'s father lost an eye trying to intervene)—and systematically attacking the houses on the *Killers*' side of the *barrio*, burning several down with Molotov cocktails.

According to both *pandilleros* and non-*pandilleros*, this conflagration was 'too much' for the *barrio* population. Several families called the police and denounced the *pandilleros*. Six *Dragones* members were arrested with the active cooperation of neighbourhood inhabitants, while another half dozen fled the *barrio*. When the case against the six who had been caught was due to come to court, however, those *Dragones* gang members that remained in the neighbourhood threatened the *barrio* inhabitants who were pressing charges with reprisals, and the case was quickly dropped. This unprecedented episode profoundly marked the *barrio pandilleros* and fundamentally changed their attitude towards the neighbourhood population. As a *Dragones pandillero* called Roger put it:

'The people in the *barrio* showed themselves to be hypocrites then, all of a sudden they hated us, and they turned against us, but before that we had been respected, liked, because we helped and protected them... without us they couldn't survive! Now they don't want to know about anything, they'll fucking denounce us if they get half a chance! Why should we do anything for such treacherous people (*'gente trucha'*)?'

The *Dragones* began to wander about the *barrio* visibly armed in order to intimidate the *barrio* population but also the *Killers*, who spontaneously disaggregated in the face of this terrorization. At the same time, however, the *Dragones* rapidly reduced in size from some forty members just after the conflict with the *Killers* to twenty members by the beginning of 2001.[23] To a certain extent, demographic factors came into play, as the peak of *pandillero* recruitment in *barrio* Luis Fanor Hernández seems to have been reached in 1995-96, and many of those who joined the *pandilla* then had been 14-15 years old, and were consequently reaching an age at which 'maturing out' naturally came into play. Another factor was that in early 2000 the municipal authorities built two basketball courts in *barrio* Luis Fanor Hernández, which—more incidentally than by design—provided an alternative focal point to the *pandilla* for neighbourhood youth, and in particular for those wavering over membership.[24] More generally,

23 Two of the twenty subsequently died from drug consumption-related health complications. The eighteen remaining were the eighteen that made up the *barrio* Luis Fanor Hernández *pandilla* in 2002.

24 This should in no way be seen as signalling an increased state presence in the *barrio*, as the basketball courts were the first public works to be carried out since

though, the conflict with the *Killers* and its aftermath also profoundly affected *Dragones pandilleros*, as one called Elvis, who had had to flee the *barrio* in order to avoid being caught by the police after the *Dragones-Killers* conflict, makes clear:

'It was horrible, I was running from here to there, millions of places, from one to the other to avoid being caught, and it's horrible, I tell you... You feel like you're being tracked, hunted, like an animal, always looking over your shoulder... I never want to be on the run again, so ever since all that, I've looked to distance myself, to avoid problems, especially as those guys in the *pandilla* have got crazier and crazier, you know, more violent and all... I began spending less time with the *pandilla*, doing my own thing, not looking for trouble. I still talk with everybody and all, but when there's going to be trouble, I do my own thing, you know, to avoid problems...'

It was at this point that the emergence of crack cocaine had a significant impact on the gang in *barrio* Luis Fanor Hernández. Crack consumption by gang members began before those who remained became centrally involved in drug dealing from early 2000 onwards, but both developments accelerated the transformation of the gang in a variety of ways. Both crack consumption and dealing led to a reduction in the number of youths involved by creating impediments for younger gang members—in particular those under 13 years old—insofar as they are both activities that are physiologically less suited for the young. The health effects of smoking crack are particularly deleterious for children, and dealing can be a problematic activity for them due to clients' lack of confidence, as well as their inability to effectively protect themselves from potentially violent addict clients. Some gang members also simply did not take to crack cocaine, as an ex-*Dragones pandillero* called Kalia told me:

'I left the gang when everybody started smoking crack, because it really fucks you up. Everybody started doing it as soon as the *narco* started selling it, and then it got heavier and heavier as the *pandilla* got involved in the drug dealing, so there was no way of staying in the gang and not doing that shit.'

---

the Sandinista regime's urban reconstruction efforts in the early 1980s, and were linked to the Liberal Party's (failed) municipal re-election campaign.

The gang's involvement in the emergent drugs trade also completely changed other patterns of behaviour, leading for example to the rapid abandonment of ritualized gang warfare with neighbouring *pandillas*, as this was an activity that could potentially scare crack clients away. The gang's ever more parochial interests also crystallized gang members' already negative attitudes towards the local neighbourhood population, and this ever-increasing antagonism vis-à-vis the *barrio* also contributed to gang members dropping out, as Ronnie told me:

'I became independent [*sic*] because I didn't like the gang's hatred towards the *barrio*… You know how we used to love this neighbourhood, Dennis, you remember, no? That's why I was in the *pandilla*, because I loved the *barrio*—we'd protect it, take care of it, people would appreciate it… When everything fell apart and people in the *barrio* and also the guys in the gang began to act like shits towards each other, I just said fuck it, that's not my thing, and left.'

The gang members that remained established themselves as *muleros* in the local drugs economy. This was of course hardly fortuitous. A drug economy cannot rely on classic mechanisms of regulation and contract-enforcement—such as the law—in a context where drugs are illicit, and inevitably needs alternative mechanisms to impose regularity onto transactions. As numerous theorists have pointed out, the most basic means of social regulation is violence, and as the dominant vector of brutality in the neighbourhood, the gang was ideally positioned to supply this violence.[25] At the same time, the exclusive nature of the drugs trade meant that to be able to provide this violence coherently the gang needed to be a small, self-interested unit rather than a large, communitarian group. Indeed, the solidaristic nature of *pandillerismo* in the mid-1990s might very well have precluded the *pandilla* from becoming involved in the drugs trade had cocaine appeared then, because gang members would most likely have been unwilling to direct their violence against neighbour-

---

25 Furthermore, as an ex-gang member, the *narco* was ideally connected to the gang in order to involve them.

hood inhabitants. When the drugs trade emerged and consolidated during 1999-2000, however, the *barrio* Luis Fanor Hernández gang was undergoing a number of endogenous changes that were leading to an organizational shakedown of the gang and an inversion of its previous solidarity with the local community that meant it was more amenable to offering the services required by the drugs trade, and also to grasping the opportunities provided by the appearance of cocaine at that particular point in time.

Conclusion: understanding social change

As Bardhan has remarked, 'an institution's mere function of serving the interests of potential beneficiaries is clearly inadequate in *explaining* it, just as it is an incompetent detective who tries to explain a murder mystery only by looking for the beneficiary and, on that basis alone, proceeds to arrest the heir of the murdered rich man.'[26] There always exists at any given time a 'repertory' of possible actions at the disposal of social actors, and the ones they choose and how these evolve are the result of a conjunction of factors that cannot necessarily be predicted in a deterministic manner.[27] Rather, as Douglas has pointed out, institutional arrangements tend to emerge through a process of 'bricolage',[28] the result of *ad hoc* combinations of pre-existing social forms and processes. It is therefore not the relationship between a given institutional form and function *per se* that is important, but rather understanding what it is that enables a given institution to articulate a given function, what the limitations are on this particular institution performing this particular function, and what are the different factors that can lead to a change either in form or function or both.

The emergence of the drugs trade in *barrio* Luis Fanor Hernández during mid-1999 clearly stands out as an important factor in explain-

---

26 Bardhan, 1989, p. 1392 (italics in original).
27 De Certeau, 1984.
28 Douglas, 1987, p. 66.

ing the profound transformation that the neighbourhood *pandilla* underwent between 1996-97 and 2002. At the same time, however, endogenous changes affecting the *pandilla* before the rise of drug dealing were clearly also just as critical, not only in terms of understanding the specific trajectory of the gang, but also for comprehending the actual development of the drugs trade in the neighbourhood. Without the gang's changing internal dynamics it is likely that the drugs trade would not have been able to take root in *barrio* Luis Fanor Hernández when it did. At the same time, there also existed something of a positive feedback loop between the two social processes that mutually transformed and consolidated their evolution, to the extent that we can talk of a real 'compatibility' between *pandillerismo* and the drugs trade. Without this 'compatibility', both the drugs trade and the gang's transformation from a communitarian social form to a more predatory institution would have been impossible, as it was in many ways this, more than anything else, that enabled them to flourish and mutually reinforce each other.

Seen in this way, it can be argued that it is not so much particular endogenous or exogenous factors, such as the internal dynamics of gangs or the drugs trade, that are important in order to explain the 'lability' of Nicaraguan *pandillerismo*, but rather the fact that these issues came together in a particular manner at a particular moment in time. To this extent, it is perhaps more accurate to talk about the existence of a 'contingent compatibility', insofar as the transformational trajectory of any given institution through time is, to a large extent, not so much determined as contingent, an improvisation from a range of possibilities. What is important to understand, then, is what determines the array of options and their potential articulation at any given point in time; while the emergence of exogenous factors or the endogenous contradictions of institutions are important to explaining social change, they do not constitute by themselves the basis upon which to explain the 'lability' of given institutions. Rather, we need to have a holistic idea of the complex interplay between exogenous stimuli, endogenous contradictions, and the particular nature of an

368

institution, its context, and the agency of the social actors involved, as is starkly highlighted by the way the vigilante gang of *barrio* Luis Fanor Hernández 'turned bad' between 1997 and 2002.

❧

Abrahams, R. *Vigilant Citizens: Vigilantism and the State*, Cambridge, 1998.

Arendt, H. *On Violence*, New York, 1969.

Bardhan, P. 'The New Institutional Economics and Development Theory—a Brief Critical-Assessment', *World Development* 17(9), 1989, pp. 1389-95.

Bloch, M. 'La "consummation" des jeunes hommes chez les Zafimaniry de Madagascar', in *De la violence*, F. Héritier (ed.), Paris, 1996, pp. 201-22.

Burawoy, M. 'Revisits: An Outline of a Theory of Reflexive Ethnography', *American Sociological Review* 68(5), 2003, pp. 645-79.

Cohen, A. 'Political Anthropology: The Analysis of the Symbolism of Power Relations', *Man* 4(2), 1969, pp. 215-35.

De Certeau, M. *The Practice of Everyday Life*, Berkeley, 1984.

Douglas, M. *How Institutions Think*, London, 1987.

Guevara, E. *Venceremos! The Speeches and Writings of Ernesto Che Guevara*, New York, 1969.

Isbester, K. 'Understanding State Disintegration: The case of Nicaragua', *The Journal of Social, Political and Economic Studies* 21(4), 1996, pp. 455-76.

Lancaster, R.N. *Thanks to God and the Revolution: Popular Religion and Class Consciousness in the New Nicaragua*, New York, 1988.

—— *Life is Hard: Machismo, Danger, and the Intimacy of Power in Nicaragua*, Berkeley, 1992.

Nicaragua Network News 'News in Brief, 9, 6, 5-11 February 2001', http://www.tulane.edu/~libweb/RESTRICTED/NICANEWS/2001/2001_0205.txt 16 June 2004.

Rodgers, D. 'Living in the Shadow of Death: Violence, Pandillas, and Social Disintegration in Contemporary Urban Nicaragua', PhD dissertation, University of Cambridge, 2000.

—— 'Globalization and Development Seen from Below', *Envío in English* 272, 2004, pp. 17-22.

—— 'Living in the Shadow of Death: Gangs, Violence, and Social Order in Urban Nicaragua, 1996-2002', *Journal of Latin American Studies* 38(2), 2006, pp. 267-92.

Suttles, G.D. *The Social Construction of Communities*, Chicago, 1972.

Turner, V.W. *The Ritual Process: Structure and Anti-structure*, Chicago, 1969.

15

LYNCHING AND POST-WAR
COMPLEXITIES IN GUATEMALA

Jennifer Burrell and Gavin Weston

Since the signing of the final Peace Accords on 29 December 1996
by the high command of the Guatemalan military and the URNG,[1]
which officially ended the 36-year-long civil war, lynching has become increasingly common in the country. Analysts from across
the social sciences have sought to understand this phenomenon in
various ways, generating a considerable literature addressing reasons
for lynching, policy predicaments, and plans for action. Significant
social anxiety has led to an understandable emphasis on causality,
and the question of why lynching happens. In Guatemala, we argue,
this has ultimately contributed to a narrowing of debate that fails to
take into account the fact that vigilantism is on the rise globally, in
response to myriad kinds of transition processes, and among groups
that span generations, gender and different kinds of local relationships to power, as demonstrated in this volume.

In response, in this chapter, we explore what we call a 'genealogy
of causality',[2] that is, some of the reasons, connections and principal
vectors of cause that have been central to debates about this issue in
Guatemala. We explore these in relation to ethnographic data col-

---

1 A coalition of four socialist insurgent groups.

2 Burrell thanks Martha Huggins (personal communication) for suggesting this
analytic concept as a way of making sense of the proliferation of recent writing
on the topic.

lected over the course of the decade that preceded and followed the cessation of armed conflict. The value in doing this, we argue, is to see the range of explanations and factors currently being discussed and to add new ones to larger debates about vigilantism. Local specificities, we show, often suggest characterizations of violence that include a range of factors that fall outside of traditional categories of analysis or expectations of post-war violence.

In proposing a widening of analytic considerations that are nevertheless based on the local, we draw attention to the myriad ways in which violence ultimately interpolates into communities, and new forms and idioms of power are brought to bear on situations for which the repertoire of local mechanisms must be expanded. Long-term militarization has lasting effects on everyday life, as do migration, intergenerational conflict, shifts in gendered subjectivities, state roles and relationships with extra-statal institutions, such as NGOs. What happens when some of these idioms and power relations are shifted into other moments and are directed to differently situated actors: a hapless Japanese tourist, for example, or a recently returned migrant?

The great hope of transition is democracy and a better life for the majority, but as many of the cases in this volume demonstrate, it often achieves quite the opposite. As fieldworkers of various sorts, we invest our own hopes and dreams in the challenges of these moments, contributing to ambiguity about how we can study violence like lynching, what to say about it, and how to best serve the people we work with. The existing tools of analysis, it seems, often pull us between the poles of alleged academic objectivity and political and humanitarian advocacy, with a slippery middle ground that is difficult to occupy. And yet, we remain convinced not only that ethnography matters, but that ethnographic interventions are essential to exploring the murky grey space between vigilantism, hopes, dreams, abuses and violations.

Guatemalan lynching hovers on the fringes of human rights. It becomes a violation of human rights through the state's inactivity in curtailing it, rather than because of the acts of violence themselves, so that Godoy calls them 'a new form of human rights abuse'.[3] Despite this marginal relationship with human rights, we are acutely aware as authors of Richard Wilson's assertion that there is a need for ethnography to help '...compensate for the individualised, a-cultural, deracinated and therefore universalistic nature of most human rights accounts.'[4] There has been a tendency to de-subjectify lynching, like other forms of human rights violation, in an attempt to engage with legalistic discourses designed to influence state policy.[5] We argue that an approach which contains a detailed account of local specificities within individual lynching is useful both analytically and in redressing this imbalance.

We come to this project of co-authorship by virtue of having done fieldwork in a town in north-western Guatemala, Todos Santos Cuchumatán, where lynching became an acceptable post-war mechanism in the aftermath of conflict and the ensuing vacuum of power that resulted.[6] Local debates over why things happened and the construction of narratives about particular incidents, as well as the failure of many existing arguments to accommodate community explanations, concerns and actions within wider networks of power, have led us to explore the different pathways through which idioms of power resonate. While we recognize the mechanisms of post-war complexity that have supported the rise of lynching in Guatemala during this period, we are simultaneously acutely aware of the urgency of widening a sphere of dialogue that addresses the concur-

---

3 Godoy, 2002, p. 641.

4 Wilson, 1997, p. 157.

5 Ibid., p. 154.

6 Burrell conducted fieldwork from 1994 to 2000 and Weston in 2002-3. Burrell has explored the aftermath of lynching and how villagers eschewed the anonymity of the mob in order to turn each other in to state investigators in the wake of the 2000 lynching of Tetsuo Yamahiro, a Japanese tourist, in the forthcoming article 'After Lynching in Todos Santos Cuchumatán,' in *Revisiting Guatemala's Harvest of Violence*, Diane Nelson and Carlota McAllister, eds, Duke University Press. Weston explores lynching more generally in Guatemala and particularly in Todos Santos in his dissertation, which he is currently writing for the Department of Anthropology at the University of Sussex.

rent rise of incidents throughout the region of Latin America, and throughout the world, as demonstrated by the cases in this volume. Through the engagement of the very local with the much broader, we come to understand specific incidents in one local community as part of a global phenomenon that is connected to war, peace processes, transitions and the promotion of insecurities of all kinds, be they political, economic, social or cultural.

Lynching as a post-war phenomenon

The construction of intellectual genealogies, elaborated and developed most famously in the work of Michel Foucault,[7] allows for movement away from a 'grand scheme of progressive history' to show more mundane turns and choices in everyday life. We employ it in order to suggest an alternative to viewing lynching as in some sense an inevitable outcome of the Guatemalan post-war experience, or 'the continuation of civil war by other means'—seeing it rather as an option in a flexible and ever-expanding repertoire of potential actions amidst a climate of increasing national and regional violence. In the first part of this paper we explore a growing consensus concerning key factors responsible for the widespread fomentation of lynching. These explanations infrequently move beyond war or the subsequent transitional phase in accounting for lynching.

Contemporary analysis of lynchings in Guatemala can be broadly split into two separate, yet interrelated sections: those that explain the lynching as in some way a continuation of violence from the civil war, and those that explain the violence as relating to the failure of the justice system within the transition to democracy. While these two aspects can be divided, more frequently their constituent parts are synthesized to express an overarching explanation for lynching relating to factors linked only to the war and the subsequent transition period that followed.

---

7 Foucault, 1977, building on Nietzsche's genealogy of morals.

Perhaps the clearest proponent of the first of these explanations—that lynchings are continuation of the violence of the civil war by other means—is Godoy.[8] Her argument is that the civil war removed existing elements of customary law, replacing them with violent modes of conflict resolution. Godoy argues that frequently those instigating or carrying out these attacks are those who were granted state authority through the civil patrol system during the civil war. While the PACs (*Patrulleros de Autodefensa Civil* or Civil Patrols) were stripped of power during the peace process, many still hold positions of respect or fear within rural areas. In some cases these ex-PAC members force the local population to participate in lynching. As Gutiérrez and Kobrak[9] note, these former paramilitary structures had a widespread familiarity with acts of collective violence from their activity during the civil war. Godoy also links the violent response to crime evident in lynching to the climate of terror that was instigated during the conflict. As Green[10] made clear, the unpredictability and all-encompassing nature of the violence of the civil war in Guatemala formed an environment in which terror became the key psychological mechanism that kept the rural population compliant, and aspects of this terror continue to burden the thoughts of rural Guatemalans as Godoy,[11] Gutiérrez and Kobrak[12] note. This would imply that the violence of crime and social deviance are feared more acutely among these populations (although spectacularly rising incidents of crime throughout the country are currently frightening all Guatemalans).

The second part of this genealogy is perhaps most clearly expounded by Daniel Rothenburg,[13] who places lynching in the context of the loosened bonds of a repressive state. Rothenburg sees the elation

---

8 Godoy, 2002.
9 Gutiérrez and Kobrak, 2001.
10 Green, 1999.
11 Godoy, 2002.
12 Gutiérrez and Kobrak, 2001.
13 Rothenburg, 1998.

that followed the peace process as masking an un-satiated '…hunger for justice […] enunciated within an environment of enormous systemic mistrust.'[14] Rothenburg sees this hunger propelling the public into acts of vigilante violence. Within the transition period following the peace accords, the high expectations for justice (and change more generally) produced an immense tension that has been vented through incidents of vigilantism. While Rothenburg places a more emotive relationship with justice at the heart of his analysis,[15] others focus more specifically on the institutions related to justice.

The justice system is singled out as the cause of lynching by a number of authors. Seider points to an effective rule of law that protects citizen rights and enforces obligations as 'one of the central challenges of peace building and democratisation common to all post-authoritarian societies.'[16] This is a challenge that has thus far eluded the Guatemalan state. As Gutiérrez and others observe, the judicial system in Guatemala is inaccessible for a number of reasons.[17] Among these reasons are the physical distances between many rural areas and the state arbiters of justice such as the Justices of the Peace; the language barrier between a largely Spanish-speaking justice system and an indigenous Mayan-speaking population it is meant to serve; the financial barrier for many who cannot afford legal representation, or travel to cities to access courts; and finally, the fact that many do not perceive the state criminal-justice system as the appropriate ground in which to resolve conflicts.[18]

However, it is not only these problems that hamper access to and use of the justice system. Public perception of the legal system is

---

14 Ibid., p. 6.

15 He states: 'People want order desperately, and it is this desperation, not poverty, a corrupt judicial system, an incompetent police force, or the claims of indigenous law which motivate mob action.' Ibid.

16 Seider, 1998, p. 97.

17 Gutiérrez, 2003; IDIES, 1999.

18 Gutiérrez, 2003, p. 205.

frequently starkly negative, and with good reason. Carlos Mendoza[19] points out that people simply do not trust the justice system, seeing it as inefficient and corrupt at every single level, from the rank and file police and prisons staff to courts. María Fernández García[20] adds that state complicity during the civil war plays a large part in this mistrust, as the judiciary throughout the civil war used its powers to protect the military state and its representatives from prosecution, rather than the public whose human rights were so grossly violated that the CEH Truth Commission Report[21] declared that the actions of the Guatemalan state in the 1980s constituted genocide against the Mayan people.

Julian López García notes that the demand for justice is so great because of the all-pervading nature of crime in contemporary Guatemala. With 18 per cent of households having experienced burglary or including the victim of a robbery (figure based on data from November 2002),[22] and with little chance of the police solving crimes unless they are committed against the rich, it is easy to see how insecurity and the absence of legal frameworks for dealing with it occupy such a prominent role in the public's collective psyche.

These explanations which contextualize lynchings as relating either to the war or to the subsequent transition period should not necessarily be seen as competing hypotheses. These two contrasting theses represent what seems to be a widely held and consensual view on Guatemalan lynching, one that reflects contemporary conditions in Guatemala. Of the authors mentioned so far, only Godoy and Rothenburg enunciate ideas representing just one side of this dual cause. Fernandez García, Gutiérrez, Kobrak, Mendoza, and López García all combine elements of each to come to what appears to be a broad consensus over the causes of lynching in Guatemala. While some of these authors do explore other factors at play in lynching

---

19 Mendoza, 2003.

20 Fernández García, 2004.

21 Comision de Esclarecimento Historico, 1999.

22 López García, 2003.

(Gutiérrez looks at power relations, for instance, and López García looks at crime), it is always in relation to over-arching war-related explanations.

There are some obvious reasons why these explanations have become so ubiquitous. Most stark is the fact that lynching began with such a sudden start in 1996, the year in which the peace process was finally completed. The fact that the war ended and 1996 was central to Guatemala's transition to peace obviously places these factors at the core of any explanation of lynching. Eyewitness testimonies place ex-PACs at many lynchings, leading some and participating in others.[23] Some lynchings such as that of Judge Hugo Martinez, who allowed a suspected rapist to walk free, are quite distinctly tied up in issues of mistrust of the judicial system.[24]

The nature of this evidence demonstrates that it should be accepted that these post-war aspects are prevalent factors in lynching, a fact which needs no debating. What needs contesting is that these factors appear to have become not only the most prominent, but virtually the only factors explored in relation to the causes of lynching. Our concern is that the over-emphasis on these approaches ignores or negates the aftermath of lynchings, their effects upon communities, and the fact that there is often substantial dissent or coercion involved in this method. In other words, not all community members take part in spontaneous mob violence, some refuse to participate, actively try to intervene, or bring potential victims to safety.

We note that there are two other factors commonly mentioned in relation to lynching. The first, which one hears frequently in Guatemala but is rejected by every single one of the authors mentioned so far, is that lynching is a form of indigenous justice. As they are not limited to the indigenous population and an equivalent mode of mob action does not exist in pre-war Guatemalanist literature, this idea can be rejected outright. The second is that there

---

23 Godoy, 2002.
24 MINUGUA, 2002; Mendoza, 2003, p. 103.

is a link between the areas worst affected by lynching, those worst affected by the civil war and their levels of social exclusion, measured according to those scoring most unfavourably on the Index of Human Development, an index which takes into account figures of life expectancy, education and per capita income.[25] However these observations are rarely taken any further. No attempt is made to show how this poverty, social marginalization and lack of education bear on lynching in a coherent way, the implication merely being that lack of provision in these areas results in crime, with lynching occurring as a result. While this is doubtlessly contributory, the specific dynamics of this relationship between social exclusion and lynching have been ignored in favour of attention to war and transition related factors.

The Foucauldian concept of genealogy rests on the construction of an archaeology, the level of knowledge and detail necessary to understand what makes an event or situation possible.[26] While archaeologies and genealogies as conceptual apparatus alternate and support each other in the explanation of particular histories, the strength of archaeologies lies in the way they function as objective neutral positions, avoiding causal theories of change.[27] When analysis of lynching is limited to this narrow remit understood within certain frameworks of causality, a number of problems become apparent. If we view the violence of the war as not having disappeared, only having changed form, we evoke old ideas of 'cultures of violence', where violence is inescapable owing to the 'nature' of a community. By prioritizing war-related explanations over all else, we deny specific lynchings their own internal or local logic, and deny community members agency in accounting for them and their sometimes unexpected, inconsistent or contrary actions in the aftermath. While the war and transition undoubtedly contributed to

---

25 MINUGUA, 2003; Fernández García, 2004 .
26 Foucault, 1994, p. 31.
27 Dreyfus and Rabinow, 1982, p. 105.

the fomentation of lynching, when we look at specific cases, other unrelated factors become at least as important.

Lynching, local power and conflict in Todos Santos

As noted in the Global Vigilantes workshop from which these contributions emanated, ethnographic fieldwork on violence and post-war tension is essential to understanding these moments. In this section, we show how ethnographic understanding gives rise to nuanced understanding of conflicts that are based in local life and, while cast differently in the post-war period, are the kinds of conflicts that have animated life in Todos Santos for generations.

Two major lynching incidents in Todos Santos Cuchumatán, a Mam Maya town located in the north-western highland department of Huehuetenango, inform our discussion. The first, in 1997, was the near-lynching of a young migrant recently returned from the United States. The second, which brought national and international infamy and new levels of internal conflict and blame to the community, was the lynching of a Japanese tourist and a Guatemalan bus driver during the large regional market in May 2000.[28]

In 1997 Jorge Mario Ramirez Matias returned to Todos Santos having spent over a year working in the United States. Newly muscular, with long hair and pierced ears, Mario mixed the visible accoutrements of migration (Nike sneakers, baseball caps, leather jackets) with the *traje*[29]of Todos Santos, in the process melding a

---

28 Narratives of lynchings can differ wildly from one account to the next depending on many factors including who the narrator is, who the audience is, vested interests, and more intimate histories of conflict. We have both collected a variety of different kinds of accounts (and Burrell was witness to one incident). Each version, including the one that we provide, is a version of events among many competing narratives.

29 *Traje* is the hand-woven clothing worn throughout Guatemala by indigenous Maya women and sometimes men. Todos Santos is one of few Mayan towns in Guatemala where men still continue the practice of wearing this clothing, which consists of red-striped trousers and white striped shirts with elaborately woven collars and cuffs.

model worth emulating for many male teenagers in the village. His new-found prestige, relative wealth and status as a returned migrant were quickly channelled into leadership of one of two so-called gangs in the village. While it would be misleading to state that Jorge Mario was not a gang member, he was not one in the context of the very real problem of *maras* (gangs) in Guatemala and throughout Latin America. Although he would occasionally invoke prior member-ship in a US gang to curious tourists, he was, to our knowledge, never involved in gang culture whilst there. In Todos Santos in 1997 when Jorge Mario narrowly escaped lynching, the activities of gangs amounted to little more than groups of youths naming themselves in ways that aped gang culture such as M2 (*Emé Dos*), the Mendoza Gang or the Pajon Gang. They were not involved in drugs or theft, they did not own guns and were not responsible for violence apart from drunken brawling (which is not limited to gangs of youths[30]). As Burrell notes, gang activity in Todos Santos, in contrast to the rest of Latin America, was a pursuit for the relatively well-off, young men who were members of families who could afford to educate them and who did not require their labour in fields or businesses. Many of their parents were noted community leaders. In other words, belonging to a gang required a substantial amount of leisure time.[31] Through loi-tering and the intimidation of other youths, the so-called gangs were viewed as threatening. Although Jorge Mario was not connected to any real criminality, outside alcohol fuelled altercations, his appear-ance and association with general trouble marked him out as a social misfit to older generations and as a model for emulation, something dangerous in a Mayan village where respect for authority, especially of elders, had historically been central to community life.

His return to Todos Santos set off new waves of rumour and gossip. He had a lot of money and spent it freely among his friends, getting

---

30 Moser and McIlwaine note that by far the most common cause of all social violence in Guatemala was the result of alcohol consumption (McIlwaine and Moser, 2001).

31 Burrell, 2005.

drunk and having fun. He and his friends would stay up late holding barbecues, listening to loud music, drinking beer by the crate-load at the ancient Mayan ruins (a local ritual centre) near to his house. Rumours soon started. At some stage these rumours encompassed recent local and regional crimes, ranging from petty theft of poultry and radios through to armed robbery of pick-up trucks on the road to the departmental capital.

The market on 20 December 1997 was the last one before the Christmas celebration and as a result was packed with people from surrounding hamlets preparing for the holiday. At some point just before the buses were to make their return to these outlying communities, the mayor began to denounce Jorge Mario before a large crowd that had gathered in the central park, accusing him of theft and of badly influencing village youth through his behaviour, long hair and disrespect for elders. The mayor publicly bated him, eventually inviting the crowd to physically attack with whatever items were at hand: fruit crates, vegetables, sticks, and rocks. Although some villagers attempted to head off the attackers, the crowd rapidly grew. After receiving a number of bad blows to the head, Mario managed to drag himself down the main street, under a continuous hail of objects, to the weaving cooperative, where his father was president. Cooperative staff and associates quickly barricaded the shop. Outside, an increasingly menacing crowd gathered and some people went off to find petrol, with the idea of burning the cooperative building, which was made of wood. Mario's father and other community members attempted to calm the crowd and eventually buses left, thinning the crowd substantially. Others phoned human rights defenders in the departmental capital and travelled there to fetch the military, as this was prior to the local installation of the National Civil Police (PNC). While all this had happened at around mid-day, it was not until 7pm that the military finally arrived to help. Mario escaped under escort, dressed in women's clothing to protect his identity from those who were still gathered outside of the cooperative calling for his death.

He spent the next two days in hospital. During this time, the mayor had lodged a *denuncia* (official accusation) against him with regional authorities, accusing him of being responsible for the hold-ups of pick-up trucks. His family says this was a change in accusations by the mayor to cover his own back for inciting the violence. Because of these accusations he had a military escort while in the hospital. He had to pay 10,000 quetzales bail[32] to remain out of detention while there was an investigation. Charges were later dropped against him when his passport and other papers showing he was not in the country at the time were produced. Allegedly the *alcalde* (mayor) had to pay a bribe to escape charges of inciting the attack. Jorge Mario returned to Todos Santos a week later and kept a low profile for the next month or so, eventually incurring additional community ire by inciting a panic among picnicking children when he drunkenly attacked their teacher. Some children were lost in the mountains and, when search parties failed to initially ferret them from their hiding places, spent a freezing night alone on the *altiplano*.

Local accounts and explanations suggest that the *alcalde's* accusations against Jorge Mario were probably motivated by ongoing battles about local sites of power and local party politics, especially relating to upcoming mayoral elections. First, the mayor is from an important *aldea* (hamlet) of Todos Santos and there is ongoing tension between mayoral candidates from various places in the township. Jorge Mario's father was a former mayor and was planning to stand again in the next elections. The accusations may simply have been an attempt to sully the reputation of the family in order to render his candidacy less feasible. After the attack on Jorge Mario, his father still ran for *alcalde* as a matter of principle, but received just a handful of votes. What ultimately seems clear was that the mayor intended to demonstrate his local power and support through inciting violence around the person of Jorge Mario. In doing so, he deliberately flaunted the absence of established mechanisms for making accusations (by using a loudspeaker in the town centre instead). In addition, he utilized

---

32 Approximately £1,000 sterling.

and exacerbated the urban-rural tension between people who live in the centre and those who live in the hamlets. While leaving himself open to accusations about the relative levels of education, civility and modernity of rural versus urban populations, and his extremely careless (albeit effective) manipulation of power and mob violence, he drew on his own standing as a resident of a large and powerful *aldea*, and his ability to wield this power in very specific ways on a variety of terrains.

Also of significance is Jorge Mario's embodiment of the increasing pace of social change occurring in Todos Santos. With a rise in labour migration, increased tourism and the challenges that these suggest to so-called 'traditional' values, Jorge Mario's obvious 'Americanized' appearance with his piercings, tattoos and long hair saw him singled out as a figurehead for '*los cambios*', or 'the changes', which were increasingly viewed as impinging upon the rural Mayan existence. While this idealistic view of a previously unchanged world is a construct, it nevertheless was a powerful idea that still holds weight, perhaps more so in the *aldeas*. The attack upon him, then, was at least in part an attack against changes that many wished to halt or, at the very least, to critique. Since before the attack, the largely undocumented migration to the US has become extremely common, and to an extent has become a rite of passage for those youths whose families can afford it. Jorge Mario was however at the forefront of these transnational flows. That his assailants were largely those from the surrounding *aldeas* rather than the 'civilized' centre, those that had the least to gain financially from some of *los cambios*, highlights tensions which compose an ongoing dimension of local strife.

A related way of viewing this conflict is in relation to power and intergenerational conflict.[33] Structural violence and widespread poverty in Guatemala and most of Central America provide youth with increasingly fewer choices to secure livelihoods for themselves. Even when jobs are available, these pay subsistence wages. In order to purchase land, build and furnish houses and educate children, young

---

33 Burrell, 2005.

men have virtually no options other than migration. Migration frees them in significant ways from the economic and social hierarchies that have structured community life. In this sense, the local linkage to wider regional anxieties about gangs may be seen as an attempt to control newfound access to economic and social power. Controlling substantial numbers of youth from the kinds of families that already have a foothold in political and economic life constitutes an effective and therefore dangerous challenge to hierarchical authority forms embedded in community life.

What we suggest here is a series of local power considerations that have been additionally coloured by the war, but are also linked to community life and have long historical trajectories. Genealogies that see the war as the overwhelming cause of new social forms like lynching run the risk of ignoring the way that these idioms of existing power gain new inflections in this period.

Rumours, mobs and unexpected aftermaths

On 29 April 2000 Tetsuo Yamahiro, a Japanese tourist, and Edgar Castellanos, a Guatemalan bus driver were lynched by an angry mob in Todos Santos. This second incident is the most widely reported lynching to occur in Guatemala, receiving press attention at a national and international level.

Most accounts agree that in the weeks before the lynching, rumours had been circulating in the departmental capital of Huehuetenago and that these intensified in the days just prior to the incident. Satanic cultists, it was said, were arriving to hold a convention outside the city where they intended to sacrifice children. At some time in the preceding years, it was told, police had attributed a murder in Huehuetenango to Satanists. According to the new cycle of rumours that circulated on radio stations and in local newspapers, quickly spreading a rising panic throughout the department, the Satanists would be kidnapping children, and would most likely try to do this during crowded market days. On 19 April 2000, the day they were allegedly arriving, levels of paranoia in the departmental capital were so intense that the military was drafted to patrol the empty streets.

While rumours may consistently circulate, they come to wider attention only when they precede tragedies. In Guatemala, rumours having to do with baby snatching, kidnapping and organ harvesting have a long historical trajectory and circulate with some frequency. Often, foreign middle-aged women are implicated in these rumours, as in 1994 when two women were attacked by angry mobs, in the highlands and the coastal area respectively.[34] Because of the immediate response that these kinds of rumours generate, they are often thought to be easily manipulated—each time they surface again there are corresponding and often-credible calculations about why they gained credence. However, generalizing across all cycles misses how these rumours are historically constituted and how historical experience makes them threatening. Kidnapping of children of wealthy Guatemalans tends to happen in waves, the rate of international adoption is quite high in Guatemala and the legitimacy of some adoption agencies is periodically questioned, boys were forcibly inducted into the army, and large-scale plantation owners took children, often against their parent's will, to work on the coast.[35] In other words, rumours may gain precedence at particular times in ways that they would not at others.

In Todos Santos, in response to this news, fear was escalating. The 19th was a Saturday. Many men were out doing the shopping at the market. This was unusual as it is traditionally the role of women, but owing to the level of fear many were staying home to protect their children. Against this backdrop of intensifying fear, a plush tourist coach full of Japanese tourists came to town as part of an organized tour of Guatemala. The driver, Edgar Castellanos, was from the capital and not known locally. The bus was jet black with blacked out windows, all lending an air of mystery and furthering anxieties about whether or not the Satanists would be recognized if they arrived at

---

34 Adams, 1998.
35 Burrell, 2005.

the market. All Asians are collectively referred to as *chinos*, in the same way that people from the US, Canada and Europe are called *gringos*. Apart from a handful of Japanese travellers who had lived long-term in the village, and were renowned for being quick learners of Mam and excellent weavers, *Chinos* were not frequent visitors to Todos Santos.

Samper[36] argues that rumour allows people 'some measure of joint control over ambiguous stressful situations; they affect the solidarity of a group, creating a public that can then participate in collective action.' The rumour spread quickly that the Satanists were in town and dressed either entirely in black or in local costume, depending on who you asked. Whether this was as a direct result of the tourists arriving or simply an unfounded rumour is unclear, but certainly there was yet another rise in tension. What is clear, however, is that there was never a consensus about whether or not Satanists were coming, what they would look like if they did come, and what should be done if they tried to snatch children. Indeed, as Burrell points out, recognizing the explosive danger inherent in these rumours, some community members were warning others to be exceedingly careful on that fateful market day.

Exactly how the attack happened is unclear. Some say that Tetsuo Yamahiro was taking photos of the baby of Catarina Pablo, others say he was comforting it as it cried, others say it was his friend who was initially attacked and it was when he tried to save him that he himself fell victim to the mob. Whatever actually occurred, it was the scream/accusation of Catarina Pablo that someone was trying to steal her baby which sparked the attack. Yamahiro was wearing a dust mask to protect him from the dusty market (according to some to protect his asthma), which added to his 'other' appearance. When the attack started he was quickly overpowered. He was beaten with whatever was nearby, hit with sticks and crates and hacked at with the ever-present machetes rural men routinely carry at their sides. Other Japanese tourists were quickly taken by other *Todosanteros* to

---

36 Samper, 2002.

the relative safety of the cells of the police station, where the crowd could be temporarily kept at bay if necessary.

Many newspaper reports claim that thousands were involved in the attack, but if you see the narrow alley-way where the attack took place, that was an impossibility; and it suggests there was no opposition to the lynching, which is not true. Many were nearby, but only trying to see what the commotion was. Some were aiding the escape of other tourists. Others were too scared to stop those that were frenziedly attacking the tourist. The geography of the space in which the attack on Yamahiro occurred would not allow for more than forty people being physically involved. Castellanos, the bus driver, tried to escape but was stoned and set on fire on the far side of the village. Weston has heard that some took the fact that he did not burn easily as a sign that he was not human, thus confirming his guilt as a Satanist. The bus was torn to pieces, right down to the fabric being torn from the seats to look for evidence of hidden children.

Eventually the military and representatives from MINUGUA (The UN Peace-keeping Mission in Guatemala) came from Huehuetenango to calm the situation. Fearing pressure from the international community, the Guatemalan government quickly initiated a thorough investigation into the incident and collected testimonies from community members in order to arrest six people held to be involved in the incident. Catarina Pablo was identified and arrested as the woman whose scream allegedly started the attack. The rest, it was claimed, were scapegoats or were accused as part of family feuds or historical conflicts. Indeed, why *Todosanteros* gave testimony against one another when there was no vantage point from which they could see what had happened in the mob that surrounded Yamahiro was a topic that animated village life and contributed to great anxiety, fear and local insecurity for months afterwards.[37] Why did community members not seek refuge in the anonymity usually provided by lynch mobs? Many people traced these actions to historic conflicts community members had with one another, often related to ongoing

---

37 Burrell, forthcoming.

struggles between families and individuals that spanned decades and generations. In other words, direct state intervention in the aftermath of the Yamahiro case was used by community members as a way of addressing past conflicts with one another.

Although accounts provided to state functionaries did lead to the immediate jailing and prosecution of six *Todosanteros*, when investigators returned to the town to confirm accounts and collect further information, no one would speak with them. The trial of four of the six eventually ended in acquittal. As the judge reported, there was simply not enough evidence to convict the defendants, and in the national context of concretizing democratic legal process, a fair trial was a priority.[38]

Relating both these lynchings to the war is relatively straightforward. Since all men over the age of eighteen in Todos Santos (and many other rural communities in Guatemala) were forced to serve in paramilitary civil patrols after 1982, many of the *Todosanteros* involved in the lynching were ex-patrollers. Although some patrolled diligently and even enthusiastically, this was not the case for all adult men across the board and various strategies were employed by those who did not wish to carry out this duty. In Todos Santos, although these men were officially demobilized in 1996, as reported in Prensa Libre[39] and written about by Burrell,[40] security committees that have risen to the forefront of community life since 2002 (allegedly to deal with the gang problem) are closely linked to this (now illegal) form.

Likewise, a desire for justice following the war, even in the face of nonexistent or bankrupt state institutions, could also be seen to play a major part in what has motivated the resort to lynching in post-war Todos Santos. However if we move beyond these expectations we see that equally some of those people involved in escorting Japanese tourists to safety were also ex-patrollers and opposed to the violence.

---

38 Reuters, 26 June 2001, and Burrell, forthcoming.
39 *Prensa Libre*, 2003.
40 Burrell, unpublished manuscript.

As in the first lynching, again rumour and social change can be seen to play key roles in the build up to the lynching.

Conclusions

Incidents of lynching are never alike, except if we attempt to categorize them in certain ways, for particular purposes such as human rights concerns or policy implications. While similarities may be frequent, and comprise a basis for comparison and for broadening our understanding of them as a form, each incident emerges at the nexus of local power and politics in larger regional and national streams. Indeed, the labelling of incidents as lynching, vigilantism or a type of popular justice is central to studying this realm. If lynching enables us to study a phenomenon[41] as opposed to a series of extra-legal actions, the specificity and local colour of each incident becomes more important to understanding why these resonate in some communities and places and not others. Moving away from wide-ranging causality to exploring beneath the surface of community life and everyday considerations, we have shown how various positions and subjectivities—age, gender, class, education, one's *aldea*, religion, migratory and/or military experiences, for example—resonate in different ways with established and dynamic idioms of contemporary power. These specificities link people to larger global phenomenon, like vigilantism, in ways that are locally distinctive and remind us why ethnography matters.

Adams, A. 'Gringas, Ghouls, and Guatemala: the 1994 attacks on North American Women Accused of Body Organ Trafficking', *Journal of Latin American Anthropology* 4(1), 1998, pp. 122-33.

---

41 Burrell thanks Amy Chazkel and discussion participants at the 'Local and Informal Justices: Case Studies and Theoretical Debates on Lynching and Vigilantism' panel at LASA 2006, San Juan, for raising this important point.

Burrell, J. '"Peace Processes": Power, Politics and Conflict after War in Todos Santos Cuchumatán, Guatemala', PhD dissertation, New School for Social Research, 2005.

—— 'After Lynching in Todos Santos Cuchumatán', in *Revisiting Guatemala's Harvest of Violence: Studying War in a Postwar Society*, D. Nelson and C. McAllister (eds), forthcoming.

—— 'Life and Death of a Rural Marero.' Unpublished manuscript.

Comisión de Esclarecimento Histórico. 'Guatemala Memory of Silence', http://hrdata.aaas.org/ceh/report, 13/01/05.

Dreyfus, H.L. and P. Rabinow. *Michel Foucault, Beyond Structuralism and Hermeneutics*, Chicago, 1982.

Fernández García, M.C. 'Lynching in Guatemala: Legacy of War and Impunity', http://www.wcfia.harvard.edu/fellows/papers/2003-04/fernandez.pdf#search='lynching%20in%20Guatemala%20legacy%20for%20war%20and%20impunity, 15/03/06

Foucault, M. *Discipline and Punish: The Birth of the Prison*, London, 1977.

—— *The Order of Things: an Archaeology of the Human Sciences*, London, 1994.

Godoy, A.S. 'Lynchings and the Democratization of Terror in Postwar Guatemala: Implications for Human Rights', *Human Rights Quarterly* 24(3), 2002, pp. 640-61.

Green, L. *Fear as a Way of Life: Mayan Widows in Rural Guatemala*, New York, 1999.

Gutiérrez, M.E. 'Los mecanismos del poder en la violencia colectiva: los linchamientos en Huehuetenango', in *Linchamientos: Barbarie o "Justicia Popular"?*, C. Mendoza and E. Torres-Rivas (eds), UNESCO/Proyecto Cultura de Paz, Guatemala, 2003, pp. 175-210.

Gutiérrez, M.E. and P.H. Kobrak (eds). *Los Linchamientos Pos Conflicto y Violencia Colectiva en Huehuetenango*, Guatemala, 2001.

IDIES. *El Sistema Jurídico Mam*, Guatemala City, 1999.

López García, J. 'Abordando Los Linchamientos en Guatemala: Del Autismo Capacitador a Consensos negociados', in *Linchamientos: Barbarie o "Justicia Popular"?*, C. Mendoza and E. Torres-Rivas (eds), Guatemala, 2003.

McIlwaine, C. and C. Moser. *Violence in a Post Conflict Context: Urban Poor Perceptions from Guatemala*, Washington, 2001.

Mendoza, C. 'Violencia colectiva en Guatemala: una aproximación teóretica al problema de los linchamientos', in *Linchamientos: Barbarie o "Justicia Popular"?*, C. Mendoza and E. Torres-Rivas (eds), UNESCO/Proyecto Cultura de Paz, Guatemala, 2003, pp. 89-124.

MINUGUA *Thirteenth Report of the MINUGUA on the Human Rights Situation in Guatemala*, 2002.

—— 'Los Linchamientos: un flagelo que persiste', in *Linchamientos: Barbarie o "Justicia Popular"?*, C. Mendoza and E. Torres-Rivas (eds), UNESCO/Proyecto Cultura de Paz, Guatemala, 2003, pp. 275-327.

Prensa Libre. 'Acciones ilegales: Medidas de seguridad en Todos Santos están al margen de la ley.' 20 February 2003.

Rothenburg, D. 'Los Linchamientos –The Meaning of Mob Action in the Wake of State Terror in Guatemala', *Native Americas* 15(1), 1998, pp. 1-7.

Samper, D. 'Cannibalizing kids: Rumour and Resistance in Latin America', *Journal of Folklore Research* 39(1), 2002, pp. 1-32.

Seider, R. 'Customary Law and Local Power in Guatemala', in *Guatemala After the Peace Accords*, R. Seider (ed.), Institute of Latin American Studies, London, 1998, pp. 97-115.

Wilson, R. 'Representing Human Rights Violations: Social Contexts and Subjectivities', in *Human Rights, Culture and Context: Anthropological Perspectives*, R. Wilson (ed.), London, 1997, pp. 134-60.

16

STATE VIGILANTES AND POLITICAL COMMUNITY ON THE MARGINS IN POST-WAR MOZAMBIQUE

Helene Maria Kyed

Introduction

On 14 August 2004, the huts of the police and local state administration in Bunga were burned to the ground by one or more local residents. Bunga is a locality on the outskirts of Dombe administrative post, Sussundenga District, situated only a few kilometres from Renamo's main base in Manica Province during the Mozambique civil war (1977-92). The incident happened only three years after a relatively stable post-war state presence had been established in Bunga. This stability came after more than seven years of unrest during which the state feared resistance from Renamo supporters. State officials labelled Bunga a *zona de confução* (literally a 'confused zone') inhabited by people who had been morally destroyed by their protracted exposure to Renamo control. Against this background, it is hardly surprising that the criminal investigation unit represented the act of arson as an 'uncivilized' form of political resistance against 'the law and order of the state'. A well-known, active Renamo member was arrested and detained for four days, before being freed for lack of evidence. This led to a series of complaints against the police from the paramount chief and a large number of Bungians. The latter were furious about the police handling of the case, the presumption that this was an act of Renamo resistance against the state, and the police preventing the rural residents from providing their own version of the story. To the residents, the arson was not a good thing, but neither was it entirely unjust. Time and again the local state administrator had abused his power in order to 'steal married women', and every time he had been tried in the community court he had refrained from paying compensation to the aggrieved husbands. The burning of state property was a last resort in a chain of actions aimed at putting an end to the local administrators' habit of 'eating' the women of Bunga—according to the public statements of Bungians, it was not because they were against the state (the police and the administration) as such.

This case raises questions relating to the inherent contradictions in the current reorganization of justice and the police on the margins of state governance in Mozambique—the subject of this chapter. Dissatisfaction with state employees, such as the local administrator in Bunga, is linked to the fact that local notions of justice are seldom catered for by state institutions. Conversely, the instances of self-redress resulting from such dissatisfaction are actively usurped by police officers to politicize criminal acts and blame 'bad behaviour' on the opposition party, Renamo. Paradoxically, the exclusionary politics of the police coincide with the PRM (*Polícia de República de Moçambique*) publicly campaigning for *unidade* (unity) between the police and the people (*povo*) and the *Vigilança do Povo* (people's vigilance), which compels each citizen to take an active part in assisting the PRM. Such police campaigning illustrates local variants of post-war national initiatives centred on democratizing the police force and decentralizing the enforcement of law and order to non-state actors. Besides the general encouragement of the *Vigilança do Povo* since 2002, the state has recognized a little over 4,000 'community authorities' from the ranks of 'traditional leaders' and 'secretaries of suburban areas or villages', who are required to assist the state in pursuing administrative tasks, policing and law enforcement. In 2004-5, the state also launched community policing forums, which also follow the principle of *unidade*. According to the Ministry of Internal Affairs (MINT), these initiatives aim to create 'a new culture of community security' where 'citizens are directly involved in the system of security and policing'.[1]

This chapter examines how such state-sponsored local vigilance and policing have been put into practice in the former war zones of Dombe in the 2002-2005 period.[2] It provides a perspective on 'vigilantism' which looks at how states in a post-war situation attempt to regain control of areas formerly lost to them, by outsourcing policing and domesticating unregulated forms of law-and-order enforcement. In areas like Dombe, where state sovereignty has been highly contested, the *Vigilança do Povo* and the outsourcing of policing to non-state authorities have become means for the PRM to (re)enforce the law in more effective and decentralized ways. At the same time, these initiatives are being employed to win the allegiance of the rural population and local power-holders.

On the basis of ethnographic explorations of everyday policing, conflict resolution and public police meetings, this chapter critically scrutinizes the inclusionary and democratic language in which the different forms of state-sponsored vigilantism have been officially cast. A core argument of the chapter is that the implementation of these initiatives has been dominated by acts of re-ordering, separation and exclusion that centre on reclaiming state sovereignty, in terms of the monopoly on both the exercise of legitimate force and defining of licit and illicit forms of conduct and affiliation. While the outsourcing of police functions to traditional leaders and community police officers centres on reclaiming the state's monopoly of force, the notion of *unidade* revolves around highly politicized attempts at delineating proper forms of citizen-communities. This happens through the criminalization of certain forms of affiliation, defined according to old war factions, namely the Renamo rebel movement and

---

1 Ministry of Internal Affairs (MINT), 25-27 July 2005, pp. 4-5.

2 This chapter is based on data collected during long-term fieldwork in Sussundenga District in June–October 2002, April–September 2004 and July–September 2005.

the Frelimo state. The *Vigilança do Povo* and the use of community police persons become entangled with a particular 'politics of policing', in which the PRM engages not merely in the pure enforcement of the law, but equally in the task of producing political affiliation to the Frelimo state. Collaboration with the PRM is cast as equivalent to loyalty to that state, and transgressions of laws are presented and acted upon as being caused by Renamo affiliation. This perspective of the police underscores the politicization of crime and also legitimizes the use of illegal and often violent police tactics, in particular against Renamo supporters. In the very name of enforcing the law, the PRM encourages practices of breaking the law and often uses state-sponsored vigilantes to do so. If, as Abrahams suggests,[3] unofficial forms of vigilantism tend to lie on the boundary between the law and illegality, then this is also true for state-sanctioned vigilantism in Dombe. Conversely, the Dombe case suggests that, in being state-regulated, vigilantism does not necessarily become less violent in practice.

Re-ordering state–society relations on the margins

The outsourcing of policing in Dombe mirrors in its own right the inherent contradictions of security sector reforms at the national level in Mozambique. Promises to democratize and de-militarize the security sector have been slow in delivery and have been pitted against preoccupations with regaining state control and political allegiance in Renamo strongholds such as Dombe.[4] In the mid-1990s, the donor-funded training of police officers centred on 'human rights' and 'good governance', but the overall reorganization of the police was carried out by the Spanish paramilitary Guardia Civil. According to Wisler and Bonvin,[5] this has meant a continuation of the centralized paramilitary model of policing that predominated before and during

---

3 Abrahams, 1996.
4 Lalá, 2003; Chachiua, 2000.
5 Wisler and Bonvin, 2004.

the civil war. On the surface this continuity contradicts the decentralization of policing that took off immediately after the turn of the millennium, giving way to the inclusion of community authorities in enforcing law and order and community police forums. In practice there has nonetheless been a tendency for community forms of policing to be seen by 'senior [police] officers as an instrument for the state to better control communities rather than as a service to communities'.[6]

This argument also holds for Dombe, where the outsourcing of policing has been ambiguously structured around reclaiming state sovereignty by co-opting, but also criminalizing, competing forms of what Hansen and Stepputat refer to as 'local sovereign power not entirely "penetrated" or governed by the state'.[7] These local sovereigns may include non-state actors who make 'decisions on life, death, punishments, rewards, taxation and territorial control'.[8] Owing to the legacies of war and the confinement of the Frelimo state's control to urban centres, such non-state actors held almost exclusive sway over the field of governance in Dombe after the war. Traditional leaders provided one form of informal sovereignty, expressed in their dealings with criminals, dispute settlement and territorial control. They operated sporadically alongside Renamo soldiers who had turned themselves into local administrators; remnants of the *mujhibas*, Renamo's local police force during the war; and finally, *curandeiros* (witchdoctors or traditional healers). These actors did not comprise a fully integrated system of governance with clearly demarcated territorial constituencies, but they did share a common history of opposition to the Frelimo state: Renamo obviously because of the war, and traditional leader and *curandeiros* because of their banning by Frelimo at independence in 1975. The rural population of Dombe generally mistrusted state institutions and the police after

---

6 Ibid., p. 11.

7 Hansen and Stepputat, 2005, pp. 30-1.

8 Ibid., p. 31.

the war,[9] and in 1995 this was expressed in pockets of overt opposition to the resettlement of police posts by a number of local residents and chiefs.[10] As Alexander suggests, despite the constitutional abolition of the one-party state in 1990, the state was still viewed as equivalent to the old enemy Frelimo. It was not associated with development and service provision by the majority of Dombians, but with the militarized governance of people and territories that had dominated state practice since the war began in these areas in 1978. This was particularly the case in remote and mountainous areas such as Bunga, where Renamo arrived before the Frelimo state had been able to implement its post-independence development programmes. Here it was not Renamo, but the Frelimo state that was seen as the aggressor.[11]

The implementation of decentralization reforms in Dombe reflects the 'profound crisis of authority'[12] that Frelimo and state institutions faced after the war. Decentralization was matched by attempts to re-establish and make effective state administrative and police posts, as well as to canvas support for Frelimo. Decree 15/2000, which provided for the recognition of traditional leaders, was the first legal measure to regulate non-state sovereigns and recruit them under the ambit of the state.[13] Rather than being confined to acts of recognition, inclusion and the outsourcing of functions, in practice its implementation has been indistinguishable from acts of re-ordering—of establishing, but also creating the boundaries between the entities of the state and society, as well as the intermediaries between them, the 'community authorities'.

Within the field of the enforcement of law and order, acts of reordering centred on two interrelated forms of boundary-making. One

---

9 Alexander, 1997.

10 *Noticias,* 29 June 1995; *Noticias,* 4 July 1995; *Noticias,* 13 July 1995.

11 Alexander, 1997, p. 10.

12 Ibid., p. 20.

13 For an analysis of implementing Decree 15/2000 in Sussundenga District, see Buur and Kyed, 2005; Kyed and Buur, 2006.

belongs to the domain of the juridical-institutional and covers strategies of outsourcing that revolve around reorganizing of hierarchies of authority and determining parameters of collaboration between state and non-state actors. The other belongs to the domain of producing a 'political community'[14] and conjures up the subtle measures involved in outlining proper forms of citizen-communities. Processes of inclusion and exclusion played an integral part in re-establishing the state (represented by the police) and the law as sovereign by outsourcing through the *Vigilança do Povo* and community forms of policing. I firstly address the domain of the juridical-institutional.

Domesticating non-state forms of vigilantism —the juridical-institutional domain

In Dombe, Decree 15/2000 led to the state recognition of eight paramount chiefs (*régulos*) and the registration of thirty-four sub-chiefs in 2002. The recognized chiefs were renamed 'community authorities' to indicate their role as community representatives, but the state regalia and the long list of obligations with which they were entrusted pointed more towards their envisaged role as the state's assistants.[15] Together with tax collection, registration, census functions and civic education, the community authorities are obliged to assist the police 'in attending to the committing of violations and the existence and locating of troublemakers, hidden arms and mined areas',[16] and to 'articulate with the community courts, where they exist, in the resolution of small conflicts of a civil nature'.[17] The formalization of the hierarchy of chiefs and sub-chiefs implied the formal exclusion of those other non-state authorities that continued to exist after the war from governing over rural communities. It also implied attempts to tame and regulate the practices and range of operation of the chiefs.

---

14 Agamben, 2000.
15 Buur and Kyed, 2005.
16 Regulamento do Decreto 15/2000, art. 5d.
17 Ibid.

Despite the vague legal framework that left implementers with no operational guidelines for how actually to include chiefs in policing and conflict resolution, the sub-district police were quick to develop their own models for practice or meta-rules.[18] These rules do not exist in writing, but have been divulged to the chiefs as if they were the law and enforced as such. They are structured around the problem of securing the PRM's monopoly of the use of force, and of defining and prosecuting 'criminal' acts (serious theft, homicide, drugs, fights in which blood is spilled, rape, stabbings, arson, murder threats and insulting state functionaries). Simultaneously, the PRM attempted to ensure that conflicts and misbehaviour not defined as 'criminal'—e.g. witchcraft, adultery, insults and threats of a minor nature, beatings without blood being spilled, minor theft, violations of customary law and land disputes—are solved only by those authorities recognized by the state and not by ordinary individuals or groups of individuals themselves. Eliminating self-redress or unregulated vigilantism has thus been a prime goal of the PRM, but it is also a responsibility that the chief of police in Dombe has placed on the recognized chiefs. In fact, in the sphere of everyday policing, a whole set of (unwritten) obligations and prohibitions has been divulged to chiefs.

These obligations include inspecting, locating and providing information about troublemakers. Chiefs are also obliged to arrest law-breakers and suspects, and bring them to the police station. They can tie people up if they resist arrest. In doing so, the PRM recognizes those traditional police officers that chiefs have used since colonial times to detain violators, but they are nonetheless prohibited from receiving the usual payment from law-breakers. Other prohibitions include the use of force and the solving of criminal cases as defined above, but chiefs are also prosecuted if they fail to provide information about criminals or to turn them in to the police. In practice, these prohibitions and obligations position 'community authorities' in an anomalous role as apparently forming part of the state, but not really doing so. They are physically outside the spaces in which state

18 Abrahams, 1996, p. 48.

officials operate—mostly limited to the vicinity of administrative and police posts in semi-urban centres—and yet are obliged to act 'as if' they were part of the state, without enjoying adequately sanctioned sovereign power. This leads to a sort of 'scale of stateness', which has a significant impact on the *de facto* authority of chiefs, as well as on the PRM's ability easily to maintain a strict boundary between the state and non-state domains of authority.

In Dombe, chiefly authority is not based solely on state recognition and/or traditional inheritance and spiritual factors. The performance of various governmental duties also gives credence to a chief's authority, which includes the use of corporal punishment and a chief's ability to deal promptly with criminal cases and to enforce justice in the form of the payment of monetary compensations. Although corporal punishment has not been used frequently, it still provides an important potential tool underlining the constitutive authority of the chiefs. Sanctions in the form of payments of compensation, in money or in kind, by perpetrators to victims, commonly employed by chiefs, are equally significant in terms of local ideas of justice. Rural people do not have (private) insurance and therefore have no means with which to recoup any monetary losses. But compensation also forms a significant part of reciprocal relations both between and within extended families, which in its absence can create social instability and violent acts of self-redress, as we saw in the Bunga case. Judgements issued by the formal justice system, where victims and/or their families receive no compensation, do not satisfy these mechanisms of social ordering based on concrete exchange relations. Many interviewees stated that imprisonment neither provided justice nor was of any benefit to a plaintiff. Imprisonment was seen a 'payment to the state', not to the victim and his or her family. For these reasons, many people in rural areas prefer to have criminal cases solved by the chief, just as some chiefs continue to flout the law and solve criminal cases in order not to risk losing popular legitimacy.

When chiefs bypass the PRM and thus challenge state sovereignty, this is not always discovered by the PRM, but when it is, it is dealt with in a particularly brutal manner. In 2004, I encountered three such cases. In one case, a sub-chief had solved a case of fighting between two men. When the person who lost the case informed the PRM about it, the sub-chief was arrested, *chambokeado* (beaten with a rubber stick) and put in prison for two days. In the second case, a chief, following what he referred to as 'ordinary practice', ordered community members to catch and beat up a man who had burned down three huts in the neighbourhood. The chief was subsequently taken to the district police, beaten and then fined for having failed to call them in. In the third case, a sub-chief was accused of having ordered the family of someone killed by witchcraft to punish the woman allegedly responsible. Members of the dead boy's family had beaten the woman up, cut off her body parts and hung her in a tree. The brother of the murdered woman took the case to the police, who arrested the chief together with two male members of the family that had committed the act. They were beaten at the police stations they passed through on their way to the provincial capital, where they were kept in prison for a year. The case never went to court.

Interestingly, such punishments involved measures that, while enforced in the name of restoring the law, lay outside the domain of the formal justice system. The particularly brutal way of punishing the formal counterparts of the PRM underlines fundamental aspects of sovereign power and its performative inscription on particular bodies.[19] It may seem contradictory to find the PRM breaking the law in the very name of enforcing it. If, however, we follow Carl Schmitt's idea that sovereignty originates in the exception (*Ausnahme*), that is, in the capacity to suspend the law, and the notion that sovereignty is constituted by the aptitude for excessive violence,[20] then it seems relevant to suggest that the above cases centred on marking out the space of the state's sovereign power. If it holds, equally, that 'sovereign power is essentially an unstable and precarious form of power, whose efficacy as a social authority capable of disciplining

---

19 Hansen and Stepputat, 2005, p.11.
20 Hansen, 2005, pp. 170-1.

and creating subjects is dependent on its constant public reiteration and performance, or rumours hereof',[21] then the publicly known oscillation between playing the legal card and trespassing on it may not necessarily be viewed as contradicting state sovereignty. It may nonetheless be experienced as highly ambivalent or even irrational, which 'adds to the mystical aura of sovereign power.'[22]

In the Dombe case, this ambivalence appears particularly strongly in the intricate space between outsourcing and reclaiming sovereign power, or in other words, between recognizing chiefs and entrusting them with powers (the productive or generous side of sovereignty) on the one hand, and criminalizing and treating them with brutality on the other (the violent side of sovereignty).[23] But the ambivalent character of performing sovereign power does not end there: it is also reflected in the intricacy of enforcing a strict boundary between state and non-state domains of authority. While the PRM is determined to ensure that non-state authorities do not challenge the state's monopoly of force, when ordered by the PRM (physical) violence can be performed by non-state actors.

The first time I encountered the direct outsourcing of force was in August 2004. A chief, who had followed the law in bringing a suspect to the police, was ordered to *chambokear* the suspect within the confines of the police station. The incident was far from being a secret, but was openly talked about in the area and referred to as an example of how the police break 'their' own laws. As the chief himself remarked: 'It is as if it is OK when the police tell us to beat people... but it is a bit confusing to understand what we can and cannot do.'[24] When I returned in mid-2005, the confusion expressed by the chief had increased, as had the outsourcing of both physical

---

21 Ibid., p. 171.
22 Ibid.
23 Ibid., pp. 171-2.
24 Chief Mushambonha, Dombe, August 2004.

and symbolic violence through the now systematic employment of community police persons.[25]

Officially, the extension of community policing or PolCom (*polí-ciamento comunitário*) to rural areas should copy the community policing councils (CPCs), which were implemented in selected urban *bairros* from 2000. According to official policy, the CPCs should comprise community members elected on the basis of criteria of seniority, confidence and knowledge of community problems. Their role is to debate problems of community crime, inform the PRM about crime and provide civic education.[26] In Dombe, however, the District Commander admitted, such councils 'will take time to form and need long-term planning, so that is why we have begun with smaller *nucléos* [units], which in the future will become subordinate elements of the councils.'[27] Incongruously, more enforcing power has been conferred on these units than is officially conferred on the CPCs and the community authorities. Each comprising eight to ten young men selected by the chiefs and sub-chiefs, the *nucléos* have been mandated by the PRM to go out on patrol and arrest alleged criminals, both when they are on duty in the chieftaincies and when doing turns at the police station. In the latter case, they are entrusted with handcuffs and *chambocos*, which they use when they are sent by the PRM to detain suspects. They are allowed to beat alleged criminals resisting arrest, but only to inflict a fixed number of strokes of the *chamboco*. Since these community police persons have been trained by the PRM, the police officers in Dombe seldom bother to make arrests themselves in the vast rural areas. In some cases they also order the young people on duty to use physical force against suspects within the confines of the police station.

---

25 In 2004 the PRM in Dombe had unofficially begun to use what the chief of police referred to as community police officers and *pessoas da confiança* (trusties), who secretly collected information about troublemakers for the PRM and occasionally assisted police officers in arresting alleged criminals.

26 Ministry of Internal Affairs (MINT), 25-27 July 2005, p. 10.

27 Interview with District Commander, Sussundenga, Sept. 2005.

The *nucléos*, in other words, do the dirty work of the police officers. This also includes nightly patrols during which the so-called *lei fora da hora* is enforced, which can be likened to a curfew imposed between midnight and five o'clock in the morning. Although this *lei* is not a proper law (it is actually unconstitutional), it is implemented as if it were, with potentially severe consequences for violators. After they have been put into a police cell, a PRM officer interrogates them. If they are suspected of having committed crimes in the past and/or of intending to do so in the future, they are *chambokeados* by a community police officer and put back in the cell 'for a few days, so they can learn not to do wrong and to respect the police', as the Dombe chief of police remarked. In other cases, those arrested do 'public' work for the police, such as cooking food or sweeping the dusty courtyard of the police post, while being watched over by a *nucléo* member.

The outsourcing of 'educative' measures, that is, physical violence, to ordinary people from *within* the local population reveals the inherently violent and illegal aspects of state-enforced and state-controlled vigilantism. But the practice of using ordinary citizens (even young ones) to act against fellow citizens also brings us to the issue of producing 'political community' and its 'other'.

Separating friends and foes: the domain of 'political community'

The PolCom *nucléos* seemed to be an institutionalized extension of the PRM's overall encouragement of the *Vigilança do Povo*, which since at least 2002 has been promulgated at public meetings in Dombe. The main message at these meetings is that each citizen has a responsibility to work with the police and inform them about 'troublemakers' in their communities.[28] In other words, citizens are encouraged to work in tandem with the police in order to enhance

---

28 For a detailed analysis of these public meetings held by the PRM and state officials, see Kyed, 2007.

their own security, as seen by the PRM conveners of the meetings. At the meetings the *Vigilança do Povo* is equated with the *unidade* between the police and the people and observance of the law. To make sure the message is received, the PRM displays prisoners to the public at these meetings, physically illustrating what happens to different kinds of violators. Usually the prisoners on display come from the very area in which the meetings are being held, meaning that people are usually familiar with them. Transgressing the law by violating the prisoners' right to respect for their persons, the public display of criminals functions to give the concept of unity a particular meaning, placing those who collaborate with the police in opposition to those who violate the law.

According to the Dombe chief of police, the overriding objective of the *Vigilança do Povo* is to combat crime by aligning good, law-abiding 'community' members with the PRM as against fellow citizens (i.e. family members, neighbours and friends) who commit crimes or who are perceived, for a variety of reasons, as potential criminals. Hence the district commander told those attending one meeting: 'It is you who know him [the criminal] ... We the police are here to protect you, but for our work to go well we have to unite. Our unity is you and you have to tell us secretly what happens. [...] You are the first police here and the thief is from your family, so you know him.' The commander consistently situated the notion of unity in opposition not only to criminals as such, but also to non-collaborators with the state. In this sense, the *Vigilança do Povo* is focused not only on combating crime, but also on questions of allegiance and forms of affiliation. There is, in other words, an underlying political strategy behind the *Vigilança do Povo*, one taking police work beyond law enforcement: the aim of combating crime from a purely legal perspective is coupled with the boundary-making practice of producing 'political community'.[29] This is centred on delineating a division between people who can be included in the state's version of the ideal citizen-community—i.e. those who collaborate with the PRM—and

---

29 Agamden, 2000.

those who cannot and do not collaborate. In this sense, a non-collaborator of the PRM was viewed, if not as an actual criminal, then as a potential criminal.

It is worth noting here that the idea of the *Vigilança do Povo* did not emerge in a historical vacuum, but is descended from the post-colonial concepts of *ligação polícia e povo* (police-people liaison), *grupos de vigilancia popular* (popular vigilance groups) and *milícias populares* (popular militias), all of which officially disappeared with the abolition of the one-party state in 1990.[30] These state-created vigilante groups were part of Frelimo's party-state structures, and apart from working for local crime prevention, their main function was to support state security by identifying political traitors or *os inimigos internos* (the internal enemies).[31] According to a key official in the Ministry of Internal Affairs, a main difference today is that the *vigilanças do povo* no longer form part of Frelimo, nor do they have to support 'the defence of territorial integrity' against the state's opponents, notably Renamo.[32] In Dombe, there seem nonetheless to be clear continuities with the past use of the *Vigilança do Povo*, if not in defending state security, then at least in providing an instrument for fending off Renamo opponents, who continue to be cast as the internal enemies.

This emerged at the public police-community meetings, and also in the statements of *posto*-level police officers, where the division between collaborators/non-criminals and non-collaborators/criminals was consistently infused with a political content. In other words, Renamo was discursively produced as the significant other of the 'political community', whereas a failure to collaborate with the police, as when people do not report criminals or are unwilling to speak about a crime, was presented as hostility towards the *hurumende*—the usual label for the state, the government and Frelimo. Hostility was explained by state officials as resulting from rural dwellers' many years

---

30 Interview with General Macamo, MINT, October 2005.
31 Ibid.
32 Ibid.

of exposure to war and their subjection by Renamo. While rural people generally explained that the reason for not taking cases to the police was their preference for sentences involving compensation enforced in the chiefs' courts, the PRM reasoned that this was because people had been 'confused' by the war. The same kind of reasoning applied to cases of self-redress and of committing of crime as such, an aspect that was also clear in the arson case in Bunga in August 2004, when state officials immediately blamed Renamo for the act. A convergence between crime and Renamo affiliation was clear in a statement made to me by the district commander:

'Crime and the lack of knowledge of the law have to do with the war. The majority of the population that lives in Dombe lived in the military bases of Renamo. And for this reason they still have this 'Renamista' mentality, this anarchistic doctrine. [...] Dombe, you know, has had a high level of serious crime and a lot of cases where people take the law into their own hands.'[33]

State officials and Frelimo secretaries constantly referred to Dombe as a 'zone of confusion' composed of people who had been morally destroyed by war and who lacked any basic sense of civic responsibility. This labelling derives from the war, when the area was a fierce combat zone, quickly taken over by Renamo fighters, and also from the early post-war years, when Renamo took full control of the area until mid-1990s. The fact that Dombe is still a Renamo stronghold (giving Renamo approximately 90 per cent of the votes in the 1994, 1999 and 2004 elections) sustains this labelling and is also reflected in state officials' continued representation of the police as part of a Frelimo-defined state project.

The idea of Dombe as a 'zone of confusion' profoundly informs policing, to an extent that goes beyond the idea of 'people's vigilance' and the PRM's representation of criminal acts as being caused by subjection to Renamo. In the eyes of the PRM, it also informs and to a large extent legitimizes the use of exceptional and illegal measures to combat crime and deal with non-collaborators. I have already described how community police members have been granted the

33 District commander of police, Sussundenga, August 2004.

authority to use violence and break the law in the name of 'educating' Dombians to abide by the law and respect the police. With regard to community policing it is unclear to me whether the PRM has an elaborate strategy of directing community police persons to target Renamo supporters particularly. The fact that many of the young men involved were the sons of Renamo members and/or former *mujhibas* or traditional chiefs' policemen in the days when chiefs collaborated with Renamo suggests that their 'incorporation' by the PRM was a matter of taming or domesticating young people who were potentially collaborators of Renamo.

Conversely, several other cases, including that described above in Bunga in August 2004, illustrate how the notion of a 'zone of confusion' and the party politicization of policing informed the ways in which particular individuals were dealt with by the police. Among Dombians, there was a general idea, real or perceived, that those who explicitly pledged allegiance to Renamo, or whom the PRM knew were Renamo supporters, were treated particularly brutally by the PRM. A middle-aged man in Chibue chieftaincy, for example, claimed to have been beaten extra severely because the police had found boot marks on his legs (indicating he had been a Renamo soldier). About this incident, he related: 'Knowing that we come from an area where we live with Renamo, they [the police] make us suffer a lot'. There was a similar case in Bunga in mid-2005, in which two young men from an area known to be dominated by Renamo were accused of arson. Although even the offended party claimed this had been unintentional, the Bunga PRM officer saw to it that the perpetrators were severely punished. They were not sent to court for trial, but were held by the Bunga police for six days and forced to build a new office for the police officer (replacing the one that had been burnt down a year earlier). They were also publicly beaten on the second night by the PRM officer. As I heard their screams and promises to respect the police in the future, the local state official assured me: 'In these areas where there is a lot of Matsangaíssas [Renamo people][34]

---

34 André Matsangaísso was the first chief commander of Renamo; he died in

there is no place for human rights. We need to use these measures as an example, so that people learn to abide by the law.'[35]

The imprisonment of Renamo members without trial and suitable evidence to support accusations happened from time to time in Dombe in the period 2004-5. According to one of the individuals who was imprisoned (twice), the PRM did this to persuade Renamo supporters to convert to Frelimo. That such police tactics also served to signal to others the dividing line between the categories of criminal/Renamo supporter and non-criminal/*hurumende* supporter was particularly clear in a case from 2004. Here a young Renamo member was taken into custody and *chambokeado* for having said bad things about the district administrator. Two days later he was publicly displayed at a police-community meeting and described as a criminal confused by the war. This too happened without a trial.

This exceptional and violent treatment of Renamo members, who are displayed and treated as the 'significant other' of righteous citizen-communities or as those outside the *unidade* of the police and the community, resembles what Agamben refers to as 'bare life'.[36] This concept refers to the 'inclusive exclusion', or the kind of simple being who is excluded from the category of citizen, has no dignity and deserves no rights, but who at the same time is included as the constitutive other of the 'political community'. The categorization of some individuals in society as 'bare life' is, according to Agamben, the most elementary operation of sovereign power.

In this light it is pertinent to ask whether the *Vigilança do Povo*, community policing and the obligations and prohibitions placed on traditional leaders are wholly about reinforcing and enacting the sovereign power of the state through exclusion and violence. As should be clear by now, the discursive production of Dombe as a risk-laden marginal area made up of anarchistic Matsangaíssas informs the treatment of Dombians as potential criminals. At the same time,

---

combat in 1979.

35 Chefe da Localidade, Bunga, September 2005.

36 Agamben, 2000.

the outsourcing of policing (and sometimes of violence) is based on the creation of partnerships and cast in the language of a state police force serving the public. This may seem contradictory, but if we view outsourcing as an inherent aspect of reclaiming state sovereignty (and by extension Frelimo allegiance) by separating out a specific Frelimo state version of citizen-communities, the contradiction appears mutually reinforcing. This does not mean that conflicts do not arise, nor that rural dwellers and community authorities do not strategically circumvent the boundary-making exercises of the PRM, as I have already pointed out: they constantly do, for example, by taking their (criminal) cases elsewhere, 'hiding' or not turning in criminals and/or exercising self-redress. As already suggested, a contradiction has emerged between the PRM's consistent presentation of non-collaboration and self-justice as being the result of affiliation with Renamo and rural dwellers' reasons for bypassing the police. As in the Bunga case, those reasons tend to rest on local notions of justice that the PRM and the formal justice system do not satisfy, namely forms of compensational exchange between parties in a case.

Conclusion

Abrahams suggests that 'the unofficial nature of vigilantism tends to make it rather labile' in the sense that it 'exists in an awkward borderland between the law and illegality' and 'is capable of slipping and sliding in one direction or the other'.[37] In other words, the distinction between vigilante action against crime and crime itself is often blurred.[38] In the case of Dombe, this also seems to be the case with state-regulated and sanctioned forms of vigilantism and the control of crime. A key difference is that in Dombe it is less the unofficial forms of vigilantism and more the local tiers of the state that reproduce this ambiguity. The state, in other words, is the prime agent in oscillat-

---

37 Abrahams, 1996, pp. 43-4.
38 Ibid., p. 45.

ing between being inside and outside the law.[39] State officials, as I have demonstrated, frequently transgress the law or authorise their non-state counterparts to do so, yet they do this in the very name of enforcing the law. An important question is whether this merely expresses a 'disillusion with the state',[40] as Abrahams suggests with regard to state officials who act as vigilantes. Hansen[41] alerts us to the inherently ambiguous character of the state and sovereign power in general as simultaneously benevolent and violent, and, following Carl Schmitt, as being vested in the ability to suspend the law. In answering this question, therefore, it may be useful to distinguish between the ideally benevolent character of the modern state and the violent character of sovereign practices.

As this chapter has shown, the outsourcing of policing is notoriously centred on re-claiming state sovereignty by domesticating unregulated forms of vigilantism and order-making. In the juridical-institutional domain, this takes the form of prohibiting non-state actors—in particular chiefs—from usurping the state's monopoly of force and of sentencing of criminals. At the same time chiefs are obliged to work actively for the police, just as community police *nucléos* are employed to exercise a sort of state-controlled violence in the physical as well as the symbolic sense. Despite, or perhaps because of, the 'capturing' or taming of non-state actors by the state, vigilante violence, it seems, has not decreased: it has merely become state-regulated and state-sanctioned. If illegal and violent means of enforcing the law may tell us something generally about sovereignty as originating in the capacity to suspend the law, then in present-day Dombe this seems to be a frequent state of affairs embodied in routine police practice. The consequence is that it is the police, in the form of its lower-ranking officers, which is acting as the sovereign.

As this chapter also shows, the recurring 'state of exception' is informed by a police perspective, which falls back on and is to a large

---

39 Ibid.
40 Ibid.
41 Hansen, 2005, pp. 171-2.

extent legitimized by the historical merger between the state, the party and the government, as well as by the discursive production of Dombe as a Renamo-created 'zone of confusion'. When compared with the historical analyses of Mozambican security measures by Chachiua[42], the politicized employment of the category crime/criminals, which this view sustains, seems to be a continuation of the police ethos that prevailed during the war. This ethos builds on the Renamo-Frelimo/state/police opposition and on a claimed convergence between crime, disorder and political opposition, which are 'seen as deserving the same response'.[43]

In Dombe this convergence not only means, as in the Bunga case, that crime is always potentially represented by the police as having been caused by the politics of war: it also has the effect of taking police work beyond pure law enforcement. Nowhere is this clearer than in the strategy underlying the *Vigilança do Povo*, where combating crime is merged with winning the allegiance of the rural population and with the boundary-making exercise of producing the political community. Collaboration with the police is represented here not as abiding by the law alone, but also as a sign of allegiance to Frelimo.

As Baker suggests for Mozambique as a whole, the Dombe case shows that although the PRM is creating partnerships, it still seems to be 'unfamiliar with the concept of being accountable to the public' and 'to some extent continues to be the Frelimo Police'.[44] In a Renamo stronghold such as Dombe, where the PRM is treated highly ambivalently, the partisanship of the police may be risky business. If not actually creating the grounds for counter-violence in the future, it is, as the Bunga arson case suggests, risky in the sense that it sustains the reappearance of self-redress and distrust of the formal juridical system, the state administration and the PRM. A pertinent question for the future also concerns the consequences of the PRM's use of young men in exercising violence against their fellow citizens

---

42 Chachiua, 2000.
43 Chachiua, 2000, p. 10.
44 Baker, 2003, p. 145.

and policing them. Discontent is rising among some chiefs, who see in the transfer of power to the *nucléos* a further threat to their powers of enforcement, some of which have already been stolen from them by the state.

🏵

Abrahams, R. 'Vigilantism: Order and Disorder on the Frontiers of the State', in *Inside and Outside the Law: Anthropological Studies of Authority and Ambiguity*, H. Olivia (ed.), London, 1996, pp. 41-55.

Agamben, G. *Means without End: Notes on Politics*, Minneapolis, 2000.

Alexander, J. 'The Local State in Post-war Mozambique: Political Practices and Ideas about Authority', *Africa* 67(1), 1997, pp. 1-26.

Baker, B. 'Policing and the Rule of Law in Mozambique', *Policing and Society* 13(2), 2003, pp. 139-58.

Buur, L. and H.M. Kyed. 'State Recognition of Traditional Authority in Mozambique. The Nexus of Community Representation and State Assistance', *Nordica Africa Institute Discussion Paper* 28, 2005, pp. 1-28.

Chachiua, M. 'Internal Security in Mozambique: Concerns versus Policies', *African Security Review* 9, 2000, pp. 1-15.

Hansen, T.B. 'Sovereigns beyond the State: on Legality and Authority in Urban India', in *Sovereign bodies: Citizens, Migrants, and States in the Postcolonial World*, T.B. Hansen and F. Stepputat (eds), Princeton, NJ, 2005, pp. 169-91.

Hansen, T.B. and F. Stepputat. 'Introduction', in *Sovereign Bodies: Citizens, Migrants, and States in the Postcolonial World*, T.B. Hansen and F. Stepputat (eds), Princeton, NJ, 2005, pp. 1-38.

Kyed, H.M. "The Politics of policing: Recapturing 'Zones of Confusion' in Rural Post-war Mozambique", in *The Security De-*

velopment Nexus, L. Buur, S. Jensen and F. Stepputat (eds), Nordic Africa Institute, Uppsala, 2007, pp. 132-51.

Kyed, H.M. and L. Buur. 'New Sites of Citizenship. Recognition of Traditional Authority and Group-based Citizenship in Mozambique', *Journal of Southern African Studies*, 32(3), 2006, pp. 563-81.

Lalá, A. 'Security Sector Reform as a Governance Issue: the Case of Mozambique', *Journal of Security Sector Management* 1(2), 2003, pp. 1-31.

Ministry of Internal Affairs (MINT). *Policiamento Comunitário e Serviços Provinciais de Bombeiros, Reunião com os Municípios*, Manica, 25-27 July 2005.

Wisler, D. and B. Bonvin. 'Human security, development and local policing', www.humansecuritygateway.com.

AFTERWORD

17

SOME THOUGHTS ON THE COMPARATIVE
STUDY OF VIGILANTISM

Ray Abrahams

When I first began to write about vigilantism in th 1980s, it command-ed little attention among anthropologists in Britain or elsewhere.[1] It was often necessary to spell out its relevance to other more mainstream concerns, and I sometimes encountered scepticism about whether it constituted a coherent category deserving of attention at all.

The situation outside anthropology was a little better. In Britain, a few criminologists mainly studied current outbreaks of individual and community self-help in Britain itself, and among them Les Johnston especially clearly recognized that he was dealing with a widespread form of social action that demanded a comparative ap-proach.[2] A small group of historians including E.P. Thompson were also interested in comparable phenomena such as 'rough music' and some of its nineteenth-century transformations.

In the United States, with its central place in the historical devel-opment of vigilantism, the field was predictably more fertile. Histori-cal memoirs and analyses of some of the main vigilante movements there were relatively abundant, and a number of these—particularly Richard Maxwell Brown's *Strain of Violence* (1975)—proved very useful as I worked on my ethnographic material and put together

---

1 A main exception was Suzette Heald who had encountered the phenomenon in her fieldwork in Eastern Uganda in the 1960s. See Heald, 1989.
2 Cf. Johnston, 1996.

my comparative study, *Vigilant Citizens* (1998). Also helpful were some of the collected essays edited by the political scientists Rosenbaum and Sederberg in their book *Vigilante Politics* (1976).

Naturally I am pleased to see that things are noticeably different today. In fact, the Sussex workshop was the first of two meetings on the subject that I attended in 2005—the second formed part of the German Anthropological Association conference in Halle in October. As this book reveals, the workshop brought together an impressively able and enthusiastic group of younger scholars breaking new ethnographic ground in Africa, South Asia and elsewhere, and it was clear to me, as a relative 'old-timer' privileged to take part in the proceedings, that the social anthropology of vigilantism was truly alive and well.

As I mentioned in my book, I first became aware of vigilantes in an oddly global situation—as a fairly typical Manchester schoolboy with a passion for Hollywood Westerns that were themselves partly the creation of middle European cinema moguls trying to create a unifying mythology for their new-found country. My research involvement arose rather differently and more directly out of maintaining contact with—and personal and ethnographic interest in—the Tanzanian villagers who had cheerfully accepted me among them during my first PhD research in the late 1950s and on a second field trip in the mid-1970s. In a way that Mr Micawber might have applauded, vigilantism as a subject of research 'turned up' for me in 1983 when I received a letter from a Nyamwezi friend.[3] He informed me that a new system for protecting property had been adopted in a village where I had lived and worked. Every man, young or old, had to be equipped with bow and arrows, and with a gourd-stem whistle to be blown only in emergencies. If a theft was committed, a hue and cry was raised and the thieves were to be followed by the young men of the village concerned. The whistles would alert the members of neighbouring villages, who would in turn forewarn others in the same way to look out for and try to intercept the criminals. There was

---

3 This was my sometime field assistant, Bernard Kalugula of Busangi.

a special village fund to which all contributed, and this was used to support the young men on such forays.[4]

This was the nowadays well-known Sungusungu or Basalama vigilante system. The letter-writer himself confirmed my own immediate reaction that the new development had something in common with earlier forms of neighbourhood courts and collaboration that I had documented in the late 1950s and that had helped to spark off my more general academic interest in relations between local communities and the state.[5] He cannot have guessed that his information would occupy me for the next twenty years.

The wide range of material presented at the workshop, and the lively discussion that it generated, have tempted me to concentrate here on a number of comparative issues. Although most participants presented detailed ethnographic case studies, a number of theoretical and methodological questions were raised for me and others that bear upon my own attempts at comparative analysis, and I would like here first to identify and comment upon some of these. Thinking about them afresh has been a stimulating and clarifying exercise even in contexts where I have not ultimately been persuaded to abandon my original position. At the same time, I hope that an increasing number of scholars will be tempted, as I have been myself, to try to complement detailed ethnography with broader treatments of the subject. This is no easy task at the best of times, and it is especially taxing in this sort of case.

Some definitional issues

A number of important questions surround the definition of vigilante activity in this context. Vigilantism—a term I use here in a relatively weak sense rather than in strict relation to an 'ism'—is for several reasons intrinsically difficult to pin down. It is commonly unstable, exhibiting a labile quality encouraged by its typical position

---

4 Subsequent enquiries also revealed that alleged witchcraft was also a fairly common focus of Sungusungu attention.

5 See the bibliography for some of my subsequent publications on the subject.

as part of the 'informal' legal and political sector and the absence of strong well-established pressures to retain its character and form. It occupies an awkward borderland between law and illegality, and the veil of secrecy that cloaks much vigilante activity also provides cover for deception, so that it is by no means always what it seems or claims to be. Again, it is a phenomenon that commonly generates strong emotions and conflicting opinions, and as I and others have noted, the very choice of the word and its immediate cognates can be problematic in contexts such as Southern Africa where it is part of the vernacular and has particular political and other connotations.

This last problem cannot comfortably be resolved, since the choice of other words is equally likely to stumble over comparable local usage, unless we coin them for ourselves and risk irritation and incomprehension among non-specialist readers. My own preference is to acknowledge the problem while at the same time claiming a sort of 'academic licence' to employ words in a semi-technical way which is neither exactly the same as nor utterly different from locally varying usage. The need for this is reinforced by the fact that there are several other contested words in this particular domain.

A number of definitional strategies are in theory possible though not, in my view, satisfactory. One is to decide that vigilantism is best looked at as if it was a form of something else that may, however, prove yet harder to pin down, a form of social banditry or mafia for example. I have discussed these and what I call 'other dwellers in the twilight zone' elsewhere, and my conclusion remains that where such phenomena are actually identifiable, comparison and contrast with them are more fruitful than a definitional 'reverse take-over'.

I am also not in favour of a strict taxonomic approach to the problem. This can lead easily to the adoption of a formula that is either too wide or too narrow to be helpful, even if we are dealing with a limited range of relatively static phenomena. Leach taught us long ago that such labelling needs special care when applied to social forms that are less stable than they look. This is true *a fortiori* when the material we are considering is as changeable and as uncertain as vigilantism often is, and I have much sympathy with Nietzsche's comment that 'only that which has no history can be defined'—at least in simple taxonomic terms.

I have found a third approach much more helpful. Max Weber was arguably the most sensitive of our early social science ancestors to the difficult relation between words we use and the often 'messy' real life phenomena to which we attach them. His strategy of 'ideal' or 'pure types' sets out to provide a measure rather than a simple picture of reality. Whatever the particular content or focus of a definition of this kind, the main point here is that we need not necessarily be too worried or surprised if one or more real cases fail to fit it. The approach can only be expected to provide us with the possibility of an illuminating comparison between our formulation and the complex and by no means always stable reality of what people say and do; and its potential to do that is its strength rather than a weakness. It allows for and can help us to make sense of social 'shifting sands'.

Within this general framework and approach, and for my own comparative purposes, 'vigilante' and 'vigilantism' have seemed to me 'ideally' to involve an organized attempt by a group of 'ordinary citizens' to enforce norms and maintain law and order on behalf of their communities, often by resort to violence, in the perceived absence of effective official state action through the police and courts. This last point is of course a key one. Vigilantism cannot exist alone but only alongside and, typically, on the frontiers—structural and/or cultural—of state power.[6] This also helps to differentiate the relative conservatism of the 'vigilante' from the radicalism of the 'anarchist'. Vigilantism is typically more critical of the state's actual performance than of the state itself. At the same time, its wide distribution warns us not to underestimate the force of popular concern for law and

---

6 It is conceivable of course that comparable structural patterns may be observable within other formally constituted authority systems such as large companies with disciplinary codes. I have also suggested (Abrahams, 2003) that international activities such as the invasion of Iraq by the USA and Britain and their coalition allies has a certain vigilante quality in the absence of a direct United Nations mandate.

order, even though other, seriously less laudable agendas are often found lurking behind vigilante assertions about this.

This formulation permits the combined examination of a wide range of cases whose reality is increasingly different from the ideal type. In my own study, it begins with a discussion of Sungusungu and other examples from Uganda, Peru and Tsarist Russia which lie relatively close to the ideal type. I then explore the first San Francisco movements and the Montana vigilantes of the 1860s which have also often been described as fairly close to the ideal, while displaying special features that partly stem from their location in recently settled and expanding communities within, but on the edges of, a complex social system, and at a time marked by high levels of social turbulence and population movement. I next discuss a variety of more politicized vigilante movements in the US and South Africa, of which the 1856 San Francisco case and the first and rather different second phase of the Ku Klux Klan's activities are the best known. From there it is a further step to the kind of pseudo-vigilantism in which government personnel in Central and South America and other areas organize counter-insurgency or themselves operate directly as death squads while claiming that the killings that ensue are popular vigilante-style reactions to their target victims.

How successful I have been in this is ultimately not for me to say. Arguably, however, there is some value in the fact that there is typically a reasonably close correspondence between the adopted formulation and at least the asserted aims or 'ideals' of the vigilantes themselves. This gives some emic weight to the choice while in no way privileging such assertions over reality in one's analysis.[7] At the same time, the fact that such assertions are not usually simply descriptive but are also thought to be attractive and legitimating is of some significance.

This point lies behind my own resistance to refocusing of the definition directly onto frequently recurring features of actual vigilante activity. I am happy to acknowledge that economic and political

---

7 Cf. In this regard, Leach's (1954) use of Kachin ideal types of polity.

considerations often underlie such actions. Vigilantism is a relatively cheap form of law enforcement and, as such, it has often been attractive to those anxious to keep taxes low. Also it is not unknown for vigilantes to gain financially from their actions. More generally, it is obvious that the frequent concern of vigilantes for the protection of property may fit more closely with the interests of the 'haves' than of the 'have-nots' in societies where economic inequality is well developed, though the violent reactions of the urban poor to theft in African cities such as Dar-es-Salaam reveal some puzzling complexities in this regard. Comparably, and connectedly, it is also obvious that the maintenance of law and order, as the term 'social control' suggests, has close connections with the power structure of societies which may in turn be marked by deep and persistent inequalities. At the same time, however, I would argue that a typically covert wish to establish or maintain economic or political inequality, or a simple desire for financial gain, is best looked at as a complicating aberration from a simple wish for order, rather than latter being seen as itself an aberration from a more complex fundamental form.

Breaking and maintaining rules

In the course of the workshop two further issues arose that seem possibly to merit closer consideration than I, at least, had previously given them. One concerns questions of the legal recognition of offences. The other relates to the character of 'the mob'.

The first issue emerged particularly clearly in material that Lars Buur presented in Halle, but it also arose in his and Stefan Jensen's discussions in the Sussex workshop. Vigilantes are commonly described as stepping in to uphold law and order when the state fails to do. Thus if the state is unable to enforce the laws aimed at the protection of its citizens' property and security, vigilantes classically 'take the law into their own hands'. In such circumstances, there is no argument between the parties as to what the law is, or where the rights to legislate and, normally, to jurisdiction lie.

There are, however, many situations, in a wide range of 'old' and 'new' states, where vigilantes are engaged in rather more than this by trying to enforce behaviour patterns and punishing 'offences' that the law itself does not demand or prohibit. Witchcraft is a classic case that frequently emerges in contemporary Africa. The state itself may not recognize it as an offence, at least as it is locally understood, and the state's penalties are much less severe when it does so than those commonly exacted by vigilantes. In other contexts, such as contemporary South Africa, there are radical differences between the state's enthusiastic adoption of international Human Rights legislation and the attitudes of rural and some other citizens to basic features of family law and the law of persons. This is especially clear with regard to basic assumptions about the rights of women vis-à-vis their husbands. Again, in Britain and North America, there has been a long and changing history in different times and places of the local vigilante enforcement of rules—of residential segregation in Northern Ireland, of racial segregation in the southern United States, of sexual morality in the American Mid-West and elsewhere—that are not recognized at all in the state legislation of the time.

In my own work I have tried to deal with this issue in two main ways. I have noted that vigilantism is a 'frontier' phenomenon and that the frontiers involved are not necessarily or simply spatial ones. Rather, some of them are 'cultural', following ethnic, religious, class or other lines, and they are specially difficult if they are combined with spatial distance or other forms of inaccessibility of the communities concerned. This may well create a double failure of the state in local eyes, when it is unable to enforce its own laws and at the same time fails or refuses to recognize the seriously offensive character that some forms of behaviour nonetheless possess in local eyes.

In addition to this notion of a cultural frontier, I have also tried to make use of a distinction between first-order rules about human behaviour and second-order rules about these. First-order rules may be prescriptive (telling people what they must do) or proscriptive (telling them what they must not do) and some of them may be defined as legal inasmuch as they are officially sanctioned by the state. Some second-order rules are legislative, defining how first-order rules are to be made, and others are 'jurisdictional', defining who is allowed to apply and enforce them. Additionally there are rules of due process that define the proper procedures for such application and enforcement. It is clear that when vigilantes seize and punish a suspected cattle-rustler, they are enforcing a first order legal rule against theft, while at the same time they may be thought of as breaking, or at least operating in ways not sanctioned by, the second-order rules of jurisdiction and due process.[8] On the other hand, if the vigilantes seize and punish someone for being a witch, or organizing a strike, or being sympathetic to racial equality, they are commonly in conflict with, or acting without authorization from, the state's first order rules. At the same time, it is clear that there is some degree of overlap between these first- and second-order zones, to the extent that the former typically prohibits the arrest, imprisonment or use of violence by unauthorized persons and thus asserts, at least by implication, the rights of citizens to be dealt with in accordance with second order procedures.

I have been reasonably satisfied with these formulations, especially since the same vigilante groups may be involved in both kinds of activity. However, I am very ready to agree that the distinctions involved here might usefully be explored in greater detail than there has been so far in my work. Whatever the merits of my own approach, it makes perfectly good sense to treat such plurality of legal and moral culture more directly as a general problem area in which vigilante activity forms only one of several ways in which difficulties arising from discrepant values can be addressed in society. This would encourage the examination of a range of structural arrangements in which differences between centre and periphery on such matters were tolerated or even institutionalized to varying degrees in

---

8 I phrase this point cautiously because most legal theorists, following Hart, tend to see second-order rules as aimed not at the populace at large but only at authorized officials, though arguably they are at least consonant with the idea that such officials are also the only persons entitled to behave in these ways.

some systems while being treated as more or less intolerable in others. It also permits closer comparison between vigilantism and more formally sanctioned local level policing and adjudication practices, including forms of private policing.

Mobs and committees

I turn now to the character of the mob. The word itself is a relatively old one, as too, perhaps more surprisingly, is 'mobocracy'.[9] It is a shortened form of the Latin phrase '*mobile vulgus*' (the unstable or excitable crowd) and, with the exception of some Antipodean usage, it has typically quite negative connotations. The Oxford English Dictionary glosses it as the 'disorderly and riotous part of the population, the roughs, the rabble' and as '...the lower orders, the uncultured or illiterate as a class...disorderly or lower class people forming a crowd'. As I shall discuss below, its use with regard to vigilantism has been contested in some of the earlier literature. Here, however, I want to deal with a more substantive issue raised in discussion by Murray Last.

Professor Last vividly drew our attention to well-known features of mob behaviour— the wild and apparently spontaneous and uncontrollable nature of mob violence that is in sharp antithesis to, though by no means necessarily more deadly than, the cool-headed application of reason and organization to the handling of alleged offences. These are of course polar points, with many stations in between, of a continuum between what Radcliffe-Brown classically identified in more anodyne terms as 'diffuse' and 'organized' sanctions. I must confess that I am not wholly sure how this opposition can be best built into the definitional framework outlined earlier, but it seems possible, and indeed within the spirit of Weberian analysis, to recognize two polar types of vigilante action, with a somewhat unclear middle ground in the 'real' world between them.[10] It seems clear,

---

9 Both date back to the eighteenth century.

10 There is in fact an intrinsic 'structuralist' element in Weber's approach, as emerges classically in his opposition of ideal types of 'formal' and 'substantive'

however, that whatever analytical strategy is adopted, this distinction deserves more attention in the future.

Words in action

As I noted earlier, the use of the term 'mob' has been contested in some commentaries on vigilantism. Social action generally is rarely if ever unambiguous and uncontentious, and the vocabulary used by actors and others to describe it often occupies a fuzzy zone somewhere between the truth and hocus-pocus, and often enough nearer to the latter. This is commonly the case with vigilantism, and I hope that other scholars in the field may be tempted to explore this important matter further in the future. I myself paid some attention to it in my book and I discussed it in more detail in a recent paper.[11] Naturally, I can only give it somewhat skimpy treatment here. A close examination of this question might appear at first sight a self-indulgent scholastic diversion from the harsh practicalities of vigilante behaviour and the conditions in which it arises. It can however usefully illuminate how language is employed to legitimate and defend or oppose and control such behaviour in important ways. It is clear that in its many guises and configurations, vigilantism commonly has very serious real world implications—often of life and death—both for its targets and for its practitioners. It also poses well-known difficulties for the governance of the state. At the same time it illustrates some puzzling qualities of local-level social life. It claims to uphold law and order and morality by typically violent and illegal means, and it often displays confusing combinations of opposing elements—sectional and common interests, elitist and populist values, and intolerance and caring decency. It is not surprising that, with such a heady and manipulable mixture, vigilantism tends to provoke conflicting responses within and be-

---

rationality, and 'charisma' and 'tradition'.
11 See Abrahams, 2002.

tween individuals and groups, and that rhetoric and labelling play a significant role in the arguments it generates.[12]

Differing characterizations of the activities of Northern Ireland 'punishment' groups, or 'squads' as they are often referred to more pejoratively by critics, are one of many cases of strongly contested usage in this context. Some claim that the groups satisfy local community needs to control activities such as drug and alcohol abuse, joy-riding, theft and vandalism among young offenders, while others emphasize the illegitimacy of their often brutal violence as they seek to gain and maintain political control of 'the streets'. 'Victim' is one of an interesting set of strongly contested concepts here. The opponents of the groups' activities see the recipients of 'punishment' as key 'victims' in this situation. For some supporters, however, these targets are unacceptable 'perpetrators' of offences and at best 'deserving victims' of just retribution, while the true victims are the communities they have disrupted. Many actors and some commentators would extend this to explain or justify these 'punishment' activities by casting their 'perpetrators' as 'victims' of sectarian violence and, for some, of state repression. It has also been suggested that all in the province may be seen to some degree as 'victims' or as 'perpetrators' of 'the troubles'. Again the term 'punishment' itself is similarly contested, with its aspirations to the moral high ground, and many would prefer to talk of brutal intimidation. Whatever one's own judgement of such activity, such key words are clearly more than the statement of fact that they claim to be.

A closer look at the word 'mob' is also useful here. For while it would be pointless to deny that it may sometimes aptly characterize vigilante behaviour, its use in strong criticism of all such activity, as in John Caughey's work, is much more problematic.[13] This point was in fact anticipated in a much earlier discussion by the American historian Hubert Howe Bancroft who devoted much of his life

---

12 Cf Chavez in this volume for an interesting example from the modern United States Southwest.

13 Caughey, 1960.

as a scholar to the documentation of vigilantism in all parts of the American West, and especially to the large-scale movements which arose in San Francisco in the 1850s. Unlike Caughey, Bancroft was favourably disposed to much vigilante activity, which he saw as filling a gap left by the absence of effective state crime control in frontier conditions such as those of the mid-nineteenth century American West. His monumental two-volume work of 1887 has the significantly mild title *Popular Tribunals*, and he argues passionately there against a mindless worship of the law, which dismisses vigilantism simply as 'illegal'. 'Law is the servant and not the master of men', he claims, and he tells us that 'Law we must have...But to talk of the sacredness of law...is to clothe rules and prescriptions with the superstitious veneration which enshrouded them of old.'[14]

Bancroft emphasizes the difference between the disciplined activities of the leading members of the city's vigilance committees and the undisciplined tendencies to 'mobocracy' of the populace at large. In direct anticipational confrontation with Caughey's later comment, he argues that the 'terms vigilance committee, mob-law, lynch-law, are not 'as many suppose, synonymous'. He admits to superficial similarities with mob-violence but claims that 'one is an organization officered by its most efficient members, aiming at public well-being, and acting under fixed rules of its own making; the other is an unorganised rabble, acting under momentary delirium, the tool, it may be, of political demagogues, the victim of its own intemperance. Underlying the actions of the one is justice; of the other revenge.'

Here Bancroft is clearly using the distinction between mobs and committees in a judgemental rather than a purely analytical way. Whatever else they do, such arguments also help to show that vigilantism is far from always simply a 'popular' response of ordinary folk to the failure of due legal process to deal with breaches of the law. 'The people' and 'the community' are, on inspection, complex concepts, and the populism of much vigilante rhetoric often conceals sectional interests, and in Bancroft's and some other cases goes hand

---

14 Bancroft, 1887, p. 36, 43.

in hand with a self-satisfied elitism. Nor are one's anxieties necessarily allayed by learning that many of the vigilante elite in question in San Francisco were businessmen or freemasons, however proud of this they were themselves, or that the 1856 committee was largely concerned with the destruction of its political opponents, however corrupt their political machine was.[15]

Predictably, it is often in the labelling of vigilante targets that one finds evidence of the truly dangerous power of words and encounters the worst implications of our capacity to classify and label. I must here acknowledge a special debt to Edmund Leach.[16] For as Michael Herzfeld has also noted, in his study of bureaucratic stereotyping and 'indifference', Leach's ideas in this particular area have been enormously insightful.[17]

The basic argument is by now well known. Central to the present context is the general fact that human beings are fundamentally linguistic, and as such classifying, animals. Language and its labels are both the key way we comprehend the world, and even put it to good use, and the way in which we contrive—either accidentally or, as John Barnes has pointed out in his book *A Pack of Lies*, often enough deliberately—to distort and misrepresent it. One does not need to take a hard-line Whorfian position to accept that we relate in highly significant ways both to the world in general, and to other people in particular, through the labels we attach to them. Herein arguably lies a great deal of our peculiarly human capacity for both good and evil and, of course, for argument between and about them.

It is so natural to us to relate to the world in this way that we can easily be led or misled to mistake the label for the labelled. What was once an alleged quality of so-called 'primitive mentality' emerges here as a fundamental feature of so-called civilized society.

---

15 See Senkewicz, 1985 for an interesting analysis of economic and, later, political interests lying behind the 1850s San Francisco movements.

16 See especially Leach, 1977.

17 Herzfeld, 1993.

And a key point is that labels often have a lethal quality—they provide us all in different times and places with a Bond-like licence to kill. It was an optimist or a fool who coined the children's chant that sticks and stones can break our bones but names will never hurt us, if only because the two are all too often intimately connected.

Vigilante targets are commonly one of many cases in point here. For in addition to the stereotyping of individuals through the use of superficially descriptive labels such as sex-offender, street-children, Black or Jew, or Australian (as main targets in the first large San Francisco movement of the 1850s), or independent-minded woman, the world is littered with examples of a deadly slippage which assumes that such terms are synonymous with others such as murderer or witch or other not quite human 'enemy within'. And as I have noted, such labels can be lethally accompanied by beatings, torture and lynchings whose victims might well have preferred the odd stick or stone.

Of course, it is not only vigilantes who in varying contexts and to varying degrees perform this kind of linguistic black magic. The state itself has been no sluggard in this field, and one can see the deadly costs of labelling, and much worse of believing in the more dehumanizing forms of label, in terrorism and in depressingly many examples of more directly oppositional politics at sub-state level in which anything from residential ethnic cleansing to bombing, military rape and attempted genocide of their harshly labelled enemies appears to be justified to their performers at the time.

Anthropology and history

I turn now to some further aspects of the kind of approach that the comparative study of vigilantism seems to require. In the age of structural-functional dinosaurs when I came into British social anthropology, there was still something of a stand-off between structural and historical explanation despite the pioneering good sense of figures like Evans-Pritchard and Schapera. To paraphrase a nice piece of nineteenth-century repartee, we might almost say

433

that if history could be caricatured as seeing life as just one damn thing after another, functionalist anthropology in turn could have been said to view it as just one damn thing over and over.[18] Since then, of course, the two fields have become much closer, and not surprisingly I see this as important both for social science generally and for vigilante studies in particular.

It is important here that vigilantism is a widespread but not universal phenomenon. Its individual past and present outbreaks tend to have their own distinctive characteristics, which merit careful ethnographic and historical attention. At the same time most of us still tend to find clearly recognizable comparabilities between these outbreaks wherever and whenever they occur.

There are general possible solutions, both historically specific and more timeless, as to why this might be so. There is the possibility of spontaneous independent invention resulting either from pure chance or more probably from a predictable response to commonly recurring problems. Another factor may be the use of earlier local experience and recourse to a pre-existing social and cultural template when circumstances appear ripe. Thirdly, the similarities in question may derive from their diffusion from elsewhere. I should say at once that I feel no need to see these possibilities as mutually exclusive, though one cannot automatically assume they will be present everywhere and in equal measure. The Sungusungu case appears to have been a genuinely local northern Nyamwezi development, partly new and partly building upon earlier local templates, that rapidly spread within the Nyamwezi/Sukuma area and eventually well beyond, in part with state assistance.

It has often struck me that the nowadays neglected term 'diffusion'—that special bugbear of Radcliffe-Brown and Malinowski—has

---

18 I actually first encountered this idea in the form of a quip that history was 'just one damned thing after another' which was variously and wrongly ascribed to Churchill, Henry Ford, and Mark Twain. The original version, about life, is ascribed to Elbert Hubbard (cf. *Oxford Dictionary of Quotations*), and the response (again about life) that it was, on the contrary, just 'one damn thing over and over' came from Edna St.Vincent Millay.

quite a bit in common with the currently more fashionable concept of 'globalization'. This point is less important in itself than as a reminder that new words do not necessarily designate completely new processes. Of course, the speed and intensity of the contemporary movement of people, information and ideas throughout the globe are quite unprecedented, but we should nonetheless not underestimate the extent to which such connections have formed a significant part of social life in earlier times.[19]

This issue commonly emerges when we study vigilantism in different places and at different times, and it is perhaps especially easy to forget when dealing with older cases. Work on charivari and 'rough music', especially by Thompson, combined with some of my own explorations, raised some interesting aspects of this for me, if only because the wide range of locations in which detailed behaviour of the same kind is found is in itself remarkable. I soon learned that 'shivari', as it was called there, was transported to the southern United States, and that similar patterns of behaviour also apparently spread into western Russia.[20] But more was to emerge when I began to look for evidence of knowledge of nineteenth century American vigilantism in the London *Times*. Having found that the index keyword to look out for was 'lynch law', I was then surprised to find several reports of 'lynch law' in places like Newcastle and Chester and in Rossshire. The patterns described fitted well with Thompson's account of later developments in 'rough music' in which men who were cruel to their wives, or cheated their work mates, and both men and women who maltreated children were subjected to beatings and sometimes more traditional forms, in the case of men, of so-called 'skimmington' treatment, such as bouncing a man up and down as he sat astride a sharpened plank. Thompson plausibly suggests that a search through

---

19 Thus Mintz, 2000, p. 176 has commented that the emphasis upon contemporary globalization ought not to lead us to forget the significance of the millions of Europeans and others, including huge numbers of black slaves, who have crossed the oceans to the New World since the sixteenth century.

20 Cf. Galeotti in this volume.

local newspapers for information on this subject would be very useful, and this conjured up for me an image of Cambridgeshire fen-folk reading a column that was in fact published in the *Cambridge News* in December 1888. The article described how so-called White Caps of Iowa engaged in punishing drunken and cruel husbands, and it seemed likely that the readers would be nodding to themselves in recognition of familiar things, rather than treating the news story, as its tone appeared to expect, as evidence of weird goings on across the sea.

Again, there is rather more evidence than has been recognized by Richard Maxwell Brown of cultural influence from elsewhere, including Britain, on the development of US vigilantism. The young prospectors who hit the American West had a wide range of backgrounds including Britain and Australia and South America, as well as the eastern states, and while they may have arrived, and sometimes left, with empty pockets, they certainly did not come with empty heads.

I hope I have said enough to make my point sufficiently for present purposes. In studying vigilantism, as in many other contexts, we are dealing both with a variety of structural levels and with various short- and long-term, narrower and wider processes. Both broad- and narrow-based historical *and* synchronic approaches can enhance each other in this study, so that it is often if not always worth one's while to look for (though not simply to assert) the possible influence of national and international as well as local factors upon the particular development of vigilantism that one is studying. I may add that Orin Starn does this in an admirably careful and open-minded way in his book *Nightwatch,* about North-west Peruvian *rondas campesinas.*[21]

Finally, let me mention one more point that appears to merit further contemporary and historical consideration. Thompson interestingly noted with regard to food riots that it may be worthwhile to ponder the apparent absence of rioting in some places as well as its

---

21 At the same time, I am puzzled how someone who must know the Berkeley Bancroft Library well could manage to ignore the concept of vigilantism and other material on the subject in his discussion.

presence when and where we encounter it. A similar thought struck me about Sungusungu which started up among the Nyamwezi and Sukuma when they were by no means the only Tanzanian people experiencing the problems that encouraged them to take this initiative. Indeed it was particularly the absence of a spontaneous Sungusungu type of reaction to raiding among the nearby Kuria people that started me thinking about this issue. My own tentative conclusion was that earlier templates were an important factor in this case.

At the same time, this is something of a minefield, if only because human societies are in no way as predictable as clockwork and they are always capable of taking us by surprise. Years ago, I reviewed a book about the Lang'o area of northern Uganda in which the author asserted that the people had little or no interest in witchcraft. Yet, not long after his research there was completed, there was a very nasty outbreak of violent witch-hunting in the area. Also, it is rather easier for people to import solutions from other societies than it might be for them to dream them up—without earlier templates or at least extremely favourable local conditions—for themselves, as indeed happened among the Kuria. Nor do the problems stop there. Maxwell Brown makes much of the special conditions that he sees gave rise to vigilantism in the United States in contrast, in his view, to Britain. Yet as I suggested earlier, this contrast seems excessively stark. Vigilante style ideas may be buttoned down by state power and ideology rather than absent, and they may suddenly erupt under pressure.

Such caveats notwithstanding, such a search might still help us to refine our understanding of the kinds of circumstances in which people do resort to vigilante action.[22]

Gender issues

The variable place of gender within vigilantism has been relatively neglected, and it was pleasing to see that a few of the workshop par-

---

22 Barrington Moore's (1979) study of injustice interestingly examines this kind of issue with regard to the attractions of the Nazi party to many dissatisfied 'ordinary' people in interwar Germany.

ticipants addressed different aspects of this question in their papers. While writing *Vigilant Citizens* I devoted first a chapter section and ultimately a special chapter to the topic, and this chapter itself, like Topsy, just grew once it became clear that the issue demanded discussion. Among the topics that I tried to address were whether we were currently witnessing a general shift in the intensity and extent of women's violent behaviour and, coupled with this, whether vigilantism was typically a male phenomenon. The paper in this volume by Atreyee Sen elegantly brings out the complex nature of this issue. It also makes it clear that the active role of women in vigilantism fully deserves its own established place both in vigilante research and in gender-focused studies more generally.

A few further comments on this and related questions may be useful here. As in other contexts, a valuable point of entry is Thompson's stimulating work on 'Rough Music' and 'The Moral Economy of the Crowd' reprinted and further explored in his *Customs in Common*. There he carefully documents the active role of women in historical food riots and in charivari, while at the same time resisting attempts to accuse him of exaggeration or misrepresentation of the nature of their role. In this regard, it seems possible that what is commonly called 'laddishness' in contemporary society is a genuinely new development, and that we ought not to assume the absence of interesting role-related differences between patterns of male and female participation in vigilantism and other comparable fields. Again, we are all by now well aware of the need to avoid lumping all of a community's—and even more a society's—women together. Rudyard Kipling's interestingly worded claim that 'the colonel's lady and Judy O'Grady are sisters under their skins' seems much more questionable than it once was among feminists and non-feminists alike.

All this seems to fit well with Michelle Jolly's research on San Francisco and with Katherine Blee's impressive 1991 study of *Women of the Klan*.[23] It is also perhaps interesting that much of

23 Blee, 1991; Jolly, 2003; Jolly, 2005.

modern British female vigilante-style activity seems to have been directed against paedophiles. At the time I wrote my book, there was interesting material on this topic concerning rough music-type behaviour against a suspected paedophile in the Rapploch Estate area of Stirling, and I was later also interested to write a little about the anti-paedophile activities of women in the Paulsgrove Estate in Portsmouth following the murder of Sarah Payne. The special role of at least some local mothers in such activities does not seem altogether surprising in this context.

Women, of course, also sometimes figure as the targets of vigilante activity. Despite the early presence of a Sungusungu 'women's wing' in some Nyamwezi and Sukuma areas of Tanzania, the organization has primarily been a male domain, and groups' activities have included efforts to keep women in their perceived proper place as faithful and obedient wives. In France in the aftermath of World War II, women who had collaborated with the German occupying forces were common victims of popular vigilantism. Additionally, it is widely documented how women have historically and recently been commonly identified as witches, and subjected to the violent attention of both vigilante and official witch-hunters.

Despite some exceptions, however, and especially those concerning alleged witchcraft, women seem to have been less liable than men to face extreme vigilante violence. Although many women have suffered deeply through the loss of their menfolk at the hands of vigilantes, they themselves seem generally to have been more liable to beatings and humiliation than to being killed. While women in gold-rush California, for example, were often the focus of a quarrel and a fight that ended in a lynching, there as elsewhere they seem rarely to have carried out the kinds of crime—murder and robbery—that typically provoked vigilante hangings. A notorious exception that provoked much outrage was the so-called Downieville Tragedy of 1851, when a vigilante mob hanged a Mexican woman, Juanita, for murdering a drunken 'white' miner. This was described by the *Sacramento Times and Transcript* as a 'blot upon the history of the state' and it seems clear that the hanging of a woman in this way ran against the grain of more sober public sentiment.

Partly similar male attitudes to women emerge from material on the murders of Brazilian 'street children' by vigilantes and 'death-squads'. These children are predominantly poor males, who are often petty criminals and drug-takers. In some contrast, poor young women with a similar background are more likely to be less visibly engaged in domestic work or prostitution, and are much more likely to be murdered by men who are close to them—brothers or lovers for example—than by vigilante strangers. The subordinate status of these young women and male paternalistic attitudes, as well as their absence from the streets, seem clearly to be involved here.

These are then a few of my thoughts on vigilantism. I hope that both my main topics and some of the issues I have passed over relatively briefly will appear to merit further discussion. Notwithstanding my remarks on strategies of definition, and on the need to look both within and beyond particular outbreaks of vigilante activity, the relation between the ideographic and the general remains a thorny and perhaps ultimately irresolvable issue within anthropology, as too does the old question of whether social structures are more easily comparable than cultures. I have also noted briefly that the relative stability of different social and cultural forms deserves further thought in this context. This is a complicated issue, which relates in the case of vigilantism at least to several different factors. Variability of demand is clearly one, and another is the serious claims that persistent vigilance makes on the time and energy of relatively large numbers of people, tending to offset the attraction of its monetary cost-effectiveness.

Whatever our different perspectives on these and other questions may be, however, I feel confident about one thing. Given the persistence of the state and the intrinsic flaws in its workings, it will be very surprising if we find ourselves short of new intellectually and ethically puzzling material on vigilantism to subject to our scrutiny.

❧

Abrahams, R.G. *The Political Organization of Unyamwezi*, Cambridge, 1967.

—— 'Sungusungu: Village Vigilante Groups in Tanzania', *African Affairs* 86(343), 1987, pp. 179-96.

—— 'Law and Order and the State in the Nyamwezi and Sukuma Area of Tanzania', *Africa* 59(3), 1989, pp. 354-68.

—— *Vigilant Citizens: Vigilantism and the State*, Cambridge, 1998.

—— 'What's in a name? Some Thoughts on the Vocabulary of Vigilantism and Related Forms of 'Informal Criminal Justice', in *Informal Criminal Justice*, D. Feenan (ed.), Aldershot, 2002, pp. 25-40

—— 'The Vigilantes Ride Again', *Cambridge Anthropology* 23(2), 2003, pp. 67-68.

Bancroft, H.H. *Popular Tribunals* Vol.1, San Francisco, 1887.

Barnes, J.A. *A Pack of Lies: Towards a Sociology of Lying*, Cambridge, 1994.

Blee, K.M. *Women of the Klan: Racism and Gender in the 1920s*, Berkeley, 1991.

Brown, R.M. *Strain of Violence: Historical Studies of American Violence and Vigilantism*, Oxford, 1975.

Caughey, J.W. *Their Majesties the Mob*, Chicago, 1960.

Herzfeld, M. *The Social Production of Indifference: Exploring the Symbolic Roots of Western Bureaucracy*, Chicago, 1993.

Johnston, L. 'What is Vigilantism?' *British Journal of Criminology* 36(2), 1996, pp. 220-36.

Jolly, M.E. 'Sex, Vigilantism, and San Francisco in 1856', *Common-Place* 3(4), 2003, http://common-place.dreamhost.com//vol-03/no-04/san-francisco/index.shtml.

—— Rogues, Patriots, Ladies, and "Vigilants": Unmasking Gendered Language in Discourses of Legitimacy in the San Francisco Vigilance Committee of 1856. Paper presented at the Global Vigilantes Workshop, University of Sussex, 2005.

Leach, E.R. *Political Systems of Highland Burma: A Study of Kachin Social Structure*, London, 1954.

—— *Custom, Law and Terrorist Violence*, Edinburgh, 1977.

Mintz, S.W. 'Sows' Ears and Silver Linings—A Backward Look at Ethnography', *Current Anthropology* 41(2), 2000, pp. 169-89.

Moore, B. *Injustice: The Social Bases of Obedience and Revolt*, London, 1978.

Rosenbaum, H. and P. Sederberg (eds) *Vigilante Politics*, Philadelphia, 1976.

Senkewicz, R.M. *Vigilantes in Gold Rush San Francisco*, Stanford, 1985.

Starn, O. *Nightwatch: The Making of a Movement in the Peruvian Andes*, Durham, NC, 1999.

Thompson, E.P. *Customs in Common*, London, 1991.

INDEX